Maidan

McGill-Queen's Studies in Protest, Power, and Resistance

SERIES EDITOR: SARAH MARSDEN

Protest, civil resistance, and political violence have rarely been more visible. Nor have they ever involved such a complex web of identities, geographies, and ideologies. This series expands the theoretical and empirical boundaries of research on political conflict to examine the origins, cultures, and practices of resistance. From grassroots activists and those engaged in everyday forms of resistance to social movements to violent militant networks, it considers the full range of actors and the strategies they use to provoke change. The series provides a forum for interdisciplinary work that engages with politics, sociology, anthropology, history, psychology, religious studies, and philosophy. Its ambition is to deepen understanding of the systems of power people encounter and the creative, violent, peaceful, extraordinary, and everyday ways they try to resist, subvert, and overthrow them.

MAIDAN

Ukraine's Democratic Revolution

SOPHIA WILSON

McGill-Queen's University Press
Montreal & Kingston • London • Chicago

ISBN 978-0-2280-2737-9 (paper)
ISBN 978-0-2280-2738-6 (ePDF)
ISBN 978-0-2280-2739-3 (ePUB)

Legal deposit first quarter 2026
Bibliothèque et Archives nationales du Québec

Printed in Canada on acid-free paper that is 100% ancient-forest-free, containing 100% sustainable, recycled fibre, and processed chlorine-free.

This publication was made possible through the financial support of the Shevchenko Scientific Society, USA, from the Olha Mociuk Fund.

We acknowledge the support of the Canada Council for the Arts.

Nous remercions le Conseil des arts du Canada de son soutien.

McGill-Queen's University Press in Montreal is on land which long served as a site of meeting and exchange amongst Indigenous Peoples, including the Haudenosaunee and Anishinabeg nations. In Kingston it is situated on the territory of the Haudenosaunee and Anishinaabek. We acknowledge and thank the diverse Indigenous Peoples whose footsteps have marked these territories on which peoples of the world now gather.

Library and Archives Canada Cataloguing in Publication

Title: Maidan : Ukraine's democratic revolution / Sophia Wilson.

Names: Wilson, Sophia Voitanik, author

Series: McGill-Queen's studies in protest, power, and resistance ; 10.

Description: Series statement: McGill-Queen's studies in protest, power, and resistance ; 10 | Includes bibliographical references and index.

Identifiers: Canadiana (print) 20250290316 | Canadiana (ebook) 20250290340 | ISBN 9780228027379 (paper) | ISBN 9780228027386 (PDF) | ISBN 9780228027393 (EPUB)

Subjects: LCSH: Ukraine – History – Revolution of Dignity, 2013-2014. | LCSH: Democracy – Ukraine.

Classification: LCC DK5419 .W55 2026 | DDC 947.706/21 – dc23

This book was designed and typeset by Peggy Issenman in 11/14 Minion Pro. Copyediting by James Leahy. Cover photograph by Max Rokotansky. Used by permission of the Archive of the Ukrainian Maidan Museum.

McGill-Queen's University Press
Suite 1720, 1010 Sherbrooke St West, Montreal, QC, H3A 2R7

Authorized safety representative in the EU: Mare Nostrum Group BV, Mauritskade 21D, 1091 GC Amsterdam, the Netherlands, gpsr@mare-nostrum.co.uk

To the people of Ukraine

Contents

Figures and Tables

Figures

Tables

Acknowledgments

My book is like Maidan itself: it became possible only because many people came to the rescue. First and foremost, I owe thanks to the many incredible Ukrainians who took part in the revolutionary events and shared their experiences. Remembering is reliving, and remembering the events of the Ukrainian Revolution meant bringing back to life both positive and painful memories. To protect their privacy, I must refrain from naming the many revolutionaries who agreed to be interviewed, but I'm forever grateful to all those who spoke with me, at times for hours, remembering what they saw and did, and to those who helped me locate multiple sources of information, from legal documents to materials on civic initiatives. I am thankful to so many for their guidance and generosity. We can't resurrect victims of social injustice, but it is in our power to record history, keeping alive the memory of the fallen. I express my gratitude to institutions in Ukraine, including the National Memorial Complex to the Heavenly Hundred Heroes and the Revolution of Dignity Museum (Maidan Museum), the Center for Civil Liberties, the Ukrainian Institute of National Memory, and the Center for the Studies of History and Culture of East European Jewry of the National University of the Kyiv-Mohyla Academy, for aid in locating and sharing records about the Maidan Revolution.

I am indebted to the Canadian Institute of Ukrainian Studies for a generous research grant to conduct fieldwork in Ukraine, to my home Southern Illinois University Edwardsville for research funding and continuing support, which enabled my work on this project, and to the US Shevchenko Scientific Society (the Olha Mociuk Fund) for aid with publication. I am lucky that my colleagues at SIUE are also my friends, and multiple intellectual discussions with them helped me grow. I thank Laurie Rice, Suranjan Wereraratne, Ken Moffett, Nicholas Guehlstorf, Anne Flaherty, and Andy Theising from the political science department, as well as Linda Markowitz, Mark Hedley, and Jessica DeSpain for their feedback on various parts of this manuscript. I am also thankful to Joshua Kryah, Alison Lamothe, Sterling Recker, Olga Bezhanova, Charles Berger, Saba Fatima, Steve Tamari, Douglas Simms, Jack Glassman, Chris Pearson, Mark Poepsel, Jeffrey Manuel, Nancy Lutz, Tara Huntley, and Tori Walters for many conversations about politics and society. Special thanks to Eric Ruckh, Jessica Hutchins, and the John Martinson Honors Program for providing support in teaching courses focused on Ukraine. SIUE students from various backgrounds became my teachers – discussing Ukrainian history and global politics with them helped me better understand my own arguments. The acute attention given to my presentations by members of the Lifelong Learning community polished my writing. I'm grateful to the university's URCA program, and thank Jordan Saner, Kaitlyn Funneman, Aliyah Price, Madison Hutchinson, Catherine Throm, Nathan Coggeshall, Megan Bagby, John Long, and Abby Mast for their research assistance.

The Harvard Ukrainian Research Institute holds a very special place in my heart. The generous Eugene and Daymel Schklar Research Fellowship in Ukrainian Studies at HURI allowed me to conduct research and meet a fascinating group of scholars committed to the study of Ukraine. Serhii Plokhy's rabbi-esque mentorship at different stages of working on the book was invaluable; his kindness was encouraging and wisdom inspiring. I am also thankful to Lubomyr Hajda, Tymish Holowinsky, Kostyantyn Bondarenko, George Grabowicz, Halyna Hryn, Nadiya Kravets, Megan Dunkin Smith, Olha Aleksic, Volodymyr Dibrova, Oleh Kotsyuba, Anna Chukur, and the 2015 co-fellows at HURI – Oksana Iurkova, Alessandro Achilli, Anton Kotenko and Huseyin Oylupinar – for often long, and always fascinating, conversations about Ukraine and the field of Ukrainian studies. Emily Channell-Justice's scholarship and friendship were symbolic of the profoundness I associate with HURI. Teaching courses for the Harvard Ukrainian Summer Institute, alongside Serhii Bilenky, allowed me to meet students from around the world, leading to many discussions that had a lasting effect on my work.

I am grateful to the following institutes for hosting me in residences, workshops, and talks in the development of this project: Weizenbaum Institute in Berlin; Polish History Museum; Harvard University Davis Russian and Eurasian Center; University of Wisconsin Center for Russia, East Europe and Central Asia; European University Viadrina Frankfurt-Oder; Kyiv Maidan Museum; National Academy of Science of Ukraine; Brigham Young University Political Science Department; Center for East European and International Studies/Prisma Ukraina in Berlin; Invisible University for Ukraine; Fulbright Program (Ukraine and New Jersey); Marshall University; National Geospatial-Intelligence Agency; and Glen Carbon Illinois Public Library. I'm thankful for having been able to present papers related to this project at conferences hosted by the Association for Slavic, Eastern European and Eurasian Studies; Association for the Studies of Nationalities; International Studies Association; American Political Science Association; Law and Society Association; Illinois Political Science Association; and Society for Military History. Particularly invaluable was feedback from Elizaveta Kuznetsova, Victoria Sereda, Joanna Konieczna-Salamatin, Alexandra Hnatiuk, Yaroslav Hrytsak, Volodymyr Kulyk, Alexander Motyl, Olena Nikolayenko, Jayanth Krishnan, Kathryn Hendley, Paul D'Anieri, Catherine Wanner, Oxana Shevel, Valerie Sperling, Sarah Philips, Olha Onuch, Dmitri Gorenburg, Peter Rutland, Kristina Hook, Daniel Beers, Cynthia Buckley, Svitlana Krasynska, Roman Krakowsky, Richard Butterwick-Pawlikowski, James Collins, Bryan Kozik, Mikhaeel Alexseev, Celeste Beesley, Elizabeth Wood, Mark Bessinger, Christina Jarymowycz, Alexandra Hrycak, Oksana Mikheieva, Yulia Bidenko, Emma Mateo, Heather Pool, and Christopher Newman. The American Association for Ukrainian Studies and Shevchenko Scientific Society offered great opportunities to engage in intellectual debates regarding all things Ukraine. Conversations with fellow scholars of Ukraine, including Vitaly Chernetsky, Marta Baziuk, Frank Sysyn, Paul Magosci, Eugene Fishel, Ostap Sereda, Victoria Somoff, Olha Khometa, Veronica Anghel, Maria Popova, Nick Kupensky, Olena Lennon, John Vsetecka, Olena Palko, Olexandra Wallo, Dominique Arel, Marko Stech, Tania Plawuszczak-Stech, helped put my research in a larger perspective.

The University of Washington played a fundamental role in shaping me as a scholar, and connections with it continue to affect me today. Stephen Hanson, the guru of post-Soviet studies and the author of a groundbreaking study on revolutions, offered priceless feedback on parts of this manuscript. Jamie Mayerfeld inspired me to study human rights when I was a grad student, and I'm thankful for his insightful comments on my current work. Conversations with Ellis Goldberg about revolutions, Maidan, and the Arab Spring were mesmerizing and had a profound effect on shaping my theoretical argument. I'm heartbroken that he will not read it – may his memory be a blessing. I am also deeply grateful to Rachel Cichowski and Anthony Gill for their mentorship and support during my PhD years, as well as Joel Migdal, Michael McCann, Susan Whiting, George Lovell, and Margaret Levi for their inspirational teaching. My brilliant UW friends – Sooenn Park, Pam Stumpo, Amanda Fulmer, Talal Hattar, Heather Pool, Jennifer Fredette, Jessica Beyer, Charles Rowling, Iza Hussin, and Robert Farley – made a great impact. I am thankful to my Utah State University professors David Goetze, Carolyn Rhodes, Michael Lyons, Peter Galderisi, Jing Huang, Dwight Israelsen, Penny Byrne, and Edward Pease for their support of a lost immigrant student. It was owing to David Goetze's mentorship that I chose to become a political science professor; the recent generous gift of his personal library on Eastern European and Soviet history helps me to not give up.

I especially thank the editors of McGill-Queen's University Press – Michaela Jacques and Richard Ratzlaff – as well as the anonymous reviewers, for their questions, comments, and suggestions, which helped substantially improve this manuscript. I am grateful to Anastasia Leshchyshyn for comments and indexing. Some of the discussion appearing in this book was previously published in the *Journal of Law and Courts*; and *Research in Social Movements, Conflicts and Change.* I am thankful to the anonymous reviewers and editors of those editions, Daniel Lempert and Johanna Solomon, for valuable feedback that influenced my discussion of the revolution. All photographs used in this volume were provided from the archive of the Ukraine's Maidan Museum, and I am thankful to Lesya Onyshko and all those who took the time to find the needed images.

My family and friends believed in me, even when I didn't, and made my life better every step of the way. My mother, Svitlana Vorobyevska, has been a role model of a strong woman; while a physician in leadership roles, she devoted a big part of her life lovingly raising me and encouraging me to do my very best. Despite the gentle disappointment that my career choice brought to my father Simon Voitanik, an extraordinary physician himself, he supported me with unconditional love, humour, advice and a mysterious faith that it's not too late for me to be a martial artist. My stepfather, Yuri Vorobyevsky, played a very important role in my upbringing, teaching me right from wrong with love. I am grateful for having Irina and Julia in my life. My cousin Helen Schneider has played the role of a dear sister. Grandma Raia, Lyusya (oh how I miss you both), Fiona, Alex, Raia, Mila, Ihor, and Illiya were always close no matter how far. Special thanks to Debby, Camille, and Connie for their warmth and love. Doug, Sue, Kelly, Eric, and Kayla became our family, helping us feel at home in Illinois. Friendships with Jackie, Luz, Andrea, Brendalynn, Tera, and Arezou made life's experiences more meaningful and enjoyable.

I fell in love with my husband Will, being overwhelmed by his extraordinary kindness. He has been my rock, holding my hand through my many tears when I worried about loved ones, mourned the passings of those dear to us, and agonized over the horrors brought by the invasion of my home country. Will made many trips to Ukraine with me, and proofread a bazillion versions of this manuscript; his undying optimism keeps me alive. We are lucky to have two amazing humans as our children. Jenia's compassion to others through charitable work and the wisdom in her poetry taught me to be a better person. Tyler, who was less than a year old when I left for my first Maidan fieldwork, tried to feed me oatmeal through the phone – his tender-heartedness was a guiding light when I was away from home, and his sharp wit keeps me young with laughter. This book would not have been possible without my family's patience and support … and oatmeal.

Table 0.1 Timetable of the Maidan and the events leading to it

Date	*State action*	*Social response*
1991	Ukraine gains Independence from the Soviet Union.	
Winter 2000–01	KUCHMA-GATE: Journalist Georgy Gongadze, who founded a news site sharply critical of the Kuchma presidency, found dead and decapitated. Kuchma is implicated.	*Ukraine without Kuchma* protests in Kyiv, challenging government media suppression (*Kuchma-gate* also dubbed *Kuchma-hate*).
2004	Systematic fraud during presidential elections. Yanukovych announced the winner.	*The Orange Revolution* – mass protests in Kyiv challenging the fraudulent elections.
2004–05	Supreme Court orders a re-run of presidential elections. New Constitution adopted, empowering the parliament and decreasing presidential powers. UKRAINE BECOMES A DEMOCRACY: Elections become free and fair, freedoms of expression and the press become a norm.	
2010	Yanukovych comes to power through free and fair elections.	
1 October 2010	The Supreme Court's powers are drastically reduced by presidential decree, which established an additional High Specialized Court for Civil and Criminal Cases.	
October 2010	Yanukovych manipulates the Constitutional Court to boost presidential powers, reversing the 2004 constitutional reform.	
Fall 2010	Yanukovych manipulates a criminal indictment and conviction of his major political rival, former prime minister Tymoshenko.	Up to 5,000 protest in Kyiv, claiming the trial was a political prosecution designed to stop Tymoshenko from running in future elections.
November 2010	A law raising taxes for small businesses is passed by parliament.	10-day protests outside parliament succeed at pressuring them to reverse the tax law.
May 2012	The government excludes HOSTYNNY DVIR from a list of architectural landmarks.	Activists occupy Hostynny Dvir, organizing classes and cultural events, keeping the courtyard lit at night and cleaning up the area.

Date	*State action*	*Social response*
2010–2013	Series of laws and executive orders restricting press freedoms are passed, including changes to defamation laws. Local authorities suppress hundreds of peaceful gatherings across the country. Local courts begin judicial practice of citing 1988 Soviet law requiring state permission for public gatherings. Intimidation practices against journalists.	Journalist movement "Stop Censorship!" is organized in 2010. The March for Freedom of Speech: about 100 journalists march through central Kyiv. 18 May 2013 *Rise Up, Ukraine!* anti-repression rally, organized by civic organizations and opposition political parties.
May 2013	Presidential Party of Regions organizes *Joining Europe without Fascists!* rally to be held during *Rise Up, Ukraine!* anti-repression rally. Government-hired mercenary Vadym Titushko violently attacks journalists during the *Rise Up, Ukraine!* rally, including a prominent Yanukovych critic, Mustafa Nayyem.	Jewish organizations: Congress of the National Communities of Ukraine and the Association of Jewish Organizations and Communities criticize the so-called "anti-fascist," government-organized marches, claiming they were "aimed to discredit the political opposition."
June–July 2013	A police officer – suspected in the case of gang rape and severe beating of a 29-year-old woman in Vradiyivka – was released from pretrial detention.	Vradiyivka residents storm the local police department in response to the news. 10-day march from Vradiyivka to Kyiv, protesting police brutality and abuse of power.
Summer–Fall 2013	Russia's trade boycott to pressure Ukraine not to sign the agreement with the European Union: Ukrainian products are claimed "too risky," blocking their entry at the border into Russia – Yanukovych declares that preparations for the EU trade deal should continue despite the pressure.	
21 November 2013	Ukrainian government suspends its plans to sign the European Union trade agreement.	Protesters gather on Maidan against the government decision (becomes known as EUROMAIDAN).
23–4 November 2013	Ukraine's parliament rejects a series of bills that would have satisfied the EU by letting opposition leader Yulia Tymoshenko out of prison to travel to Germany for medical treatment.	The number of protesters in Kyiv reaches 50,000 on 24 November. A pro-government rally reaches 10,000 people (becomes known as Anti-Maidan).
29 November 2013	Government stands firm on decision to abandon the EU deal.	Representatives of political opposition call for an end to the EuroMaidan protests, encouraging a focus on forthcoming elections. The protest stage is taken down. Only around 300 protesters remain on Maidan Nezalezhnosti square.

Date	*State action*	*Social response*
30 November 2013	*Student Beating* At 4:10 a.m., Berkut riot police surround and beat the remaining group of protesters, detaining some, injuring seventy-nine people, including students, seniors, and reporters.	Tens of thousands of Kyivans gather on Maidan. Approximately 800,000 protesters gather on Maidan and surrounding areas on 1 December 2013, forcing police to retreat from the square.
1 December 2013	Police violence and detentions of protesters on Bankova Street. 50 protesters injured and detained.	Mobilization of civic groups to organize food, housing, transport, legal and medical aid to maintain resistance and communicate the resistance message. A stage is set up for resistance communication, multi-denominational prayers, and entertainment. Activists build barricades around Maidan "to protect protesters from further police attacks" (Maidan Occupy). The Maidan movement demands now focus on the release of the detained, end of repression, resignation of Yanukovych, and return to the 2004 constitution.
December 2013	State violence continues, resulting in severe injuries to protesters and journalists. State relies on detentions and systematic violations of due process. *Titushky* (government-paid mercenaries) are now regularly involved in violence against revolutionaries.	Approximately 500 lawyers mobilize to provide pro-bono aid to the detained. Lawyers, activists, and journalists work to record human rights violations and publicly expose them. Revolutionaries form self-defence units. Multiple initiatives and marches are organized to criticize undemocratic measures and state violence – including the Million's March, and the caravan to Yanukovych's residence.
11 December 2013	Police violently storm Maidan Occupy.	Bells are rung at the Mykhailivskyi Monastery. The number of protesters increases from several thousand to 25,000 to prevent a violent dispersal.
25 December 2013 – 7 January 2014		Holiday gatherings on Maidan.

Date	State action	Social response
16 January 2014	The government passes the 16 January laws, de-legalizing protests, increasing penalties for participation in civic unrest, and granting immunity to police officers who used force against protesters. Repressive measures include a prohibition to wear hard headwear, and drive in columns of five or more cars.	Approximately 100,000 protesters on Maidan. People carry signs challenging the constitutionality of the 16 January laws. Protesters wear pots, scuba diving and other head gear to mock the repressive laws.
January 2014	Police use stun grenades, rubber bullets at revolutionaries indiscriminately. Snipers use rubber bullets to blind. Police openly target journalists, medics, and makeshift hospitals. Torture and humiliation of revolutionaries (torture and mockery of Havryliuk is recorded and becomes public). Kidnapping of activists (Verbytskyi found murdered with signs of torture, Bulatov found with signs of "crucifixion-style" torture). FOUR PROTESTORS MURDERED BY BERKUT OFFICERS.	Revolutionaries use sticks and throw rocks and Molotov cocktails during violent clashes on Hrushevskoho street. Maidaners create a protective smokescreen between them and police by burning tires. Firewood and tires taken in large quantities to Maidan.
23–5 January 2014		Revolutionaries besiege administrative buildings in Chernivtsi, Ivano-Frankivsk, Lviv, Rivne and Ternopil, Khmelnytskyi, Lutsk, Sumy, Uzhhorod, and Zhytomyr.
25 January 2014	Yanukovych meets with the leaders of political opposition parties Klychko, Yatsenyuk, and Tiahnybok.	Opposition party leaders call for an early presidential election.
30 January2014	Ukraine's parliament adopts *quid pro quo* law offering amnesty to arrested protesters, demanding that Maidaners vacate occupied government buildings and demolish barricades in 15 days.	Maidaners clear one area of their territory and relinquish control of a number of government buildings.
14–16 February 2014	All 234 revolutionaries arrested since December released due to amnesty law.	Maidaners vacate Kyiv City Hall.
18–19 February 2014	Clashes between revolutionaries, police, and titushki in central Kyiv. State forces storm Maidan Occupy, shooting demonstrators. Around 30 revolutionaries killed, several hundred severely injured, and many go missing.	Revolutionaries continue to hold parts of Maidan Square, organizing violent resistance. Resistance activism in the cities of Lviv, Ivano-Frankivsk, and Khmelnytskyy, storming offices of regional police and the SBU.

Date	State action	Social response
20 February 2014	Government opens fire on revolutionaries using snipers, targeting head, neck, and vital organs. 53 REVOLUTIONARIES KILLED, nearly 1,000 injured, 215 hospitalized.	Maidaners continue resistance.
21 February 2014	Agreement signed between the government and opposition party leaders, and including foreign ministers of Poland, France, and Germany, announcing new presidential elections in 10 months, a return to the 2004 constitution limiting presidential power, new amnesty law.	Maidaners denounce the deal. A revolutionary from a self-defence unit threatens an armed offensive if Yanukovych did not resign by morning.
22 February 2014	Yanukovych flees Kyiv by helicopter, eventually surfacing in Russia. Police violence stops, a number of Berkut officers flee the city/country.	
23–6 February 2014	The Ukrainian parliament votes 328 to 0 to remove Yanukovych from office. Parliament vote for speaker Turchynov as interim president. Arrest warrant issued for Yanukovych. Berkut police unit disbanded. Civic rights restored.	Maidaners abandon resistance.
22–7 February 2014	A return to the 2004 version of the constitution. Interim government in operation (including professionals and civic activists).	Maidan representatives approve interim government.
25 May 2014	Presidential elections held – declared free and fair by local and international observers.	
26 October 2014	Parliamentary elections held – declared free and fair by local and international observers.	

Maidan

1

Introduction

"I yelled at them!! You should have seen me yelling at these policemen: *Quiet! Stop this horror, armed police surrounding and beating people! Let's agree: we'll offer you aid as well, but if a person falls down, you can't beat them. It's inhumane!* … I shocked myself that I mustered that much bravery," recounted a pediatrician-turned-revolutionary. The Maidan was Ukraine's social movement to restore democracy in the winter of 2013–14. In the course of resisting state oppression, people also debated the meaning of protest, types of political regimes, and methods of resisting suppression. As a Maidan participant shared, "It was a great place to be. We went there to talk about democracy." This book tells the story of the Ukrainian Revolution from the perspective of the revolutionaries. It is a carefully researched and detailed account of the underbelly of the resistance process, offering a unique look at how different people contributed to the mass uprising, challenged the state in multiple arenas, and negotiated revolutionary ideology. It also explores how the resistance process changed those who came to change the country.

How are revolutions fought? Especially when there are no leaders organizing it; when events are driven by popular discontent with the state? That is the point of this book: to look into the details of how participants self-organized the resistance, and how they managed to form a unified ideological front. While the common idea of resisting authoritarianism united the revolutionaries, diverse people and groups didn't agree on how to do it or what should be the new rules bounding the state. As a result, this notable event in Ukrainian history is a challenge for researchers. Due to the grassroots nature of the Maidan Revolution, ideology can't simply be traced to leaders' speeches. This book embraces the challenge of tracking the formation of the Maidan's revolutionary ideology, following continuing debates and evolving ideas among the participants, and shows that a grassroots revolution is a complex process of ideological formation of rights' boundaries in a society. In other words, a revolution is a dialogue about rights, and the resulting regime depends on the ideas negotiated during these interactions.

The Maidan – a revolution named after the Ukrainian word *maidan*, a main square (as it took place on the *Maidan Nezalezhnosti*, or Independence Square, in Kyiv) – was a turning point in Ukrainian history. This book supplies a wealth of new empirical data, presenting an unparalleled opportunity to see the writing of a nation's *social contract* in action. If social contract is an agreement about the boundaries of power between state and society, then who decides? Revolutions become a decisive moment in a country's history when boundaries are fundamentally renegotiated. While Ukraine became a democracy in 2004 (after the Orange Revolution – social protests triggered by rigged elections), a new president attempted to assert authoritarianism through state violence and repressive laws in the winter of 2013–14. But the people pushed back – with protest signs, tire burning, and court cases, they turned resistance into a grassroots revolution. It was not led by a charismatic leader, but was rather a self-organized resistance movement against state oppression, which succeeded in reverting the state back to democracy. Moreover, the revolutionary socialization process transformed the participants themselves, affecting future social discourse in the country. Thus, the process of the Maidan Revolution fostered the creation of a new Durkheimian "moral community."

The detailed analysis in this book also sheds new light on how Maidan revolutionaries managed to maintain peaceful resistance during the initial stage, and why they eventually embraced political violence. Thus, this study looks at one of the core questions in political science: why a previously peaceful civic society may embrace political violence to counteract the state. This book uncovers that it was the process of continuing interaction with security forces during the winter months of 2013–14 that led to a realization among participants about the true aims of the state. More specifically, as revolutionaries' perceptions of the state changed during the events, it led them to believe that anti-state violence was their only choice to return the country to democracy.

Eight years later, in 2022, the invading Russian army destroyed books on Ukraine's Maidan Revolution. True accounts of Ukrainian history became illegal within the occupied territories: books were systematically seized from schools and libraries and mocked by Russian media. Similar actions had taken place in Russian-controlled Ukrainian territories since 2014. Truth about the revolution was likewise eradicated throughout Russia. A post-Maidan democratic Ukraine was simply incompatible with the Kremlin's imperialist ambitions. The 2013–14 Maidan Revolution prevented the consolidation of an authoritarian regime in Ukraine, and fundamentally changed the country. If the Maidan had failed, President Yanukovych would have prevented free and fair elections, suppressed freedom of expression and the press, and crippled the judiciary. If the Maidan had failed, the Ukrainian state would have been controlled by the Kremlin via an authoritarian puppet regime. But the Maidan succeeded.

Around four million people participated in the Ukrainian Revolution, many knowingly risking their lives and security. In December 2013, after a month of state brutality and disregard for protester demands, activists delivered a creative message to the state. They recorded a "National Address to the President of Ukraine," mimicking the annual address traditionally given by the president just before midnight on New Year's Eve. Their version featured Maidan protesters behind the podium, who – with some humour, but in all seriousness – criticized state violence and declared that the victory of democratic forces was inevitable. In January 2014, the Ukrainian government passed laws legalizing repression: freedoms of the press, assembly, and expression were severely limited. The laws included numerous prohibitions, including one on wearing helmets (many Maidaners wore helmets to protect themselves from police beatings). A few days later, several hundred thousand people came to Kyiv's centre to protest the repressive laws, many wearing cooking pots or other self-made headwear to mockingly emphasize the extent of growing state repression. These are some of many imaginative social messages delivered during the revolution. In fact, the entire revolution was a dynamic exchange between state and society: state actions, such as violence, were interpreted as a sign of growing repression, followed by a social response – manifesting social rejection of repression (which, in turn, was followed by more severe state repression).

The Ukrainian Maidan Revolution, also known in Ukraine as the Revolution of Dignity, was a true democratic revolution. It was far more than just protests – it was a system of complex social networks of mutual assistance to maintain anti-authoritarian resistance, a true grassroots movement. After police beat and detained peaceful protesters in November 2013, hundreds of thousands travelled to the capital to protest, and many decided to stay. They cooked food and organized logistical operations to connect revolutionaries with those offering free rent and pro bono legal and medical aid. Activists organized marches, vehicle caravans, printed illegal brochures, and launched social media campaigns against the state. They fought police and thugs, who were hired by the state to beat protesters, argued in courts against due process violations, and debated the meaning of democracy with their countrymen.

Ukraine's Maidan Revolution had multiple arenas: the protest square, hospitals, courtrooms, churches, mass and social media, and so forth. Revolutionaries utilized these arenas to challenge the state about its repression and demanded that the state follow the constitution. A pro-democratic revolution is a state–society dialogue about the terms of legality, a negotiation of social contract. We are familiar with the process of judicial review: the power of judges to decide whether a given law is constitutional. The Ukrainian Maidan Revolution became a form of social review: activists questioned the constitutionality of new repressive laws, unlawful detentions, excessive police violence and shootings. Not only activists and lawyers, but religious leaders appealed to the state, drawing lines of morality along lines of constitutionality, claiming that the violent acts of the state were in violation of citizens' human rights. There were revolutionary hubs in various parts of Ukraine, in which activists spent sleepless nights putting together survival kits or sowing protective leather gear for those in Kyiv. Diaspora volunteerism also flourished, as Ukrainians in North America helped newcomers to Kyiv navigate the city over the phone.

Consider the resistance operations taking place inside Kyiv hospitals. Revolutionaries, injured by policemen, were forced to go to hospitals. However, after beating protesters, police would often go to hospitals to arrest their victims. Or so they thought. In reality, Maidan was there as well. Police would search medical records for the types of injuries they had inflicted, but physicians would avoid recording any suspicious details, at times changing the names of the patients or the nature of their injuries. Police often couldn't find injured revolutionaries, as staff would hide them in X-ray rooms. Revolutionaries who couldn't be hidden had volunteer guards – either lawyers, or those who could summon lawyers – to point out the illegal nature of arresting a hospitalized patient. Often, this was not enough: police knowingly and openly continued to violate the law. But activists had another move up their sleeve: they called the press. Journalists appeared, pointing video cameras in policemen's faces. Such public shaming of policemen for their illegal actions was often an effective method of preventing arrests.

This study of Maidan teaches us that a democratic revolution is a continuous process of value negotiations, and actors often discover their opponents' values during their ongoing interactions (rather than having a clear understanding of the opponent's moral principles at the onset of the conflict). It's a dynamic exchange between state and society consisting of violent and non-violent acts, in which society acts according to their continuing *interpretations* of state actions. Growing state violence and the open humiliation and torture of protesters through the winter months changed the dynamic of the protests, affecting the means of resistance. Not only did the state continue to ignore protesters' demands to end severe police violence and illegal detentions, it eventually resorted to live ammunition. Moreover, police systematically humiliated and degraded revolutionaries, stripping them naked in sub-zero temperatures, forcing them to kneel, and so on. Severe violence, torture, and humiliation were interpreted by activists as an indication of Yanukovych's determination to consolidate a terror regime in Ukraine. This fundamentally changed their response: support for political violence began growing among protesters. It was the combination of social resistance and political violence that forced Yanukovych to flee and his criminal regime to crumble. Not all police beatings of peaceful protesters result in revolutions. This study shows that the outcome depends on how police violence is interpreted by the people. Since Yanukovych kept stretching his powers, changing the constitution, violating constitutional rights, and then bluntly breaking the law to beat and shoot protesters, social angst grew. Many of the activists I interviewed said they believed that if they hadn't resisted, Ukraine would have become dictatorial, "just like Belarus or Russia."

The study also shows that another essential element of a democratic revolution is a process of value negotiations among the revolutionaries themselves. Maidaners were a diverse group, representing different social and economic classes, and various ideologies, beliefs, and ideas about what needed to be done. While some advocated political violence from the beginning, continuous deliberation led to agreement and substantial efforts to pacify the protesters and prevent violent clashes with police (even after some had taken place). For example, handing candles to the protesters was a conscious and carefully designed move by activists: candlelight "pacified people," and "kept their hands occupied." Disappointed by opposition politicians, Maidaners formed a council of the multiple social groups present on the square, coordinating anti-state actions, initiatives, and marches. Maidan included multiple religious, ethnic, and regional groups. There were Orthodox, Greek Catholic, Catholic, and Evangelical Christians, Muslims, and Jews; some spoke Ukrainian, some knew only Russian; while there were more people from the west and centre of Ukraine, there were revolutionaries from all regions of the country, as well as foreigners (including from Russia). Importantly, Maidan encompassed a wide variety of ideological views: liberal, conservative, feminist, leftist, and ultra-right. This ideological assortment presented an obvious challenge for the resistance movement. While ongoing debates, and at times violent interactions, continued throughout the winter, a pro-democratic consensus prevailed, producing a unified front.

Revolution became the process that changed society: Soviet-era social beliefs were challenged, giving way to a reconceptualization of civic duty, nation, and belonging. As a multitude of social networks were built to resist police violence and prevent detention, this led to the growth of interpersonal social trust. As activists debated means of resistance on the protest square, they de facto participated in a reconceptualization of *democracy*, one necessitating constant social oversight of state functions. As they fought against the unlawful detention of protesters in courts, they asserted new boundaries of state–society relations, engaging the concept of inalienable rights. The extensive grassroots social movement, which brought Ukrainians from various social backgrounds, identities, and regions, defined the new post-Maidan Ukraine.

Revolutions have two defining features: mass movement (distinguishing a revolution from a coup), and a political regime change (distinguishing it from an unsuccessful revolt, but also from other social movements seeking a change within a regime). Some have suggested that the Maidan Revolution was not, in fact, a revolution, as there was presumably no regime change. The argument here is that Yanukovych came to power via free and fair elections, and since post-Maidan Ukraine was democratic, and some politicians were even re-elected after the revolution, there was no regime change. However, if we are to discuss the regime type (and its change), we need to address, firstly, the fact that after coming to power, Yanukovych took overarching measures to suppress democracy in Ukraine: changing the constitution to increase his powers, undermining the Supreme Court and judiciary, and running a "mafia-style syndicate" of government tax agencies and criminal organizations. Freedoms of assembly and the press were systematically targeted via new policies and court decisions. Secondly – and vitally – during the winter months of 2013–14, the Ukrainian state institutionalized full-scale authoritarianism: new laws deprived citizens of civil liberties, courts violated basic rights of due process to imprison activists, and police used excessive violence, live ammunition, and torture to repress protesters. The authoritarian regime was short-lived, thanks to the Maidan, but it does not change the fact that it was institutionalized, and severe repression was used in an attempt to eradicate social opposition and consolidate authoritarianism for the foreseeable future. The Maidan Revolution succeeded at ousting the Yanukovych administration, putting an end to these laws and practices. With that victory, a democratic regime replaced an authoritarian one. Shootings, beatings, and detentions of protesters came to an end; constitutional freedoms were restored.

This book breaks down the anatomy of the Maidan Revolution: as Lawson argues,[1] to fully understand a revolution we have to analyze how it began, unfolded, and ended. While providing a detailed account of the events, strategies, and effects, I present an interpretative and, thus, explanatory argument: a more nuanced understanding of revolutionaries' perceptions helps us better understand the *causes* of their participation and changing strategies, and the outcome of the revolution. I challenge, however, the positivist explanatory approach: I argue that activists' decision to rely on political violence depends not only on power dynamics, or established set of identities, but on their continually altering image of the state (dictated by their understanding of morality). The positivist reading of identities is also challenged through this nuanced study: participation in the revolution shifts activists' perceptions of self and their sense of belonging.

For constructivists, grassroots revolution presents a new challenge in tracing the development of ideas and ideology. Rather than tracing the formation of ideology as elite-driven, it is vital to analyze the negotiation of revolutionary ideology among participants with various beliefs. The terms of a new social contract depend on the dynamic of these revolutionary debates: the successes and failures of these negotiations among the participants, and the effect of the revolutionary process on multiple actors' perceptions of social justice. A strict positivist approach assumes pre-determined knowledge of the participants' motivations (i.e., many scholars assume that revolutionaries have a clear idea of who they are, what they want, and what they think the state wants). This book's more nuanced interpretive study of the Maidan shows that these perceptions are subject to change during the process of revolution. I show that actors' motivations (to use political violence, for example) change as a result of interactions with state actors, which leads to a change in perceptions about the state, and, in turn, affects revolutionary motivations and actions. Moreover, participation in the revolution affects their perception of self and their community.

Maidan Nezalezhnosti and Ukraine's Resistance Movements

The word *maidan* in Ukrainian means an open space or main square, and *Maidan* usually refers to the Maidan Nezalezhnosti (Independence Square) in the centre of Kyiv. The centre squares of Kyiv tell a history of Ukrainian anti-state resistance: including the anti-Bolshevik war in 1918 and political rallies during the Soviet era. As Serhii Plokhy emphasizes, Ukraine's autonomy movement was a major factor behind the collapse of the Soviet empire.[2] In the last years of the Soviet Union, Maidan (there is some irony in the fact that it was then called October Revolution Square) was the place for social protests and expressions of Ukrainians' public discontent with the Soviet state. For example, a pro-ecology gathering in 1988 was triggered by the consequences of the Chernobyl accident, a tragedy which the Soviet state augmented with an attempted cover-up and gross mismanagement.[3] While academicians and activists carefully avoided anti-state rhetoric (being monitored by the KGB), they communicated ideas in support of reforms.[4] Such protests were an essential manifestation of Ukrainians' growing disillusionment with the Soviet state.[5] The so-called Revolution on Granite in 1990 (tents were set up on the granite surfaces of the Maidan) was led by students who organized hunger strikes to call for reforms, including multi-party elections, and challenged the new union treaty with the Soviet republics – with dissidents, intellectuals, and the local population showing support.[6] As Olga Onuch points out, the Revolution on Granite was a "trend-setter": it had a profound effect on the scope and strategies of post-Soviet revolutions in Ukraine, including the use of the main Kyiv square, tent city, and a stage-centred protest.[7]

In post–Soviet Ukraine, protest movements on the Maidan challenged authoritarian measures of the Kuchma regime such as fraudulent elections and suppression of the press. The *Ukraine without Kuchma* protests in the winter of 2000–01 took place in the aftermath of *Kuchma-gate* (dubbed by the Ukrainians as *Kuchma-hate*), which involved the murder of journalist Georgiy Gongadze, and recordings implicating president Kuchma as having ordered it.[8] The Orange Revolution of 2004 saw hundreds of thousands of people on the Kyiv square – with many in Ukraine referring to the event as the *first Maidan*. It was also a mass protest movement, challenging fraudulent elections in Ukraine which followed Kuchma's repressive measures against the press, and the suspicious poisoning of the opposition candidate, Victor Yushchenko. The protests successfully placed pressure on the Supreme Court to order a re-run of the elections. While the protests saw multiple activist groups leading social discourse about the rules of democracy,[9] the protests were organized by Yushchenko's campaign team.[10] As the government lost legitimacy, citizens joined the opposition political elite and mobilization activists, who promised change.[11] As Aslund and McFaul put it, the Orange Revolution was "Ukraine's democratic breakthrough."[12] Indeed, it brought democracy to Ukraine: elections in the aftermath of the revolution were free and fair, and the administration no longer provided *temniki* to the press (instructions, with accompanying pressure, on how to cover the news). The irony of the success of the Orange Revolution was in setting up a democratic system that allowed Yanukovych – the same candidate who was declared a winner as the result of fraudulent elections in 2004, and who lost to Yushchenko after the re-run – to come to power through free and fair elections. Yanukovych was elected by a populace who were well aware of his criminal record.

Yanukovych's Growing Hold on Power prior to the Maidan Revolution

After taking office in 2010, Yanukovych began taking overarching measures to suppress democracy in Ukraine. His extensive changes included constitutional revisions to increase his presidential powers, institutional revisions to control the judicial and prosecutorial system, and the connection of government tax agencies with criminal organizations. Ukraine's democracy took an especially hard hit under Yanukovych as freedoms of assembly and the press were systematically targeted via new policies and court decisions. Through manipulation of the judicial system, he also jailed his major political opponent, Yulia Tymoshenko.

Yanukovych directed a massive transformation of Ukraine's legal system, which included a substantial institutional makeover, creation of new key positions, and multiple appointments of judges and prosecutors. Notably, institutional transformations included an immediate return to the 1996 constitution, which replaced the existing parliamentary governmental structure with one that guaranteed extensive presidential powers. This went hand in hand with Yanukovych's attack on Ukraine's judicial system through undercutting the powers of the Supreme Court and establishing tight control over the judges of lower courts, which led to a number of judicial decisions suppressing political opposition.[13]

The first obvious assault on democracy by Yanukovych's administration came in the way of meddling in local elections during his first year in power. The elections were rescheduled from May to October 2010, while suddenly changing electoral rules shortly before they were held. Moreover, manipulations of the process took place on election day, notably disqualifying the opposing party – the Tymoshenko Block – in one city.[14] Such manipulations were enabled because Yanukovych had a solid grip on his party (the Party of Regions), which quickly gained a majority in the parliament, likely involving illegal schemes (forcing parliamentarians to defect from other parties).[15]

Within months of coming to power, Yanukovych curated constitutional changes, gaining substantially more powers, and structural changes that fundamentally undermined judicial independence. Four judges of the Constitutional Court who opposed the changes proposed by Yanukovych suddenly resigned, reporting pressure from the presidential administration, some under visible pressure from criminal investigations against their relatives.[16] With its new composition, the court immediately invalidated the 2004 constitutional amendments (implemented after the Orange Revolution), depriving the parliament of considerable powers, and shifting them to the president.[17]

The Yanukovych administration substantially reduced the jurisdiction of the Supreme Court, which had ruled in 2004 to rerun rigged presidential elections, and was expected to offer resistance to abuses of state powers. This was done by creating a new High Specialized Court for Civil and Criminal Cases, High Council of Justice (to replace the existing Council), and centralized High Judicial Qualification Commission (to replace regional ones).[18] Not only did these institutional changes drastically deprive the Supreme Court of powers, they allowed Yanukovych to have control over the judicial educational testing process and appointments.[19] Subsequently, judicial appointments in high-profile cases often went to probationary judges who ruled to Yanukovych's liking.[20]

Control of the judiciary for political gain became especially evident in Yanukovych's prosecution of his main political opponent, former Prime Minister Yulia Tymoshenko, in 2011. A young judge, with barely two years' experience and still in his probationary period, was transferred to Pechersk District Court from a regional city court by presidential decree "to hear the most salient criminal case in the nation."[21] Soon after he delivered a criminal verdict, imprisoning Tymoshenko for allegedly overstepping her role as prime minister by signing an unfavourable contract with a Russian gas company, the young judge was quickly promoted. The nature of Tymoshenko's criminal accusation, and poorly hidden manipulations of the judicial system in the criminal proceedings against his political opponent, sent a sure sign to many in Ukraine about Yanukovych's authoritarian inclinations. A number of international organizations, including the Council of Europe, called the verdict an example of politically motivated selective prosecution and politicization of the criminal justice process.[22] On 24 August 2011, Ukraine's

Independence Day, around 5,000 people protested in Kyiv against the trial, marching towards the presidential administrative buildings before police broke up the march. Tymoshenko's supporters saw the trial as designed to prevent her from running in future elections.[23]

Growing social discontent with Yanukovych's increasing authoritarianism was met with state repression. Note that after the 2004 Orange Revolution, constitutional freedoms of peaceful assembly became much better protected. Lower courts stopped ruling in favour of authorities, who would attempt to ban protests, and by 2007, human rights monitoring organizations noted that freedom of assembly was widely enjoyed in Ukraine.[24] Under Yanukovych, however, the pattern was reversed. The freedom to assemble began to be repressed through the lower and appellate courts.[25] Thus, every 2010 court decision in Donetsk, Zaporizhzhya, Kyiv, Lviv, Odessa, Poltava, Summy, Ternopil, Kharkiv, and Cherkassy regions upheld local authorities' bans on local gatherings.[26]

Repression continued throughout the Yanukovych presidency. In 2012, authorities attempted to suppress 354 peaceful gatherings through the courts, and succeeded in 90 per cent of cases. Court rulings included such explanations as "the protests might damage the nation's image."[27] Bizarrely, in order to circumvent constitutional guarantees, the courts began citing a Soviet law from 1988 that required protest organizers to seek permission from authorities to hold public gatherings.[28] As Ukraine's Human Rights Helsinki Association noted in its 2012 report, the Soviet-era decree regulated "non-existent constitutions of non-existent entities [Soviet republics]," violated the Ukrainian constitution, but was used by the majority of courts to ban peaceful gatherings in Ukraine.[29] This practice of the lower courts continued, despite the High Administrative Court's 2012 conclusion that the 2010–11 administrative courts' handling of peaceful assembly cases was incorrect. The courts also stopped referencing rulings of the European Court of Human Rights (the practice had been common under the Yushchenko administration, and was codified in 2006).[30] In yet another blunt move, the courts under Yanukovych ruled opposite to ECHR decisions while pretending this was done in accordance with them. For example, while the ECHR ruled in *Bukta v. Hungary* that authorities may not disperse protests even if they were not notified, the Ukrainian administrative courts ruled that according to the ECHR ruling, organizers were required to inform the authorities about the gathering.[31] In 2012, the state started arresting and prosecuting protesters, relying on Soviet-era decrees (a state practice found unlawful by the ECHR).

Freedom of the press in Ukraine also drastically declined after Yanukovych came to power. New restrictive laws and executive orders, censorship measures, limitations on access to information, and blatant intimidation were the new norm, reflected in much lower rankings for press freedoms under Yanukovych in comparison with previous years.[32] A series of restrictive laws included The Law on Protection of Personal Data, the Law on Protecting Public Morals, most notably the Law on Court Fees (which made it much easier for plaintiffs to seek large monetary damages when filing defamation cases), amendments to the code regulating classified information, and increased fines for both civilians and officials if they are convicted of mishandling state secrets.[33] Journalists reported being afraid of losing their job for government criticism: intimidation became a widespread government tactic, and a part of the system. One characteristic suppression tactic was to work in collaboration with tax police, who would conduct searches to intimidate journalists. A prominent Ukrainian journalist, Mustafa Nayyem, known for his strong government criticism, was beaten by the guards of a member of Yanukovych's party, the Party of Regions.[34] Another prominent case of a journalist being beaten took place during the *Rise Up, Ukraine!* opposition rally on 18 May 2013, as the journalist was attacked by Vadym Titushko, who was hired by the authorities.[35] The last name of the attacker was later repurposed by Maidaners, as the term *titushka* (*titushky*, plural) was used to describe hired thugs who attacked civilian protesters and journalists, and provoked clashes between the police and protesters.[36] After the Maidan, lists of targeted journalists were found in Yanukovych's residence.

Protests continued over the years of Yanukovych's presidency. In 2010, protests succeeded at pressuring the Yanukovych government against passing a new tax code. According to the proposed law, taxes were to be raised for small businesses while giving tax breaks to his wealthy industrialist backers.[37] After over ten days of mass protests by thousands of businessmen in Kyiv and across the country, amendments were made to continue tax breaks for small businesses.[38]

Another notable state–society stand-off prior to the Maidan involved depriving Hostynny Dvir (Hospitable Courtyard) of its status as an architectural landmark in 2013, while a private company with offshore roots presented a multimillion-dollar reconstruction project.[39] For nearly three months, activists – a handful of Kyiv intellectuals – occupied Hostynny Dvir to save it from destruction and preserve it as a city landmark and a rare cultural public space. This small-scale resistance effort involved a number of grassroots activities to maintain presence, socialize, raise social awareness, and gain support. For example, activists picked up garbage, and organized classes and art events. They collected thousands of signatures from Kyivans in support of preserving the landmark, as well as several thousand hryvnia in donations to light the courtyard at night, buy food, and clean the facilities. As one activist shared, they "took away ten trucks of garbage to make this place look more aesthetic."[40] Importantly, Hostynny Dvir became a place of socialization, hosting numerous events such as "language… classes, lectures and seminars, art performances, literature presentations, movie screenings and concerts."[41] Despite eviction attempts and police tear gas, the activists continued to occupy Hostynny Dvir. Many of them acquired mobilization skills that later proved useful during the Maidan Revolution.

In the words of a post-Maidan chief prosecutor, Yanukovych ran a "mafia-style syndicate" whose crimes likely cost Ukraine "up to $100 billion."[42] The entire state apparatus worked for specific officials to profit from state-funded projects and money laundering, according to Mykola Holomsha, deputy attorney general of Ukraine.[43] Stolen government assets were found in European banks, often registered to Yanukovych's family members or close partners.[44] The corruption schemes involved tax evasion, fraudulent tax claims, bribery, and extortion. While corruption was a Soviet legacy that flourished in Ukraine since the Soviet collapse, the Yanukovych administration developed a systematic way of extorting and embezzling, working with criminal gangs and tax agencies.[45] Systemic corruption was enabled through Yanukovych's centralized governing hierarchy, which controlled the operations "from town, to municipality, then regional, to the ministry [level] and then up to the president," in the words of Andrei Marusov, chairman of the board of Transparency International Ukraine, an anti-corruption organization.[46] This centralized system of government corruption targeted businesses, forcing them to participate in illicit schemes and/or pay bribes.[47] Notably, corruption under Yanukovych relied heavily on tax police and inspectors, who systematically extorted money from private businesses via threats and intimidation.[48]

While the exact scale of systemic corruption under Yanukovych was unknown until after the Maidan, it touched many lives, stifling businesses. Public discontent grew over corruption, and the impunity of those involved in criminal state activities. Opposition parties organized a series of *Rise Up Ukraine!* anti-Yanukovych protests in 2013, which drew tens of thousands of protesters over several months. But perhaps the best-known anti-state protests under Yanukovych – prior to November 2013 – took place in the town of Vradiyivka in July 2013, when five hundred protesters broke into the local police station. The protests came in response to the release of a policeman who had been accused of gang rape and severe beating, causing skull injury to a local twenty-nine-year-old woman. The release was widely believed to be due to his familial connection to the regional police chief.[49] In the previous year protests erupted in the same region (Mykolaiv) when a teenage girl died after being raped and set on fire.[50] After storming the police station in Vradiyivka, a group of activists organized a ten-day march from the town to Kyiv to protest police brutality and abuse of power at large.[51] The protests reflected growing public concern with *mazhory* (those benefiting from nepotism) and their impunity for criminal activity, which had intensified under Yanukovych.

During Yanukovych's tenure, public concern over corruption and his handling of media rights grew. A majority in Ukraine disapproved of the president's handling of corruption (77 per cent disapproval) and oligarchical influence (63 per cent disapproval). A majority also disapproved of the administration's denial of broadcasting frequencies to selected private TV channels (55 per cent disapproval). Notably, an overwhelming majority of Ukrainians approved of Yanukovych's handling of relations with Russia (66 per cent). The salience of "pro-Western" issues was minimal prior to the Russian invasion in 2014 – a fact often left out of analyses of Ukraine. Prior to Russia's invasion in 2014, only 3 per cent of Ukrainians listed "status of Ukraine and EU" as an important political issue, and only 1 per cent of Ukrainians listed "status of Ukraine and NATO" as an important political issue for future presidents in 2009.[52] When rating the most serious problems facing Ukraine in

2010, "prospects of Ukraine joining NATO" were of concern to only 3 per cent of respondents, and "problems with Russia" of concern to only 3 per cent of respondents – the latter was a decline from previous surveys.[53] Thus, prior to the Maidan, Ukrainian citizens were concerned with the loss of rights and growing corruption under Yanukovych's regime. Moreover, separatist parties never received more than a small percentage of the vote, even in Donbas and Crimea; and even those who sought closer ties with Russia rejected integrationist projects (insisted on by Russia).[54] Therefore, the division of Ukraine into pro-West and pro-Russia camps prior to the Maidan is a misleading narrative, which obfuscates the reasons behind social resistance in Ukraine against the Yanukovych regime.

Throughout his presidency, public pressure against the Yanukovych government continued to mount. A few factors helped ameliorate public dissatisfaction: the prospect of presidential elections at the end of 2014, when Yanukovych could be voted out of office, and the Ukrainian trade deal with the European Union, with the expected consequent leverage applied by European countries to restrain government corruption and aid democratic development in Ukraine. The economic deal with the European Union was in the works for years, and was planned to be signed in November 2013.

Russian Interference and Trade Boycott

Public desire for a democratic Ukraine, however, ran against the Kremlin's plans: a democratic Ukraine meant a sovereign Ukraine. An economically strong Ukraine with close ties to Europe meant the Kremlin could not dictate its terms. Aleksandr Tsipko, a former adviser to Mikhail Gorbachev, let slip a secret in his 2008 interview: Boris Yeltsin agreed to Ukrainian independence on the eve of the referendum in December 1991 because he believed that an independent Ukraine would "crawl back on its knees" after he took the Kremlin from Gorbachev.[55] Tsipko claimed: "Ukraine's 'Western path,' prompted by the disintegration of the Soviet Union, might die off amid the economic collapse awaiting Ukraine in the conditions of the global crisis."[56] One of the most reliable ways for the Kremlin to maintain its control was through upholding authoritarianism in Ukraine. Indeed, Ukraine's president

Kuchma turned to Russia when facing pressure from Ukrainian society after the *Ukraine without Kuchma* mass protests. As a result, the Russian government openly supported Kuchma in the 2000s, after he increased authoritarian measures.[57]

The Orange Revolution's success at bringing democracy to Ukraine foiled the Kremlin's plans for continued control of the country. In the words of Yaroslav Hrytsak, the Orange Revolution "created the impression that Ukraine had reached the point where its return to Russia was impossible."[58] According to Putin's former adviser Andrey Illarionov, the first serious plan for a military solution to the "Ukrainian question"[59] appeared in 2004, when Kuchma refused to suppress the Orange Revolution by force. While the military take-over was shelved, Russia's FSB and the Kremlin played a decisive role in fostering political crisis in Ukraine after the Orange Revolution, to bring Kremlin-friendly leadership to power in Ukraine, according to the Russian nationalist ideologue Aleksandr Prokhanov.[60] In fact, Russian political technologists invested greatly in the Ukrainian election campaign, pitting the eastern and western regions against each other.[61] After Russia's success in promoting the campaign of Kremlin-friendly Yanukovych, its grip on Ukraine's politics, military, and economy further tightened. According to Ukrainian intelligence reports, presented to Yanukovych, an interdepartmental government commission was formed in Moscow in order to "create political, humanitarian and economic conditions favorable for intervention in Ukraine."[62] The major objectives of the Kremlin commission were "the establishment of the dominance of Russian energy companies in the Ukrainian market and the broadening of influence in the communications, machine, and shipbuilding industries, and other key sectors."[63]

After the Orange Revolution, Moscow sharply raised gas prices for Ukraine, and the crippling effect of high prices allowed Russia to pressure Yanukovych into a twenty-five-year lease extension to Russia's Black Sea Fleet military base in Crimea, in exchange for reducing the rates.[64] Speaking about the deal, Yanukovych said it was key to Ukraine's economic survival: "Ukraine's … gas contract was driving us into the grave. That was the main problem. We had to find a way out."[65] In the summer of 2013, as the official signing of the Ukrainian agreement with the European Union approached, the Russian border patrol began baseless full checks of all Ukrainian trade transport to

Russia, causing long delays. The owners of forty Ukrainian companies whose products were declared "risky" without justification were the same ones who were considered to have lobbied for Ukraine's political choice to sign the trade agreement with the EU, including companies run by Poroshenko, Kolomoiskiy, and Savchuk.[66] On 24–5 July, the Russian Customs Committee labelled forty large Ukrainian companies as "risky," subjecting them to comprehensive checks.[67] On 22 August 2013, the Kremlin openly threatened Ukraine with cutting off all trade if the country concluded the Association Agreement with the European Union.[68] Yanukovych resisted at first, by proclaiming a pro-European economic direction in two big speeches: on Ukraine's Independence Day on 24 August[69] and at the opening of the parliamentary session on 3 September.[70]

On 14 September, the Russian customs service declared all Ukrainian imports to be "risky," causing nearly 1,000 trucks to be held at one Ukraine-Russia border control post the next day.[71] A number of Ukrainian companies reported problems with customs documents and the sudden addition of new requirements, such as receiving permissions from certain Russian agencies.[72] This de facto blockade forced many Ukrainian companies (such as those transporting perishable products) to cease their exports to Russia entirely.[73] Ukrainian fruit and vegetable export companies expected to lose $30 million due to the Russian blockade. Eventually, Russian presidential adviser Glasev stated that the actions on the Ukraine–Russian customs border were carried out in preparation for changes to requirements and will worsen "if Ukraine makes the suicidal move to sign an agreement with the EU."[74] There are two fundamental differences between the EU's and Russia's economic agreements with Ukraine. First, the EU never forced Ukraine to give up its trade with Russia. Neither did it impose blockades on Ukraine's products for manipulation purposes. Secondly – a vital point for many Ukrainians – the EU's conditions involved putting pressure on the Ukrainian government to promote selected human rights issues. The Russian government, on the other hand, took advantage of and further encouraged undemocratic practices by Ukrainian leaders. Public pressure against Yanukovych's growing authoritarianism, and Ukraine's potential to gain economic strength, meant the Kremlin would lose its chance to control Ukraine. The Kremlin made its blunt moves: by blocking Ukraine's trade products on the border, Russia successfully forced Yanukovych to abandon the EU agreement. Taking advantage of

Yanukovych's weakness, Putin wanted to establish control of Ukraine by locking in its economy and, as before, encouraging authoritarianism. As a detailed account in the Epilogue shows, the Kremlin unleashed systematic propaganda to undermine Ukraine's social opposition to the repression that followed.

November 2013: EuroMaidan

On 21 November 2013, Yanukovych's prime minister issued the dramatic order to suspend the process of signing the trade agreement with the European Union, in the interests of "national security" and to renew "active dialogue" with Moscow.[75] EU officials, who had been preparing to sign the long-negotiated deal, said Yanukovych cited fears of Russia, which had threatened retaliation, crippling trade sanctions and cutting energy supplies in new "gas wars."[76]People in Ukraine saw Yanukovych's refusal to sign the EU deal as a strong sign of growing authoritarianism.[77] Closer ties with the European Union offered a useful mechanism to reinforce democracy in Ukraine: European Union diplomacy often applied pressure for pro-democratic and anti-corruption reforms in Ukraine. Just as many citizens in Europe who rely on European Union organizations such as the European Court of Justice to have an additional check on their own government, many Ukrainians expected that the EU would play a stronger role in promoting democracy in Ukraine. As one activist put it, "We want closer ties with the EU not necessarily because we expect we'll live better, but because we want our politicians to live worse."

In the next several days of November, following this unexpected announcement, Ukrainians started gathering on the main square in Kyiv – Maidan Nezalezhnosti (Independence Square). Social demands included (1) signing of the association agreement with the European Union; (2) cancelling orders of the government to suspend European integration processes; (3) adopting the necessary legislative acts concerning European integration; (4) incorporating the request to the European Commission, European Parliament, and EU member governments to remove all additional terms and conditions that prevent the signing of an agreement on associate membership with the EU; and (5) incorporating requests to the European Commission, European Parliament, and EU governments not to put the future of Ukraine's dependence on those individual Ukrainian politicians.[78]

On 24 November, approximately 50,000 people came to Maidan Square to protest the government's move to delay the association deal with the EU.[79] On 27 November students of the Kyiv Mohyla Academy, a major university in Ukraine, went on strike with the support of their administration. Students from other universities were prevented from striking or even attending the protests, with administrators encouraging students to turn in fellow classmates for protest participation.[80] The jailed former prime minister, Yulia Tymoshenko, announced a hunger strike in support of protesters.[81] Many students took part in the protests during the next couple of days. Opposition political parties held separate gatherings, eventually joining the protests on the Maidan. For several days, protests and peaceful marches continued, with tens of thousands of participants. A stage was set up, where politicians and activists offered public speeches, and popular musicians helped keep the crowds going. By 29 November 2013, however, protests died down, the stage was taken down, and the resistance movement announced that it would focus their energy on campaigning against Yanukovych in the next presidential election. Only a couple of hundred protesters were left on 29 November 2013, when Ukrainian authorities deployed hundreds of riot police to central Kyiv.[82] The unprecedented police violence that followed, characterized by cruel and excessive use of force, was unleashed on the small peaceful crowd in the middle of the night, shocking the conscience of Ukrainian society. This extreme state violence, which became systematic and grew over the winter months, was the major reason behind the anti-state Maidan Revolution in Ukraine. This book tells the story of this revolution and its effects.

Contributing to Scholarship on the Maidan Revolution

There is growing scholarly literature on the Maidan Revolution of 2013–14. This book supports that scholarship, which has placed an emphasis on the role of ideational factors during the Maidan Revolution – such as the effects of support for democracy on protest participation;[83] social notions of human dignity on mass mobilization during the Ukrainian Revolution;[84] the role of democratic values in the mobilization of Ukrainian diaspora;[85] and the role of ideational,[86] religious,[87] and media[88] discourse. Likewise, it supplements literature on the ideological origin of anti-authoritarian movements in Eastern Europe.[89] This body of scholarship is juxtaposed with studies that emphasize structural and economic factors as explanatory variables behind the revolution,[90] such as Ukraine's geopolitical position, the interests of competing outside powers,[91] as well as an "unstable world order."[92]

Major contributions of this book to the existing literature on Maidan are the following. It is the first detailed account of the Maidan as a democratic revolution – including a step-by-step analysis of the state's repressive methods and social actions that led to regime change. Secondly, it depicts a continuing process of state–society dialogue during the Maidan via communication and violence, proving the most detailed analysis of the causes of evolving resistance strategies and growing political violence. Thirdly, the book presents a detailed picture of the nature of resistance, including an account of revolutionaries' motivations, grassroots self-organization and effective co-operation, as well as extensive negotiations of revolutionary ideology among the participating social groups. I also demonstrate that the revolutionaries were not deterred by force: they knowingly risked their lives and security to restore democracy. Finally, I contribute to the literature on post-Maidan change in Ukraine by explaining how the revolutionary process contributed to social change, such as perceptions of national identity and civic duty.

To underscore the pro-democratic nature of the Maidan resistance movement, I emphasize the legal aspects of state–society interactions during the revolution. This entails the most detailed, up-to-date account of the repressive methods utilized by the Yanukovych administration against the opposition, as well as the revolutionaries' use of constitutional discourse and the courts. Maria Popova argued that, due to a lack of political and legal opportunities to challenge the state, Maidaners in 2013–14 turned to violence – in contrast to 2004 events, when the Supreme Court offered an institutional path to redress the injustice.[93] While it's correct to identify the role of the Supreme Court in the outcome of the Orange Revolution, this perspective leaves out the fact that revolutionaries actively included the courts as a method of resistance during the winter of 2013–14. My detailed account of legal resistance during the revolution builds on McCann's socio-legal framework, showing that resistance can flourish not only with the presence of institutional routes, but despite the lack of these routes, and can in fact expose their inadequacy. Uncovering judicial violations was a core method by which Maidaners acted to challenge the state and reaffirm social commitment to civil liberties.

The causes behind the use of political violence remain debated by Maidan studies. Onuch and Sasse, who briefly examine the dynamic of resistance tactics, argue that activists and political opposition failed "to control protests" due not only to state violence, but also to "ideological diversity," which contributed to the radicalization of the resistance.[94] Others also overemphasize the role of radical groups during Maidan. As my study provides a more detailed analysis of state–society and intra-society interactions, a more intricate picture emerges: the process of these interactions with the abusive state forced many participants (not only the radical ones) to change their perceptions of the state and its intentions. The account in this book shows that ideological diversity was not the source of the problem, but simply an expected phenomenon of mass resistance. It is vital, however, to trace how ideological debates are carried out, and how methods of resistance are negotiated among revolutionaries. This book analyzes the *process* of changing perceptions among the participants, showing that not only radical individuals, but also pacifists tell of their transformation and their growing support for violent methods of resistance as the only means to overcome state repression. While not becoming fighters themselves, many started looking for ways to aid the violent resistance – collecting bottles for Molotov cocktails or digging up cobble stones to use as projectiles, rather than looking for ways to stop those who agitated for and used violence. In other words, I show that political violence was not a failure of the pro-democratic activists to control the masses, but rather their successful strategy to defeat an authoritarian state. I also analyze the underbelly of the ultra-right formations during the Maidan, and show why they failed to hijack the movement.

The importance of social discourse is discussed in several recent books on Maidan. Emily Channell-Justice (*Without the State: Self-Organization and Political Activism in Ukraine*) focuses on leftist and feminist groups during the Maidan, and shows a "constant process of negotiation" in their interactions with other revolutionaries, and in adapting their previous ideological tenets to engage a larger debate on equality and tolerance.[95] Catherine Wanner explored the role of religious actors in her book *Everyday Religiosity and the Politics of Belonging in Ukraine*.[96] She also discovered ways in which participation in the revolution transformed their perceptions and sense of identity. Tanya Lokot's *Beyond the Protest Square: Digital Media and Augmented Dissent* identifies not only the important role social media played in mobilizing protests, but also as a platform for social discourse.[97] While these studies focus on certain aspects of the Maidan, they bring to light the vital role of socialization on transforming existing perceptions. I embrace guidance from these anthropological studies (which focus on certain groups/aspects during the revolution) and dissect interactive social processes to analyze the causes, development, and outcome of the Maidan Revolution as a whole. This approach allows a closer look at the origin of ideas during a revolution, when the pace of idea exchange and negotiations for rights is accelerated.[98]

Recently, some attention has been given to analysis of the Maidan as an active negotiation of the social contract.[99] The Maidan movement resembled Poland's Solidarity in the 1980s. Solidarity leaders also referred to their movement as "a revolution of dignity, a celebration of the rights of the vertebrae, a permanent victory of the straightened spine."[100] As Krapfl points out, building on the Durkheimian model, the heightened social interaction of the revolutionary period "facilitates the collective articulation of a body of ideas and ideals that the assembled community accepts as defining."[101] But how do diverse groups of revolutionaries agree on this goal? Brier, who asserts that we cannot simply assume human rights discourse is an "inexorable outcome of seeds planted in antiquity or Enlightenment,"[102] shows the intellectual path of Solidarity members, who contextualized their experiences and "developed a politics revolving around social self-organization and based on human dignity and rights."[103] Cirtautas provides a fascinating analysis of how the concept of dignity – central to Solidarity's goals and the "presentation of a particular conception of citizenship based on the natural right of man to live in dignity" – emerged as a product of continuing discourse, and was a "fusion of Catholic and socialist humanism."[104] This book explores the process of a negotiation between different ideological groups, as they determine the means and goals of their common movement. I demonstrate how concepts of rights and limits of legality are argued with the state and other social actors – on the protest square, in courts, via protest signs and social media. This account of Maidan events shows that a revolutionary process resembles a complex dialogue about the ideas of governing and civil rights, and the development of that dialogue determines the political regime that follows. In other words, the ideas that are debated by civic groups and the state are essential in determining the outcome and the consequences of the revolution.

Importantly, I build on anthropological and political science literature that sees violence as a form of political communication and apply it to the study of Maidan. As Calabrese puts it, "it is idealistic to say that violence happens when communication breaks down, for this view presupposes that the two are somehow dichotomous, and the violence itself cannot and does not function as a form of communication."[105] Relying on Hanna Arendt's argument that violence can bring grievance to public attention, he asserts that communicative intent underlies many acts of violence – and this applies to the state as well as its opposition.[106] Scholars of terrorism and civil war point out that violence against the state and/or civilians underscores the "communicative" function behind these acts.[107] Even "corpse messaging" in a drug war is much more than a random act of violence, but a "vivid illustration."[108] As a discussion of the state–society interaction will show, the nature of violence used by the Yanukovych regime (including torture and humiliation) during the winter of 2013–14 was interpreted by revolutionaries as a message that the state was ready to assert new legal boundaries – that is, to rewrite the existing social contract by extending state powers and limiting civil liberties. I will also show that, in return, the social response to this repression – via peaceful protests and court battles, as well as later violent battles with police – was aimed at preventing the state from imposing these new terms of legality.

Resource mobilization scholars focus on the role of structural factors – institutional resources, such as oppositional parties and social mobilization organizations – for the success of social movements, including the Orange Revolution.[109] The peculiar aspect of the Maidan Revolution, however, was revolutionaries' ideational rejection of the political elite,[110] volunteer engagement not triggered by activist groups, as well as reliance on multiple individual donations. I explore this aspect of Maidan mobilization, detailing how individuals volunteered their time and skills, which helped overcome a lack of monetary and institutional resources. Thus, the role of pro-democratic revolutionary dialogue and co-operation helped to build new interpersonal networks, to share skills, information, and knowledge, and to create a successful resistance movement. The detailed account in this book describes how resistance to state repression in Ukraine developed into a grassroots movement with multiple civic groups coordinating security, logistics, legal, and medical efforts to maintain dissent.

Marci Shore presents a compilation of personal stories to make a "lyrical and intimate book," about the Maidan Revolution, *The Ukrainian Night*, in which ideas and solidarity are shown to overcome selfhood and fear.[111] She notes "how little [the Maidan] revolution was understood," pointing out that Western media and politicians "commented on NATO policy, oil pipelines, and international finance, but not on the transformations of human souls."[112] While Shore's account, in her words, does not present a systematic scholarly study of the revolution, the emerging scholarship on post-Maidan Ukraine has pointed to the fundamental social transformation that took place in Ukraine after the revolution. Thus, scholars have shown that civil society has flourished after 2014, and Ukrainian citizens have changed perceptions of their ethnicity,[113] historical memories,[114] and political preferences.[115] Otrishchenko emphasized the change of post-revolutionary perceptions of Maidan spaces, stating what Ukrainians often expressed: "we looked for Europe, but found Ukraine."[116] Mychailo Wynnyckyj's book *Ukraine's Maidan, Russia's War: A Chronicle and Analysis of the Revolution of Dignity*, in the words of the author, is a "highly personalized" account, involving a "biased ... contribution"[117] that sees the Maidan as a "bourgeois" revolution against Yanukovych's "neo-feudal" regime. The author contemplates the role of emerging "civic worth and civic responsibility" discourse during the Maidan. While various aspects of the social transformation have been addressed, the contribution of this book is an examination of *why* Maidan had that effect. Some scholars, in fact, point out that it might be challenging to disassociate the effects of the Maidan and the Russian invasion on social attitude and engagement after 2014.[118] My account, on the basis of in-depth interviews with the participants, shows the *mechanism* behind social change – how the experiences of Maidan, and the social discourse that took place during the revolution, shaped new attitudes for those who participated. The process of revolutionary engagement with the state and other activists, and a sense of self-power that came with the democratic victory, affected participants' perceptions of Ukraine, "civic duty," and interpersonal trust. Through this change of social perceptions, Maidan fundamentally altered the totalitarian legacy of state–society relations, where the state was seen as a guarantor of social goods, contributing to social apathy.

Methodology

This study asks several core questions about the revolutionary process: why did people participate in the anti-state movement, and why did peaceful methods of resistance eventually give way to political violence? How did multiple ideological groups negotiate a common ideology, and sustain mobilization (overcoming resource scarcity)? Finally, how did the revolution affect social values? The book's major contribution is a systematic account of events from the perspective of the revolutionaries, which offers crucial insight into the motivations and strategies of social actors during the pro-democratic uprising, and explores the role of ideational factors on methods of resistance. I argue that Ukraine's state repression affected activists' perception about the state as willing to violate constitutional rights, forcing them to rebel in order to force the state to abandon civic rights suppression. The state's decision to legalize rights suppression and increase repression by extra-legal means, such as torture and killings, convinced the revolutionaries that the state had turned fully authoritarian, and therefore peaceful methods of resistance couldn't be effective, thus pushing them to resort to violence to deliver regime change. I rely on interview data and records of revolutionary communication to analyze social perceptions as a vital element in understanding the effect of repression on mobilization and political violence. Moreover, the nature of resistance, such as revolutionaries' use of courts to challenge new terms of legality, also captures revolutionaries' intention to restore a regime that respects civil rights. In keeping with the approaches of Brier and Cirtautas, who trace the development of ideas among actors of the Solidarity movement, I follow the process of ideological negotiations throughout the revolutionary events of winter 2013–14, and explore how diverse groups of Maidaners achieved consensus on the means and goals of resistance. I show that pro-democratic ideology – support for a civil rights regime – became the consensus resulting from these negotiations. Finally, I explore how this socialization process moulded participants' values as a result, bringing to prominence the role of civic duty in sustaining democracy. This in-depth exploration of the revolutionary process underscores that the Maidan was a democratic revolution: not only because it brought down a regime that embraced dictatorial laws and practices, but also because it was democratic in nature.

This is an inductive study. This approach allows me to begin the research process having delineated a clear phenomenon of interest, relying on theoretical assumptions to make provisional claims about causal relationships.[119] In order to produce a theoretically grounded explanation, it is necessary to assess the compatibility of the collected data with the initial proposition "in explicit context with rival theories and arguments."[120] Finally, an inductive process of study prescribes continuing analysis of theory–data compatibility, to "judge when the causal argument has become plausible, persuasive, and presentable."[121]

My research aims to capture the importance of state–society dialogue, changing social perceptions about the state, and evolving resistance ideology to show that this socialization process results in a change in the level of support for political violence, and affects post-revolutionary social values. This necessitates a combination of methodological tools, developed within political science and anthropology. Firstly, I will use elements of the process-tracing inductive method, to identify the logic of inference.[122] "The process-tracing method is the analysis of evidence on processes, sequences, and conjunctures of events within a case … [it is a] key technique for capturing causal mechanisms in action."[123] The strength of this method lies in spotting how variables interact, a causal mechanism that leads from a source to an outcome.[124] The method is an "especially powerful empirical approach for distinguishing between ideational and material effects."[125] The method should not involve a chronology of events[126] but, rather, should (1) reveal conjunctures, indicating the logic of inference, and (2) provide a rationalization as to why causal explanations, suggested by alternative theories, do not stand.[127] In other words, process-tracing is an inductive approach that analyzes not only the mechanism of causality, but also addresses and eliminates plausible alternatives.[128] Most importantly, it unfolds the causal mechanism behind the claimed variables, rather than just assuming and testing the relationship between them.

Secondly, in order to study the gradual change of social perceptions and tactics, and trace the effects of ideational factors, I incorporate an anthropological interpretive approach.[129] Political science methodologies are often dictated by rational choice approaches, which see humans as motivated by security or materialistic (self-interested) concerns. Structuralist analyses, which dominate studies of revolutions in political science, focus on grand factors that cause state collapse: financial emergency, severe division among elites, and the potential for certain groups to mobilize.[130] As Migdal points out, structuralist theories "remove agency, the power of people to affect the course of history."[131] The dominance of these approaches does not offer tools to trace the gradual change in activists' perceptions throughout the mobilization process, as they are assumed to be constant.[132] As a result, the field of political science lacks methodologies to analyze the process of change in perception as a result of socialization processes. In contrast, anthropological approaches explore the cumulated, embodied symbols to search for meaning and "deeper saliences,"[133] which is reflected in Geertz's postulate that humans are "suspended in webs of significance." Kubik and Aronoff point to cases where political scientists gained from "observing 'actual' human behavior, rather than relying only on interactions of variables in abstract theoretical spaces," giving attention to the symbolic-cultural microscale.[134] While I could not observe participants during the revolutionary events, I did conduct many in-depth interviews with the participants and performed a detailed examination of state–society interactions in courts, the protest square, and other revolutionary arenas. Consequently, I was able to study the dynamic of changing social perceptions and their effects on mobilization tactics. As Kubik and Aronoff teach, an interpretive inductive approach is a powerful tool for implementing constructivism, as "human sociability and politics are expressed and facilitated through the cultural construction of bonds of collective identity, which assumes that various groups with conflicting values negotiate their internal and external social boundaries by publicly communicating and demanding 'respect' for cultural constructs."[135] Attention to activists' negotiations with the state and other social actors helped me discover the process of morphing in the conflicting values of Maidan groups, as well as the process of negotiation of social contract with the state – through violent and non-violent means.

The goal of this study is to trace the role of ideas and social interactions in social mobilization, as well as the after-effects of these processes. In chapters 2 and 3, I trace the causal mechanism between state repression and the methods of resistance. More specifically, I examine interview data and state–society interactions to determine the causes behind the shifts from overwhelming support for peaceful resistance to strong support for political violence following severe state violence. To identify the causal inference, I rely on a constructivist theoretical approach to examine the intervening variable: activists' changing perceptions of the state. I address plausible alternatives, brought by rational choice theory: fear of retaliation from the state and a lack of institutional opportunities. Applying an anthropological method in these two chapters helps trace the interpretive role of political violence. Thus, the chapters will explain how state violence was interpreted by social activists, and how this interpretation motivated them to eventually adopt violent methods of resistance. Applying the interpretive method in chapter 4 helps examine the revolutionary socialization process, allowing me to discover how multiple groups negotiated a consensus political ideology for the resistance movement. It also helps to understand the importance of ideas over financial and institutional resources. Chapter 5 traces the effects of revolutionary social discourse on post-revolutionary activists' values of civic duty. This is juxtaposed with the alternative constructivist explanation: the legacy of a totalitarian communist regime on state–society relations. The interpretive method is crucial here, as it helps trace the effects of revolutionary socialization on post-revolutionary social change. While the development of the ideological basis for previous movements for democracy and social justice can be traced via charismatic leaders' speeches and writing – from Solidarity leaders to Dr Martin Luther King, Jr – the key developments of the ideological discourse behind the Maidan movement are better understood through the discourse among the Maidan participants and the exchanges between the state and revolutionaries.

Ukraine's Regional Diversity and Support for Maidan

Scholars debate how to interpret the fact that the Maidan movement had higher support in the centre and west of the country compared with the eastern and southern regions. In the west of the country, popular support for the Maidan was 84 per cent, in the centre 66 per cent, while 33 per cent in the south of Ukraine, and only 13 per cent in the eastern regions approved.[136] This is often brought up to suggest that the Maidan was a conflict between the various regional identities of Ukraine. A more detailed look, however, shows that support for the Maidan Revolution is intertwined with democratic values.[137] In other words, support for Maidan in the centre and west of the country is more likely due to higher democratic values in those regions, rather than regional identities. Those who supported democracy as a regime were more likely to approve of the Maidan protests. Moreover, those who were strongly dissatisfied with the status of Ukrainian democracy were 38 per cent more likely to approve of the Maidan protests than those who were strongly satisfied.[138] Region had no influence on whether the Maidan movement was seen as legitimate; when partisanship and policy preferences were controlled for, respondents in eastern Donetsk, for example, were significantly more likely to approve of the Maidan protests than those in Kyiv.[139] In fact, age mattered more: younger people across Ukraine were more likely to support the Maidan.[140] Surveys, however, don't capture *why* democratic values brought support for the Maidan; nor do they explain how different ideologies within the movement were settled. This book examines in detail how social perceptions of increasing state repression were interpreted, and why revolutionaries believed they were saving democracy. It also shows how a pro-democratic ideology was negotiated within the anti-state movement.

Limitations of the Study

While this inductive study exhibits strong internal validity, its major limitation is weak external validity. Focusing on the intricacies of communicated meanings and their shaping of subsequent decisions of certain actors limits our ability to generalize a common framework and apply it to other cases of social resistance. Nevertheless, a discussion of potential theoretical implications on the basis of the lessons learned from this Maidan study are offered in the concluding chapter.

A second limitation is that the current study focuses on events in Kyiv, as a decisive platform for state–society dialogue. While some events and examples of regional Maidan mobilization in different parts of Ukraine (as well as diaspora-led protests) are mentioned, it would be methodologically impossible to provide a systematic study of all these events within the scope of this book. For a similar reason, the so-called Anti-Maidan (endorsed by the state) is not systematically addressed in this book. This book's focus on Kyiv allows a systematic and in-depth analysis of the revolutionaries' actions and debates that took place in the capital. Firstly, it provides for methodological consistency, with which I trace the changing perceptions and competing ideologies among civic actors who were in closer proximity to interact throughout the winter months, challenging the state and each other. Secondly, since the aim of the resistance movement was to challenge the Kyiv-based regime, mainly the presidential administration and the law enforcement it controlled, all the actions outside of Kyiv were aimed at helping maintain the resistance. Indeed, it is the final events in Kyiv – the fleeing of Yanukovych, his apparatus, and the Berkut forces – that were decisive in a successful transformation of the regime. Future studies should address Maidan-related protests in various parts of Ukraine,[141] and abroad,[142] to fully understand the complexity of this social revolution.

Sources of Data

I conducted in-depth interviews with revolutionaries, transcribed multiple existing oral histories, collected legal documents, attended court hearings, and recreated maps of violent battles. During my four field trips to Ukraine between May 2014 and July 2016 to study the Ukrainian Revolution, I conducted 102 in-depth, semi-structured personal interviews. The interviews were held in either Ukrainian or Russian, for which I performed the translation. The interviewees were approached through "snowball sampling," a method by which new respondents are recruited through recommendations from existing respondents.[143] While this technique has been criticized for its potential to provide bias in sampling, this concern was outweighed by the diversity of the respondents it provided, and the high willingness of interviewees to comment extensively on sensitive information as the interviewer was recommended to them by people they trust. In order to assure a representative sample (and learn extensively about the process of the revolution), I targeted revolutionaries who had different tasks, including leaders and members of civic initiatives who performed defensive, logistical, medical, legal, transportation, entertainment, and other functions. The study was conducted in full compliance with the SIUE Institutional Review Board's committee, which is responsible for reviewing and approving research involving human subjects and ensuring the ethical treatment and protection of participants. Please note that while initially, in 2014, the IRB had approved a disclosure of names of the interviewees who chose to do so (and who signed the according documentation), as this book was getting ready for publication in 2024, the board voted to protect the names of the participants, even if they had previously preferred to be public.

The interview data also drew on comprehensive collections of interviews with revolutionaries conducted by Ukraine's Judaica Center and edited by Leonid Finberg and Yuliana Holovach,[144] as well as a collection of interviews with revolutionaries, conducted by the Ukrainian Institute of Memory (a total of forty-seven interviews were provided to me from the collection), as well as printed collections by the Institute.[145] I performed translations of all the cited interviews into English. In the period after their personal interviews were conducted, between April 2016 and September 2017, I conducted follow-up online surveys with interviewees. Unfortunately, I wasn't able to reach all of those previously interviewed via this method (fifty of the recipients provided responses, forty-four of whom answered most of the questions in the survey). However, the survey respondents represent a wide variety of revolutionary participants, presenting linguistic, ethnic, and gender diversity, as well as a wide variety of revolutionary activities.[146]

Plan of This Book

Chapter 2 depicts state–society dialogue during November–December 2013. It shows how state violence was interpreted during these months, and the social response to the interpretation of state actions. Moreover, I trace activists' debates on the means of the resistance, and their efforts to maintain its peaceful nature. The chapter details excessive police violence against peaceful protesters on 30 November, as well as the state's continuing rights' suppression and the process of interpreting these actions as a manifestation of growing authoritarianism. The chapter describes how citizens mobilized to deliver a pro-democratic message to the state, despite continuing police violence. On the basis of extensive interview data, it is shown that the resistance movement went far beyond protests, including an analysis of court battles and civic initiatives.

The third chapter traces the transformation of state–society relations in Ukraine during January and February of 2014, after the passage of the repressive 16 January laws. Rather than yield to protesters' demands to end severe police violence and repression, the state intensified its humiliating and degrading treatment of the revolutionaries. The chapter details the methods of state violence, including torture of protesters and eventually the use of live ammunition. I trace how degrading treatment and severe violence eventually led protesters to conclude that the state was determined to consolidate a terror regime in Ukraine through any means possible. I demonstrate how this understanding of the state's intentions fundamentally changed social response, leading to growing support for political violence within the resistance movement.

Chapter 4 explores the growth of grassroots resistance during the Maidan Revolution by providing a detailed account of multiple civic initiatives born during the revolution. I analyze how revolutionaries gained leverage by volunteering their time and skills, relying on a continuous flow of public donations, creating new social networks, and continuously developing new strategies in response to growing state violence. The process of creating civic resources, drawing on pro-democratic consensus of the protesters, facilitated deeper co-operation and overcame a lack of financial and institutional backing. Thus, I demonstrate that social groups were at the wheel of considerable transformations, contributing to the success of the revolution and affecting the dynamic of the state–society dialogue.

Chapter 5 discusses the transformative effects of the Maidan Revolution on the political regime and society in Ukraine. First, I discuss the transformation of the political regime in the aftermath of the revolution, which ended severe state repression and re-established a democratic regime. Secondly, I analyze how the mechanism of mobilization, and revolutionary social discourse, altered previously dominating social concepts. This chapter demonstrates that perceptions of "civic duty" and communal trust changed among those who participated in the revolutionary events. Through this change of social perceptions, the revolution of 2013–14 fundamentally altered the communist legacy of social communal distrust. The Maidan Revolution became a discussion forum for the active citizenry, where participants watched each other sacrifice money, health, security, and ultimately life for a shared goal. These experiences led to a sense of community on the basis of democratic ideals, breaking the primal importance of existing trust networks. Moreover, it transformed the totalitarian legacy of state–society relations, where social apathy had led to viewing the state as the guarantor of social goods.

The concluding chapter discusses how the current study of the Maidan Revolution supplements scholarly literature on contentious politics. I conclude that constructivist theoretical approaches, which see contention, including violent acts, as a form of dialogue, and a democratic revolution as a negotiation of social contract as most useful to understand the Ukrainian Revolution. I also discuss how a constructivist framework for understanding a revolutionary process as a state–society and intra-society dialogue helps us comprehend the mechanism of the transformation of state–society relations, overcoming the totalitarian legacy where the state was seen as a guarantor of social goods, and therefore contributing to social apathy. I show how this theoretical framework, informed by the Maidan study, can be applied to analyze the success or failure of other pro-democratic social movements in other cases (such as Belarus and Russia).

I call it *the curse of Ukrainian scholars*: hardly any book on Ukraine is written without mentioning the effects Russia had on developments in Ukraine (peculiarly, the opposite has not been true). During and after the Maidan Revolution, the Kremlin unleashed propaganda campaigns to dehumanize the participants of the Maidan Revolution and all of its supporters. In the Epilogue, I demonstrate that Russian propaganda about the Ukrainian Revolution contained systematically false accounts about Maidan events in order to justify its invasion and provoke mass violence. Its effectiveness in influencing the Russian populace should not be understated and is vital to comprehending Russian aggression and the atrocities committed by Russian forces in Ukraine.

Terms and Concepts

State

My study is instructed by Joel Migdal's framework of state–society relations, which looks beyond the dynamic of power between the actors in the processes of institutional change, but builds on sociological approaches and emphasizes that aside from coercion and incentives, state and social organizations use symbols and values concerning how social life should be ordered. "These symbols and values either reinforce the forms of social control in the society or propose new forms of social life."[147] This approach instructs us that not only power but also legitimacy is vital in sustaining order, and therefore its loss is detrimental for state–society relations. I use Migdal's comprehensive definition of the state as "a field of power marked by the use and threat of violence in attempting to control people's behavior and shaped by (1) the image of a coherent, controlling organization in a territory, which is an outgrowth and representation of the people bounded by the territory, and (2) the actual practices of that organization's multiple parts."[148] Migdal emphasizes that the state is a multi-layered, complex phenomenon, "a far cry from that of a centrally controlled organization using a monopoly over the legitimate use of violence in order to get its way."

State Repression

Some have defined repression as actions that increase the costs of protest,[149] by preventing, controlling, or constraining protest, including its initiation,[150] thus, focusing on opportunities for dissent. As the purpose of this study is to point out the key importance of social perception of state actions, Davenport's detailed definition of repression provides deeper insight. He specifies repressive state actions, including "harassment, surveillance/spying, bans, arrests, torture, and mass killing by government agents and/or affiliates within their territorial jurisdiction," and points out that the concept of repression involves a violation of freedoms of expression, due process in the enforcement and adjudication of law, and personal integrity or security.[151] In other words, the concept of state repression stipulates the essential element of the illegality of state action. Legality should be measured not by the laws of the country, but rather by international legal principles of protection from arbitrary arrest and detention, fair trial, and freedom of expression (as stipulated in the International Declaration of Human Rights, International Covenant on Civil and Political Rights, and the European Convention on Human Rights; Ukraine is a party to all three of these international conventions). This more detailed account explores the basis for social outrage in response to state repression.

Society

Migdal points out that scholars who study social change "need an approach that brings this struggle for social control into stark relief," encouraging models that depict society "as a mélange of social organizations rather than a dichotomous structure." Society involves formal and informal institutions, "ranging from families and neighborhood groups to mammoth foreign-owned companies, [and] use[s] a variety of sanctions, rewards, and symbols to induce people to behave according to the rules of the game. These are the norms and laws that define the boundaries of acceptable behavior, and they may include at what age to marry, which crops to grow, which language to speak, and much more."[152] Thus, society is a complex structure in which communities communicate meanings that inform how power between the various groups is exercised. In the theoretical framework presented in this book, I discuss state–society dialogue. As in the revolutionary context, I treat participants of the mass protests as representatives of social concerns, akin to the concept of political representation in a democratic republic. They also, inevitably, become representatives of their respective groups, whose rights they defend when negotiating on their behalf (for example, religious or LGBTQ groups).

Revolutionaries, Activists, and Protesters

I use the term revolutionaries to refer to any persons who participated in the anti-state resistance movement during the winter of 2013–14 in Ukraine. I distinguish between protesters, who were physically present at the protest venues, such as Maidan Square, and activists, who were engaged in maintaining the resistance but were not necessarily present at the protest venues. Activists formed civic initiatives, including but not limited to those that organized housing, food, funding, public relations, and legal, psychological, and medical aid. The majority of protesters came from outside the capital,[153] making newly created social networks crucial in maintaining the protests.

Dissent/Resistance

The terms dissent and resistance are used in this study interchangeably. The concepts of dissent and resistance both (1) involve collective/mass activity and (2) possess an "antisystem character, in the sense of being at odds with existing political authority" and "must pose a threat or at least severe inconvenience to the normal operation of the political elite."[154] Both concepts include peaceful and violent means to challenge state operation. Peaceful dissent activity includes (1) protests, or anti-government demonstrations, which are "organized, non-violent gatherings of a large number of people for the purpose of [expression of dissatisfaction with] a government, its actions or policies, or one or more of its leaders,"[155] as well as (2) other peaceful measures, including but not limited to organizing legal and medical aid, food, or housing for protesters, and other logistical services to help sustain the anti-government protest.

Political Violence

In this study, political violence implies actions that rely on the use of physical force against state actors. While at times, the term may be used to include destruction of property, in this study political violence involves physical force against state representatives. Political violence may be initiated with the purpose of defence from violent police attacks, but also involves a conscious understanding that utilization of violent defence tactics may injure state agents.

Support for Political Violence

Supporters of political violence may or may not use (or be willing to use) violent tactics themselves. Supporters of political violence who are not willing to use force themselves, support the idea of others within the dissent movement who do utilize force against state agents. The purpose of this study is not to predict when individual acts of political violence are likely to occur. For example, initial violent acts were performed by some protesters, but were not supported by the majority of revolutionaries. Rather, I aim to examine when support for political violence within the movement becomes significant, even if most revolutionaries did not utilize violence themselves.

Maidan, Revolution of Dignity, and EuroMaidan

In this book I use the terms Maidan and the Revolution of Dignity to describe the revolutionary events in Ukraine throughout the winter of 2013–14. I use the term EuroMaidan to refer to the protests in November of 2013 in response to Yanukovych's refusal to sign the trade deal with the European Union. This helps distinguish between these protests and the revolution, which began after the state used violence against peaceful protests. This allows me to be consistent with the views expressed by many of the participants I interviewed. When describing their motivations to take part in the events, many pointedly stated: "It was *not* because of the treaty with the European Union, I came there in the aftermath of state violence against peaceful protesters." As this book's main aim is to describe the events from the point of view of the social actors, this nomenclature becomes important to distinguish and emphasize the causality of revolutionaries' motivations – as a pro-democratic movement. Thus, EuroMaidan has a narrower meaning – referring to the November protests that died down and would have become unremarkable if the Ukrainian security police forces had not beaten defenceless, stunned youth. While the terms Maidan and EuroMaidan are at times used interchangeably, even in Ukraine, the author of this book is deeply concerned with identifying the causes of the revolution and therefore chooses to be deliberate and thoughtful about their use.

2

State–Society Dialogue, Part I

30 November–31 December 2013

> If they start limiting the freedom of peaceful citizens to express their thoughts in public squares, I can't be silent. We can't allow the scenario of Russia and Belarus in our country.[1]

This declaration by a Maidan participant summarizes the view of many in the centre of Kyiv after the aggressive actions of Berkut special police on 30 November 2013. The excessive use of police force against a peaceful crowd was unprecedented in the history of independent Ukraine.[2] Social shock was exacerbated by the fact that unarmed protesters were surrounded and then severely beaten. Police violence was even more surprising since the larger EU-related protests had diminished by the end of November to only several hundred people. Before the violence, activists had already announced that protests had come to an end, and the stage had been taken down.[3]

Police violence was seen by many in Ukraine as a sure sign of the government's decision to establish an authoritarian regime. In other words, the brutality against protesters was understood in the context of continuing steps by the Yanukovych administration to consolidate power. According to those gathered in the aftermath of police brutality, a lack of social action would lead to dire consequences. Limited activism was no longer an option, only a mass movement was seen as capable of preventing the state from taking an autocratic route. Examples of neighboring post-Soviet authoritarian regimes offered a tangible, undesirable alternative.

Police violence against peaceful protesters in the early morning of 30 November was the main trigger of the revolutionary pro-democratic movement in Ukraine. The dynamic of protests during the revolutionary period is depicted in figure 2.1. As seen in the chart, protests in response to Yanukovych's refusal to sign the EU agreement were moderate in number and wound down by the end of the month, leaving only a few hundred protesters in tents on Kyiv's Maidan Square. In the aftermath of the 30 November police violence, however, the number of people who came to protest is estimated to be 800,000. The protests continued until Yanukovych fled the country on 20 February. Aside from additional people joining for the New Year's holiday, major spikes in protesters' numbers came in response to state oppression: police violence at the end of November, police's attempted storming and dispersal of the protests in the middle of December, and the passage in January of "dictatorial laws" that severely limited freedom of expression and assembly. Even after the state resorted to using live ammunition and torture, causing hundreds of injuries in January and a reduction in the number of activists present at the square, opposition continued. Multiple grassroots initiatives were adopted or expanded to maintain the resistance movement, including a visible presence in Maidan Square.

According to public polls conducted by the Kyiv Institute of Sociology throughout the protests, "cruel repression of protest participants" was the major motivator of protest participation throughout the winter of 2013–14.[4] The major demands of Maidan protest participants (expressed by 82 per cent) were the release of detained protesters and an end to repression. Other major demands included an end to state violence, a push for democratic reforms, and the government's resignation. Polls and extensive interview data demonstrate that protests were not focused on a single policy.

The nature of social resistance was drastically transformed in the aftermath of 30 November. It was no longer merely a protest, but rather an extensive grassroots movement – the first of its scale in Ukraine's history. Activists mobilized to aid and sustain the protests and to challenge the state in other arenas: from car caravans to legal challenges. Activism included, but was not limited to, makeshift kitchens and hospitals, art and entertainment, internet streaming and communication, security and offensive operations, as well as legal mobilization (a detailed account of the formation and operation of grassroots movements is provided in chapter 4). Some referred to the area occupied by protesters in the centre of Kyiv in December as the *Maidan-sich*, a reference to the historical fortified self-governed community of Zaporizhzhian Cossacks. On 15 December 2013, the activists dubbed their protests

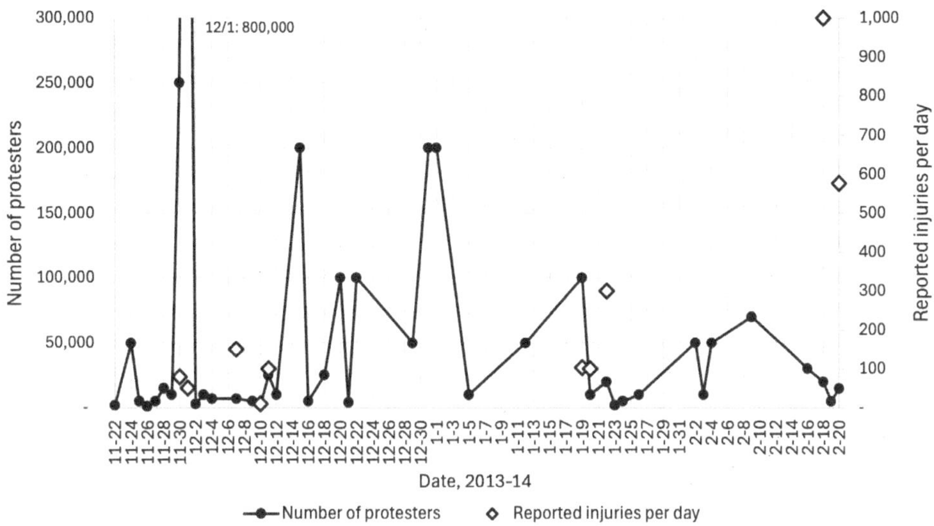

Figure 2.1 Number of Maidan protesters and protester injuries over time.
Sources: Media reports, November 2013–February 2014; see appendix 2.

the Day of Dignity, emphasizing the state's repression of constitutional rights and leading to future references to the resistance movement as the Revolution of Dignity.

What follows is a tracing of events from 30 November through the end of 2013, divided into three aspects of state–society dialogue: state repression, social interpretation, and social response.

State Repression

The Night of 29–30 November 2013: "Maidan Dispersal" "The Student Beating"

It remains unclear why the state chose to use excessive police force and mass detentions, when it was obvious that the EU-deal protest movement had come to an end. Two government officials admitted to having played a role in the events of the early morning of 30 November: Kyiv mayor, Olexander Popov, and Kyiv police chief, Valeriy Koryak. They testified that they followed directives from officials close to the president, and that the dispersal was coordinated by the deputy secretary of Ukraine's National Security and Defense Council (NSDC), Volodymyr Sivkovych. More specifically, the orders to follow Sivkovych came from Andriy Klyuev, the NSDC secretary and Yanukovych's right-hand man, and Vitaliy Zakharchenko, the minister of internal affairs.[5] Kyiv's mayor Popov stated that Klyuev called him on 29 November and ordered him to immediately "set up the city New Year's holiday tree" in Kyiv's square (where the small group of remaining protesters were centred), saying that all subsequent orders regarding setting up the tree were to come from his deputy, Sivkovych. Notably, Sivkovych did not have jurisdiction to regulate such city matters. However, Popov said he accepted the directive since "Klyuev was a serious authority in [Ukraine's] power circles."[6] Police head, Koryak, received the same directive from Minister Zakharchenko: to follow Sivkovych's lead during the operation. When facing shocked colleagues the morning after the violent dispersal, Koryak allegedly stated: "I won't be able to say I was framed. I must, therefore, take responsibility."[7] Koryak, indeed, publicly took responsibility for the police violence,[8] offering his resignation, which was granted sometime later.

Public statements from state officials were contradictory. On one hand, police press secretary Olha Bilyk justified the police raid by claiming it "was carried out with the purpose of guaranteeing unobstructed movement of technology for continuing works to prepare for New Year holiday celebrations."[9] Both she and police chief Koryak claimed that the violence was carried out in response to protester violence, which was false, as the only violent actions that night (throwing small rocks at police officers) were carried out by individuals who came to Maidan only *after* the police's violent actions. On the other hand, President Yanukovych and Prime Minister Azarov distanced themselves from the events of the police violence. Azarov stated that the government "was absolutely not interested in such a scenario," because "people who lawfully and peacefully express their protest are our citizens, whose rights we are supposed to protect."[10] Yanukovych stated that he was "deeply outraged" by the riot police violence against peaceful demonstrators. Moreover, he appeared to continue the rhetoric of European integration, saying: "We are united in our common choice of a European future."[11] It remains highly unlikely, although possible, that Klyuev and Zakharchenko would choose to orchestrate violent suppression of peaceful protesters without the knowledge of Azarov and Yanukovych. Rather, the events described below suggest a calculated state choice to restrict civil liberties by relying on intimidation tactics and seem unlikely to have taken place without the knowledge of the president.[12]

The city holiday decoration procedures began early morning, 29 November. City workers in yellow vests set out metal sheets along Khreshchatyk Street in preparation. Some protesters were in proximity, watching the process, but stayed out of the way. In the evening, a truck with a large load of decorations and equipment was moving from Instytutska Street toward a food tent, which had been provided to protesters by State Emergency Services. Several people approached the truck driver to figure out how to help him get through the crowd. One protester laid down in front of the truck when it stopped moving. Within around seven minutes, Berkut troops (the special, or riot, police of Ukraine's Ministry of Internal affairs) moved into Independence Square, while multiple police buses appeared on Instytutska Street. Seeing these troops, many people started gathering on the stairs around the monument, discussing the situation. A demand from the forces to "free the driveway" was heard (even though the driveway was not blocked).[13]

The violent dispersal began at 4:10 a.m. on 30 November. Approximately a thousand Berkut troops surrounded several hundred people next to the Independence Monument. The police and Berkut forces surrounded all who were in the square on three sides, using the Globus store as the fourth wall. Hundreds of people in the square were let out through a corridor created by Berkut troops. The troops then moved in toward the monument, surrounding approximately two hundred remaining people.[14] Those who were surrounded under the monument began singing the Ukrainian national hymn. While someone offered to pass flag holders to the front for protection from the troops, others refused on the basis that this was a peaceful gathering. Berkut forces attacked the surrounded protesters, employing excessive force by pushing some to the ground, pulling out others, and severely beating many, causing broken limbs and head injuries.[15] As one witness recalled:

> The remaining hope was that as the [Berkut] would get close to the monument, they'd let us out one by one … However, they came to the monument steps – people did not resist – and began

> hitting with both fists and batons, and then kicking those who fell. They began to pull people from the stairs … People were trying to move back, but there was no place to go … We fell … The first Berkut officer started beating me … Blood was pouring down my face, and I said [in Ukrainian]: 'Stop, what are you doing? … Nobody is resisting." They were yelling only four words [in Russian]: "bitch," "whore," "scum," "corridor."… From the left, they yelled "corridor." When I tried to get up to move there, they'd yell [in Russian]: "On the ground, bitch!" and "Lie down, bitch!" and continued beating me.[16]

Berkut forces acted systematically and consistently: the beatings appeared to purposefully inflict maximum pain and injuries.[17] One witness shared their understanding of the violence used against protesters:

> They were not beating in a way to cause pain and force people to leave. These were special forces: these were well-trained troops, they'd do only what was ordered … Three hundred police troops were plenty enough if they'd wanted to push people out without causing harm. But the order was to disfigure and to cripple. They were hitting the legs, the knees and the spine … While I was trying to carry this girl out, they kept hitting me on the back.[18]

The excessive number of troops discharged to deal with relatively few peaceful protesters in the middle of the night, and their tactics, suggest that the operation was planned by state authorities. Excessive police violence against protesters, systematically inflicted to cause severe physical trauma (which was unprecedented since Ukraine's independence) suggests that the purpose went beyond "clearing off the square in preparation for the winter holidays." The purpose may have been an attempt to draw a new boundary of state–society interaction: to establish a new norm, where indiscriminate excessive state violence was commonplace, a hallmark of authoritarian regimes.

The violent attacks were also committed without regard for age, gender, or whether they were members of the press. A number of witnesses commented that officers applied force indiscriminately: "old and young people, men and women, they were indifferent."[19] As witnesses described:

> I was yelling: "Don't hit her, she is dying! She'll die! Don't hit … And at that time I saw … how girls were lying on the asphalt, heads stuck under the fence, so they would not get hit. Berkut guys ran onto these girls, who were lying under the fence, and started fiercely beating them. Some of these girls were beaten cruelly.[20]

The police also chased people who managed to get away, trapping many, repeatedly beating them, including those who fell to the ground.[21] Injuries included broken limbs and noses, knocked-out teeth, and head and rib injuries. While some were taken to the hospital by ambulance, others, despite severe injuries, chose to avoid hospitalization for fear of repercussions from the state.[22]

After beating the protesters, Berkut troops continued to use excessive force to chase all remaining protesters from Maidan Square as far as the Bessarabskyi Market to the south and Mykhailivskyi Monastery to the north (each approximately a mile way).[23] Berkut forces chased and beat many people along Khreshchatyk Square south all the way to Bessarabska Square.[24] A witness described how police were "chasing us to Bessarabska Square and beating us. We were running around downtown, the small streets."[25] Likewise, another protester recalled, "I was in the first row. They dragged me out and beat my head. [They] used indiscriminate, excessive and unjustified force – even chasing down fleeing demonstrators to assault them."[26] After their violent attack, a Berkut officer was witnessed showing off their battery of protesters: "I got him between his legs, and he was, 'Oi-oi-oi,' followed by laughter from his peers."[27] Some protesters found refuge in the Hotel Kyiv to the east of the square.

Approximately 150 people who were chased by Berkut north to the Mykhailivskyi monastery received refuge there.[28] Mykhailivskyi monastery, in fact, became the most prominent sanctuary against Berkut aggression on the morning of 30 November.[29] Even as people reached the monastery, Berkut troops neared. To avoid further beatings and likely detention, many climbed over the fence into the yard of the monastery. The clergy, witnessing such an unprecedented scene, were naturally caught off guard. The rector of the monastery related to me that they were completely lost at first as to what to do next.[30] As he described:

> Nothing like this ever happened before. We were shocked, witnessing what was happening … But the young people asked for help, they were scared, so we invited them in, and made hot tea … We were then trying to figure out whether the police would storm the monastery … We watched them outside the gates deliberating; it seemed that they were calling their superiors … We decided to call the police and negotiate with them, asking that Berkut riot police not storm the monastery. This appeared to have worked.[31]

As a result of this successful negotiation, and the monastery's ability and willingness to offer refuge to a large number of protesters, the Mykhailivskyi Monastery (St Michael's) Square became a gathering place for Kyivans protesting police violence during the day on 30 November.

Thirty-five people were detained, including those with severe injuries, and taken to the police station. This was in violation of procedural code, which dictates that injured detainees must first receive medical aid. In fact, there was some resistance at the police station against admitting detainees with severe injuries. According to a witness, police staff at the station were questioning the actions of Berkut troops:

> I had a bone sticking out of my leg, blood was pouring, police workers did not want to admit us because we were brought in by Berkut troops. They were asking: "Who did you bring? Are these detained, or are they from a war zone? How are we supposed to register them if they are beaten?" For an hour they did not want to admit us.[32]

The prosecutor, who approached him during this time, however, turned out to be less concerned about detainee rights: after brief questioning, he hit the protester directly on his (visibly) broken leg.[33] Witnesses said violence was used mostly by Berkut troops, recalling that several municipal policemen saved a protester by shoving him under a car, after he was thrown to the side by the force of a blow from a Berkut officer.[34] On the other hand, when one protester called police at the beginning of the aggressive Berkut assault to report that her security was being threatened, her report was rejected and the policeman's response came with a good dose of profanity.[35] Thus, we see a dichotomy in the behaviour of state forces. On one hand, Berkut troops relied on excessive use of force and humiliation in what appears to have been a prepared tactic. On the other hand, it seems that other police were taken by surprise (or did not approve of state aggression), since they occasionally sided with protesters.

Another notable feature of state violence on 30 November was the use of insulting and vulgar language by Berkut officers, as well as destruction of the Ukrainian flag.[36] When one woman addressed the Berkut troops, telling them they were using excessive force, they yelled, "Go away, whore!"[37] Similarly, one interviewee recalled that when asking a Berkut officer whether he had any pity on the people they were beating, he responded: "I have no pity for morons."[38] Accounts of insults toward protesters have a common thread: while witnesses gave their accounts in Ukrainian, all witnesses quoted Berkut troops' responses in Russian. Moreover, during the post-revolutionary trial of the former Kyiv mayor in relation to the violent dispersal, one witness recalled his shock as he watched the troops rip a Ukrainian flag off his car, tear it down, and stomp on it.[39] Such animosity toward protesters and Ukrainian national symbols is worth noting, since, firstly, it stood in high contrast to any police–protester exchange that took place since Ukraine became independent; and secondly, the destruction of a national flag by the nation's security forces is baffling. Some witnesses were reported as saying that the Berkut officers were brought to Kyiv from the Chernihiv, Luhansk, and Crimea regions (predominantly Russian-speaking areas),[40] while another speculated that they were brought from Russia.[41] Either explanation is plausible. Many troops were brought from the eastern regions, given that Ukrainian patriotism has been lower in the eastern regions of the country, and the state might have chosen the proven Soviet tactic of bringing in anti-protest security forces from other regions. A Council of Europe report of the events in January–February also mentioned witnesses speculating that a limited number of security forces were from Russia.[42]

As a result of the raid, seventy-nine people were injured, thirty-five detained, and ten hospitalized.[43] The events of police violence on the morning of 30 November began to be commonly referred to as the *student beating (pobyttia studentiv)*. While many of the protesters attacked by police were not students, it was widely acknowledged that (1) young people dominated the protests against Yanukovych's decision not to sign the EU trade deal, and (2) the protests were peaceful. Thus, the term *students* evoked the impression of defenceless participants driven by ideals of justice.[44]

Continuing State Repression Throughout December

As asserted previously, the unprecedented state violence against peaceful protesters on 30 November triggered protests consisting of hundreds of thousands of people. Their major demands were the release of detained protesters, resignation of the administration, and the investigation and prosecution of those responsible. The state responded with detentions, due-process violations, ignoring of protester demands, false characterizations of the nature of the protests, and additional use of excessive force, attacking even local and international journalists who were recording the abuse.

On 1 December, a small number of activists engaged in clashes with police on Bankova Street. As a result, Berkut troops employed excessive and indiscriminate force against all protesters on the street by chasing many who sought shelter and beating those who were on the ground.[45] In less than an hour, at least twenty-two people were in the hospital with chemical burns and bodily injuries.[46] Serhiy Pantiuk, secretary of the Writers Union, who took a dozen people inside the Union's building to hide them from police violence, described details of the indiscriminate violence used by Berkut troops:

> While I was taking the women to one of the halls [for safety], some young men, running from police, ran into the building after us and blocked the entrance. Riot police officers tried to get in. And then … they ran around the building and broke in through the windows. Once inside, officers started beating everyone in the building. There were up to fifty people hiding inside.[47]

Another writer, Bohdan Humeniuk, who witnessed the attack recounted:

> I happened to be the first one in their way. I met them with my Writers' Union ID in one hand, and journalism ID in other hand, and asked them to calm down. For that they struck me in the ribs with a club.[48]

Forty journalists[49] were specifically targeted and beaten by Berkut troops. The troops attacked journalists despite being fully aware that their targets were members of the press. For example, Roman Kupriyanov, cameraman for the Euronews TV channel, was taken to the hospital after he was beaten by Berkut when he refused their order to not film a beaten protester.[50] Another journalist, Olexandr Perevoznyk, who informed Berkut troops that he was a member of the press, was attacked by six Berkut officers, who took turns beating him.[51]

The presidential administration's response to the public's shock and demands for social justice was evasive. The official justification for the violence was based on the need to prepare the New Year's tree, and (false) claims that force was justified to combat protester violence.[52] While Yanukovych publicly condemned the violence, adding that Ukraine "is united in its European choice,"[53] Zakharchenko promised that if calls for mass violence were heard, the state would "act harshly."[54] Moreover, Kyiv's District Administrative Court banned further protests in downtown Kyiv at both Maidan Nezalezhnosti, European Square, Bankova, Hrushevskoho, and Bohomoltsya streets, as well as in front of the Presidential Administration[55] and Interior Ministry buildings, until 7 January 2014,[56] upholding the Kyiv city administration's request to prohibit the meetings.[57] Multiple buses were parked around the perimeter of several government buildings in an attempt to block potential protests.[58]

Violent state suppression of the protests continued throughout December. Tiger special forces and police broke the protesters' blockade in early December, and under the pretense that they had received anonymous tips of subway stations being mined, subway stations in the centre of Kyiv were closed.[59] This announcement was followed by security forces and firefighter trucks taking over Bessarabska and Mykhailivska streets.[60] Working alongside titushky – thugs, hired by the state – police continued to take down protester barricades, pushing away protesters on Hrushevskoho and Liuteranska streets.[61]

While these measures were unsuccessful at breaking up the protests, security forces attempted to disperse protesters with a major operation on 10–11 December. Once again, in the middle of the night (1:00 a.m.), police forces stormed the protesters' encampment. Beginning from Instytutska Street and European Square, police pushed the protesters back. Around 3:00 a.m., forces attempted to storm the Kyiv administrative building, which had been occupied by protesters. While many were injured, protesters were only further motivated and protests continued.

Rights Suppression by Police and Judges

State manipulation of police and courts increased dramatically in December 2013. All lawyers I interviewed who offered pro bono defence during the revolutionary period, related multiple violations of detainee rights, constituting a drastic change even from the previous years of Yanukovych's presidency. A comprehensive analysis of judicial and police practices from December 2013 to February 2014 showed systematic violations of Ukraine's Constitution, the Criminal Procedural Code of Ukraine, the European Convention of Human Rights, and the Court's binding decisions.[62] The state's decision to swiftly suppress growing opposition via mass detentions led to multiple violations of procedural regulations and the rights of the detainees. For example, on 29 December, a car caravan travelled to Yanukovych's residence to peacefully protest. In the aftermath, arrest orders were issued to the owners of all participating cars, which did not always correspond with the participants who happened to drive those cars during the protests. Moreover, records involved massive falsifications of police signatures, to the point where the same policemen would have had to be present in different locations at the same time.[63] Legal records also show failures to inform detainees about the cause of detention, identically worded police reports purportedly written by different police officers in different cases, and detention decisions being made by unauthorized personnel.[64]

Blunt massive violations of detainees' rights were also committed in courts in violation of the ECHR, Ukrainian Constitution, and the procedural code. Judicial decisions were often made with disregard to evidence, neglecting the presumption of innocence, dismissing conditions for bail,[65] and failing to inform detainees about the Center of Free Legal Help.[66] The defence lawyers I interviewed reported that medical help was often denied, even in cases of severe skull injuries, which prevented defendants from providing proper testimony in court. Recent official investigations conducted in Ukraine indicate state pressure on the courts during the revolutionary period, with some judges recounting directives from the presidential administration to apply the maximum punishment for some activists.[67] The state did not shy away from the appearance that the courts were manipulated. Because the Federation of Trade Unions had issued a statement criticizing state violence against peaceful protesters and had allowed protesters to occupy the Trade Union building, the Kyiv Pechersk Regional Court prohibited the trade federation from entering their own building.[68]

A major state strategy to justify state violence was the public misrepresentation of the concerns and actions of protesters. On 20 December, Prosecutor General Victor Pshonka spoke in Parliament, justifying the police violence on 30 November by claiming it was "provoked" by protesters:

> Currently, the investigation has revealed that the opposition of individual protesters to the installation of a New Year tree on Independence Square has become a direct reason to involve law enforcement officers. Preparation of the square for the New Year holidays began long before these mass actions, and their occupation significantly complicated the work of public utilities … At 3:51 a.m., utility vehicles arrived at the square to clean up the area and install a [New Year] tree. However, the aggressive participants of the action did not react to their requests, started pushing communal services, blocking the movement of the vehicle, and knocking down the installed fence. Under such circumstances, for about four hours, the foreman of the Shevchenkivskyi District Road Maintenance Department in Kyiv appealed to police officers with a statement about the offense and a request to ensure that working conditions were appropriate. (*Noise in the parliament meeting room*) … At 4:10 a.m., Berkut officers began evicting protesters from Independence Square. Due to active resistance of the protesters, some Berkut employees began to use special means individually.[69]

While, later in the speech, Pshonka informed of the ongoing investigation regarding excessive use of force by Berkut troops, the number of false statements about the nature of the state–society interaction on 30 November sent a strong signal that the state was not willing to accept criticism, or release detainees. A pro-Yanukovych parliamentarian, Balytskyi, falsely stated that the anti-government protests were unconstitutional, adding a threat: "Don't mistake our politeness for weakness."[70]

Another strategy the state utilized in the attempt to weaken dissent was to conduct a dialogue with their political opposition, rather than address the protesters. This approach helped construct a government-led narrative that undermined the mass nature of the dissent, suggesting instead that is was a power struggle among the elites. On 13 December, Yanukovych organized a "round table" with leaders of the political opposition, Klychko, Yatseniuk, and Tiahnybok. No Maidan protester demands, however, were addressed. Rather, the causes of the protests were presented only as a response to the police violence on 30 November, and Yanukovych named a few officials who were supposedly responsible for the police violence on 30 November.[71] He refused to free detainees and rejected responsibility for the violent dispersal on that day, for continued state violence, and for mass rights violations.

Social Interpretation

The state's assault on peaceful protesters was a notable break from the norms of independent Ukraine, even if we take into account its previous authoritarian stages. Even during the *Ukraine without Kuchma* movement in 2001, when activists were detained, there was no public excessive police violence against the masses of unarmed protesters.[72] The 2013 Maidan scenes of young people climbing over gates to seek shelter from police beatings at a nearby monastery evoked images of Europe in the Middle Ages. It was, therefore, at St Michael's Square, adjacent to the monastery, that thousands of Kyivans began gathering to protest the police violence on 30 November.[73] The cradle of the Maidan grassroots revolution, in fact, can be traced to the doorsteps of the monastery. A symbol of protecting the people against state aggression, it also became a tactical place where medics offered free aid to the injured, lawyers interviewed victims to collect evidence, and activists discussed steps to effectively demonstrate public rejection of repressive state behaviour. By the end of 30 November, there were around ten thousand people in St Michael's Square alone. By 1 December, hundreds of thousands of people travelled from various parts of Ukraine. A consensus can be traced among protesters: they came in response to state violence to prevent the establishment of a violence-based regime in the future.[74]

Repression as Unconstitutional

The protesters and civil organizations that issued statements condemning police violence emphasized that the actions were in violation of constitutional rights. As the Professional Writers' Association of Ukraine declared:

> The notorious Berkut units committed a brutal, bloody massacre of student youth who exercised their constitutional right to freedom of assembly and demonstration. Dozens of Ukrainian and foreign civilians were seriously injured. The fundamental democratic principles guaranteed by the highest law, the Constitution of Ukraine, have been brutally trampled upon. The international prestige of the Ukrainian state has suffered irreparable damage … Ukrainian writers are shocked and deeply outraged by the events of *Bartholomew's Night*[75] on November 30, arranged by the insolent security forces against peaceful protesters.[76]

Public statements emphasized that the actions of law enforcement were unconstitutional, in violation of laws and regulations of Ukraine, and, therefore, unacceptable in a democracy. The statement also called separate attention to violence against journalists, prohibited by Ukrainian law:

> We support the right of citizens to express their views through free media and peaceful protests. It is cynical to use force and illegally obstruct the activities of journalists in the performance of their professional duties, which is a violation of Art. 171 of the Criminal Code of Ukraine.

The Federation of Trade Unions of Ukraine declared its "strong protest against the violent dispersal of a peaceful assembly of Ukrainian citizens," emphasizing that the state had overstepped the acceptable boundary of state–society relations by violating constitutional rights of citizens:

> The right to peaceful assembly, rallies, marches and demonstrations is guaranteed by basic law – the Constitution of Ukraine – and must be unconditionally ensured by all state structures. *However, as the events of November 30 showed, the law is not written for everyone. Young people suffered only because they believed in the Constitution and their legal right.* We call on the authorities to ensure unconditional observance by law enforcement agencies, every public official of the citizen's right to peaceful assembly, free and public expression of his opinion. We call on the leaders of all political forces to adhere to the principles of European democracy and respect for the rights of citizens.[77]

The criticism of state actions by religious leaders was an essential part of the Maidan resistance movement: religious authorities showed an act of civil disobedience and drew the lines of morality along lines of liberalism. Representatives of numerous religious organizations in Ukraine described the violent acts of the state as a violation of Ukraine's constitution and human rights of citizens. The Ukrainian Catholic University issued a statement saying: "The government order to disperse peaceful protests of students contradicts the Constitution of Ukraine and the rights of citizens for peaceful gathering. Therefore, the president of Ukraine and the government which gave these orders placed themselves above the law."[78] The spiritual leadership of Ukraine's Muslims, UMMA, also expressed its condemnation: "Ukraine is a democratic country, where it is necessary to sustain the rights and liberties of citizens."[79] The statement of Filaret, the patriarch of the Ukrainian Orthodox Church, similarly included a concrete discussion of state violations of the Constitution:

> The use of force to limit constitutional rights of citizens for peaceful gatherings and the freedom of expression, which was witnessed by the whole world tonight, is unacceptable … The consequence of the violent actions can only be radicalization of the protests and turning our state into a full-scale civil conflict … Court decisions could not be considered sufficient condition for perpetrating, especially at night, forceful actions, directed at limiting constitutional rights for peaceful gathering and freedom of expression. Let's not forget that the crucifixion of Christ, and the sufferings of times old and new, and numerous

> repressions of the twentieth century also took place under court decision – but this did not make lawlessness lawful.[80]

The statement of leaders of Evangelical Christians also emphasized the lawlessness of state actions: "Evangelical Christians cannot stay 'neutral' when state organs abuse their powers – when students' blood is spilled, courts make illegal decisions, and legal enforcement agents protect the government rather than the people."[81] Thus, many religious and minority groups in Ukraine interpreted morality along the lines of civil liberties, and violation of these rights by the state was pointed to as unconstitutional, and therefore immoral. Such active engagement in state–society dialogue was a vital part of the revolutionary battle.

Human Rights as the Defining Border of State–Society Relations

The dissent underscored that human rights – basic life and security – delineate state–society relations, rather than state orders. In other words, law enforcement should not use excessive force, and should rather focus on minimizing harm to protesters. Article 12 of the Law of Ukraine "On the Police" stipulates that in case of impossibility to avoid the use of force, it should not exceed the measure necessary to perform the duties assigned to the police and should minimize the possibility of harm to offenders and other citizens. Thus, the national Army Officers Union demanded to bring "to criminal responsibility all officials who gave and carried out criminal orders concerning inhuman, bloody beating of people, violating Art. 60 of the Constitution of Ukraine, according to which 'No one is obliged to carry out clearly criminal orders.'"

Public dissent emphasized that human rights, rather than state orders, should define state–society relations. As a Greco-Catholic priest, present at the protests, recalls:

> We, priests, were standing on the stage, the prayer was interrupted … It was understood that Berkut troops were not here to look at us, and that they will not look carefully – whether or not you were a priest – they will beat us just like everyone else … I went to talk to them … There were lots of them … I told them that there will be a dictatorship. That they have no right to call themselves men if they beat people – people who do not pose any threat. People who are just standing, expressing their protest,

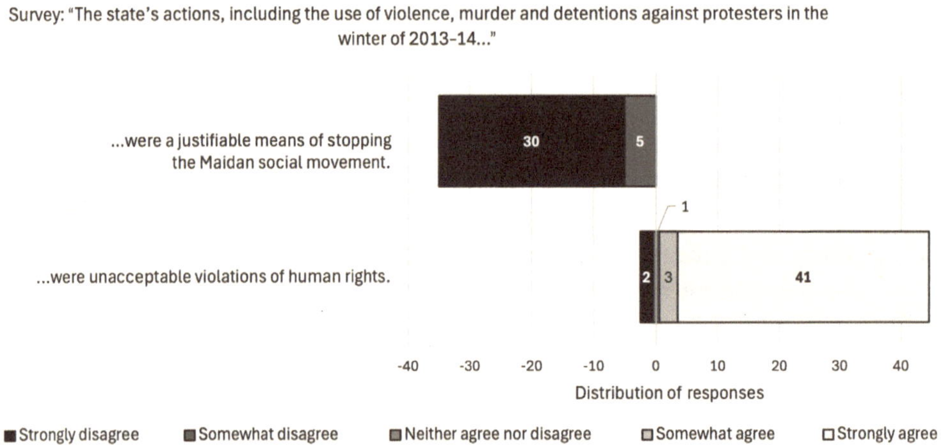

Figure 2.2 Interpretation of state action against the Maidan as violating human rights.
Source: Author's survey of Maidan protesters.

> which does not threaten neither the life nor safety of others. To beat defenseless people like that – that's not manly. That's unworthy … I was saying that they would be ashamed to look their children in the eyes when the dictatorship comes … Many of them were telling me that it was their job, so to speak, to leave us alone as they simply must do that. I answered them that during the Nuremberg trials, the Nazis who were on trial also said that they were following orders. However, they were executed – for breaking human and God's law, "Don't kill!" For torturing the defenseless, they broke these human norms.[82]

Repression as a Continuation of Presidential Attempts to Usurp Power

The unconstitutional violence perpetrated by the state was seen as a continuation of the Yanukovych administration's attempts to consolidate authoritarian power. The Army Officers' Union of Ukraine issued a statement that police aggression against peaceful protesters was an extension of an established pattern by the state:

> In the period from November 30 to December 13, 2013 in Kyiv, Ukrainian authorities used brutal physical force, violated the

> constitutional rights of citizens of Ukraine to peaceful assemblies, rallies, demonstrations. Thus, so-called law enforcement agencies violated Art. 28 of the Constitution of Ukraine, according to which "no one may be subjected to torture, cruel, inhuman or degrading treatment or punishment," and Art. 29, according to which "everyone has the right to liberty and security of person." These actions are a continuation of:
>
> - illegal decisions of the Constitutional Court of Ukraine on a change of the constitutional order in Ukraine – the transition from a parliamentary-presidential form of government to the presidential-parliamentary form, which gave Viktor Yanukovych unlimited power …
> - mass, systematic, gross violation of the constitutional rights of citizens by public authorities.

In other words, state aggression was seen in the context of previous actions by the Yanukovych administration to centralize power and to suppress political opposition and the rights of citizens.

Repression as a Manifestation of State Attempts to Consolidate Authoritarianism

Crucially, police violence against peaceful protesters was seen as a sign that the government was consolidating its authoritarian means of control. In other words, police violence was not seen as a temporary malfunction of the system, or a misunderstanding between the state and security forces. It was a continuation of an existing pattern of usurping democratic power. The new, harsher authoritarian means of control meant that Ukraine was on its way to dictatorship. Protesters related that state aggression meant the country was "turning into a dictatorship," similar to the regimes in Russia and Belarus.[83] A protester, who was interviewed on 30 November, voiced it this way:

> I'm here because what happened last night was brutal. They have beaten not only those at Maidan, but every one of us … We thought that we are different than Belarus, but we are not. We will be slaves … that is exactly what will happen.[84]

Another protester put it simply: "Taking into account the night's events, it will be a dictatorship for sure."[85] A protester described, "Hard to say what's happening: either this country is turning into a type of a dictatorship we can't even imagine, or there is some cunning plan we don't know about or maybe both … Staying at home these days is a betrayal of yourself. The fact is, we have no right to just swallow this." In other words, not only was state violence perceived as unacceptable, it was interpreted as a sign of growing authoritarianism.

Protesters conveyed their belief that a lack of social action to restrain the state will lead to consolidation of an authoritarian regime. One man explained his participation in the 1 December protest: "I have lived most of my life in Kyiv, but I am in fact [ethnic] Russian … This is my home … I want my children to grow up in a democratic country where they can feel safe and have their voices heard … rather than live with the … despotism [akin to what] Putin is trying to impose on Russia." Thus, protests were an attempt to prevent consolidation of authoritarianism, which was seen as firmly established in neighbouring Russia.

Popular protesters' chants were now "Away with the Gang" (*Bandu Het'*), "We will not Forgive" (*Ne Probachymo*), and "Revolution,"[86] implying social shock with the state, and the need for it to be replaced. An eighty-two-year-old woman explained: "You see what happened overnight to our children! Not in the day, but at night. They hide behind the back of Bandiukovych [a portmanteau combining "bandit" and "Yanukovych"] and if we do not stop it now, no one knows how it can end."[87] Interviewees emphasized the need to "consolidate … stay united by all means,"[88] for "the whole society should respond now."[89] Resistance, therefore, was seen as paramount in deciding the fate of Ukraine and its political regime. A protester who was present at Maidan Square, said: "We should make them (authorities) respond to us for what happened overnight. We should stay here until they do, no matter how long it takes. If we don't, all this will end badly, very badly."[90] Another demonstrator voiced her opinion as to the consequences if society does not protest: "if people … [don't] come out now … we will lose Ukraine." Activists expressed the belief that their involvement was a necessary action to prevent the establishment of a repressive state apparatus. As one of them related:

> I'm a criminal lawyer – when I represent a person in a murder case, I understand there is cruelty on his part; he is the problem. But when a government machine beats, tortures, murders people, and law enforcement behaves as if nothing happened, I can't stay uninvolved, because I understand that tomorrow I, or my family, could end up in a situation like that.[91]

Police brutality, detentions, and rights' violations in court were interpreted as a sign of a growing repressive state that, if not stopped by social action, would consolidate into full dictatorship. The discourse and the justification for further protests lay not only in opposition to the violence per se, but in the interpretation of what the current violence meant for the future political regime in Ukraine. A brochure distributed by revolutionaries included the following reasons to come to Independence Square:

> I am a proud and free human, I am Ukrainian, I am Kyivan
> I want to defend my children from the sticks of the bandits;
> With my presence I will not allow the gang to even think about violent actions in the future.

The brochure ends with "Remember: the fate of the nation depends on your personal presence!" Calls for mass mobilization were explained by the need to defend freedom and prevent future state violence. The "future of our children" was often evoked, eluding to the belief that a lack of social action would lead to the establishment of a dictatorial regime.

A Drop in the Ocean (*Kraplya v Okeani*) was an initiative by a Kyiv marketing firm that created a digital platform to allow people to express their reasons for participating in the resistance movement. These individualized posters were either shared electronically or printed for protests. The image was that of a drop of water, promoting the idea that individual contributions are vital to the resistance. As one *Kraplya* organizer related: "People would write the simplest things: 'because I have little kids and I want them to grow up in a normal country.' Or 'if not me, then who, the elderly?'" Social action was seen, in other words, as essential in preventing the consolidation of authoritarianism and protecting a democratic future.

Social Response

Systematic state repression from police violence and mass detentions (followed by rights violations in courts) in the winter months were an attempt to establish a new boundary of state–society relations and to normalize and legalize suppression of basic rights: freedom of expression, freedom of the press, and due process. In depriving citizens of their rights and the institutions to challenge their infringement, the state attempted to establish authoritarianism and create new expectations of what is expected from the state (repression), and what is expected from society (compliance) in the new regime. Ukraine's social response to these attempts was to push back, to reject the new terms of legality.

Social response to state repression was overwhelming. First, hundreds of thousands of people joined protests in the aftermath of the Berkut's 30 November violent dispersal. As police violence, detentions, and severe rights violations in courts continued, activists mobilized to aid protests (with food, shelter, and medical aid, etc.), organized multiple civic initiatives, and challenged the state in court. All of these served a specific function: communicating to the state, the rest of society, and the international community that Ukraine's state repression, their human rights violations, were unacceptable, and would be challenged. The protests were overwhelmingly peaceful, and activists, in fact, invested a lot in maintaining the peaceful nature of the resistance throughout December. Peaceful methods were used as one way to communicate social superiority in the state–society exchange, while the state chose to violate constitutional rights, laws, and regulations. Below is a discussion of (1) protests as an essential part of social response; (2) public statements by various social organizations; (3) activists' strategies to maintain peaceful means of resistance; (4) court battles as an arena for revolutionaries to contest new state-imposed terms of legality; and (5) religious leaders' contestation of repression through interpreting morality in line with human rights. A detailed account of civic initiatives organized by the growing grassroots community to communicate grievances to the state is provided in chapter 4

Figure 2.3 Around 800,000 people gathered on the Maidan and surrounding areas on 1 December 2013 to protest police brutality against unarmed protesters. This day marks the beginning of the anti-state revolutionary movement.

Protests

Protests were one of the most visible and essential ways to push back against government attempts to establish new terms of state–society relations. A notable feature of the protests, following the 30 November violence, was the sheer number of people who came to Maidan Nezalezhnosti (Independence Square). On 1 December the Maidan hosted half a million protesters predominantly from Kyiv but also from various parts of Ukraine. Such a large number of people articulated a clear social shock in reaction to repression. The focus of the 1 December march was the Berkut violence of 30 November.[92]

With at least a half-million and possibly up to one million protesters in Kyiv's centre, people occupied the Maidan Square, adjoining roads, the roof of the mall, the bridge, and a nearby hill.[93] The spontaneity of the mass gathering on 1 December was visible in the lack of a stage, which had been present for earlier protests as well as for the 2004 Orange Revolution. A single car was used to guide the march, and then served as a platform for prominent figures and politicians to address the crowds. From atop the car, actor Eugene Nishchuk yelled out revolutionary chants, singer Sviatoslav Vakarchuk led the hymn and gave a speech on citizens' rights suppressed by the police, and opposition politicians spoke of peaceful resistance.[94] Singer Irena Karpa, as well as former interior minister Yuri Lutsenko, encouraged a national general strike on 2 December to take to the streets and continue asking for Ukraine's leaders to resign.[95]

At noon, the All-Ukrainian Viche (rally)[96] began in Shevchenko Park.[97] This was followed by a march to the Maidan (Independence Square). Many banners referred to the Bloody New Year's Tree.[98] Interestingly, the protesters' banners and the ensuing social discourse used the term *yolka* – a Russian word for a fir tree, transliterated in Ukrainian, referring to the time when Yanukovych famously misspoke, not being able to remember the Ukrainian word (*yalynka*), and using the Russian one in a Ukrainian sentence. The chant "Away with the Gang" summed up social discontent with government actions. The chant was widely used during the rest of the winter months. Police troops who were guarding Lenin's monument on Khreshchatyk Street, were greeted by protesters' chants of "Shame!" and a plea to "Join the People."[99] The sheer multitude of protesters forced police forces to retreat from the Maidan. The barricades next to the unfinished New Year's tree structure were pushed away, and people "decorated" it with mourning wreaths, national and party flags, and posters with a *yolka* theme.[100]

The number of people in the centre of Kyiv continued to rise throughout the day. Many were there to see where the Berkut violence took place, and "look the cops in the eye."[101] Protesters chanted, "Kyiv rise up."[102] On one hand, over one thousand activists mobilized to form self-defence units to prevent further Berkut attacks.[103] On the other hand, the hope to peacefully restore state–society relations along democratic lines was evident in the protesters' attempts to continue dialogue with the police. People brought flowers to hand to the police, and glued print-outs to the newly erected metal fences with excerpts of the police code, specifying officers' rights to not follow "knowingly criminal orders of the administration."[104] Yuriy Lutsenko, the former interior minister, called for protesters to block Kyiv for a week, to pressure the parliament to adopt an impeachment law.[105] A parliamentarian from the opposition parties announced that on 2 December, the opposition in parliament was planning to hear a report from Interior Minister Vitaliy Zakharchenko and demand his resignation.[106] As one of the protesters asserted, "This

EuroMaidan would probably end itself in a couple of days, but what they did will now make millions rise. And they are going to regret. And there is no chance that people won't come out. They will. I have talked to many people, many were indifferent earlier, but now they are shocked and they are coming."[107] Throughout the following days, barricades were built around the perimeter of Maidan Square in an attempt to protect protesters from police violence. Major civic resistance initiatives, such as EuroMaidan SOS, Maidan's Self-Defence (*Samooborona Maidanu*), and AutoMaidan (*AvtoMaidan*) were formed on 1 December.

The following Sunday, 8 December – when people from various parts of Ukraine were able to travel to the capital – saw another massive gathering of approximately six hundred thousand people, dubbed The March of Millions. Protesters occupied the streets and squares near government buildings, and blocked traffic across a major central street, Hrushevskoho.[108] The protesters continued to set up a fortified tent city.[109] Thousands of volunteers delivered food, hot drinks, and clothing.

Notably, the rally was led by the political opposition elite, and also included prominent cultural figures, including Ljubomyr Husar, Yurij Andrukhovych, and Serhii Rahmanin, signifying the wide scope of social opposition. As activists grew distrustful of opposition political elites, cultural figures played a more pronounced role in the protest movement. The writer Andruhovych read protesters' demands to the government: freeing political prisoners (those detained after the Bankova events and those around the country); taking special forces off Kyiv streets; ending current repression; reducting dictatorial presidential powers by restoring the 2004 Constitution; changing the election law; signing the agreement with the EU; and implementing lustration (transparency and accountability) laws to reduce corruption in courts and law enforcement.[110] As seen in table 2.1, other major demands of the protesters, communicated to the state, included dismissal of the government, the resignation of President Yanukovych, and early presidential elections. The demands had a clear pro-democratic revolutionary character: the focus lay in replacing the regime of political repression with the rule of law, which would uphold state accountability. Regime change, in the eyes of the revolutionaries, necessitated a change of the state apparatus through government resignation and dissolution of the parliament as the existing elite were seen as the instigators of the systematic repression during the winter months.

Table 2.1 Demands of the Maidan protest movement and their support among protesters

Protest demands	*Support on 8 December 2013*
Release of political detainees, end to repressions	82%
Resignation of the government	80%
Resignation of President Yanukovych and early presidential elections	75%
Initiation of criminal proceedings against those guilty of beating Maidan protesters	58%
Dissolution of the *Verkhovna Rada* and calling early parliamentary elections	56%
Signing of the agreement with the EU	71%
Lustration laws to reduce corruption in courts and law enforcement	45%
Reduction of dictatorial presidential powers by restoring the 2004 Constitution	38%

Source: Kucheriv Democratic Initiatives Foundation and Kyiv International Institute of Sociology, 2013.

The monument to Lenin in the capital's centre was taken down by protesters in harmony with the anti-authoritarian tone of the protest movement. While approximately four thousand of 5,500 monuments to Lenin were demolished after the Soviet collapse, eighty of the monuments were, in fact, restored by the communist party of Ukraine by 2011.[111] While on 1 December the police thwarted an attempt to demolish the Lenin monument, this time they chose to stand down when a group of people in balaclavas marched toward the monument.[112] Crushing a ten-metre-high statue, with its head flying off, was compared by those responsible (the Ukrainian nationalist party, Svoboda) with the fall of the Berlin Wall. However, a member of the Maidan Council made a statement that the demolition had not been sanctioned by the opposition.[113] This contradiction reflected the internal social debate surrounding the demolition and its role in the resistance. As Kateryna Gornotsai's documentary short film *Lenin's Teeth* shows, Kyivans who gathered after the 8 December fall of the Lenin monument inevitably engaged in a conversation with strangers about the meaning of this event.[114] As Serhii Plokhy summarized, many Ukrainians "did not welcome the manner of the removal or share the nationalist ideology of those who carried it out, but they did not doubt that it was high time for Lenin to go."[115] It was only after the 20 February state shootings of protesters that the demolition of Lenin statues spread widely across the country. With 320 monuments destroyed that month,[116] a creative popular term was coined to accompany the phenomenon – *Leninopad* ("Leninfall"), sounding like Leninabad, a city in Soviet-era Tajikistan. While the demolition of Soviet-era monuments was never an agreed-upon strategy or tactic of the revolutionaries, it came as an expression of social frustration in response to Yanukovych's authoritarian methods of repression.[117]

Social response to the police storming of Maidan Occupy on 11 December was also remarkable: protesters' pleas via phones and social media called for residents to come to the square. While the number of protesters decreased to between 3,000 and 10,000 throughout the beginning of December, state violence on 7, 10, and 11 December (causing over 250 injuries) brought 25,000 protesters on 11 December. Taxis drove around Kyiv, with chants of "Kyiv Rise Up!" The bells were rung at the Myhailivskyi monastery: a rare move reserved for alarming inhabitants of monumental threats or tragedies. Prominent singers Ruslana and Vakarchuk performed through the night to inspire the masses. Public figures and opposition politicians, wearing "parliamentarian" vests locked arms to shield the protesters. Members of the national parliament have immunity from police and special forces, which law enforcement chose to honour during the entirety of the winter events. This turned the clash into a pressure game: protesters against police, who could not use violence against parliamentarians as they shielded protesters. Thousands of Kyivans continued to join the protesters, and by 11 a.m., police forces left Khreshchatyk.[118] Minister of Internal Affairs Zakharchenko publicly announced that there would be no forceful dispersal of Maidan.

Multiple initiatives and protest actions continued through December in Kyiv's centre. Their message was a condemnation of authoritarian means of control. For example, on 6 December, the Democratic Alliance organization led a protest in which protesters laid down in front of the Prosecutor General building to support those who were detained on Bankova Street. The protesters claimed, "you stepped over the law, step over the Ukrainian citizens."[119] People were decorating police shields with flowers to emphasize the peaceful nature of the protest movement, and attempted to communicate with police, as did a woman

Figure 2.4 Protesters used fires in metal drums to deal with the bitter cold. People carrying firewood to the city centre were subsequently targeted by police and titushky.

who addressed policemen with the following: "I've come here because I don't want a repeat of last week, when the blood of innocent people was shed. I'm old enough to be your own mother, and I don't want to see you hurt. Are you going to beat me and the others here?"[120]

Public Statements by Social Organizations and Regional Political Governments

The breakdown of social trust in regard to the national government's democratic commitment also comes through clearly in a number of statements issued by civil society and professional organizations. As demonstrated in the previous section on social interpretation of repression, the statements of multiple civic organizations emphasized that repression was unconstitutional and was a sign that the Yanukovych government continued a pattern of power usurpation that couldn't be tolerated. A group of cultural figures issued a condemnation of state violence, with a demand for the presidential administration to resign, signed by several hundred writers, artists, and musicians. Moreover, the statement boldly encouraged social protest:

> We, Ukrainian artists, writers, musicians, cinematographers, journalists, public figures, people of good will, are outraged and strongly condemn the repressive actions of the authorities against the Ukrainian people.
>
> We demand the immediate resignation of President Yanukovych and Azarov's government, whose shameful actions are radically contrary to the interests of Ukrainian citizens. We demand to bring to justice the security officers who bloodily dealt with the activists of the peaceful Euromaidan, and those who gave them orders.
>
> We call on all conscientious Ukrainians to resist, unite and repel the criminal actions of the authorities in any way permitted by the Constitution.[121]

The Ukrainian Sociology Association emphasized the breach of the rule of law by the state, placing the burden of responsibility for social unrest on the state's lack of accountability:

> The Board of the Sociological Association of Ukraine, an organization that unites professional sociologists from all regions of Ukraine, addresses you as a guarantor of compliance with the Constitution by all branches of government. We consider it absolutely necessary to take immediate measures to punish those who gave the order and used excessive force during the dispersal of Euromaidan participants. This is the main reason that led to the mass appearance of people on the streets, and without resolving this issue it is impossible to resolve the situation. Ten days have passed and none of the perpetrators has been punished. Every day of procrastination complicates the situation, increases tensions in society and makes further developments less predictable.[122]

Based on growing distrust with the administration as an entity that is meant to uphold the rule of law, the solution presented by these organizations was to demand its resignation. In fact, the statements were in line with protesters' discourse, which highlighted that Yanukovych crudely violated one of his major presidential duties as "the guarantor of the Ukrainian Constitution." The term "guarantor" was often invoked in a sarcastic manner by protesters in reference to Yanukovych, suggesting his failure to uphold citizens' basic constitutional rights.

A stark response also came from a number of regional governments. Opposition in the Ukrainian parliament forced a parliamentary vote of no confidence in the administration, which failed to pass. Regional councils of several Western regions showed more unity, issuing official appeals to President Yanukovych, the office of Presidential Administration, and the Ukrainian parliament, "categorically condemning the use of violence against peaceful protesters."[123] While some of them advised the president more generally to "use all means possible to prevent any force against peaceful citizen gatherings," other councils declared the use of force on 30 November a crime, and demanded the dismissal of Azarov and Zakarchenko:

> We, the deputies of Zakarpattya regional council … express outrage at the brutal dispersal of a peaceful assembly held in Kyiv on November 30, 2013. We consider a crime the bloody dispersal of peaceful gatherings of Ukrainian citizens … by armed state authorities. Therefore, we demand an urgent and objective investigation, and bringing the perpetrators to justice. We appeal to the President of Ukraine, Yanukovych, to immediately dismiss the Minister of Internal Affairs, Zakharchenko, and Prime Minister, Azarov.[124]

Moreover, the Zakarpattya regional council statement called on law enforcement officers "not to carry out criminal orders, not to commit any acts of violence against civilians and not to take part in attempts to disperse peaceful protests."[125] Ternopil regional council demanded the resignations of President Yanukovych and Prime Minister Azarov.[126] Not all the regional governments issued statements critical of state violence: while some were evasive, others expressed support. Thus, councils of several other regions issued statements in which they avoided mention of the police violence; for example, Kherson regional council called on the opposition "not to divide the country into 'us' and 'them,'"[127] while Crimea council called on Yanukovych to "take all the necessary measures to restore public order, and, if needed, impose a state of emergency."[128]

Maintaining Peaceful Resistance

Activists made deliberate efforts to maintain peaceful resistance.[129] While the protests were overwhelmingly peaceful, social anger was also manifested by occasional use of violence by small groups of participants. In the face of this challenge, leaders of newly formed civic initiatives within the Maidan consciously invested in maintaining the peaceful nature of resistance efforts.

As one activist described:

> We came from an understanding that we had to keep the demonstration of the people, who were angered by the arbitrariness of state power, from violent actions. One of the practical ways was to hand people something to hold. We then decided to give everyone candles … I spent ten thousand hryvnas to buy candles. Firstly, it was visually powerful. Secondly, it is hard to beat a person who is holding a candle. And thirdly, holding candles pacified people.[130]

The approach was taken to assert that the movement was within legal bounds and thus maintained moral superiority over a state that continually overstepped legal bounds and suppressed activists' constitutional rights.

Some notable examples of the movement's inner discourse about the use of violence involve the first days in December, prior to activists' tailored steps to prevent it. On 1 December, several masked men attempted to take over the administration building. In response, other protesters who were marching past the building, pushed them away, asserting that the meeting was peaceful, and that anyone willing to use violence was a "provocateur." Interestingly, the building was actually later controlled by peaceful Maidan protesters. Another group of protesters utilized the Trade Union building,[131] after the Trade Union Federation announced it would provide use of the building for the movement.

Figure 2.5 Several pianos were set around the Maidan by the Kyiv Conservatory. Maidaners gathered, and sometimes sang along, as professional and amateur players alike took their turn to play. The blue and yellow piano became one of the symbols of the Maidan resistance movement.

Yet another group of masked men (a notable feature, as on 1 December almost no protesters were wearing masks) used a front-end loader in an attempt to knock down the metal fence guarded by Berkut police, near the Presidential Administration building on Bankova Street around 2:30 p.m.[132] An activist recalled:

> These were simple men who wanted to act. I did not stop the loader, but on the contrary, started directing it to go forward … If the fence was gone, there'd be nothing left to separate activists from the police … but they [Berkut] were refusing to leave … We told them, but they refused … I don't know why, but among the activists, a person appeared that asked us to stop … I supported him: we got onto the loader and yelled "Stop." My friends did not understand … I was stopped by humanism and the desire for those soldiers not to end up under the arm of that loader.[133]

This incident demonstrates the internal struggle of many protesters: a desire to express social anger on one hand, and empathy toward

Figure 2.6 A protester offers chocolate to riot police. Revolutionaries continually attempted to convince the police to join their side.

policemen on the other hand. It also shows the trust toward other protesters, and willingness to respond to their pleas, as they felt united by a common goal. As a result of pressure from the majority, who were not supporting violent actions at the time, and continued to shout "Only peaceful action," those driving the loader on Bankova Street were stopped.[134]

The resistance movement insisted on separating itself from the violent incidents of 1 December. Opposition politicians, who were speaking at Maidan Square soon after the incidents, also declared the action with the loader a "provocation."[135] Civic organizations issued statements to "avoid provocations to participate in violent actions."[136] Then-parliamentarian Poroshenko filed a case with the prosecutor general, claiming that, according to presented video documents, a few hours prior to mass protests, six buses of masked men with knives were taken into the courtyard of the presidential administration, in order to present a false picture of bloody clashes, justify Berkut violence, and discredit the peaceful nature of the protests.[137] Many anti-state media outlets in Ukraine sided with the theory, claiming that aggressive activists were visibly different from other protesters, as they were wearing black masks, or balaclavas, and had nationalistic armbands.[138] Some declared the provocations were organized by the nationalist group Bratstvo,[139] while others argued that most of the (fifty to sixty) aggressive attackers spoke Russian or were Berkut themselves,[140] suggesting that aggression was staged to justify future violent Berkut attacks.[141] Even if these speculations weren't true, this approach proved to be effective in December at suppressing a small minority of activists who would have preferred a violent approach.

As time went on, and the state continued its repression throughout December, increasing social distrust, the task of stifling social anger remained vital. The activists, indeed, succeeded at this uneasy task via continuing discourse. This becomes visible in the example of the massive 29 December caravan to Yanukovych's residence. The message of the automobile protest remained the same as the earlier December protests: "We have a large, critical mass of people who are expressing protest. You need to pay attention to us, and our demands."[142] There were some 3,500 cars, spread over kilometres, occupying a large portion of the highway. Dmytro Bulatov, the Auto-Maidan initiative leader, described his predicament as the car caravan neared the residence:

> When I got on top of the car, I saw that there were so many of us. People were irritated, ready for aggression. I told everybody that this was a [peaceful] action. But we were not organized by anybody, we were just together, driven by the same misfortune. We were not an organization, so nobody was required to follow our lead. We were united by an ideological common cause. We were worried that some people might try to stay. We were worried that if somebody would set up a tent, or 20–30 tents at night, they would be beaten and taken away … I asked people to turn around: now that we managed to show our position, it was time to end. Turning people around appeared to be the most challenging task. I was trying to convince people, speaking through a microphone, I felt responsible … I saw that people turned around … I saw that our people, countrymen, could be convinced, persuaded … I couldn't get off the car for some time because I was shaking from tension. I had to stay there for five minutes, because I simply couldn't hold on to the ladder to get down.[143]

This account demonstrates the major challenges of leading a grassroots movement: those who guide are not charismatic leaders whose personalities could at times be sufficient to direct the masses. Rather, grassroots leaders are followed only as long as they are trusted to represent the common cause. Importantly, it was the common cause of the Maidan pro-democratic movement that empowered the message of peaceful means of resistance: to demonstrate to the state the legality of their actions in contrast with the illegal and unconstitutional means of state repression.

Resisting State-Imposed Terms of Legality

As discussed above, violations of detainees' rights became systematic during mass detentions and court trials. Over seven hundred lawyers mobilized to offer pro bono help to protesters. The initial move to file criminal cases against the state's excessive use of force in the 30 November attacks resulted in serious backlash. The state aggressively responded by framing the victims of police attacks as instigators of mass unrest and therefore susceptible to criminal prosecution.[144] This was a clear message from the state that the regime was transforming, openly adopting repressive methods of control.[145] In other words, the legal opportunity structure (LOS) became extremely unfavourable for litigation. Nevertheless, as will be shown in this section, lawyers unleashed a legal resistance by pursuing and appealing cases, exposing systemic police and judicial violations (in courts and in the media), thwarting police attempts to detain activists in hospitals, and so forth. Their litigation strategy was specifically aimed at challenging the newly imposed legal structure. Defence lawyers used courts as an arena of resistance, voicing social refusal to accept the new political order.

During the Ukrainian Revolution, lawyers actively resisted the imposition of new rules in a political game dictated by the state, becoming agents to broker dialogue between state and society, and participating in the construction of social meanings of justice. The goal of *cause lawyering* (legal defence for a larger social cause) in revolutionary Ukraine was to create an additional avenue of social resistance against the state's attempt to consolidate authoritarian methods of control, and to assert the moral boundaries of state–society interaction. To assert these moral boundaries, lawyers actively resisted attempts by state agents to reconceptualize the norms of state behaviour vis-à-vis citizens' rights. Moreover, attorneys actively participated in the construction of social meanings of justice in their discussions with activists, and condemned state violations when addressing national audiences, asserting that state actions constituted violations of citizens' rights. Thus, cause lawyers in revolutionary Ukraine aimed for fundamental political change through asserting concepts of legality.

Similar to civil rights movements in the United States, where the NAACP approached activists to challenge segregation law in court,[146] cause lawyers in Ukraine persuaded people to challenge state actions in courts.[147] They informed activists of the potentially serious repercussions as well as the longevity of the pursuit, and yet this came with encouragement. As one lawyer relates:

> I always asked them the following questions: "Are you sure you want to take it to the end? Do you understand that [these events] will be followed by a period of repression? Neither you nor I can predict how long these repressions will last, one or two days, or a month … or years and decades as in Belarus and Russia. Are you aware that as soon as you submit your application, you will be filed? You will be on the list. Do you understand that the prospect [of winning this legal battle] is zero until the regime changes?" And then I would add: "Do you understand that what you are doing is heroic? It is necessary. It is the only way to neutralize the system."[148]

This statement is revealing: on one hand there is consciousness of the inability to punish state offenders in the existing legal environment, and yet there is a determination to break the system through communicating social refusal to accept the new repressive order. Moreover, such communications between lawyers and activists played a role in constructing social meanings. By emphasizing the necessity to transmit social protest into legal action, defence lawyers in Ukraine highlighted the unconstitutionality of state actions and contributed to the loss of the state's legitimacy among the populace.

Another form of challenging the state in the new repressive environment was appealing court decisions of pre-trial sentences. While many lawyers bargained charges of inciting mass unrest down to charges of simple hooliganism, reducing a potential decade-long prison sentence to fines or short sentences,[149] scholars of cause lawyering point out that, not only does plea bargaining "systematically fragment political resistance through the individualization of cases,"[150] it also legitimizes the regime by complying with its terms.[151] Meaningfully, a number of Ukraine's cause lawyers chose to appeal even relatively minor sentences, such as house arrests, in order to emphasize that the state, and not protesters, had violated the law.[152] While some of these appeals were rejected, some sentences were successfully reduced.[153]

A major strategy of cause lawyering during the Ukrainian Revolution focused on increasing social awareness that the state was a violator of inalienable rights. To this end, they continually exposed judicial violations in court.[154] One lawyer recalled her victory that resulted from a combined effort with the public defender, and allowed her to represent a client:

> The judge would not let me represent the client on the basis that the person already had a government lawyer. The government lawyer stated [to the judge], "Since there is a private defender, I have no right to represent the client in court. And without defenders, you have no right to have a hearing." The judge responded, "I will file a complaint – you [government lawyer] have no right to leave as I did not dismiss you from the case. So you have to represent him, and you, private defender, will be a private observer." Then I got out two hundred pages of the [detainee's] detention file [which the court had previously provided to me], and said, "Under which part of the procedural code did you give these case documents to a private observer?"[155]

These seemingly small victories of lawyers' ability to establish what counts as acceptable interpretation of law are essential in a state–society discourse that determines the legitimacy of state actions.

Some of the most successful exploitations of the state's legal facade were lawyers' attempts to prevent detentions in hospitals. Police often raided hospitals after each round of attacks against protesters. So, defence lawyers would take turns being "on duty" at hospitals where injured protesters were treated, ready to face the police.[156] While on the streets, the riot police could corner groups of people and detain them en masse, hospitals provided a new space of interaction. Police had to face only a few detainees at a time, giving an opportunity for lawyers to demand documents necessary for lawful detention, as well as for hospital staff to object to the arrest on the grounds of the seriousness of injuries. The hurdles of detention procedures in hospitals gave time for lawyers and activists to contact the press, whose appearance would offer additional pressure on individual policemen.[157] Notably, journalists in their interviews with me talked about being repressed, and as discussed elsewhere in this book, many were physically targeted; however, several outlets and newly launched internet forums were committed to participating in the resistance.

Defence lawyers' resistance to the state's imposition of new terms of legality was also evident in their construction of a discourse with detainees. Even when bargaining with the state, lawyers insisted on reassuring their clients that the state was at fault.[158] Lawyers crafted hand-outs for the protesters, emphasizing that (1) a peaceful gathering does not require permission from the state, only a notification; and (2) a state official is allowed to do only what is provided in the law, while a private citizen is allowed to do anything that is not prohibited.[159] Likewise, various lawyers' press statements asserted that the state violated constitutional order. Thus, an open statement by lawyers and legal activists asserted that the "use of unlawful violence by Ukrainian authorities" was akin to a "legal collapse."[160] Lawyers expressed no confidence in the judiciary body, asserting that it supported "doubtful, unprincipled, and dangerous government actions rather than protect[ing] human rights and freedoms."[161]

Ukraine's defence lawyers didn't limit themselves to lessening the pain of detained protesters, but rather actively challenged the new terms of legality promoted by the state. By exploiting the legal facade of trials, they exposed judicial violations, appealed sentences, and publicized state violations of constitutional order. Defence lawyers in Ukraine actively resisted the newly imposed legal structure, and shaped social conceptions of legal rights, greatly contributing to the revolutionary resistance against the consolidation of Yanukovych's authoritarian regime.

Religious Morality and Liberal Constitutional Discourse

Religious organizations played an active role in providing physical protection to revolutionaries by offering shelter for those who were sick and/or targeted by the state, quarters for organizing medical supplies, urgent care, and, in the last days of the revolution, a makeshift hospital for treatment of severe wounds from firearms. These actions were a clear show of solidarity with protesters, as churches openly offered shelter to those persecuted by state authorities. Offering an alternative to hospitals, where police raids were routinely conducted, was also an open act of defiance against the state.

The anti-state stance of religious organizations was more than an act of solidarity. Leaders of Christian, Jewish, and Muslim communities in Ukraine maintained their presence during the Maidan Revolution, asserting their moral authority over state–society interaction. They openly criticized the state for the use of brutality and bloodshed, describing it as unjust and immoral. Many denominations openly encouraged civic protest against the state. They also called on revolutionaries to utilize only peaceful means of resistance.

Churches aimed to establish themselves as moral authorities and openly challenged the state. Thus, the Ukrainian Revolution went beyond the protests on the main square in Kyiv. The Ukrainian experience shows that revolution should be seen as a dialogue between the state and society, where moral and legal boundaries are drawn. Religious organizations in Ukraine chose to side with the people, but their support went beyond offering sanctuary. They participated in the struggle against the state by moulding the ideology of the resistance, by pushing back against state aggression, and drawing the moral boundaries of state–society relations along lines envisioned by liberal democratic thought.

In these variances, these religious organizations remained united in their condemnation of state actions. The Orthodox Church of the Moscow Patriarchate was the only one that did not criticize state violence, but rather emphasized the legitimacy of the current state, suggesting that the students-protesters were paid for their participation, and criticizing the churches who "organized prayer tents" (5 December 2013, 6 December 2013, 14 December 2013). While many religious organizations expressed support for civil acts of disobedience and protest in response to state injustice, all emphasized the importance of peaceful resistance. Many called for constant prayer, all-confessional prayers, and fasting in the name of peace. Clergy present on the Maidan square stood between protesters and Berkut officers to prevent clashes from either side. In doing so, they asserted moral authority over citizens' actions.

New Year's Address to the President: Defining Transformation of State–Society Relations

The Soviet Union was a totalitarian regime governed by Leninist ideology. Leninism dictated the supremacy of the ruling group (the party). The Soviet state was held superior at determining the path and then leading society toward eventual communism. Such assumed superiority was reflected in all aspects of the Soviet regime: from state ownership of production, services, and housing, to state guidance of economy and politics, to state control of social choices and interactions. As predicted by a number of scholars, the Leninist legacy had a strong hold on state–society relations for decades after the Soviet collapse. On one hand, Soviet citizens grew to distrust the state and any civic organizations – as they were all directed by the state. On the other, however, they grew to expect state provision of employment, housing, and most certainly politics (i.e., society did not develop the skills of monitoring the state). As discussed above, democratic values, which presuppose the state to be continually guided by society, continued to increase in Ukraine. However, civil society, an essential element that allows democracy to function because it serves as a watchdog of the state, was still rather weak in Ukraine by the beginning of the revolutionary events in the winter of 2013. After the Orange Revolution, protests contesting the results of the rigged elections in 2004, most citizens withdrew from political involvement, expecting that pro-democratic leadership and fair rules would be enough to guarantee democracy. Backsliding into authoritarianism under Yanukovych affected these preconceptions. Many interviewed revolutionaries emphasized a newly gained perspective regarding their civic duty to watch over the state.

One exploit of the protesters leveraged a popular tradition. New Year celebrations gained a central importance in the Soviet Union. Based on Leninist ideology, religion had no place in Soviet society, and celebrations of religious holidays were suppressed. New Year became a major state-sponsored holiday in the successful attempt to deflect Christmas. Minutes before midnight on New Year's Eve, the Communist party secretary (Soviet leader) would address the Soviet nation, followed by an image of a clock striking midnight. This legacy was carried into modern Ukraine: the annual New Year's presidential address about the administration's achievements still attracts large audiences. A variation on this tradition was at the core of one revolutionary initiative. Activists closely imitated the classical rich celebratory background of a typical presidential national address, including the holiday decorations and the national symbols, and implemented expensive technology for recording and digital imagery. Instead of the president giving the address, however, the activists featured protesters addressing the president. Opposition media outlets, Hromadske and Zik, aired the address, and the YouTube post of the address quickly gained viewers.

The New Year's Address of the Ukrainian Nation to the President of Ukraine, which imitated the traditional presidential address, summarized major social grievances: excessive police violence against peaceful protests, repression of the freedom of the press, and violations of detainee rights. The address also represented the major message of the resistance: that the border of state–society relations has to be outlined by the constitutional rights of citizens. Here is an excerpt:

> Dear Mr President,
> In a few minutes we will greet the new year, 2014.
>
> I wouldn't choose to be here, on Maidan square in the cold, I would rather be on a warm couch with grandma … But my grandma kicked me out to the Maidan when she saw kids being beaten.
>
> This year I found out that our kids can be thrown behind bars without any proof and be on trial like criminals … This year I understood that in the country where I was born, journalists can be persecuted and women shamefully beaten; that when asked for a dialogue, you can give orders to violently disperse students right under the nose of European politicians …
>
> Mr President, I understood that the future of the country is now in our hands, not yours. You said that this year will become a year of development and social justice; that all branches of government will guarantee maximum social effect,

> from economic growth to legal transformations. On the night of November 30, our students felt the effect [of these supposed transformations] in full power. An effect which does not let us sleep now.
>
> Mr President, during the three years of your rule, the Ukrainian nation understood that your words and your promises are empty. When you are living in a 620 square-metre palace, with piers for yachts, a house in Kyiv, tennis courts, hunting areas, an army of guards, it might be hard to think about anything else. For example, about the future of Ukraine.
>
> I wish in the New Year we can wake up in a strong free country rather than a Soviet republic … Mr President, we have unbroken trust in our nation; and with this we are going into the New Year. So we will never have in the New Year what happened in the old one.
>
> Happy New Year, Viktor Federovych! We are Europeans. We will be in the European Union with you or without you.[162]

The address encapsulates the loss of social trust in the corrupt president, who oversaw severe violations of freedoms of the press and expression. It also captures social determination to prevent the state from overstepping legal boundaries guaranteeing human rights. Crucially, *The New Year's Address of the Ukrainian Nation to the President of Ukraine* symbolically represented the social transformation that was taking place via revolutionary events: society, not the government, was becoming the leader in determining the nation's path and the terms of state–society relations as a functioning democracy.

Conclusion

Excessive police violence against peaceful protesters on 30 November and continuing rights suppression by the state were interpreted by many as a manifestation of growing authoritarianism. Ukrainians who formed the new resistance movement believed that a lack of social action would guarantee a consolidation of Yanukovych's dictatorial regime. Social shock was manifested by the significant number of protesters – measuring in the hundreds of thousands on some days – and their opposition to state repression was expressed in their demands for the release of detainees, the punishment of state officials, and, beginning in December, the resignation of the president.

In tracing social perception of state actions throughout the first phase of the revolutionary events, we see that the violence of Berkut police was decisive in triggering and sustaining the revolutionary movement. As discussed, Yanukovych's decision not to sign the treaty with the European Union prompted protests that died down by the end of November, and it was declared that further opposition efforts would be invested in the presidential election campaign. The Berkut violence on 29 November against peaceful protesters led not only to hundreds of thousands on the Kyiv square, but also to the creation of a social movement – multiple grassroots groups, functioning to communicate to the state social disapproval of the violent repression. Multiple civic initiatives on the Maidan Square were formed to organize protest walks, drives, and presentations to deliver messages to the state and galvanize support from others. Volunteer lawyers challenged judges and appealed the cases of the detained in an atmosphere of apparent legal repression, resisting newly imposed terms of legality. Religious leaders spoke of the state's unconstitutional actions along lines of spiritual morality.

A small number of participants in the social opposition, especially those who experienced police violence first hand, agitated for violence (and a limited number of violent clashes took place in December); however, the overwhelming majority of participants advocated peaceful resistance methods. Socialization among the participants yielded a discussion about the methods of resistance. Violence directed toward police on 1 December was dismissed by the Maidaners and activists who were invested in maintaining peaceful methods of resistance. Most participants at the time perceived that peaceful mass social resistance was likely to be an effective path to convince the state to stop police violence and repression and to affect the eventual release of detained protesters.

Social communication with the state via protest signs, public statements of multiple civic groups and organizations, and court cases showed a pattern of articulating protesters' vision of state–society relations as asserting the principles of natural rights. Central to this articulation was an emphasis on discussing excessive police violence as a violation of constitutional rights of citizens: protesters had the "right to peaceful assembly" and "suffered only because they believed in the Constitution," while "state organs abused their power." Not only civic organizations, but multiple religious communities, issued statements drawing the lines of morality along the concept of liberalism, condemning police violence and repressive court decisions. They underscored that the use of state force was "directed at limiting constitutional rights for peaceful gathering and freedom of expression." Natural rights were the delineating line of legality, as even conservative Christian leaders emphasized that numerous forms of oppression from the "crucifixion of Christ" to "twentieth-century repressions" "took place under court decisions," thus asserting their entitlement to conduct a *social review* – social oversight over the constitutionality of state actions, including laws and court decisions. Finally, communications via public statements and on the Maidan Square were formulated in light of Yanukovych's previous abuses of power and conveyed their belief in the necessity of social action to prevent further repression.

3

State–Society Dialogue, Part II

January–February 2014

> Those people … were orcs from the *Lord of the Rings*, because they laughed in our faces, yelling: "Good riddance!" and I understood that these guys were ready to kill many more.[1]

This perception of special forces' behaviour on 22 January, after the first killings of revolutionaries, is very telling of the transformation of state–society relations in Ukraine at the time. It provides insight into why the revolutionaries, who consciously maintained peaceful methods of resistance throughout the winter months, began to support political violence over time. Not only did the state continue to ignore protesters' demands to end police violence and repression in the courts, it started using ammunition to kill protesters. Severe police violence and killings were accompanied by notable dehumanizing treatment. As this chapter describes, Berkut troops systematically humiliated and degraded revolutionaries, from stripping them naked in sub-zero temperatures, to forcing them to kneel and sing. As is apparent in the account above, such severe violence and mockery eventually led protesters to conclude that the state was determined to consolidate a terror regime in Ukraine through any means possible. This understanding of the state's intentions fundamentally changed social response, and support for political violence grew.

This chapter is divided into three sections: the 16 January laws and its effects, the first wave of state violence, and the more severe second wave of state violence (beginning 18 February). Each section of the chapter is further divided into three aspects of state–society dialogue: state repression, social interpretation, and social response.

The 16 January Laws

Repression as the Aim of the Laws

The date 16 January 2014 marked a significant new step in state–society relations in Ukraine. Parliamentarians of the Party of Regions, Yanukovych's party, violated major procedural rules in order to adopt laws severely restricting freedoms of expression, press and protest, confining the function of NGOs, and offering impunity for violations committed by law enforcement officers. The adopted law[2] contradicted the Ukrainian Constitution, as well as international treaties, including the European Convention on Human Rights, and the Organization for Security and Co-operation in Europe. A purposeful disregard for basic parliamentarian procedures was shown through (1) the "voting by hand" procedure (which is permitted only in cases of technical malfunction); (2) an unrealistically short time to count the votes; (3) refusal to count individual votes (counting was instead done on the basis of present parliamentary groups); (4) lack of prior consideration in parliamentary committees; and (5) denial of allocation of discussion time in the parliament.[3] These blunt procedural violations sent a message that the state was determined to continue repression.

The laws pushed the boundary of state–society relations by allowing state agents to arrest and impose fines in cases of social criticism of state activity. This new boundary shifted toward the type of dictatorial relations not present even during post-Soviet authoritarian-era regimes, when the press and political opposition were suppressed but public protests were allowed. The 16 January laws repressed basic civil liberties, severely limiting dissent. Suppression of dissent was now justified on the basis of broad categories of "showing insolent disrespect" for law enforcement and "extremist activity," punishable by years of imprisonment.

The most drastic encroachment of civil liberties was the introduction of criminal liability, punishable by three years' imprisonment, for "storage … and dissemination of extremist materials" over social media and other sources, and other "extremist activity," which was broadly defined to include "disruption of public order," "hooliganism," and "illegal interference in the activities or obstruction of the lawful activities of public authorities."[4] A further encroachment on the right of free expression was the criminalizing of defamation (amending the

Table 3.1 The 16 January laws with corresponding punishments, and violations of the Ukrainian constitution and European Convention on Human Rights

Targeted activity	*Punishment*	*Violations of Const. and ECHR*
"Storage … and dissemination of extremist materials" over social media and other sources, and other "extremist activity," which was broadly defined and included "disruption of public order," "hooliganism," and "illegal interference in the activities or obstruction of the lawful activities of public authorities."	Up to 3 years' imprisonment.	Article 34 of the Ukrainian Constitution, ECHR, Article 10
Defamation	Up to 1 year correctional labour, and up to 2 years' imprisonment if it included accusation of corruption (a typical criticism by the revolutionaries of those in power), or other crimes.	Article 34 of the Ukrainian Constitution, ECHR, Article 10
Spreading information that "showed insolent disrespect" toward police or judges, or influencing them "in any other form"	Up to 6 months' arrest or up to three years' imprisonment.	Article 34 of the Ukrainian Constitution, ECHR, Article 10
"Blocking of entrance to person's residence"	Up to three years' restriction of liberty	Article 39 of the Ukrainian Constitution, ECHR, Article 11
"Blocking of administrative buildings and premises"	Up to five years' imprisonment	Article 39 of the Ukrainian Constitution, ECHR, Article 11
Installing of a tent, stage, or any small construction for holding a rally "without permission of the Ministry of Internal Affairs"	Up to 15 days' incarceration	Article 39 of the Ukrainian Constitution, ECHR, Article 11
Participation in a rally when wearing a helmet.	Up to 15 days' incarceration	Article 39 of the Ukrainian Constitution, ECHR Article 11

2001 Criminal Code), punishable by up to one year of correctional labour, and up to two years' imprisonment if it included an accusation of *corruption* (a typical criticism by the revolutionaries of those in power), or other crimes.

The laws targeted specific activities adopted by the dissent. Since many activists addressed the police to convince them to join the resistance, and attended the trials of detained activists as a form of resistance and application of public pressure on judges, the laws stipulated that spreading information that "showed insolent disrespect" toward police or judges, or influencing them "in any other form" were to be punished with up to six months of arrest or up to three years' imprisonment. AutoMaidan initiatives included caravans to politicians' residences to expose their luxury lifestyles via social media, or calling for their resignation. The 16 January laws criminalized "blocking of entrance to person's residence," punishable by three years of restricted liberty. Yet another form of resistance was to protest in front of the parliamentary building; hence, "blocking of administrative buildings and premises" could now result in up to five years' imprisonment.

The laws were extensive in their reach to penalize all those engaged in dissident activity, including those who aided protesters. Selective amendments were almost comical in their specificity of targeting the ongoing dissent. Maidan-sich, a Protesters Occupy area where a stage, tents, food stands, medical aid, and multiple other aid and information centres were set up by volunteers to maintain the protest, became an explicit target: installing of a tent, stage, or any small construction for holding a rally "without permission of the Ministry of Internal Affairs" would lead to arrest for up to fifteen days. Holding assemblies and facilitating such assemblies by providing premises, transport, or any other help, was now also illegal. In other words, according to the 16 January laws, multiple Kyiv residents who offered free housing to protesters were now engaged in "illegal activity." Perhaps the most ironic provision was a response to Maidan protesters wearing helmets to prevent injuries inflicted by police: participation in a rally while wearing a helmet was now punishable by fifteen days' incarceration. Amendments to the Code of Administrative Offences also made it illegal to drive in columns of over five vehicles "without prior agreement with the road police," responding to the AutoMaidan initiatives, which often included driving in groups of cars to show protest.

The 16 January laws repressed NGO activism and means of personal communication, allowing state agencies to track activists, suppress NGOs, and block internet media sources. The use of prepaid mobile cards, which did not require identification, was now illegal. NGOs receiving foreign funding were branded "foreign agents," required to pay 18 per cent income tax, and provide detailed reports. Moreover, NGOs and religious organizations could now be shut down on the basis of "extremist activity."[5] As described in the previous chapter, even prior to the passage of the 16 January laws, en masse violations in courts became a major method of state repression. The new Amendments to the Criminal Procedure Code now allowed pre-trial and trial proceedings to be conducted in the absence of the defendant legalizing suppression of the rights of defendants.[6]

A particularly harsh blow to state–society dialogue was the state's blatant disregard for calls to bring to justice those responsible for police brutality against peaceful protesters. The laws provided amnesty to all crimes committed from 21 November to 26 December 2013. Thus, no one in the administration who organized the attacks, or police and special forces troops who harassed and attacked the protesters, medics, or journalists, were criminally liable.[7]

The implementation of the repressive laws in the courts immediately followed, with multiple violations of due process and executive pressure on judges. The number of detentions rose significantly in January. Attempts by some judges to circumvent the law or order less severe punishments were stymied by higher authorities. On 23 January, the chairwoman of Obolonsky District Court, the only court in Kyiv that ordered house arrests for some of the detained protesters, abruptly resigned.[8] A judge from Vinnitsya oblast held a press conference after his resignation, at which he reported executive pressure on judges and stated that any judge who stepped out of line could be fired within four hours.[9]

The new laws were bluntly repressive: if you criticized the state or supported those who did, you would be severely punished according to the new law. The state crossed the previously established line of state–society relations firmly into the realm authoritarianism. Since the liberalization following the Orange Revolution, press freedom and freedoms of expression had experienced historic highs: blossoming civil liberties pushed the boundary of state–society relations in Ukraine, limiting the reach of the state. The 16 January laws were a fundamental step backward, giving the state all-encompassing power to restrict speech, expression, movement, activity, and interpersonal communication; police violence was now immune. It was meant to profoundly shift the power dynamic in the state's favour: legalized authoritarianism gave the state carte blanche to repress the current movement and any future dissent.

Social Interpretation of the 16 January Laws

On 19 January, the Sunday after the 16 January laws were enacted, some of the most vivid mass expressions of the social interpretation of the state's repressive policies occurred. Society's interpretation was simple: state suppression of the freedom of protest was unconstitutional, unjustified, and too obvious in its attempts to repress civil liberties. It was the ridiculousness of the state's obvious repression that was underlined in social response to the state. Social reading of the laws was that the state was overstepping the existing boundary of state–society relations, attempting to take it into the authoritarian realm.

The legitimacy of public frustration with the 16 January laws was emphasized by statements from Western governments and rights organizations. Opposition news sources in Ukraine published statements of European and US government officials decrying the laws, such as US Secretary of State John Kerry's statement that the Verkhovna Rada (parliament) vote violated all norms of the Organization for Security and Co-operation in Europe and "took from the people of Ukraine their right and their chance to the future;[10] and statements of EU representatives also decried the laws as repressive. A statement by the High Representative of the European Union for Foreign Affairs and Security Policy, Catheryne Ashton, was published in detail, including her assertions that the laws were limiting the rights of Ukrainian citizens and were adopted with disregard to existing parliamentary procedures and democratic principles. She also expressed concern for changes to the criminal code, which included "alarming restrictions" on the rights of gathering, freedom of expression, and the means of mass information, contradicting Ukraine's international guarantees and seriously restricting the actions of civil society organizations. The press cited Ashton's statement calling on the Ukrainian president to guarantee that these decisions would be revisited and changed in accordance with Ukraine's international guarantees. Similarly, the press published

Figure 3.1 Protesters marching with signs against the 16 January laws. Around 100,000 people came to Kyiv to protest January 16th Laws, which delegalized protest and government criticism. Here, a woman (*centre*) carries a poster "Future Freedom Is against the Law," while another reads "Ukrainian Women Stand against Slavery in the Future."

a statement from Nils Muižnieks, the Council of Europe's Commissioner for Human Rights, who called on Yanukovych to veto the bill, expressing his concern that the legal changes would restrict human rights, including the rights of expression, gathering, and association.[11]

Social Response to the Repressive Laws

January 2014 saw a wide range of social resistance that questioned state repression via law enforcement. The new laws met an immediate and notable manifestation of social frustration. Tens of thousands of people gathered in Kyiv, travelling from other parts of the country to express their disapproval. Protesters picketed the courts, where political prisoners were held on trial, and blocked police movements.[12] Along with signs specifically addressing the unconstitutionality of the new laws, protesters mocked the laws, including its restrictions against wearing

Figure 3.2 Protesters wearing makeshift headgear to mock the 16 January laws, including a prohibition to wear helmets. Throughout the winter months, many revolutionaries wore helmets in anticipation of police brutality against Maidaners.

hard headwear, by placing kitchen strainers, pots, saucepans, cake plates, and scuba-diving gear on their heads. The social message was clear: the laws were called "dictatorial," and protesters' signs and actions emphasized the authoritarian nature of the laws, outlining its blatant violations of the Ukrainian constitution and international norms.

On 17 January, the day after the passage of the bill, a number of actions were led by activists decrying the law's violation of freedoms of expression. A large banner carried in the front of the column said "dictatorship." A protest column heading to the presidential administration, calling on the president not to sign the bill, used vivid symbolism to underline the autocratic nature of the 16 January laws: faces painted with blood and mouths painted to appear to be sewn shut, and the wearing of chains and handcuffs.[13] Journalists also organized a symbolic action near the presidential administration, imitating a funeral to lament the death of freedom of the press, with large funeral-style wreaths with ribbons reading, "Freedom of the Press," "Freedom of Expression," and "Democracy, [born] August 24, 1991."[14] Over a hundred civil society organizations announced mobilization on the Independence Square

Figure 3.3 A Maidan revolutionary with a sign protesting the loss of democracy. An overwhelming majority of revolutionaries believed that if the Maidan movement failed, the state would consolidate authoritarian practices, and there would be no free and fair elections, free press, or freedom of expression.

(Maidan), and called for a public viche, to be conducted on Sunday, that would "begin the movement to reconstruct the constitutional regime in Ukraine."[15]

On 19 January, the day tens of thousands of people came from different parts of the country to protest the repressive 16 January laws, intra-society dialogue regarding the use of violence began to shift. Several factors came into play. Firstly, not only were many of the protesters severely injured, detained, and thrown in jail without due process, the state had legalized this repression via unconstitutional laws. Secondly, weeks of peaceful resistance in the bitter cold Kyiv winter demanding an end to police brutality and the release of political prisoners, appeared to have borne no fruit. On the contrary, the legalization of oppression via the 16 January laws was interpreted as the state's desire to worsen and consolidate oppression rather than end it. As a result, while it was still a minority of revolutionaries who supported political violence on 19 January, less energy and means were invested in stopping radicalized groups. Finally, the activists' ability to constrain those who would engage in political violence was becoming impaired by escalating police violence.

The eighth public viche on 19 January brought tens of thousands of people who felt threatened by the state's legal and violent aggression and concerned about growing authoritarianism. A continuing dialogue about the means of resistance continued among the revolutionaries, and included leaders of anti-state parliamentary political parties: Vitaliy Klychko, leader of the UDAR party, Arseniy Yatsenyuk, leader of the Batkyvshchyna party, and Oleh Tiahnybok, leader of the Svoboda party. After the revolutionary movement gained momentum at the end of November, the leaders of opposition parties tried to serve as liaisons between the state and the revolutionaries. While state sources often referred to the trio as "leaders of the opposition," suggesting they were the organizers of the movement, it is important to note that they were neither the organizers, nor were they perceived as such by the protesters. Thus, the term "leaders of the opposition" should be understood only in its narrow sense: as leaders of opposition parties in the parliament.

During the viche, when the opposition trio took the stage, the protesters shouted "leader, leader," demanding swift action to challenge the state.[16] Maidan activists posted a video online of the last few minutes of Martin Luther King Jr's final speech, in Memphis in 1968, as he talked forcefully about not giving in to the police or authorities when freedom of speech and assembly are at stake (and also, incidentally, criticized the Soviet Union).[17] "We need such a leader," said one of the activists. Volodymyr Viatrovych, an activist and a scholar, said King was inspiring because he was a spiritual as well as a political leader. Ukraine "absolutely" could use such a leader today, Viatrovych said.[18]

The crowd's chants demanding a leader expressed dissatisfaction with the performance of opposition politicians.[19] The revolutionaries were concerned that the actions proposed by opposition politicians were inadequate to stop the state's consolidation of authoritarianism. Thus, when Klychko announced that he and the other two party leaders planned to meet Monday to discuss a strategy, one activist said, "That's too late … Yesterday the police took our licences," she said. "Tomorrow they'll take our cars. The day after tomorrow they'll probably take us."[20] Thus, the politicians' actions were seen as no match for the speed of the state's growing aggression. "They should have created a provisional government months ago," said another activist in response to the politicians' proposal to create a special council from opposition politicians in the parliament and a referendum on early presidential elections. "We need to do something else. This isn't effective. Everybody understands that," said another protester.[21] The revolutionaries did not see opposition politicians as representatives of the revolutionary movement; some were worried that the politicians were looking out for their own interests.[22]

Crucially, the repressive laws, the immediate escalation of police violence, and crude violations of due process in the courts deprived activists of the ability to contest the state via legal processes.[23] While lawyers kept challenging the state in courts, legalization of authoritarian means of repression, including criminalization of protest and government criticism, punishable by years in prison, led to despair among many activists as to the possibility of a peaceful victory.

According to public polls, the majority of revolutionaries were still against political violence in the aftermath of the 16 January laws. This is also evident from the fact that only a small group from the tens of thousands present on Maidan during the mass protests responded to a call by a notable activist Koba to head to the parliament building on Hrushevskoho Street to demand action. Yatsenyuk, in response to the chants demanding a leader, said: "There is a leader here. It's the Ukrainian nation." This may have been interpreted as politicians' inability to act swiftly in the pressing circumstances, as some protesters left the march and headed toward the parliament.[24] At 3 p.m. on 19 January, some of those who headed to Hrushevskoho attempted to storm the police barricade – resulting in days-long violent clashes with the police, known as the "Events on Hrushevskoho." Opposition politicians who remained on the stage immediately pronounced those who turned to disturbances on Hrushevskoho as "provocateurs," insisting that the revolutionary resistance movement continued to be peaceful. Notable attempts were taken to prevent the groups from resorting to violence. One revolutionary recalled:

> [Opposition] parliamentarians and Afghan vets stood facing us: "You can't do this, go back to Maidan." I said, "Vitalik [Klychko], we are standing a month and a half already; lead this movement or provide a normal alternative." He couldn't say anything coherent … During this moment my friend starts winding up the people. This wasn't organized by anyone. This was an act of anger.[25]

Thus, while the majority of revolutionaries remained against political violence, despair, exacerbated by the repressive laws, prevented constructive dialogue within the resistance movement. The "draconian" laws, as they were dubbed by the populace, triggered hopelessness and concern that if no decisive action were taken, democracy would be lost in Ukraine. Attitudes toward peaceful means of resistance as the only option began shifting. "We have no legal means to fight back against the government, given the new laws," said one activist to a *Washington Post* journalist in January. "So what can we do?" said another. "Maybe, the nationalists who went off to pick a fight with the police at the Rada have the right idea."[26] Moreover, the threat of losing democracy was reinforced by the fact that, under the new law, the special forces, who at this point had used excessive force causing severe injuries, were given impunity, rather than being punished. As a result, the effort to stop those who decided to storm the police barricade on Hrushevskoho Street was not as strong as before. A number of clergy from different denominations came to Hrushevskoho with the purpose of preventing violence on both sides. However, even among the clergy, who played a notable role in preventing violence to that point, some grasped the injustice of the state's repression, doubting their "right" to stop the protesters. A Greek Catholic priest (*protoyerey*) recalled:

> I was certain that not all means of peaceful protest were yet utilized … But … No, you can't stomp on people's dignity like that, you can't abuse people, you can't continuously threaten them and frame their actions as illegal. The protest was framed as illegal as a result of using the law, voted in Verkhovna Rada on 16 January. That was the use of law to infringe on people's right to protest. Specifically peaceful protest. And the government, starting with the president, to the Verkhovna Rada (all institutions of power), demonstrated that it disregards people, their rights, their ability to peacefully express their protest. And people concluded: either fifteen years [of prison] as a participant of mass disturbances, or go until the end, because we won't live under such law … I realized I needed to pray alongside the priests [on Hrushevskoho] … There was clanging of [police] shields from one side, and banging on pipes and other metal objects from the

> other [protester] side. The prayer appeared to be a live shield for both sides … And there appeared a sense of premonition that the storm was coming. While there were many protesters, who were ready to storm, more aggression and force was felt from the police side … Some journalist approached me and said, "thank you for being here … You've protected lots of people from being injured, but believe me, right now a death or an injury of one of you will be used as an excuse for a forced dispersal of entire Maidan"… And somehow I started feeling that I don't have the right to prevent people from expressing their anger.[27]

The First Wave of State Violence after 16 January

State Repression: Physical and Psychological Violence

The nineteenth of January marked the beginning of lethal clashes between revolutionaries and the police, commonly referred to in Ukraine as the "Events on Hrushevskoho," which brought the first shootings of revolutionaries by the police and other mass injuries. Some among the small group of revolutionaries who headed to Hrushevskoho Street started throwing cobblestones and Molotov cocktails. Immediately, the violence of state forces against the entire resistance was raised to a new level, as they committed a number of violations of already stretched legal bounds. In obvious violations of protocol, police started throwing flash-bang grenades with nails tied to them at people, used water cannons, illegal at such low temperatures, and fired "non-lethal" hard bullets, causing severe injuries. As a result, the activists' ability to stop those wishing to engage in political violence was now also heavily impaired by the escalated police violence. In other words, energy now had to be invested in sustaining protection from the state.

According to a case filed in the European Court of Human Rights, violent attempts to disperse the protests in Kyiv included live ammunition, explosives, and water cannons despite low temperatures.[28] They reported the widespread practice of police deliberately tying metal objects to flash-bang grenades. Cases of the use of force combined with humiliation and torture were numerous.[29] The injuries received

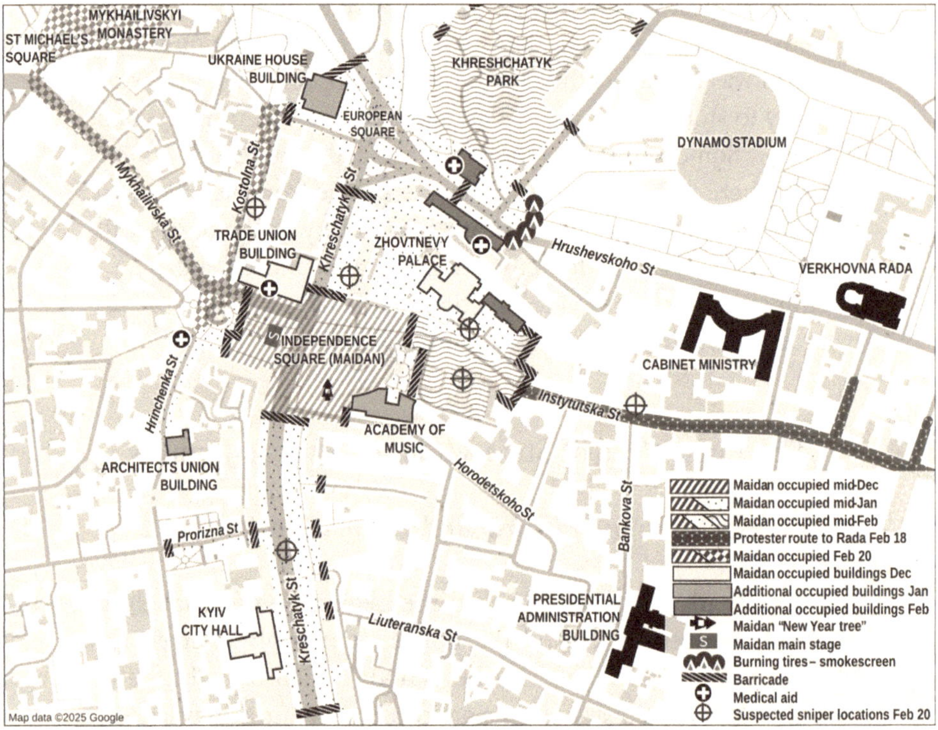

Figure 3.4 Map of the Maidan with protester-occupied areas.

as a result of riot police brutality included broken bones and skulls, concussion, severely injured internal organs, and other wounds.[30] According to my personal interviews with medical personnel who offered volunteer help during the protests, an inordinate number of eye injuries suggested that eyes were targeted as a deliberate method of harm and intimidation.

According to the European Committee for the Prevention of Torture and Inhuman or Degrading Treatment or Punishment (CPT), which conducted an investigation of law enforcement's treatment of protesters during the winter of 2013–14, ill-treatment of the protesters was deliberate, became an acceptable means of enforcing operations, and in several instances could be considered as amounting to torture.[31] An excerpt from the report reads as follows:

> In many such cases, the persons with whom the delegation spoke alleged that they had been the subject of particularly excessive use of force during the apprehension (e.g., extensive beatings involving the use of batons or other hard objects until they were unable to move by their own means or until they lost consciousness). In a number of instances, during the period immediately following apprehension, reference was made to being lifted and thrown to the ground, being dragged by the feet down stairs, repeated kicks and punches, receiving large amounts of tear gas, blows with batons, gun butts or bullet-proof jackets, strangulation, stabbing and shooting with rubber bullets at close range. This violence was allegedly deployed even though the apprehended persons were apparently not offering any type of resistance and complied with orders given by law enforcement officials, had allegedly been brought under control, and/or were in a poor state of health. The aim of the various types of alleged ill-treatment was apparently to inflict the maximum possible pain or damage to the health of the apprehended persons.[32]

The CPT report also noted numerous instances of the use of force combined with humiliation:

> [A]pprehended persons being stripped naked in cold weather and photographed; having their hair cut; toothpaste, shoe cream or other products being spread on their faces; having their trousers cut and being mocked; being made to kneel and sing to the glory of "Berkut" special police. …
>
> Some persons interviewed also claimed that, once apprehended, they had been hit with batons whilst being forced to run through a "corridor" formed by members of Internal Affairs special forces or had been initially asked by law enforcement officials to choose with which "special means" they would like to be "dealt with" (e.g., being shot at with a rubber bullet gun or receiving baton blows).[33]

Local and foreign journalists reported being the target of police beatings specifically because they were recording violent police behaviour.[34]

Figure 3.5 Police surround and beat an unarmed protester. Police violence often involved special forces, including Berkut.

Social Interpretation of the First Wave of State Violence

The interview data below shed light on the causes behind shifts from initial support for political violence among some protesters to overwhelming support for peaceful resistance throughout the winter months, and then strong support for political violence in response to severe state brutality. The data show activists' fear that, if the resistance were to fail, the state would halt the function of democratic institutions and establish a repressive authoritarian apparatus. As seen in figure 3.6, 81 per cent of the activists I surveyed believed that if the revolutionary movement failed, violent repression and detentions of peaceful demonstrators would become standard state practice. Likewise, 81 per cent believed that suppression of the freedom of expression would become standard state practice, and 88 per cent believed that future election results would be rigged by the state. As a number of activists described, they feared that state violence and the repressive January laws produced an expectation that their children would come of age in an authoritarian regime.[35]

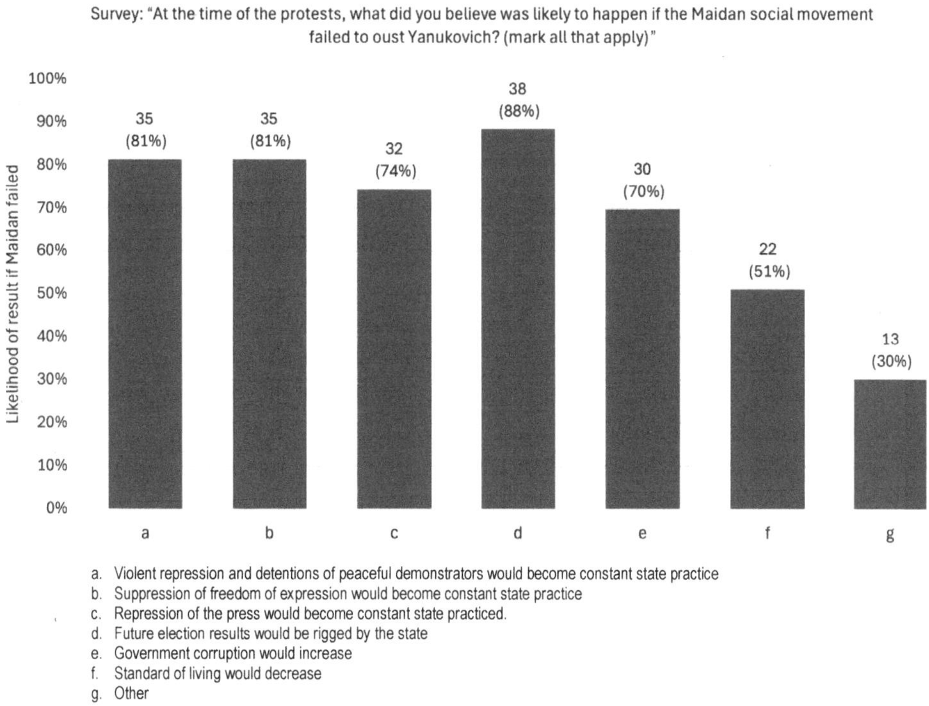

Figure 3.6 Revolutionaries' perceptions of expected outcomes if the Maidan failed.
Source: Author's survey of Maidan protesters.

Social discourse and the efforts of multiple activists to maintain peaceful resistance were largely successful: while limited incidents of violence appeared throughout December (responsibility for which was claimed by radical groups), the major Maidan Square protests retained their non-violent character until mid-January. However, in the aftermath of the first shootings of revolutionaries on 22 January, more people were likely to support violence. As an activist put it, political violence by protesters in response to state violence was seen as a struggle for freedom: "those first deaths – that turned everything around, and we began reacting differently to everything. Innocent people, who sacrificed their lives. So, what was left for us to do? The idea of earning freedom, wooden shield, a stick and some courage – and you go. But on the other side there were bullets."[36]

The police force was now perceived as enforcing arbitrary state power:

> They swore an oath to protect the people … I became different. In reality, I am a pacifist. I was always against violence, against war. But one can't remain a pacifist when an automatic weapon, baton or grenade or something like that is pointed at you.[37]

Discourse about the meaning of state aggression continued throughout the winter months. As one Evangelical Baptist leader, a philosophy PhD, put it:

> The fact that the state strengthened its aggression, meant for the people that only the last tools were left. On the other hand, this showed the illegitimate character of the state. "Tsar, then, isn't real." But it was rather difficult to justify it. We needed to make sense out of some of our interpretations of some of the texts and actions … We constantly debated. We applied hermeneutics to analyze references in the Bible, where it said that Christians must bow their heads before the state and do everything it orders. We preached a lot on this topic. And in the sermons in the church, I often referred to Constitutional provisions which say you are not supposed to follow obviously criminal orders. And when you show the Bible in this context, Christians are freed from a false responsibility before villains, and understand all their responsibility before the nation … It was obvious that the courts – are lawless, and the Constitution was rewritten to serve [their] purpose, appropriate authority, not bestowed upon them by the people … When we applied hermeneutics to analyze all these [Bible] texts, it showed new interpretation. People saw the light. And they understood that God blesses their protest.[38]

Social dialogue with the state continued with attempts to get through to the police, even as they engaged in torture and abuse of the activists. Peaceful walks on the Maidan, some including thousands of people, continued.[39] Other forms of communication with the state included attempts to communicate with special forces by showing what the resistance movement is fighting for. Activists set up a large screen to stream news from various non-state news agencies that covered the events. Police forces responded by preventing visibility of the screen and blasting Russian pop music. Most importantly, as the accounts below demonstrate, security forces continued to respond to any attempt to raise a discussion with crude violence. One revolutionary who was captured by police stated:

> The police formed a corridor, through which I was led … First, they all yelled, in one word, humiliating us. And then stepped out of that corridor and were beating us … they undressed me to T-shirt, while taking me through … I was telling them: "You don't understand what we are fighting for. [We are fighting] for your future as well."[40]

Political violence was supported by the people as an attempt to show that aggression "can't be tolerated," in the hope that government officials would hear their message and cease the aggression.[41] Attempts to be heard by special forces continued but were met with excessive violence, torture, and/or detentions:

> I had not realized the extent to which our police were sadists … it's like they were having fun in a shooting range …You could see a scar on Oleg's head – a plastic bullet does not leave a scar like that; they were shooting with metal bullets as well; they used metal bullets which are meant to stop car engines … At some point I felt that this needed to be stopped – I witnessed so many people getting hurt, including police who would start on fire [from Molotov cocktails], I felt bad for them too. It was also very hard to see injured people being carried out. So I asked my friend for a white shirt, put it on a staff, and went to talk to the police. Talking didn't work, because eight policemen grabbed me, started beating me, undressed me, ripped the shirt, pulled on the helmet so I couldn't breathe, in short they just mocked me … There are lots of weird stories that I learned from people who were detained on the same day as me (in courts, or when we were kept in the paddy wagon) – one man in his [late] 50s … was going home. He walked by the police post, and said: "I need to get to the subway station. Can I go by here?" They said, "Sure, right here" – they let him go through, and then grabbed him and threw him in the van. Turned out it was Zakharchenko's birthday – so I guess they were preparing a birthday present for him … The most paradoxical

> thing is that there were policemen from Russian-speaking regions [of Ukraine] – the expression we use now – more specifically, people who detained me were Dnepropetrovsk Berkut police. I am ethnic Russian, I told them I was from Odessa; so I couldn't understand why I was called a Banderovite, a Nazi, a fascist, and I said "I am coming to you to talk with my hands up, and you are beating me" … When I was trying to tell them that they act more like fascists themselves, I would get beaten even more on my head; so then I preferred to be quiet.[42]

Such negative experiences with security forces led to disillusionment among revolutionaries regarding the objectives of state agents. They no longer believed that law enforcement agents were serving to protect the people's and nation's interests, and therefore could not be convinced to "join the people" – as was heard in chants during the revolution, appealing to the police – in the fight for democracy.

Revolutionaries started seeing the state as an aggressor that would not stop until the democratic movement (and democracy) was destroyed. One activist related: "We understood very clearly that, in reality, we attempted to maintain the peaceful nature of the resistance until the end … Apparently, our government did not want that."[43] Another stated: "When the first deaths came, they started shooting, throwing flash-bang grenades with nails attached, it became clear: this was it – they would not stop, they had no way back, [and] at that point they would only continue to squash."[44] A number of activists who were previously engaged in peaceful resistance efforts communicated their support for political violence after the February shootings.[45]

Social Response to the First Wave of State Violence

According to a survey of protesters conducted by the Kyiv Sociological Institute (KIIS) during the revolution, while a majority of revolutionaries were in support of demonstrations as a form of protest throughout the winter months, the number decreased over time, and individual willingness to participate in violent resistance increased: support for picketing government agencies and preventing their function grew from 35 per cent on 7–8 December to 56 per cent on 3 February, while willingness to create non-governmental armed forces grew from 15 per cent to 50 per cent. This fundamental change, affecting a sizable portion

Figure 3.7 A woman appeals to the police on 23 January 2013 to end the violence in the aftermath of police killing revolutionaries.

of the revolutionaries, came after the first killings of protesters by the police, and the perpetuated cruelty of Berkut special forces. As discussed earlier, the 16 January laws offered impunity to police when dealing with protesters, unleashing unprecedented excessive violence, torture, kidnappings, and mockery of protesters by police forces. Many interviewed revolutionaries identified the first killings as a shift that altered their understanding of the state's intentions: "The switch was turned on: our people were killed ... When your countrymen kill your own, especially so arrogantly, so cynically ... But even at that moment it didn't feel right to kill ... We just wanted to stop what was happening, to prevent new losses."[46] People began shifting their grasp of what those in the government intended to do. In other words, rather than assuming that police (and especially Berkut) violence was excessive due to abuse of power of certain individuals within power structures, the popular perception was shifting toward the understanding that the government is determined to consolidate the authoritarian regime, and is taking measures to do so via changing laws, and using violence to suppress resistance to it.

Even after the first deaths (and the growing fear that the state was determined to establish a repressive regime), the revolutionaries continued to disagree on whether political violence was justifiable:

> When they killed Serhii, who lived in the tent next to mine, with whom I used to shake hands … And when in the morning they killed him, and then the Belorussian guy … Our Maidaners began to arm with sticks … The news [about the first deaths] got around quickly. Next to us there lived an artist who was drawing portraits. He also drew Serhii Nihoian. We made copies from this pencil drawing, and wrote that on such date Serhii was killed for defending the rights and freedom of the Ukrainian nation. I continued to support non-violent resistance. If they killed people, we must rise up others and strengthen the protest. I believe that there was space for non-violent resistance. And the majority thought the same. But part of the Maidan began to radicalize.[47]

Rather than deterring further protest by indiscriminate and unconstitutional state-sanctioned violence, government aggression pushed many to join the resistance:

> On January 19 … I was at home, in Khmelnytsky. My girlfriend said: "Perhaps you shouldn't go?" I said, "I can't not go." But she said, "Stay here." When the first [revolutionaries] died, my girlfriend no longer said anything, I began to pack. She said, "Just take care of yourself."[48]

An one activist put it, state aggression was seen as illegitimate, and continuing resistance was the only way to be saved from growing repression. "After the twenty-second, there were more people. These deaths became a push – we built new barricades … People spent two and a half months in critical circumstances: they were arrested, their cars burnt, the injured were taken out of hospitals to jails. How long could this go on?"[49] On one hand, some protesters were deterred from continuing participation by state aggression and the resulting deaths. On the other hand, however, many joined in, and/or embraced political violence as the only means of preventing the establishment of an oppressive regime. "Lots of people disappeared or died prior to [18 February].

It became clear that there was no other way it could end – this had to be ended with force, tough and done right," said one participant.[50] Another activist recalled:

> When the first deaths came, they started shooting, throwing flash-bang grenades with nails, it became clear: that's it – they will not stop, their way back is cut off, now they will only be squashing us. We mainly tried to save the detainees or talk to the police, while it was still possible … At some point it became clear that it was impossible to argue with them, there was no sense in talking. When real criminals showed up, who were supported and protected by [the police], we came and said: "Do you understand what they are doing?" [They replied,] "This is Maidan." We gathered and left. There were no longer any discussions with them.[51]

Thus, the first killings and the collusion of state forces with *titushki* drastically affected activists' understanding of state intentions.

State–society dialogue took another twist at the end of January: the government attempted to present the appearance that they were responding to social pressure by (conditionally) annulling the 16 January law and extending amnesty to all previously detained protesters (as well as police engaged in violence during the events). With this, Yanukovych declared that the government did everything possible to put an end to the existing crisis.[52] However, the amnesty law was challenged by the resistance movement. Activists believed that accepting the amnesty law would amount to admitting that those who had been detained were criminally responsible.[53] Secondly, according to the amnesty law, the state would begin to release detainees only after the activists vacated all protest sites, including streets, squares, and occupied buildings. This condition was interpreted as a government tactic to gain control while holding the detained as hostages, rather than a sign of a possible democratic future. The leading reason revolutionaries distrusted the idea that the state would reverse oppression was the continuation of illegal state repressive activities. While the government was publicly announcing the potential for amnesty, police and their collaborators on the ground continued to circumvent legal bounds to injure, kidnap, and torture multiple activists.

The end of January, in fact, was characterized by the disappearance of multiple Maidan activists. Kidnappings were often carried out by Berkut security forces in collaboration with titushky.[54] Some of those kidnapped were eventually taken to detention centres, albeit with numerous, often severe, injuries. A number of revolutionaries were still not accounted for years later. Some were found dead, while those who survived had signs of torture. The kidnappings of several notable activists – Yuriy Verbytsky, Ihor Lutsenko, and Dmytro Bulatov – markedly affected social discourse about state intentions. First, the disappearance of Bulatov was immediately announced by major opposition media and social media on 22 January, and since he was a leader of the AutoMaidan civic initiative, a very active and influential anti-state resistance group, society interpreted the move as the state's determination to repress the Maidan movement by all means. Secondly, when Bulatov was found abandoned in freezing temperatures outside of Kyiv on 30 January, the level and type of prolonged torture he was exposed to shook the public. With blood running down his head and face, and his ear cut off, he told reporters he was hung up in a manner similar to crucifixion, with nails punctured through his hands.[55] On 31 January, Amnesty International called Bulatov's treatment "a barbaric act" and demanded an immediate investigation. The Ukrainian government's dismissive response came when the Interior Ministry placed Bulatov on its wanted list for involvement in "mass riots."[56] "It is very hard to see a way out of the current crisis when such horrific abuses against protest organizers are taking place," Amnesty said in a statement, while also referring to the case of Verbytsky, who was found dead with signs of severe torture.[57] A similar sentiment was spreading in Ukraine: the current government was determined to exercise repression in its severest form to maintain its hold on power.

Torture and ridicule were, in fact, a major tactic of state repression during the winter, as reported in the Council of Europe report, discussed earlier. One instance of torture was captured on video by a Berkut officer who fled after the incident. In the video, watched by the nation, it was clearly seen that Berkut officers were enjoying the torture as the pain was accompanied by purposeful humiliation and the laughter of Berkut officers. Mykhailo Havryliuk, who was captured by the Berkut, was thrown on the ground and beaten for an extended period of time. After that, Berkut forces undressed him entirely (in freezing temperatures) and began to kick his head like a soccer ball, while taking pictures of the torture scene. In the video it was seen that, while naked and with snow in the background, he was forced to hold a symbolic Ukrainian hatchet, while Berkut forces took pictures and then kicked him into a police van.[58] The video became representative of state–society relations during the protests, more specifically, the state's disregard for human dignity and the suppression of basic human rights. To the revolutionaries it meant that peaceful protest was meaningless, as the current state was there to bluntly repress and humiliate. A protester recalled his personal transformation:

> When the guys died, then, obviously, Ukrainian humanity rose up … I was against that people from Maidan were going there … There was shooting, there was fire, how is it that Maidan would stay uninvolved? … We all saw that guy … the entire Ukraine knows that Cossack, how he was kicked when he was naked … I wrote then on Facebook that I will not forgive them for that. I took it personal, as humiliation. To undress a man, and then kick him like that in the stomach … I will not forgive that! I will fight, I will go to war. I did not believe until then that I would do that.[59]

Another crucial symbol of the torture scene was Mykhailo Havryliuk's *oseledets* hairstyle, a reference to the Cossacks, who in Ukrainian social discourse often serve as a symbol of Ukraine. The decision of Berkut forces to take pictures with the undressed Cossack-looking Havryliuk, who is holding a symbolic Ukrainian hatchet, was undeniably designed to show a subdued Ukrainian nation. Moreover, Bulatov's statement at the press conference in Lithuania, where he was taken for treatment, expressed another social concern – that the Russian government was assisting Yanukovych in the brutal repression to consolidate an authoritarian regime in Ukraine. Bulatov stated multiple times that the captors had a characteristic accent as spoken by those in Russia, and tortured him to record a statement that he was an American spy:

> "They interrogated and beat me every day," Bulatov said at a press conference in Vilnius … They hit me very hard, very painfully, and for a very long time … [After torturing], they made me say into a camera that I was a spy for the United States, that I was

> a spy for the CIA, that Americans were giving me money, that AutoMaidan was funded by Americans and that I was specifically hired to organize the AutoMaidan and the riots against the current government.

While many revolutionaries considered whether the Kremlin was involved in assisting the repression, the essential inference from the abundant state violence, including killings, kidnappings, and degrading treatment, was that the current presidential administration could not be trusted, as it would turn fully into an authoritarian regime, unless stopped by the revolutionary movement.

In addition to the activism in Kyiv in reaction to January state violence, revolutionary activities spread to various regions in Ukraine. Administrative buildings in Chernivtsi, Ivano-Frankivsk, Lviv, Rivne, Ternopil, Khmelnytskyi, Lutsk, Sumy, Uzhhorod, and Zhytomyr were besieged by Maidan supporters during 23–5 January. In some of areas, governors appointed by President Viktor Yanukovych were forced to resign, and some regional councils passed legislation in support of the Maidan.[60] In several cases, revolutionaries were met with little resistance from police.[61] In Lutsk, the capital of Volyn region (northwest Ukraine), after a thousand protesters surrounded the administrative building, police declared, "We are Ukrainians – we are with the people!," allowing demonstrators to enter the building.[62]

The Second Wave of State Violence

Mass Shootings

On 13 and 16 February, two EU officials, Stefan Fule (the European Commissioner for Enlargement and European Neighborhood Policy) and Catheryne Ashton (High Representative of the European Union for Foreign Affairs and Security Policy), called on the Ukrainian government to close all court cases against Maidan activists. Fule stressed the need to begin investigations against security forces involved in the beatings and torture of activists. This concern was also expressed at the Maidan viche, where it was announced that revolutionaries would march toward the Verkhovna Rada on 18 February to demand the closing of some two thousand cases against activists, and the adoption of measures to end the crisis, including a return to the Ukrainian constitution of 2004, prior to Yanukovych-led changes.[63] The Peaceful Walk began at 9 a.m. on 18 February with a few thousand activists (many from Maidan Self-Defence units) from Independence Square toward the Verkhovna Rada via Instytutska Street. Maidan activists wanted to see changes in government actions after freeing some of the Kyiv and regional administrative buildings, in compliance with some of the government demands of the amnesty law. In his interview, one activist related to me that he saw the walk as "a show of the Maidan's power" to force the government to take the resistance movement into account.[64]

The path to the Verkhovna Rada was blocked by large numbers of security forces. Near Maryinsky Park violent clashes took place with police and hired thugs. The latter, titushky, threw rocks from behind the ranks of police. Police opened fire and used flash-bang grenades against the Maidaners. Revolutionaries set fire to the official building of the pro-Yanukovych Party of Regions, with one office worker dying as a result. Many activists were thrown into police vans and taken away.[65] While ambulance vehicles appeared, there were not enough to take all the injured, while some ambulances accepted only policemen. Maidan activists were allowed by members of the Army Veteran Officers to occupy the first storey of the Officers' Building, turning it into a makeshift hospital. A number of the injured were taken there, and a small group of volunteer medics offered medical help. Notably, Berkut officers who were taken there were not denied aid.

Under the premise of a terrorist threat, Kyiv subway stations were closed by the authorities at 4 p.m. on 18 February. Berkut forces, with the co-operation of Ukraine's security forces (SBU), mounted a massive offensive operation, pushing revolutionaries into the courtyards of administrative buildings.[66] A group of titushky were located a few blocks away, preventing protesters from retreating in that direction. Maidaners attempting to retreat were beaten by armed police and titushky. During their violent attack on the Maidan revolutionaries, police forces and titushki burned tents and used violence against a wide range of activists. They purposefully targeted over thirty journalists, beating many with sticks, while also destroying or removing their video cameras.[67] Maidaners were pushed from Instytutska and Hrushevskoho streets into the Maidan Square.[68]

State forces declared an ultimatum to the protesters: all resistance activity must be stopped by 6 p.m., and the streets cleared, or the state would engage in violent dispersal. At approximately 8 p.m., police forces began the attack using water cannons and personnel carriers. The presence of titushky was especially notable at the time in Kyiv's centre, as they were using ammunition, attacking passers-by and journalists and shooting out the tires of ambulances.[69] Police forces took over the Trade Union building, which was used as a headquarters for many Maidan groups and a major makeshift hospital. After the building started on fire, the evacuation of the injured (and the ability of firefighters to access the building) was hindered by the continuing police storm of the Maidan. Approximately thirty revolutionaries were killed during clashes with police from 18 to 19 February. Several hundred were severely injured from live ammunition, while many went missing.[70]

Yanukovych placed the blame for the violent clashes on opposition political leaders, and state forces declared it an "anti-terrorist operation" to fight the Maidan resistance.[71] Diplomatic convoys arrived in Ukraine to pressure the government to de-escalate the situation. While Yanukovych met with opposition politicians on the evening of 19 February and appeared "willing to negotiate,"[72] state forces began using live ammunition again to shoot protesters the next day.

The mass shooting of protesters by law enforcement the next day became known as the 20 February massacre. At approximately 9 a.m., revolutionaries attempted to push police back from the Maidan, many armed with clubs, sticks, and improvised metal shields. State forces began indiscriminately shooting the revolutionaries.[73] Within three hours that morning, forty-eight protesters (and two police officers) were killed. While law enforcement retreated behind their barricade at the intersection of Instytutska and Olhynska streets, the shootings did not entirely cease; the last victim was shot and killed at approximately 5 p.m.[74] The use of snipers, who targeted civilians from buildings in the centre of Kyiv, was in obvious violation of local and international human rights law. Over fifty people died as a result of state violence on 20 February. Snipers targeted vital organs – heart, liver, or stomach – limiting the chance of survival, as testified by volunteer medics and hospital surgeons.

Social Interpretation of the Second Wave of State Violence

After the shootings, many revolutionaries began to see political violence as the only means of reversing the consolidation of an authoritarian regime. As seen in figure 3.8, only 13 per cent of surveyed activists somewhat or strongly supported the use of violence against the state in November, while 73 per cent were likely to support political violence after the shooting of protesters on 18–20 February.

Security forces, who aimed to humiliate, torture, and then shoot unarmed revolutionaries, were now seen as the tool of a repressive regime. One revolutionary recalled:

> I was glad that the people rose up from their knees … Clashes on the night of the [February] 18 to 19, when an armored car started to attack on Khreshchatyk. It seemed this was the end – they will crush us. What I appreciated was people's spirit and attitude to go until death. I saw the atrocities, committed by the cops. And what was done by the snipers – to shoot the unarmed! The guys who were standing in turtle formation with batons! And they were shooting [people] in the heads, shooting when people were helping to save the injured … They threw a gas grenade under my feet on Maidan, right in the moment when I was carrying a person, trying to drag him out. I don't know what was motivating them. Such atrocities I saw only during the war [in the Middle East], and even during the war it was easier because I was armed as well as the other side. But to attack people who were standing on the barricades with an armored car … The most important thing – I was glad that people showed the state that they were the strength, because it's not people who should be afraid of the state, but the state that should be afraid of the people.[75]

Thus, the major objective of resorting to violence was to stop state aggression and return to democracy. As another revolutionary put it, "I hope [Maidan] achieved such that in ten years, my daughter will not have to stand on Maidan, the way I did at the time. That is the most important thing. In other words, that the government would at least in some ways start to take people into consideration."[76]

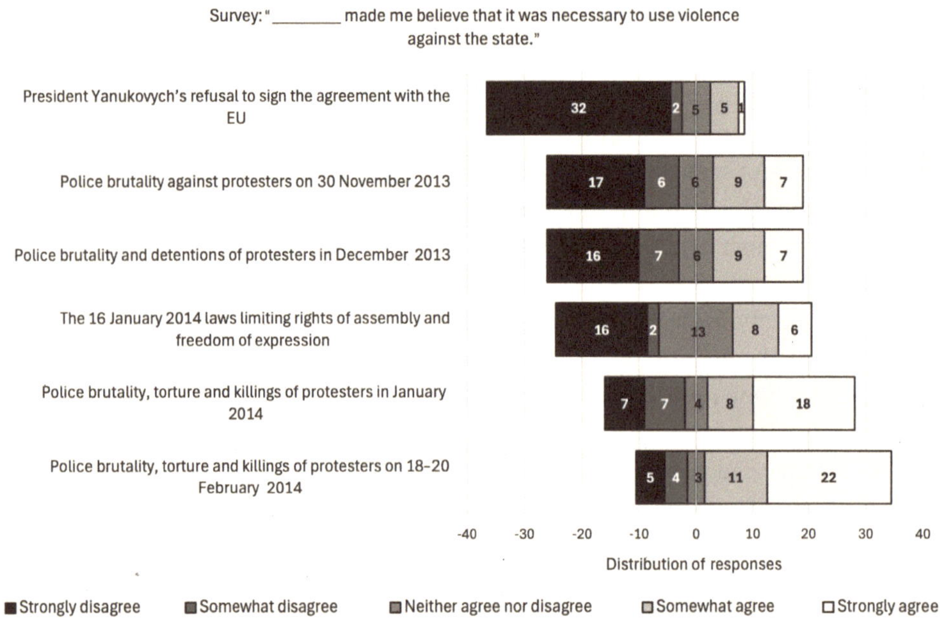

Figure 3.8 Increasing support for violent resistance among Maidan revolutionaries.
Source: Author's survey of Maidan protesters.

As more Maidaners perceived the killings of revolutionaries on 18–20 February to be a sure sign that the state was determined to consolidate a terror regime,[77] the efforts of multiple Maidan activists to maintain peaceful methods of resistance began to lose their appeal. All self-defence (*samooborona*) groups started to shift their tactics in the aftermath of the mass shootings against revolutionaries. While self-defence groups initially saw their purpose as protecting peaceful protesters from state violence,[78] the mass shootings affected their understanding of the state's intent. A fighting group leader recounted that he contacted his unit members to offer them help with arranging accommodations in case they wanted to quit and cover up their participation. As he explained, he expected severe state repression to continue, and Maidaners, especially those who participated in clashes with police, would be shot, tortured, or prosecuted. Those who chose to continue the resistance believed they had to shift tactics. Prior to that day, some of the revolutionaries had guns, which they used to fire at government forces, but these were individual occurrences. As one revolutionary recounted, it was in the aftermath of mass killing of Maidaners that they actively started searching for live ammunition: "On February 20, we left the capital in search of guns on the black market. We were planning to come back to the capital armed."[79] In the aftermath of the mass shootings, samooborona leaders started developing strategies of violent resistance – rather than focus on defence of the Maidan protesters. A sotnyk (self-defence unit leader) recounted in his interview: "I had a list and phone numbers of people who expressed willingness to engage in violent fights with the government forces 'in case things get serious' … On February 19, I was beginning to contact them."[80]

Social Response to the Second Wave of State Violence

Peaceful resistance walks were no longer organized and carried out. Many "ordinary" protesters (those not previously volunteering in self-defence units or as fighters) became more likely to support violence.[81] Previously peaceful protesters now participated in a group effort to remove cobblestones from the Kyiv streets to provide it as ammunition to the fighters.[82] A physician who previously volunteered by offering medical aid to protesters related that after the state shootings she participated in this effort.[83]

Another activist who participated in logistical organizations for the peaceful resistance recounted her activities after the state shootings: "I never could have imagined myself doing that: we were digging through trash receptacles to get glass bottles" [to make Molotov cocktails].[84] This collective consensus for violent means of anti-state resistance led Maidaners to support groups who had propagated the use of violence from the beginning, including Pravyy Sektor. As Maidaners recounted, the ultra-right ideological basis of the latter was unfamiliar to most participants, as the group's leaders chose to keep it concealed, publicly focusing on anti-corruption and pro-violence rhetoric.[85]

While many still were not willing to participate in violence against the state themselves, they did justify the use of violence against the state, and many engaged in maintaining anti-state violent efforts, including collecting cobblestones and bottles for Molotov cocktails. In other words, the vital point of revolutionary development was the micro-mobilization of social efforts, which maintained the protest resistance that was turning increasingly to political violence. As one revolutionary explained:

Figure 3.9 Maidaners burning tires as a smokescreen to protect protesters from police forces, including snipers.

> Maidan became a fortress ... and it was the last trump card held by the people ... Because if not for [Maidan], then everything would be in the hands of the state, in Yanukovych's hands ... Talks that we had to wait for the 2015 elections ... The question was – whether by the time we'd have those elections, civil society and Ukraine as a whole would arrive in the condition of scorched earth in terms of civil liberties. That's why, even though I am not a supporter of political violence as an idea, I understood that in the existing situation it was appropriate for me to take part in ... a non-peaceful Maidan.[86]

The mass shootings of civilians by state forces served as a major turning point in state–society dialogue during the revolution. Several pro-presidential party members withdrew their support. At 10 p.m. on 20 February 2014, the Verkhovna Rada adopted a law, "On Condemnation of Violence Which Led to the Death of Peaceful Civilians of Ukraine," according to which the security forces were required to leave the centre of Kyiv, and return to their stations.[87] This was followed by a nine-hour meeting, resulting in the signing of an agreement "On

Figure 3.10 Protester throwing Molotov cocktail. Maidaners resorted to sticks, rocks, and Molotov cocktails to counter police violence on 22 January 2014.

Regulating Crisis in Ukraine" between Yanukovych and the major leaders of political opposition parties Yatsenyuk, Tiahnybok, and Klychko. The signing of the agreement was attended by the ministers of foreign affairs from Poland, Germany, and France, who arrived to Kyiv for this purpose. The parties agreed to advance a law on returning to the 2004 Constitution, and to hold early presidential elections by December 2014.

While the agreement was encouraged by Western powers, and was celebrated by opposition politicians as a major achievement, Maidaners rejected its premise. The mood on Maidan on 21 February was starkly different: it was a ground for mass funeral processions. Over fifty thousand people from various parts of Ukraine gathered on the main square, listening to the prayers offered to those killed by the state, and watching the coffins of dead revolutionaries as they were carried out. While the passing of the constitutional changes by the Verkhovna Rada was met with approval, opposition politicians, who tried to speak about the signed agreement, were met by revolutionaries with disapproving whistles and shouts of "shame," and "traitors." An activist explained, "That's not an agreement. It's a shame. We expected something entirely different. We expected Yanukovych's resignation."[88] The agreement between the opposition party leaders and Yanukovych might have worked previously to address revolutionaries' discontent as a result of earlier state actions. However, the mass shootings undermined social trust in Ukraine's presidential administration. Yanukovych's resignation was seen as the only possible path to assure murders of civilians would not be repeated. Following an appearance by the opposition politicians, one Self-Defence unit leader (*sotnyk*) came to the stage to voice an ultimatum: "If Yanukovych does not resign by morning, self-defence units will storm his residence." The decision to maintain social resistance appeared to be a decisive point of the revolution's outcome. Yanukovych did not resign. He fled Kyiv overnight in a helicopter, which he packed with blocks of gold.

Addressing Alternative Explanation: Fear of Persecution?

It might seem counterintuitive to continue resistance after the cost of participation becomes so high. As seen in figure 3.11, which draws on data collected through my survey, the resistance endured, in spite of protesters' expectations of being harmed by the state. As many as 86 per cent of protesters thought it likely they would be injured as a result of their participation in the resistance movement, 79 per cent of protesters expected to be detained, and as many as 52 per cent thought it likely they could be killed. This commitment ended the revolution in activists' favour: Yanukovych fled the country, and severe state violence and mass detentions came to an end.

Revolutionaries whom I interviewed, said they were aware of the risks of staying in Maidan Square as government forces intensified the means of repression. One activist expressed, "It was clearly safer to stay at home than go to Maidan."[89] An example from court testimony where Berkut police troops were tried for the murder of protesters on 20 February illustrates this point. The wife of a murdered revolutionary recounted that her husband travelled to the Kyiv protests from his hometown in response to the first killings on 18 February: "He was appalled. He said, 'I can't understand how the government could do this. It is wrong. I have to go there.'"[90] The revolutionaries were fully aware of the severe violence the state was launching. They resisted not

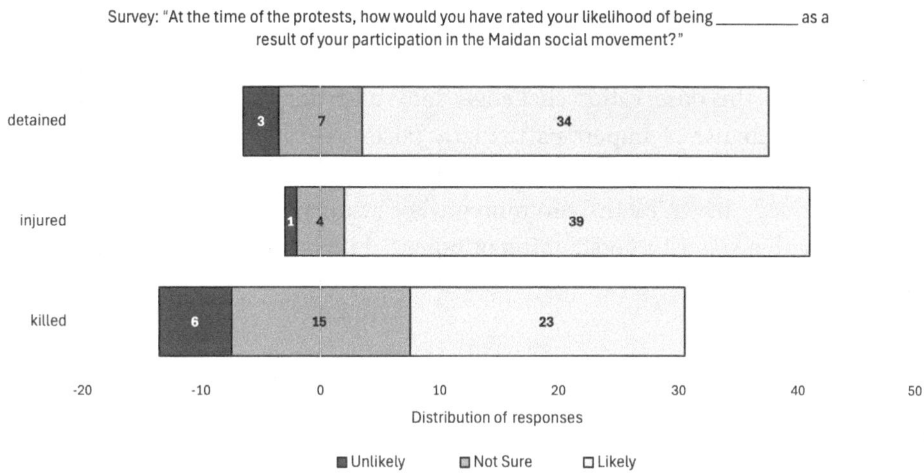

Figure 3.11 Revolutionaries' expectations of being detained, injured, or killed during the revolution.
Source: Author's survey of Maidan protesters.

Figure 3.12 An injured elderly Maidan protester is led away by police. Indiscriminate use of force by police against Maidan participants increased throughout the winter months.

simply despite severe repression, but in direct response to it, wanting to end a regime that relies on violent repression. As discussed further in chapter 6, this observation challenges some assertions of rational choice theory. The use of snipers particularly raises stakes for activists, since one does not need to be at the frontline to become a target. Yet activism continued, driven by the common goal of restoring democratic order, and with a sober understanding of potential high costs.

Conclusion

The 16 January laws, which severely restricted civil liberties and gave immunity to police, and the extreme police violence that immediately followed, were interpreted by revolutionaries as further consolidation of authoritarian power, leading to mass protests. Severe state violence led the activists to assume that open repression and violence would become standard state practice unless they employed political violence to stop it. To understand revolutionary dynamics, it is vital to examine the social reading of state repression. Is repression interpreted as a malfunction of the system or as a sign of consolidation of an authoritarian regime? As Migdal points out, a state's image is essential in state–society relations.[91]

Socialization during the revolutionary events and, most importantly, interactions with security forces and state-hired thugs, had the strongest effect on discourse among activists, affecting the tactics adopted to battle the repressive state machine. While conscious and continuous efforts initially were made to maintain peaceful resistance, state terror tactics convinced a number of activists that the current regime was consolidating into a more severe authoritarian regime. As the data in this chapter show, Ukrainian revolutionaries overwhelmingly believed that if they had failed in ousting Yanukovych, control tactics would have become routine state practice and change would not have been possible through electoral means. Thus, a lawyer who participated in the revolution pointed out the right to a revolution (with its use of force) is engrained in the International Declaration of Human Rights as people's last resort against a repressive government. Many revolutionaries started to believe that peaceful methods were exhausted, and force became the only chance to defeat the new terror regime.

The Maidan's social communication with the state continued to centre on their vision of state–society relations, asserting the principle of natural rights. As state repression increased after the passage of the 16 January laws, including the use of torture and live ammunition, revolutionary social discourse emphasized reclaiming the dignity of man – similarly to Solidarity activists, who claimed that the 1980–81 Polish events were "a revolution of dignity, a celebration of the rights of the vertebrae, a permanent victory for the straightened spine."[92] Maidan activists painted their faces to appear bloodied, with their mouths sewn shut, to symbolize the repression of their natural rights; they brought a funeral wreath to "mourn democracy." This also recalls Solidarity movement activists, who wrote letters from the communist prisons that "impotence in the face of armed evil is probably the worst of human humiliations. When six hulks pin you to the ground, you are helpless. But you do not want to give up your natural right to dignity."[93] Maidaners asserted that they were not willing to give up their natural rights even in the face of "sadist police." Similarly to Solidarity, principled action and grassroots movement were seen as the path to social liberation;[94] however, unlike the Polish Solidarity movement, and the Ukrainian Revolution on the Granite of 1990 and the Orange Revolution of 2004, Maidan protesters eventually began justifying the use of violence. The socialization element of the Maidan Revolution – more specifically, personal interactions with and observations of the security police who now systematically beat, tortured, kidnapped, and killed – stimulated Maidaners to utilize violent resistance to restore democracy. These encounters transformed revolutionaries' perception of state actors. Law enforcement agents were seen as agents of terror, and thus force was the only remaining tool to affect freedom, because "it's not people who should be afraid of the state, but the state that should be afraid of the people."

4

Grassroots Movements as State–Society and Intra-Society Dialogue

> I was wounded during the revolution ... I was taken to Austria by volunteers for surgery ... When I was recovering in a Vienna hospital, lots of people came to visit me, bringing food. [It was] local diaspora. Hospital staff kept asking me, "Who are you? Are you a celebrity in Ukraine?" I said, "Yes; I'm a volunteer."

This story, from a medical volunteer, reveals vital aspects of the Maidan Revolution. First, even medical aid activists were subject to state violence. Secondly, the volunteer movement was extensive, encompassing multiple self-organized initiatives, which appeared on the basis of current protester needs. For example, as the state began using live ammunition, multiple volunteer groups collaborated to negotiate with foreign embassies to take the wounded abroad for medical treatment and safety. Thirdly, while many people were not able to be physically present at the epicentre of the revolution, their contributions were profound: from feeding or housing protesters to staffing hotlines. Finally, revolutionaries' effective negotiation of their common goals led to new effective social trust networks. Such collaborations helped overcome the lack of resources ordinarily expected for successful mobilization.

The Ukrainian Maidan Revolution produced bottom-up civic initiatives that affected the dynamic of state–society dialogue. Social groups were at the wheel of considerable transformations, contributing to the success of the revolution. Why did Ukraine's grassroots social movement flourish, despite limited financial and institutional resources? Negotiating a consensus around a pro-democratic cause, the revolutionaries gained leverage by volunteering their time and skills, relying on a continuous flow of public donations, creating new social networks, and continuously developing new strategies in response to growing state violence. A society-wide grievance against the usurpation of state power mobilized the masses. Even with a lack of institutional resources, the mobilized public formed new initiatives with the goal of maintaining anti-state protests. Public donations and indirect involvement made the movement possible.

This chapter presents an in-depth study of the formation and maintenance of grassroots mobilization activities during the Maidan Revolution, providing a detailed analysis of how new initiatives were formed, and which role they played in (1) communicating social demands to the state, and (2) maintaining anti-state protests until those demands were met. Throughout the chapter, I show how revolutionaries overcame a lack of financial resources with an unceasing amount of social creativity, volunteer work, and public support; and overcame a lack of institutional resources with reliance on social media, newly formed initiatives, and collaboration.

Grassroots Initiatives: Formation and Function

Most revolutionary civic initiatives were formed in response to the event that became known as the "Student Beating": police violence against peaceful protesters on 29 November 2013. The initiatives were either newly created or built on existing organizations or social clubs. While the latter could have some experience working with the state, they were operating within an entirely new institutional setting and performing new tasks. Table 4.1 provides examples of major civic initiatives organized during the Maidan Revolution, and their functions. It is important to note the fluid and decentralized nature of these initiatives, as many evolved over the winter months to accommodate the needs of the movements – mostly reflecting the level of state suppression and violence. For example, medical aid initiatives, which began immediately following the events of 29 November, involved medical and non-medical personnel in stationary locations to offer aid to protesters. In January, some of these had evolved into makeshift medical brigades, accompanying the fighting and offering mobile first aid in case of severe injuries. Others were formed in late January in response to the state use of live ammunition and had highly trained physicians. The multiple medical aid groups, like many other task-oriented initiatives, did not have one centralized authority to navigate their function within the movement, and the groups occasionally had disagreements over "jurisdictional" boundaries.

A small group of initiatives were led by volunteers who were previously engaged in human rights NGOs. For example, the Euromaidan SOS, an initiative that became one of the leading groups coordinating legal aid, was organized by members of the Center for Civil Liberties (CCL). The CCL was created in 2007 to provide education about and promote human rights, as well as monitor electoral and other state functions in Ukraine and neighbouring post-Soviet countries.[1] While the organization was hardly known to the masses prior to the revolution, its EuroMaidan SOS initiative gained fame and trust during the events. Their experience as international observers of elections and the suppression of post-election protests in Russia and Belarus affected their members' decision to mobilize after the police violence on 29 November.[2] State aggression and the detention of peaceful protesters "suggested the need for a mechanism that would bring together those who needed legal help and those who could offer it."[3] Another legal aid group was formed by an NGO group for refugee rights, No Borders. Lastly, some were formed on the basis of existing clubs. For example, AutoMaidan, the initiative whose major functions were transportation and providing security from police violence, was formed from an automotive enthusiast community.

On 30 November, many Kyivans came to protest against state violence, gathering next to the Mykhailivskyi Monastery, where protesters received refuge from police the night before. Unlike the preceding November demonstrations, whose purpose was to protest Yanukovych's refusal to sign the EU agreement, 30 November marked the shift to "do something" against state violence.[4] Many started organizing in groups to provide an applicable function. Lawyers were collecting witness testimonies of state aggression, medics were now gathering in expectation of having to treat the injured, and a large number of people started building barricades around Maidan Square to prevent further police attacks. Most initiatives were newly formed, building on the skill sets of their new members. Thus, AutoMaidan's Legal Protection was initiated and led by a bank lawyer who had no previous experience with civil rights anti-state litigation.[5] While one medical aid initiative built on an existing connection with the Red Cross, others had no institutional affiliation. Most volunteers had no previous experience with community organization or volunteer work.

Many initiatives emerged from groups of individuals who gathered to protest state violence. AutoMaidan's founder Dmytro Bulatov described how one of the major initiatives was launched in response to November police violence against peaceful protesters:

> I saw the horror on TV, I got into my car, put a flag, and invited people to join in a car caravan to express protest against the violence. We were protesting in support for civil freedoms, a free country. [State] violence is what pushed me and others. [As I drove], people joined in. We gathered a column of about 200–300 cars and drove around, honked, telling people to come to Maidan to protest … We were driving around, gathering drivers, via [Kyiv's] Left Bank, through Obolon region, [Pivnichnyi] bridge, Perov Street, then we came to the Lebedi monument, then up through Khreshchatyk, Instytutska Street … and finally to the Ministry of Internal Affairs[6] – there were lots of us, showing protest. Next day we agreed on Facebook to meet again. So, there was a group of different people; we met so fast, and self-organized a civic initiative.[7]

The civic initiatives had two major overlapping functions: (1) communicating to the state – via protest and other means – that it had crossed its constitutional boundaries in suppressing social freedom of expression; and (2) aiding the masses in maintaining protests until the demands (release of political prisoners, punishment of the responsible state agents and resignation of the president) were met. Aid was multi-faceted: initiatives were formed to offer physical security, legal, medical, and psychological aid, food, clothing, housing, and so forth.

Mass protest was the essential form of communicating with the state: people continuously arrived to the capital from various parts of the country to express their civic position against state violence. Therefore, continuing the presence of protesters on the square became a major objective. To sustain the protests for a lengthy period of time, activists organized to provide protesters with lodging, food, safety, medical and legal aid, and other needs. Protesters' needs were provided not only by activists present on the Maidan, or those who arranged help remotely, but also by Kyiv residents, who offered food, housing, clothing,

Table 4.1 Examples of major civic initiatives organized during the Maidan Revolution

Civic initiative	*Function*
Food stands	Free food provision to revolutionaries
AutoMaidan • car owners offering help • car protests • security	Secure transportation for revolutionaries Transportation of revolutionary material Dialogue with the state through civic actions
Legal aid • EuroMaidan SOS • Legal AutoMaidan • No Borders	Aid for detained revolutionaries Dialogue with the state through legal defence/action Connecting detainees with pro bono lawyers Spreading information about the needs of protesters
Medical aid • Professional and newly trained volunteers • Churches	Aid to injured or ill revolutionaries Shelter and security for treatment of the injured
Housing aid • *Hromadskyi Sektor Maidanu* • *Zhytlo dlia Euromaidanu* • Churches	Housing for revolutionaries Aid and security for injured or ill revolutionaries
Logistics	Promoting collaboration between civic initiatives
Makeshift kitchens	Food for revolutionaries
Hromadskyi Sektor Maidanu Hromadska Rada Maidanu *Kolo Narodnoi Doviry*	Communication with the state via civic actions Communication with pro-revolutionary political elite Organization of public protest
Donation seekers	Collection of donations from large businesses to maintain protest
Kraplya v Okeani • Marketing	Communication with the state via protest media Advertising the revolutionary cause to the public
Education & Information • Stage • Open Maidan University • Brochures • Streaming Initiatives, such as *Spilno*	Exchange of information about protester needs Communication with the public about the aims/plans of the resistance movement Provision of entertainment to maintain the protest Intra-revolutionary dialogue
IT Groups	Provision of internet, communication
Samo-Oborona	Security of the protesters Violent resistance

transport, and donations. In addition to protests in Kyiv's central square, activists organized marches and mass drives to other locations in the city, such as politicians' residences and the city of Cherkassy. Most of the protests that were held in other cities across Ukraine, however, were organized independently.

Other forms of delivering the revolutionary message (to the state and a wider population) involved legal battles, various forms of marketing, and art expressions. The message was distributed via posters, information booklets, videos, drawings, sculptures, etc. Volunteer legal aid was based on the immediate need to offer legal protection from arbitrary state detention and violations of due process. However, a substantial pro bono legal movement that was formed also became an arena for protest: fighting for the rights of the detained, lawyers communicated to the state the social refusal to accept newly imposed terms of legality (see chapter 3). Similarly, a number of activists would travel to court hearing locations, and while they were not permitted to attend the hearing itself, their presence outside of courtrooms became an expression of civic position. Finally, multiple forms of broadcasting the events by the press, activist-organized streaming, and communication over social media served as a tool to expose state aggression.

Maintaining the Protests and State–Society Dialogue

Newcomers to the Maidan sought ways to contribute to the growing volunteer community, adding a self-help dimension to the mass movement. In order to maintain mass protest, volunteers continually formed and improved ways of providing safety, basic needs, and entertainment to the protesters. On 30 November and 1 December, many arrived to Maidan Square to build barricades, surrounding the square, and formed squadrons to protect from further state attacks. In addition, AutoMaidan was formed to offer secure transportation to and from the Maidan Square. Later, this initiative expanded to block police cars from getting to the Maidan Square, and to offer secure transportation to and from hospitals after instances of police violence, as well as transporting tires and gasoline for barricades and violent resistance. With approximately 800,000 protesters arriving in Kyiv on 1 December, a number of initiatives were formed to offer basic needs to the arriving masses, such as housing, food, clothing, medical aid, and even haircutting services. Multiple initiatives continued to form throughout the winter months to expand existing accommodations, and to reflect the growing needs of the protesting masses, including offering electronics charging booths or transportation from other cities to the capital. Volunteers formed initiatives to provide communication, entertainment, and education to the protesters on Maidan Square. This included weekly protester meetings, or viche, announcements, and performances on the stage, as well as public lectures and musical performances throughout the square. On 1 December, the revolutionaries captured and occupied several government and community buildings surrounding the square, which served as headquarters for a number of these initiatives. Others operated in booths set up on the square, or remotely.

Grassroots and Dispersed Leadership

Leadership of the revolutionary movement was dispersed and built on grassroots initiatives. The initiatives drew leaders who were dedicated to the cause, but not necessarily experienced with leadership roles. In November (prior to police violence) multiple protests were held, including an unaffiliated protest on the Maidan Square, and one led by politicians from opposition parties on European Square. Politicians advocated to combine the two protests. A council of activists was formed, debating three solutions to the unorganized structure of the protests: one group (led by Viktoria Tsumar, Oleh Grybeichuk, and Egor Sobolev) supported combining with politicians, another (led by Olexander Doneljuk from the Syla Ljudej civic group) advocated for radical solutions, such as a march to the Verkhovna Rada (parliament) and encouraging students to organize a lying-down strike. A third group (led by Volodymyr Vetrovych, Igor Lutsenko, Bohdana Babych, and Denys Ott) advocated against combining forces with the political groups, while avoiding radicalization. The first group prevailed when negotiating the compromise: politicians were allowed to join in the unaffiliated protest, but could address only the question of European integration, not party politics. Throughout the protests, political flags were continually present, but public addresses of opposition politicians focused on the Maidan events and avoided party political rhetoric.

To maintain resistance after 29 November, Maidan activists organized several civic councils, such as *Hromadska Rada Maidanu*, *Hromadskyi Sektor Maidanu*, and *Kolo Narodnoi Doviry*. The aim was to coordinate resistance strategies, holding meetings at the Trade Union building and other locations around Kyiv. Politicians and political organizations were banned from participation, as the activists feared Yanukovych could influence politicians through their donors, such as Dmytro Firtash.[8] *Rada Maidanu* became one of the a decentralized bodies of collaboration of civic activism, rather than a top-down command. The Council's main function was to coordinate the action, as well as discuss social issues pertaining to the revolutionary change. It was a gathering place of activists who knew what was going on, to reflect on possible warning signs or to advertise upcoming resistance actions, rallying other groups to attend and show support. A number of coordination issues were discussed, such as the need for more volunteers in certain areas. These coordinating efforts also became an arena of social discourse about state–society relations: the meetings often involved a discussion of theoretical issues about potential political change. Participants often turned to discussions about a constitutional means to end Yanukovych's rule prior to the next election cycle, as well as means to restore the 2004 constitution.[9]

Logistics: Coordinating Volunteer Services

As the number of protesters, tents, and barricades grew, so did the number of the civic initiatives to aid revolutionaries with lodging, food, and transport. With that, volunteers formed groups to notify incoming participants about such initiatives, as well as to coordinate the efforts of these initiatives more effectively.

> We put an information tent next to the Main Post Office, made a Maidan map, by that time we knew there was an eatery, a [makeshift] hospital, and other services. We'd ask people if they were new, and invite them to come to our tent – we had a big poster, "Ne Zlyi Maidan" (Not an Angry Maidan). We also provided information about where volunteers were needed: in the [makeshift] hospital, kitchen, or security. We were trying to make a somewhat organized structure.[10]

Another civic group (more specifically, a married couple) set up a hotline. Callers were prompted to choose between lodging information, transport, or they could speak with an operator. This initiative operated online, via a closed Facebook group, a telephone hotline, and at their headquarters in the October Palace on the Maidan Square, where they distributed informational pamphlets, referring newcomers to use the hotline. As previosly mentioned, they also collaborated with one of the lodging initiatives to screen people. As the police force would strategically attack at night – when the number of the protesters and observers on the square was substantially smaller, activists invested effort in maintaining as much presence on the Maidan as possible. The Logistics initiative came up with an ingenious solution to accommodate night callers:

> My husband is an IT specialist, so he created a system similar to Skype, which allowed online [call routing]: you didn't have to be in Kyiv to help Ukraine. So, Ukrainian-speakers … [from other places] could help the revolution efforts … When it's night here, immigrants in Canada, America were able to help. You wouldn't even know if she was in Toronto arranging your lodging [in Kyiv]. You could call the hotline, a Ukrainian-speaking girl would respond, you would never know that she was in Toronto. A girl from New York is arranging housing in Kyiv, it was awesome. These were people from Kyiv, they knew the city really well, knew where everything was located. A man from Kolomyia could call, or an elderly woman [who didn't know their whereabouts in Kyiv].[11]

The same initiative coordinated some of the revolutionaries' transportation efforts, through initiating a Facebook page, *Transfer Maidan*. They organized internal social media, promoting collaborative efforts. Eventually, they organized transport for injured revolutionaries to different cities to avoid being discovered by Kyiv police in the city hospitals. They coordinated with volunteers to transfer the injured to Chernihiv or Bila Tserkva, for example, where the volunteers knew a physician they could trust.[12] Notably, many other grassroots initiatives provided transport for the revolutionaries, such as AutoMaidan, and some focused solely on transporting the injured – such as E-plus (both discussed later in this chapter).

Logistics were mainly carried out by each separate initiative, to collect donations and seek volunteers. EuroMaidan SOS, a major initiative that guided pro bono legal aid to detainees through the Center for Civil Liberties, started with a Facebook post. As Oleksandra Matviichuk[13] described, the first post addressed those detained (and their relatives), offering to connect them with lawyers. The second post was addressed to lawyers, encouraging them to volunteer. Their trust in local attorneys paid off: over 500 lawyers responded within a few days. Similarly, another initiative, the AutoMaidan's Legal Protection,[14] was formed when two volunteer lawyers announced a search for volunteer attorneys via Facebook. They received over 300 requests to aid AutoMaidan activists.

A number of volunteers brought food and supplies to the newly formed centres, sustaining their around-the-clock mode of operation. Notably, coordination of these efforts was decentralized, and often decided on the spot. Donation boxes and bank account numbers for suggested donations were provided on social media and on the Maidan. For the purpose of transparency, some civic initiatives provided a detailed account of donations and spending via social media.[15] Certain initiatives refused to take monetary donations, and redirected new volunteers to find their own mode of contribution, encouraging further civic engagement. As one described:

> Maidan didn't need leaders ... People asked how they could [donate] money. We said, we didn't need money: "go around and see where your help is needed." So, one person who had a furniture business brought friends, and started helping ... We didn't have warm clothes, so a pile of twenty winter outfits were brought ... On Hrushevskoho we had injured people ... we send notifications that we needed bullet proof vests, they were brought to us. When snipers [appeared] – we asked for flashlights to point at their eyes to prevent them from shooting us.[16]

Public donations also included phones and phone payments to help the protesters as well as volunteers in other locations.[17] Numerous civic initiatives collected public donations by posting information about the needed items via social media, and delivering them to those who needed them. One activist who volunteered at a hospital where injured revolutionaries were treated stated: "Clothes were brought here. Initiative *Varta v Likarni* [Hospital Guard] called and asked what we needed – we said we needed phone accounts to be refilled. We received 6,800 hryvnas overnight. Then we asked for water – so much water was brought, we couldn't fit it all in."[18]

Several IT companies collaborated to provide an *IT Tent:* a post with wi-fi routers, which provided free internet access for those on the square. The post also enabled streaming video from the square. The organizers relied on public donations of laptops and other technology.[19] Some groups focused solely on aiding communication among the revolutionary initiatives. Many built on existing skills, but adjusted them to the needs of the revolution. For example, Moto Help, which existed before the Maidan Revolution as a volunteer group in Kyiv, relied on motorcycles and radio transmission to aid communication in case of car accidents. They also had knowledge of dealing with specific traumas. During the revolution, they worked closely with the teams of *Mykhailivskyi Medics* and Red Cross–affiliated medics.[20]

A vital revolutionary strategy during the Maidan was constant mobilization in order to counteract the state's round-the-clock repression. Defence lawyers, as well as volunteers and members of civic groups who mobilized to organize legal help, adopted a "revolutionary mode" twenty-four hours a day, withstanding subzero temperatures when waiting outside of courtrooms.[21] Lawyers conducted systematic documentation of injuries, even in a growing atmosphere of fear where some journalists were unwilling to assist in recording abuses.[22] The need for resources to build networks and coordinate legal aid was overcome by a surge of volunteer initiatives dedicated to the task. Thus, a large mass of volunteers collected information about those detained, injured, and missing, and connected the detained or their relatives with volunteer attorneys.[23] Pro bono lawyers and human rights groups were engaged in printing hundreds of thousands of leaflets to offer legal education pertaining to protest conduct.[24]

Shelter and Clothing

The buildings occupied by revolutionaries, including the city administration building and the Trade Union building, were run by certain initiative groups and offered shelter to the revolutionaries. Tents were also set up by the revolutionaries, where they self-organized into regional affiliations, and many took turns sleeping in the tents (despite freezing winter temperatures).

Several initiatives were formed to aid revolutionaries in finding shelter, or to get temporary rest and a shower from living in tent conditions. Activists would put incoming revolutionaries in touch with local organizations and individual residents, who volunteered to house them. The initiatives were formed as some activists considered the need after the 29 November police aggression. Two major initiatives reported having housed hundreds of thousands of protesters. They were initiated and operated separately, but co-operated as the events unravelled. One was part of a larger initiative, *Hromadskyi Sektor Maidanu*, which also focused on communicating social demands to the state. In an interview with me, a Hromadsky Sektor activist in charge of housing arrangements within the initiative relates the process:

> We housed approximately 200,000 people, including in churches, sport facilities … We used three little wooden houses, which were set up for the New Year's holiday fair. We occupied these after December 4. We put carpets, somebody brought an infra-red lamp for warmth, [others] – a table, big notebooks. Later, I was recording the information into our computer data base. Some people came to offer their housing, others – to request it. Those who offered housing gave their phone number, and when we called them, they would come to pick up the person. This [process] allowed us to screen the people: are they titushky, are they from SBU? There was a big Greco-Catholic church on the Left Bank, and an Orthodox church on Lvivska square, and there were sport facilities who'd shelter people for the night. If a person was sick, somebody could drive them to one of the churches, as there were medics there and an opportunity to sleep. The smaller church sheltered those who were more ill and elderly; those who had a hard time moving around. We'd help people get to Mykhailivskyi [monastery]; we'd send groups of ten people with a volunteer, as it wasn't safe otherwise. If [they came] before midnight [subways still in operation], – we'd send them to the Left bank, as it was big, and could fit lots of people … People who offered [to house somebody] … we'd ask them to write down [their] name, how many people they could house, for how many nights, home pets? Gender? A couple of times apartments were robbed, a woman came and cried, for one of those cases we had contact info – we gave it to the woman, she could say to police she rented it (we couldn't obviously), but for another a volunteer didn't write it down. We were very sorry, collected money to help. Only two times that I witnessed such cases.

Similarly, a Lutheran church in proximity to the Maidan Square offered housing to sick revolutionaries. A church building worker recalled with humour that somebody approached him:

> "Hi, I am Olya," she said, and stared at me – I guess she thought I'd recognize her. But I hadn't heard of Olha Bohomolets prior to this. So, I said, "Hi, I'm Vasya." She then explained that she was a medic, and they were trying to find a place to shelter revolutionaries who were ill. I talked to the priest, and he agreed.

Activists sought out organizations, churches in particular, to help shelter revolutionaries who became ill (many reported pneumonia cases during the revolution). The story above is telling for another important reason: while prestige and connections were previously expected to play an essential role in getting things done on such a scale, now the purpose of immediate institutional arrangement (a church being turned into a shelter) overshadowed other factors. People were likely to respond to what was seen as morally right, even if it bore potential risks in dealing with state authorities. With such a trivial beginning, the Lutheran church became one of the churches that sheltered the sick during the events. The dispersed leadership proved to be exceptionally effective at finding resources, as religious organizations were sympathetic to the cause of the revolutionaries. In fact, the Lutheran church literature, distributed later, engaged in a social contract philosophical discourse, defending the morality of the citizens' choice to resist an abusive state (see chapter 6).

Another major housing initiative, *Zhytlo dlia Euromaidanu* (Housing for EuroMaidan), was part of a larger logistical initiative that also provided coordination of transportation and medicine/food delivery. As an activist reported, just ten minutes after the Facebook page was created, people volunteered to house people in their homes. While *Zhytlo* and Hromadskyi Sektor functioned separately, they later coordinated for the purpose of screening. As *Zhytlo* operated completely online, they were able to screen those who requested housing via video chat: as they explained, this allowed them to see if they were titushky or if they were drunk. "We had to protect those people." She noted that the initiative was built on the idea and experience of the Orange

Figure 4.1 Protester initiatives connected those in need of housing with those offering a place to sleep, from Kyivans offering a room in their apartment to churches, to warehouses, pictured here, which were converted to temporary housing for Maidan participants.

Revolution of 2004, when locals offered housing to the revolutionaries: "We did it in our place; there was no distrust; we were all together. Strangers lived in your house. The beginning here was similar." While the experience of the Orange Revolution was short-lived, the length and the tragic aspect of the Maidan Revolution had more profound effects on the bonding between protesters from other cities and locals who offered housing. Several fitness centres also offered lodging for revolutionaries. *Zhytlo* organizers worked with one, Academy Fitness, accommodating lodging for approximately one hundred people every night. The initiative collected donations online and purchased sleeping bags for those lodging in the fitness centre.

A number of housing arrangements were organized without the aid of the specialized initiatives, as local revolutionaries would offer their own housing or workplace to fellow activists. "My workers knew where my office was … I fed them, gave them tea, they were in self-defence.

I invited them, some slept there, I brought them clothes; they were providing security."[25] In addition, there were continuous public donations of clothing, especially warm clothing as temperatures dropped throughout the winter months. There were several posts on the Maidan Square where donations were collected and then distributed by volunteers. One volunteer recalled, "When I made it to Maidan for the first time, there were two of us carrying groceries, home canned goods, and fur coats. I asked somebody where to donate them. Even though he was leaving, he grabbed the bags and showed us the way to the Trade Union building post."[26] Volunteers often carried scarves, hats, and other items to offer them to the protesters. As one described: "Fascinating people, how they helped each other, fed each other. People would appear out of nowhere and changed your gloves for you, put on masks."[27]

Food

There were multiple makeshift kitchens set up following 29 November. Many volunteers took shifts to cook soup, slice bread, and carry tea to protesters. Donation bins were set up in front of each makeshift kitchen, and money that was donated by hundreds of individuals was sufficient to continually provide food for the protesters. One Kyiv restaurateur, who organized and ran a makeshift kitchen on the Maidan Square, tells his story:

> We thought it was going to end [in November] … Then [I received] a phone call: kids were beaten … We started making sandwiches, feeding them, offering emotional support. It was shocking … On the morning of November 30, people started bringing tea, coffee, bread … We … set up a work line behind the seminary building. People would bring groceries, we'd sort them out. The monastery brought out tables, we asked people to bring tables and chairs, they brought everything [we needed]. When we needed something, I'd post it on Facebook … On one occasion, somebody came and asked what we needed. I said that we needed large generators, five to seven kilowatt. People brought generators. One architecture student built shelves from [materials that were brought]. Somebody who had an office on Instytutska Street, said we could keep our stuff in their office; we didn't know them at all … At first we had workers from our restaurant, then other

Figure 4.2 Revolutionaries running a makeshift kitchen on the Maidan, with the burnt-out Trade Union building in the background.

> volunteers joined. People were bringing donations: groceries, money. We had a donation box – next to all our locations, there were a lot of people to feed. Another fascinating phenomenon: volunteers who helped volunteers. There were people who brought us a warm dinner every evening.[28]

Thus, behind every initiative was a network of intertwined grassroots initiatives to sustain it. New initiatives appeared to meet the needs of the ones established earlier. An activist shared the process of joining an already established makeshift kitchen:

> I wanted to help more. Somebody mentioned they had a kitchen, and volunteers were needed. It was *Maltiiska Kukhnya* by Maltiisky Krest, founded in Lviv. They needed people who can work at night. While others had to rely on the subway, I had a car [which allowed me to volunteer at night]. We set up a work line. We had the best tea, because we sliced fresh ginger and lemon, among other things … Some guys came and asked whether we needed gas … People brought tea, coffee, a bunch of businesses helped out. Elderly women, who could barely walk, brought us what they

> could afford. We never asked anybody who came [to eat] what their function was on the Maidan. A bunch of people would just come to hang out.[29]

Another volunteer described her experience at a food post as a process of communal bonding:

> I'd bring groceries and other items regularly, and then I would be in the kitchen two or three hours. It was difficult because the work had to be done while standing. People were close to each other; somebody would slice bread, pass it to you, you'd smear what you have there on top, and then pass it the next, who'd have a pickle. It was very fast. It was also amazing: women sang Ukrainian folk songs. The atmosphere was so wonderful.[30]

The process of communal participation and various social exchanges – between the activists on the square and those who sponsored, bought, or delivered food, clothing, and gadgets acquired a reasserted mode of social dialogue. The activities to find small individual and large business donations was a time-intensive activity, which contributed greatly to the resistance efforts. Moreover, these activities communicated support for the cause and fostered further participation in the movement:

> We once mentioned there was not enough honey in the kitchen, so a barrel of honey was delivered. I then joked when streaming, we got everything, just missing some chocolate for good mood, so people brought us chocolate. People are treating us so well. They saw we worked 24/7.[31]

The donations also served as an emotive message to the participants, evoking an atmosphere of communal support. Individual communication during the donation process served as reaffirmation of the revolutionary efforts:

> When you see an elderly woman who brings her own medicine [to donate], with two pills already missing from the package, and saying, "Daughter, that is all I have," how can you not go back [to Maidan] after that?[32]

Housing and food arrangements played a fundamental role in sustaining the anti-state protests in Ukraine. Grassroots initiatives developed in attempts to ameliorate the hardship of the protesters. Activists who were motivated to resist the state were driven to help others who shared their aspiration in preventing the consolidation of an authoritarian regime. The sentiment conveyed in the above statements – "We never checked which function those who came to eat played on Maidan," "wonderful atmosphere," "fascinating phenomenon" – is telling: not only were the activists aiding each other to achieve a common goal, they were enjoying the newly growing community of like-minded participants. This sentiment was echoed in other testimonies of the participants, who used the terms, "positive energy of Maidan," "light-filled faces," "being recharged by positivity," etc. (see chapter 6). In other words, temporary arrangements to aid the revolutionaries created a *Maidan-sich* – a social institution of its own, which could not only sustain itself, but also serve as the headquarters of a tangible ideational community.

Medical Aid

Medical volunteers played a fundamental role in maintaining the protests. Importantly, while medics chose to volunteer, because they supported the revolutionary cause, they also treated police, who were often neglected by the state. While initial medical aid was focused on offering first aid for physical traumas and common colds, in January and February medics were battling to save the lives of revolutionaries as a result of the growing aggressiveness by the state.

Several medical aid initiatives operated simultaneously during the revolution. One, initiated by a member of an opposition political party, was loosely operated by the revolutionary headquarters located in the Trade Union building. Others operated separately, asserting their independence. The account below is a vivid representation of volunteers' continuing adjustment to the growing needs of revolutionaries in the face of increasing state aggression, and the collaboration process with other initiatives:

> On November 30, I saw that Mykhailivskyi monastery [where protesters hid from police] had a sign seeking medical aid. I came saying I had experience during the Orange Revolution.

This was my point of no return, I went through the entire revolution. Many people came with injuries – head injuries, in particular. Many didn't think it was necessary to go to the hospital, while others felt safer here. We were cleaning wounds. My friends and I, who started there at the St Varvara corner, organized a medical group, *Mykhailivskyi Medics*. We came up with our own symbol: since we could not use the Red Cross symbol, we had a candle in the symbol … On December 1 … on Bankova [Street] … we were on the steps offering aid, we were taking in only people who needed aid … Bohomolets team brought lots of medications. The Red Cross team also joined … now we became like a family. We took the rest of the medication to the Mykhailivskyi monastery – they gave us a small room … By the next weekend, we had eighty people, we taught them how to offer first aid, including Pirohov's technique, bandaging, how to wash the face in case of gas attacks. In just one day, we had vests made with names and reflectors, crosses drawn by markers; people offered to print the emblems. It seemed seamless: people would come and ask what they could do, somebody would come asking which medications were needed … there was so much trust … we didn't control who took what. There were fifteen people who were "active volunteers," altogether we had a hundred people. Our group was separate from the Red Cross, but we had collaborated. We coordinated actions, we knew we could trust each other, cover each other, say where we were. We were *Mykhailivskyi Medics* group, they were the Rapid Response team, affiliated with the Red Cross, organized by Logginov. They put on their jackets, and were saving people … When there were no active events, we'd patrol on Maidan Square. A million people would ask for help … We were not allowed to administer medications, our task was acute necessities … Our task was to be ready … We had four groups: one group working until 6 p.m., another group worked half of the night, checking people into hospitals, etc. If there was an emergency situation: reserve was called (2nd, or 2nd and 3rd, or all) if the situation was really bad, all would join in.[33]

Other medical volunteer groups operated within the Maidan Square, with physicians and medics reporting to the Trade Union Maidan headquarters or the Ukrainian House building. Each medic reporting to the Trade Union HQ was assigned to a self-defence unit. Their main task was to examine the protesters, and if acute medical conditions were found, they were encouraged to go to the hospital. Medics coordinated with the housing groups to find shelter for those who were sick, and with the AutoMaidan initiative to offer safe transport to the hospital or to their shelter.[34]

In January, the police started actively raiding hospitals to jail injured revolutionaries. Many (but not all) physicians and medical staff chose at the time not only to offer treatment to protesters, but also to hide the presence of injured activists. During the raids, they would hide the injured in X-ray rooms, etc. Some falsified records regarding the nature of treatment; for example, they recorded hernia rather than broken limbs. One physician recalled: "When an injured revolutionary arrived, I'd ask which name I should write down, he'd say 'My name is so and so. I'd say, what should I *write down*? They would understand [my insinuation] and give me a fake name."[35]

As the number of injuries grew and the dangers of being treated in a hospital increased due to police raids, a number of volunteers were stationed in hospitals, coordinating their efforts with other civic initiatives. Ambulances were also no longer trusted as they would record the nature of the injury, and/or deliver to the nearest hospital rather than one with more pro-revolutionary staff. The developed safety net incorporated a multi-layer security system: AutoMaidan drivers transported the injured, volunteers performed security checks at the entry, Varta v Likarni (Hospital Guard) volunteer groups guarded hospital beds, and in the case of police appearance could inform media to put police on the spot (and thus, often prevent arrests by applying public pressure). Volunteer lawyers were often present to prevent arrests as well. In February, during the active state shootings, self-defence groups patrolled Kyiv City Hospital No. Seventeen, which specializes in firearm injuries and had a number of supportive physicians.

Rapid growth in the number of injuries also meant a severe shortage of medical supplies. Volunteers rushed to bring medical supplies to hospitals, but with an over-abundance of some supplies: "there was so much zelenka [disinfectant], it was unreal." As a result, some activists

Figure 4.3 Medical aid volunteers also became targets of state violence.

volunteered to organize the incoming flow of supplies, collaborating with medical staff. This collaboration yielded a more effective coordination of mass donation efforts. Other initiatives were contacted to collect monetary donations to purchase needed surgical equipment. A hospital volunteer reflected on the effectiveness and speed of the collaboration: "We wrote on the internet we need pharmacists to sort the incoming medications, in the next half hour there were twenty pharmacists to do it … Clothes were [also] brought here."[36] Similarly, volunteer medics on the Maidan shared about their reliance on other motivated revolutionaries: "The input from people was unbelievable: they kept carrying medications, even in the middle of the night."[37] Grassroots mobilization became the fundamental strength of the Maidan movement: the fluidity and bottom-up self-organization helped with continuous provision of medical supplies, and with that, maintained the social resistance movement.

The most important message heard from medical volunteers, and all those who sustained the logistics for medical aid, was to support the resistance and maintain the revolutionary movement. The medics, however, also engaged in a more direct dialogue with the state (and beyond) about the boundaries of state powers:

> At the first press conference [with Maidan movement representatives] it was discussed that people with the sign *Press* can't be beaten. I called Olha Bohomolets,[38] saying we can't go on like that, and we did our first press conference on December 3, in which I described that … Berkut troops were beating everybody without regard … I stated that the medics shouldn't be beaten either. We wrote a letter to the European community, describing the situation, and stating that we needed support: press and medics should not be attacked.[39]

The interaction of volunteer medics with the state was often more direct and dangerous:

> On December 1, I ended up in the middle of events … Berkut [troops] were beating everybody indiscriminately: medics or not medics. When they ran into the apartment building [where people and medics found refuge], the guys protected us with their backs. Their plastic backpacks were destroyed, even though they had Red Cross markings … We kept bringing people in, bandaging their injuries … It was scary, I was yelling, watching people running, falling down and then being beaten by Berkut. I filmed their attacks, a group of them beating someone with sticks. This wasn't normal. When we found a place and I sat down, I thought to myself: "How could these horrible things be taking place? These beatings, it's horrific." My friend said, let's go talk [to them]. We came to that wall [of Berkut troops], saying, "Step aside." Berkut leader started yelling [switches to Russian]: "They beat my boys …" [switches back to Ukrainian]: You should have seen me: short, yelling at these huge policemen: "Quiet! Stop this horror, armed police surrounding and beating people! Let's agree: we'll offer you aid as well, but if a person falls down, you can't beat them. It's inhumane!" I shocked myself that I mustered that much bravery. He listened and said: "Guys, did you hear? If there is Red Cross, if you need help, use it."[40]

Thus, the medics' main task was to offer free medical aid. However, their participation in the protests meant that they were revolutionaries themselves. They stood up for their compatriots' human rights, and were communicating to the state their message, calling for the end of injustice and indiscriminate violence.

Medics collaborated closely with multiple Maidan initiatives. One, E-Plus, focused on the transportation of ill and injured revolutionaries. As an E-Plus organizer described, the activism itself was a civic position:

> After the December 1 beatings – the protest of the million – we understood that … we had to fight for our rights. Euro-integration moved to the second front, and the most important objective was justice … To show our civic stand, we understood that we had to unite, get more people and engage in activism, to get more people, and set specific goals. In December … we were on Maidan almost twenty-four hours [per day], we brought food, we organized housing, brought our own money. I made forty-five sandwiches and took them there. This was a civic revolution, sponsored and organized by the people of Ukraine. It was partially a revolution and partially a festival, a festival of popular resistance.[41]

As state violence against the resistance grew, the needs of revolutionaries widened. With that, the risks for participation and different forms of activism increased. However, rather than decreasing their aid to protesters, activists found ways to adapt and increased the range of their aid:

> On January 21, I understood that the [resistance acquired] a different structure: [we needed to figure out] how to help people, save them. We organized a safety and medical aid volunteer group – E-Plus Bezpechne Transportuvannia (E-Plus Safety Transport), with some twenty Kyiv activists. We had ten cars, bought ten phones, and made a hotline. We coordinated with Olga Bohomolets; we had fifteen people on the hotline – seven to twelve people per point on Maidan. They had our poster, E-plus, and three cellphones. We were called twenty-four hours with pneumonia, minor injuries, even gunshots. Since now, people were kidnapped, arrested in hospitals … we couldn't take them

to hospital ER departments, instead we agreed with monasteries, churches, such as the Lutheran church, where twenty people were sleeping every night for two months. Exhausted, morally tired people who lived in tents for a long time, food was good there and medicines; everybody was sick after those gases. Then we agreed with Mykhailivskyi monastery, the Greco-Catholic church – St Basil (on the Smyrnoho-Lastochkina Street), and the Catholic church (Kaputsynov Street) – they had a small hotel, which they opened for all injured people; we transported five to ten people there; so we transported out of Maidan more than 300 people; personally I transported fifty or seventy; we all had a schedule, divided. Here, there were doctors, medical necessities; we organized this structure, shelters with showers, but after two to three days, the revolutionaries all went back to Maidan. After Maidan won, we started taking people to the airports to transport them abroad for medical treatment; we took people en masse, around 200 people. We had agreements with foreign embassies – Czech republic took thirty-eight people, Poland over 120 people, Romania ten, Austria twelve people, Germany twenty-five people, Israel twenty people, Italy around twenty people. We took them all to the airport and then we would pick them up after they came back.[42]

Activists' extensive collaboration and continuous adaptations to the needs of protesters, allowed by the organic nature of the grassroots organization, empowered the revolutionary resistance. Even initiatives organized for transport adapted to the new needs of revolutionaries: organizing not only transport, but housing where they could be transported, working with others to assure there would be food and medical aid. They also brought the revolutionaries to safe places where they could debate the meaning of the revolution. Churches provided not only food but spaces for discussions about resistance. Some religious literature created during the protests addressed the question, justifying civic resistance against a repressive government.

Security and Political Violence

Self-Defence: "Samooborona"

Samooborona [self-defence] units started emerging on 1 December 2013, and included those who arrived to Maidan to protest against state violence and offer protection to peaceful protesters. The initial function of these units was to "prevent [police violence] from happening again,"[43] by offering security to the protesters, tents, stage, and buildings on the Maidan Square and surrounding streets. Eventually, samooborona was also engaged in defence operations outside of Maidan Square and organized violence against police and titushky as well as spying on law enforcement. Self-defence units became known as *sotnya* (translated as "hundred" or "brigade"), named after Cossack regiment units of the Zaporizhian Sich, a semi-autonomous polity and proto-state of Ukrainian Cossacks in the sixteenth to eighteenth centuries.[44] Each major organized violent state attack against protesters, notably those on 10–11 December, 19–22 January, and 18–20 February, led to high numbers of people signing up to samooborona.[45]

One of the objectives of samooborona, as described by one member, was "to have a critical mass of people, so we'd be taken seriously, to negotiate, to have a dialogue, and finally to deliver our point of view to those who are making decisions."[46] As large numbers of people started gathering on 30 November, some discussed the necessity "to have a commanding group, people who could solve problems, have a discussion, and prevent misunderstandings and provocations."[47] It was agreed that Andriy Parubiy, a member of the Ukrainian parliament, would become the Maidan commandant, coordinating volunteer security corps for the protesters.[48] In the evening of the same day, Parubiy announced that "those who want to stand and defend Maidan, may come to the [established] tent to sign up."[49] While many responded and consequently organized into sotni (plural of sotnya), many other revolutionaries ended up performing similar tasks without sotnya membership. As one revolutionary recalled, "I was not part of any sotnya, I attended the viche, cleaned garbage, built barricades. [Later] I became a security guard at the Trade Union kitchen."[50]

As seen in table 4.2, sotni were often organized around certain affiliations and camaraderie, such as regional affiliation, or membership in certain civic organizations, or a certain group function during the

Table 4.2 Examples of Maidan Sotni [Hundreds] self-defence units and their functions

Number	*Title/roots*	*Function*
1st Sotnya		Institutska Street, barricade under the bridge, next to the October Palace building
2nd Sotnya		Initially: protection of the 2nd barricade, after events on Hrushevskoho Street: overseeing European Square and Hrushevskoho Street.[a]
3rd Sotnya		Overseeing the 3rd barricade (from the Trade Union building to the Main Post Office building)[b]
4th Sotnya	Cossack Sotnya (organized by members of Ukraine's Cossack Organizations Council)	Overseeing the Cossack Redut barricade (from the Main Post Office to Horodetskoho Street)[c]
5th Sotnya		Overseeing the 5th barricade (Horodetskoho Street)[d]
6th Sotnya	Medical Sotnya *Shvydka Medychna Dopomoha Maidanu*	One of the organized groups that offered medical aid to revolutionaries
7th Sotnya	"Sotnya Leva" (Lviv region)	Maidan Stage, 1st barricade on Institutska Street
8th Sotnya	"Afghan sotnya" (war veterans of the Soviet war in Afghanistan)	Multiple locations
14th & 15th Sotni		Protecting protesters, and in reserve for when needs arise
Jewish Sotnya	Identity-based	General participation
Women's Sotnya		Feminist message, general participation

a Yurchenko In Ukrainian Institute of National Memory 2015: 146.
b Samooborona Maidanu, 3 Sotnia, https://www.facebook.com/pg/3sotnya/about/?ref=page_internal (accessed 14 July 2020).
c Yurchenko In Ukrainian Institute of National memory 2015: 146.
d Yurchenko In Ukrainian Institute of National memory 2015: 146.

revolution. For example, sotnya four was organized by members of the Ukrainian Cossack Organizations Council, which relied on existing leadership and promoted revolutionary participation among the members; the fifteenth sotnya was organized on the basis of the Ukrainian version of the Boy Scouts organization, Plast.[51] War veterans of the Soviet war in Afghanistan formed the eighth sotnya, claiming their battleground experience was now needed to protect Ukraine's civilians from the state.

Zhinocha Sotnya, or the Women's Hundred, was formed by female revolutionaries to promote a feminist message within the Maidan resistance movement (see chapter 6). Revolutionaries emphasized a democratic, even organic, selection process of sotni leaders: "There was a barricade, people organized there, did something, and among them appeared a leader."[52] As Parubiy started going through Maidan on 1 December, he "started giving numbers to barricades and sotni,"[53] as well as asking who was chosen as a sotnyk (sotnya leader).[54] There were five initial sotni, but the number grew throughout the winter months, and by 13 February 2014, there were thirty-nine sotni. Samooborona leadership included the commandant, sotni leaders, and komendatura – seven to ten persons responsible for information, food, clothing, registration, defence, and other training.[55] Sotnya leaders gathered daily to exchange information and participate in "constant dialogue."[56] Following the samooborona leadership meetings, there were meetings of the sotnya leadership, which included a sotnyk, a quick-response team, and *chota*[57] leaders, where samooborona leadership decisions were discussed and alternative solutions contemplated.[58]

In addition to the money each sotnya collected in donations and received from business sponsors, they usually received food, clothing, and a modest sum from the collected public donations received at the Trade Union building headquarters, which could be spent on lighting for their tent, phones and phone accounts, cigarettes, and other needs.[59] Sticks and bats were often self-made, protection gear included bikers' equipment or leather protection, hand-made and donated by the public.[60] Some shields were appropriated from police during the Hrushevskoho events.[61]

One of the most critical tasks for samooborona and other protesters was *vystoiaty*: to maintain protests, and prevent violent dispersal by the police, who almost always attacked during the night. During the day, revolutionary-controlled territory always had a considerable number of protesters, activists, and visitors, but most would leave while subway trains were still running. The danger of being there at night was the threat of *razgon* (dispersal). By 6 p.m., most would leave Maidan to make it to the subway.[62]

Security issues covered by samooborona, as well as those not affiliated with the self-defence units, included controlling access to revolutionary-controlled territory on the Maidan Square, securing a number of revolutionary-controlled buildings from open public access, and turning away intoxicated people (the use of alcohol was discouraged). Entrance to revolutionary-controlled buildings, including the Ukrainian House and the Trade Union building, required proof of affiliation with one of the revolutionary groups housed inside, whether it be the medics or samooborona headquarters. The "quick response team," for example, could be called (mostly at night) to handle a drunk person: "he kept taking his clothes off, and we'd dress him ... We talked to him for almost four hours, until he left."[63] Samooborona also handled occasional internal fights.[64]

Former military troops, police, and even Berkut members were involved in defence training, including "how to stand together, how to hold the crowd, how to prevent [the police] from pulling one of us out, how to handle sticks and shields, possible forms of attack and retreat. For example, if retreat is necessary, one shouldn't run but slowly back away while facing the enemy, to prevent leaving one of your friends, who would be arrested."[65]

The quick-response team also responded to defend the activists from police and titushky raids outside of the Maidan territory, and engaged in fights with titushky. For example, the team responded when titushky started destroying protesters' cars on Mykhailivska Street.[66] Samooborona and AutoMaidan ran occasional investigation operations: certain teams researched locations of titushky groups, apprehended them, and brought them to Maidan for questioning. A member of the third sotnya described:

> Sometime in the middle of January – at the time when Hrushevskoho was burning – titushky were bused in en masse. Together with AutoMaidan, we drove around to visit hostels, dormitories, gave our phone numbers, and asked to let us know if there will be big groups of suspicious people. Sometime at night, January 21–2 we received a call. All AutoMaidan [folks] had radio transmitter Zello, since cellphones were tapped. Via Zello, we were told the address, and decided to go ... we apprehended some 280 persons. Brought them to Maidan. Then took them to the Trade Union [building]. After questioning them, we either handed them to police, or just let them go. What were we supposed to do with them? Among those titushky there

> were some thirty who had aggressive demeanour. Yelled chants, threatened, behaved in an inadequate way. So we made them clean the grounds. Talked to them, found out where they were from, how they coordinate, gather. Then we received information about their superiors, and called them. We said we were letting their people go – they had to come and pick them up.[67]

Another revolutionary described getting information about titushky whereabouts via Zello radio transmission: "A taxi driver would see a group of athletic-looking people,[68] near a certain subway station, it was obvious – they were paid … We'd jump out of nowhere, beat them up, and pull them by the ears to find out how much they were paid. [They said] they were instructed to come and scare those *maidanutye* (a derogative Russian term for Maidan revolutionaries)."[69] A member of the "special op" team, which had members from multiple sotni, recalled the operations and violent tactics they used: "We went through sewers, got into their territory at night. I spent hours in Maryinsky Park in white camouflage. We'd wait for a policeman, grab him and throw him down, take him to the Ukrainian House." The captured policemen would then be (possibly violently) interrogated to gather information, and often traded for arrested revolutionaries after contacting Ukraine's intelligence agency.[70]

AutoMaidan

The civic initiative group AutoMaidan (from *automobile*) encompassed many people, and played multiple notable functions during the revolution. In a way, it was exemplary of the multi-systematic Maidan resistance: the drivers' group started on 1 December as a show of protest, and continued to organize protest drives and actions during the winter months; facing police violence against protesters, however, the drivers used their cars as a form of physical protection and to form obstacles against state agents. As described earlier, AutoMaidan was formed from local automobile club members who drove through Kyiv, collecting a caravan of over 200 cars, in order to show protest against police violence on 30 November. In addition to stating the civic position on 1 December, they also played an active role in agitating other Kyivans to join; as Dmytro Bulatov described: "We drove around the city, calling people to come to Maidan." Within a couple of days, they had taken on another function – protection of the protesters against police violence. At first, AutoMaidan drivers coordinated their efforts to prevent Berkut forces from reaching the Maidan protesters:

> We [parked] cars in between the Cabinet Ministry and Verkhovna Rada (parliament) – to block Berkut buses from reaching Maidan Square, and [prevent them from] beating people ... We stopped our cars [in the middle of] the street, lifted the hoods, pretending something was broken, to avoid [immediate] jailing. If ambulances or pregnant women, or other people, had to go through – we'd immediately organize and move to the side – but not for police cars ... In this way, we were trying to defend people in the city centre, and at the same time, we showed protest. It was a civic position ... We were protecting people, we didn't have any other way of doing this. Policemen came daily threatening us, claiming that we'd have serious problems, that we'd be jailed.[71]

After a week, Maidan protesters' presence grew, and while the revolutionaries started building barricades on the Maidan, police installed barricades using buses, and AutoMaidan activists could no longer access the street. Their resistance efforts, however, only intensified and involved more complex operations. One major AutoMaidan function remained protecting the physical security of the revolutionaries. AutoMaidan drivers offered free rides to Maidan participants – not only delivering transportation aid, but preventing the arrest of those carrying Maidan-related items, such as firewood, tires, etc. As described earlier, AutoMaidan activism also involved driving the injured, searching for titushky, and guarding the hospitals. They offered protection to buses that drove revolutionaries from other regions, as police would not let them get through to Kyiv – a large quantity of cars around such a bus physically prevented police cars from pulling it over. Many car owners joined AutoMaidan, driving protesters and transporting tires and other revolutionary gear.

AutoMaidan also became an ardent and noticeable critic of the Yanukovych administration. As was discussed in chapter 2, AutoMaidan activists organized a protest caravan to drive to Yanukovych's residence at the end of December. AutoMaidan activists also organized a number of protest drives to other members of the presidential administration, mocking their corrupt and anti-democratic policies and practices. Bulatov's team drove to Prime Minister Azarov's residence, delivering a funeral wreath to "commemorate the death of his political career."[72] AutoMaidan revolutionary resistance activism, including open and notable criticism of politicians, led to severe state persecution of their members in the form of violence, kidnapping, torture, detentions, and destruction of their cars by Berkut and pro-state mercenaries. As described in chapter 3, Bulatov was kidnapped, interrogated, tortured, and left to die, eventually surviving the attack.

Legal Aid

Over seven hundred lawyers mobilized to offer pro bono help to protesters. While many lawyers relied on a revived professional organization to connect with clients, new civic initiatives were formed to aid with the task. Prior to the revolution, the Center for Civil Liberties attracted only tens of lawyers per year for volunteer work. During the revolution, however, the centre's initiative, EuroMaidan SOS, which was created to link the detained with free legal help, attracted approximately five hundred lawyers for the cause. A lawyer-led initiative created during the revolution, AutoMaidan's Legal Protection, attracted over forty lawyers to assist over three hundred AutoMaidan activists. In post-revolutionary Ukraine, some lawyers continue to offer free help for Maidan activists and families of those killed to receive state compensation.

A vital-cause lawyering strategy in revolutionary Ukraine was constant mobilization to counteract state repression. Defence lawyers, as well as volunteers and members of civic groups who mobilized to organize legal help, adopted "revolutionary mode," working twenty-four hours a day and withstanding subzero temperatures while waiting outside of court buildings. Lawyers conducted systematic documentation of injuries, even in a growing atmosphere of fear where some journalists were unwilling to assist in recording abuses.[73] As discussed in detail in chapter 2, lawyers in Ukraine aided detainees, often persuading them that challenging state actions in the courts is a vital mode of resistance. Lawyers often appealed court decisions of pre-trial sentences, continually exposing judicial violations in court.

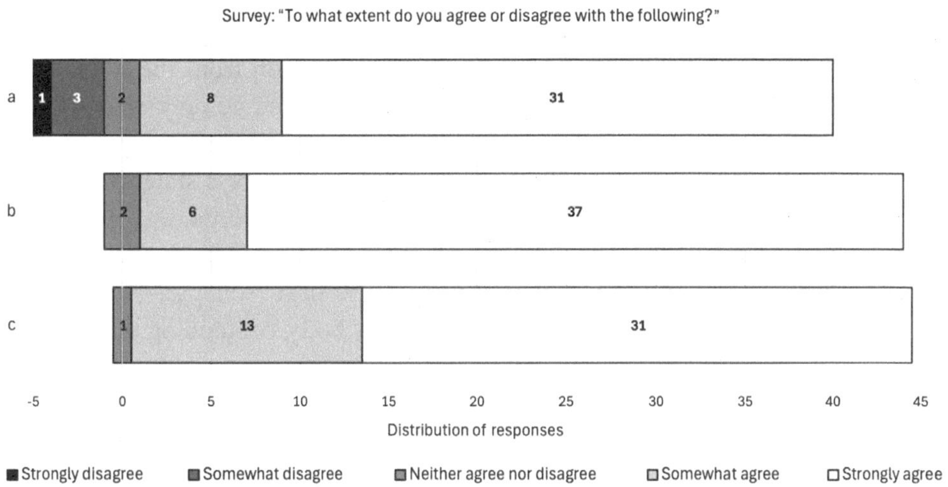

a. The efforts of lawyers to defend the detained protesters have confirmed my belief that violence by the state and arrests of demonstrators represented a violation of human rights.
b. Although lawyers defending detained protesters were not able to win each case, it was important for them to keep fighting in court to make it clear to the state that suppression of human rights is unacceptable.
c. State violence and detentions constituted an attempt to establish a new legal order, where human rights are violated to promote the will of the state.

Figure 4.4 Revolutionaries' opinions of cause lawyering and legal resistance.
Source: Author's survey of Maidan protesters.

Some of the most successful exploitations of the state's legal facade were lawyers' attempts to prevent detentions in hospitals. Police often raided hospitals after each round of attacks against protesters. Defence lawyers would take turns being on duty at hospitals where injured protesters were treated, ready to face the police. While riot police on the streets could corner groups of people and detain them en masse, hospitals provided a new space of interaction. Police had to face only a few detainees at a time, giving an opportunity for lawyers to demand documents necessary for lawful detention, as well as opportunity for hospital staff to object to the arrest on the grounds of the seriousness of injuries. Moreover, the hurdles of detention procedures in hospitals gave time for lawyers and activists to contact the press, whose appearance added pressure on individual police.

Lawyers' resistance to the state's imposition of new terms of legality also lay in their construction of a discourse with the detainees. Even when bargaining with the state, lawyers insisted on reassuring their clients that any legal violations lay on the side of the state. Lawyers crafted information hand-outs for the protesters, emphasizing that (1) a peaceful gathering does not require permission from the state, only a notification; and (2) a state official is allowed to do only what is provided by the law, while a private citizen is allowed to do anything that is not prohibited.[74] Likewise, various lawyers' press statements affirmed that the state was the violator of constitutional order. An open statement by lawyers and legal activists asserted that the "use of unlawful violence by Ukrainian authorities" was akin to "legal collapse."[75] Lawyers expressed no confidence in the judiciary body, contending that it supported "doubtful, unprincipled, and dangerous government actions rather than protect[ing] human rights and freedoms."[76]

Revolutionary activism included the continuing presence of protesters at the trials of those who were detained. The leaders of social initiatives promoted the idea of protesters attending and monitoring court hearings. Attempts to place pressure on the courts did not cease even after the state engaged police to prevent the public from being present at hearings. A representative of Euromaidan SOS described their co-operation with the public:

> We constantly informed protesters of the locations of each trial … It was difficult because they would often be moved to a different location at the last minute – to make it more challenging for the public to keep track … Young people, who were not let inside the courtroom, stayed outside the building and continued to chant: "Individual rights above all." Local Kyiv residents provided food and hot tea … to the chanters.[77]

Ukraine's lawyers didn't limit themselves to lessening the pain of detained protesters; they actively challenged the state's newly promoted terms of legality. The state attempted to legitimize repression by trying activists in court. Lawyers fought against the state by exploiting the legal facade of trials. They used the court setting to expose judicial violations, appeal sentences, and publicize state violations of constitutional order. Lawyers in Ukraine actively resisted the newly imposed legal structure and shaped social conceptions of legal rights, greatly contributing to the revolutionary resistance against Yanukovych's attempted formation of an authoritarian regime.

Education, Information, Entertainment

The Stage

The stage *(stsena)* played a vital role in maintaining protests, information exchange, and social discourse. Famous singers, like Ruslana and Vakarchuk, sang there in freezing temperatures to keep people on the Maidan. Religious and community leaders offered communal prayers, activists called for action, opposition politicians described their negotiations with the presidential administration (and were often booed off the stage). One of the most common uses for the stage was logistical announcements: the need for certain food and medical supplies for certain groups. Stage time slots were allocated to different groups at all hours. At night, with less competition for stage time, activists often set up "open mic" sessions, during which people could express their views on the state or the Maidan movement, whether positive or critical. It was from the stage that activist Parasyuk announced on 20 February, after the state shootings, that the Maidan resistance movement would not give up, and would head to the presidential residence, causing Yanukovych to flee the country.

Open Maidan University

A smaller stage was set up by activists for general education purposes. Called Maidan University, it served the function of maintaining protests by providing a form of entertainment, but it appeared to mostly serve its intended function: social intellectual discourse. Its origin showcases the Maidan approach: if you'd like to help the resistance, bring your ideas and talent. One activist, decided to bring her passion for public education to Maidan, setting up an "educational platform with interesting lectures and films … because students were the major force behind the resistance, so Maidan had to have an educating element." Her partner, a successful businessman, soon joined by other volunteers, helped to bring her innovative idea to life: using his tech-savvy business contacts, they arranged for a small stage to be brought to the Kyiv centre. Even the processes of bringing this stage to the Maidan involved state–society exchange: "As they were delivering the stage to the Maidan square … police stopped them … and we

Figure 4.5 A student revolutionary studying on a burned-out bus, 24 January 2014. This image became symbolic of a large number of university-educated people participating in the revolution.

went there, trying to explain that the driver had the right to go into the centre of the city. The protests are taking place, and you need to let us express our ideas."[78] The activists stood their ground. And even though the police did not give permission, the activists managed to deliver the stage the next day, setting it up overnight with the help of Maidan volunteers. "We'll never forget it: we set up a stage in the middle of Kyiv without any approval of city administration, but at that time we did not consider the Kyiv city administration to be legitimate, because they went against the people."[79] Thus, multiple uncoordinated acts of civil disobedience became a vital form of communicating social refusal to accept new terms of authoritarian legality. Certain tensions of human exchange during grassroots organization were often overcome due to the common cause shared by the participants: it had to be "agreed with the [main] political Stage, to avoid being accused of being traitors who organize their own Maidan." The project ended up attracting thousands of listeners, promoting intellectual exchange about politics, economy, and society – even if attracting a different crowd than anticipated by the originators:

> We organized ... over two hundred lectures during the Maidan events, inviting not only university professors but also many experts and successful Ukrainians ... The first lecture was given by Pavlo Sheremeta, who became the minister of economics after the Maidan Revolution ... There was a wide variety of topics, for example, 'organic marketing' – how to distribute the message through social media, engage famous people, send your friends, engage all people all over the country; to our surprise, the lectures attracted mostly elderly people rather than university students. People from different parts of the country – cities, villages ... We got the feeling that people lack communication with experts and influential people. People were very engaged, listened attentively, even during freezing temperatures. [Most] lectures had around two thousand listeners, and approximately the same amount joined the live online stream.[80]

While it was set up to engage students, Maidan University became an arena for social discourse about state–society relations and civic engagement. To maintain this social exchange, the organizing activists invested efforts to support the audience. "While people were listening, me and the guys were running around, getting tea and bringing it to the listeners, so they could keep listening. We bought plastic foam, as it was cold to stand on the granite – to allow them to stand there longer; and with time we set up a fire pit, so people could keep themselves warm." The project resulted in wider co-operation: the nearby Oliva restaurant began providing water. Businesses started helping financially, including alumni of the Luhansk business school.

Kraplya v Okeani/Strike Plakat

Artists played an active role in channelling a social message to the state. Numerous art projects were carried out by volunteer artists, who drew posters and street art, and created projects that scorned state political repression and mass corruption and emphasized the pro-democratic nature of the resistance. Artists were involved in doing make-up for protesters during the December March of Millions – people walked with their mouths painted to appear "sewn" shut, criticizing censorship and repression under Yanukovych. Some artists worked together to aid the protesters in developing efficient ways of communicating with the state. For example, artists from a Kyiv marketing firm stopped their usual business to devote all their time and effort to the resistance, creating *Kraplya v Okeani* (Drop in the Ocean), also known as *Strike Plakat* (Strike Poster). One of the artists behind the project described the process of aiding the social protest:

> I came to Maidan after students were beaten … when we started feeling that it is wrong and unjust, and we ought to show protest. That very night we threw ourselves into making poster drawings … The first night we met with many other … artists, painters, those working in advertising; we continued discussion over Facebook, sent each other images. It was difficult to simplify the [resistance] message; eventually, we decided on *Ia Kraplya v Okeani* (I'm a Drop in the Ocean) as the most concise. In the morning we got wooden boards, and were cutting them out. We were all afraid … we all understood we could go to jail, at a minimum … We gave away around two hundred of those posters. That was the beginning of our design … We kept going every day. We pretty much stopped working with our clients, understanding this was more important. We just couldn't think of anything else. We started the initiative Strike Plakat – we had a Facebook community, where people could ask us for help … We decided to do something digital, so people could share. We made poster generator, because there just wasn't enough time. We created a digital platform on our website where … with a blue background, every person would appear as a drop, and people could write in, finishing the phrase, "I am walking [taking part in the March of Millions] because …" and everyone would add what they wanted. For example, "I am taking part in the protest … against corruption." "I am walking so I wouldn't be scared." Another, employing a play on words: "I am walking … so others won't sit [in prison]."[81] We came up with some ideas, but people picked up the idea really quickly … This … led to an electronic ocean … There were two or three thousand posters printed in one or two nights … There were also many funny ones. [For example], we created a file with instructions on how to recreate the Maidan New Year tree at home: you could print the pieces,

> and attach to wooden boards at home … This had many shares [on social media]. My parents from Lutsk described … [someone] putting this together, and they had no idea I was the artist behind the project.[82]

Artists enabled effective social communication with the state. As Klubnikin described, they spent hours, days, designing the most concise and elegant message to represent social grievances. Their task was to apply their professional training and experience to come up with the most succinct expression of the protest message. The state–society dialogue itself became celebrated. As the artist described:

> Another favourite poster of mine: "Never before has a little printer felt like such a hero." Indeed, it was fun to see these [Kraplya posters] on the Maidan: you could see that they were printed on old poor-quality printers, but it made the experience even more emotional. Another one we made: "Information is our main defence" with an iPhone pictured as a shield, because filming the truth [was a form of defence] … And it was true: journalists, for example, played a huge role [in the revolution].[83]

The artists' initiatives contributed to intra-society and Ukraine–Russia dialogues about the aims and means of the revolution: "We built on our professional contacts … and produced short documentaries … to tell a story about the 'little' people. For example, one about folks from Mukacheve, who got together and were cooking *bohrach* on Maidan." As the activist described, they were counteracting Russian propaganda by showing that these people were contributing without any direction. However, their main task was "to inspire people who felt insignificant."

Those behind the resistance art were in danger of prosecution. It was particularly difficult to find print shops willing to take the risk. As the artist recalled:

> If you were found with a poster like that, you'd be jailed immediately. You would get five years. So if Maidan had not won, we'd all be imprisoned right now … Many print shops refused to print the posters. We printed posters with an image of a tree covered with blood – to symbolize the police beating, and images

> of Yanukovych with a red [clown] nose … That was considered brave. We printed these posters at night, we didn't even know where it was printed: we didn't know the person and never met them, somebody just recommended him; he asked for images to be emailed to him, and then he would send the printed posters by taxi courier.[84]

Not only did the activists take the risk of designing and printing anti-state posters, they found creative ways of disseminating the messages by making them appear to be supported by the state:

> There was a video ad that ran in one of the cities, featuring resistance art, such as "*Kraplya v Okeani* will change Ukraine." A mayor didn't understand that it was revolutionary. As soon as they realized, they stopped it, but the effect was powerful … Since we'd printed advertisements for the city before, we had keys to the official bus stop displays. We found an empty one right next to the mayor's office, and, covering our faces, placed the poster picturing Yanukovych with a red nose. This was shocking: an official venue … making fun of the president. It gave an image of substantial support from above, so it impressed people, and had a strong effect: people would even take pictures of this "official" poster.[85]

Communicating the revolutionary message to the state became a form of art itself by using multiple forms of visual expression, activating multiple talents, and, most importantly, becoming an expression of genuine social frustration: an artistic state–society dialogue.

Streaming

Most media sources were controlled by the state, preventing the spread of truthful information. Moreover, Russian media invested in propaganda to provide purposefully misleading information about the revolution's goals and efforts.[86] At the same time, the viewership of actual events was increasing in Ukraine and abroad. To accommodate the demand, and to counteract Ukrainian state and Russian propaganda, volunteers organized direct streaming from the square. Direct streaming of the events on the Maidan Square was used to inform about the need for additional support against police attacks:

> There was no streaming technology available, so we set up people to take turns staying next to the camera … Direct streaming added hope that if the [Berkut] storm of Maidan began, people would see it and could save us. A Spilno.tv link was [created] and provided on the Euromaidan site. Because of our example, Hromadske, Espresso TV also did live streaming. When the first clashes on Hrushevskoho started, we set up, starting with one camera, and one tent. By the New Year we had a full studio, three cameras, and invited lots of people to provide commentary on what's going on. Thus, we developed new technology for civil journalism. After six million views, we received a bill from the streaming company for $200,000 since we did not have advertising to rely on. We said, "Sorry, we are having a revolution, and have no money." When they saw what we did with the streaming, they wrote off our debt, in return for permission to use our approach – to stream civil action. We allowed them, and set up a school of streaming. And on Maidan, everyone began to stream. We provided "how to" booklets for others. During the first police storm, on December 11, only two thousand people were present at the beginning. We had approximately 100,000 viewers. I described what was happening during the storming [of protests by police]. Taxi drivers were driving people to Maidan. In just a few hours, thousands of people came. We understood that streaming gave a colossal mobilization strength. We didn't have censorship, video editing, just streaming. We'd ask people from different countries to walk with us, and provide commentary – as a result, people provided commentaries in seven different languages. Overall, more than sixty million people watched us. In addition, our stream was also used by BBC, CNN, Al Jazeera.[87]

Ukrainian revolutionaries' commitment to the revolutionary cause led to the discovery of multiple methods of digital communication, which empowered the resistance movement. As described earlier, social media was another essential tool to organize logistics, but also to inform about state repression and to call for social action. Tetyana Lokot's work about Maidan activists' use of social media shows how it was used to share information and present witness accounts of the events (in different languages), organizing protests and social networks. Lokot concludes that in the case of the Maidan Revolution, digital media augmented the dissent movement by bridging the physical space of the protests with global audiences and "enabling different modalities of participation."[88] The account in this chapter of the revolutionaries' creative use of digital media for grassroots mobilization additionally demonstrates the evolution of social skills to communicate the anti-state message and galvanize the resistance movement.

The Press

The opposition TV network, sponsored by anti-state economic elites, provided coverage of the resistance. A number of journalists also tried to pressure the editors of state-owned media, with some quitting in protest.[89] While state-owned channels avoided coverage of revolutionary events, and/or presented them as disorderly vandalism and right-wing violence, truthful coverage, or just streaming of the Maidan Square, empowered revolutionaries, and became a resistance in itself. Internet and YouTube streaming allowed affordable coverage of the events. The most popular video internet source was Hromadske, led by famous journalist Mustafa Nayyem. Nayyem was also known for his Facebook post calling for protests against Yanukovych's refusal to sign the EU agreement in November. (Famously, Nayyem's post encouraged Kyivans to come to the square "to drink some tea.") Hromadske provided video coverage and interviews conducted in a small Kyiv studio.

As described earlier, journalists played a vital role in publicly shaming police to prevent detentions. When police prevented detained protesters in hospitals from getting legal help, attorneys would notify the Euro-Maidan SOS. Their representatives would then contact the press, which were often successful in placing pressure by filming police actions, leading to lawyers being allowed to see the detainees or even preventing detention.[90] As one activist described: "We received subpoenas in the mail, were called in to be interrogated by the police. I was called several times, I invited journalists every time. They filmed how I would enter the police building, so if I were jailed, it would not be done in silence."[91]

Opposition Politicians

Opposition politicians, including Klychko, Yatsenyuk, and Tiahnybok, became visible due to the media spotlight on their participation in negotiations with Yanukovych's government. They were often referred to as "the leaders of the opposition" in international media, because of their leadership of the opposition parties: UDAR, Batkyvshchyna, and Svoboda. However, this reference misleadingly suggested that these politicians led resistance efforts on the Maidan. In reality, they were participants on equal footing with the revolutionaries, as the organizing of Maidan efforts took place without their leadership or consent. Their speeches on the Maidan stage were often booed by those on the square, and their negotiated agreement with the presidential administration in February after the live shooting of protesters was rejected by revolutionaries (see chapter 3). In fact, Klychko knelt on the Maidan stage after signing the agreement, "to ask revolutionaries for forgiveness." Nevertheless, opposition politicians played a notable role in presenting the case of the Maidan resistance, setting up the stage, informing the resistance of parliamentary decisions, and at times liberating the detained.

Politicians from opposition parties and activists formed two parallel councils. As described earlier, the activist-formed civic councils were prominent in coordinating grassroots resistance efforts. Opposition politicians formed their own council, *Rada Maidanu*, inviting select activists to participate, and attempting (but not succeeding) to establish their leadership over resistance efforts.[92] The presence of multiple councils, both maintaining revolutionary organizational and communication functions, reinforced the decentralized nature of the revolutionary organization.

The most effective co-operation between activists and opposition parliamentarians involved parliamentarians' legal immunity. On 10–11 December, when the police took active measures to forcefully disperse the Maidan protesters, opposition parliamentarians and other public figures locked arms and stood in front of the protesters to prevent the police attack (see chapter 2). Similarly, while special police forces prevented the public from entering courtrooms (in violation of Ukraine's legal code), they nevertheless chose to respect the immunity of parliamentarians. This was occasionally utilized by parliamentarians to support activists in courts. A Euromaidan SOS activist described:

"The Sokol Police force stayed on guard to prevent us from entering the courtroom ... A parliamentarian from the opposition party was walking into the courtroom, noticed me ... grabbed my arm and pulled me through the row of Sokols."[93] While there were notable disagreements between opposition politicians and the resistance movement at large, it didn't prevent their productive collaboration.

Intra-Society Dialogue: Negotiating Belonging

Multiple exchanges between the revolutionaries and society at large represented an intra-state dialogue. As discussed in earlier chapters, while resisting the state, revolutionaries continually debated the methods of resistance, developing ways to maintain peaceful means of resistance. As this chapter has emphasized, activists also invested a lot into communicating the aims of the anti-state movement to Ukrainian society at large, and debated the meaning of the democratic revolution among themselves. The democratic structure of the grassroots organization assured continuing pro-democratic discourse. Revolutionary discourse about individual rights vis-à-vis the state simultaneously involved a discussion about rights of various minority groups within the larger Ukrainian society. While some succeeded at promoting their message, others failed. Religious groups and ethnic minorities asserted their belonging in the larger social milieu of Ukrainian citizens. Women played an active role, yet a feminist discourse failed to take root. Likewise, the LGBTQ community failed to promote dialogue of their social belonging during the revolution.

Ethnic and Religious Minorities

The leaders of Jewish, Muslim, and non-Orthodox Christian communities successfully asserted their belonging in Ukrainian society during the Maidan Revolution. The leaders of Jewish and Muslim minorities participated in communal prayers on Maidan's stage. A leader of an all-Ukrainian Jewish organization asserted in an interview to the press that Jewish people of Ukraine participate in the Maidan, and that the danger to the Jews of Ukraine comes not from the revolutionaries but from the violent state.[94] The statement of the Muslim community portrayed Ukraine as a state with "political, ethnic and religious tolerance," while questioning whether the current government would be likely to sustain this. Priests and pastors from non-Orthodox Christian religious organizations, including Catholics, Lutherans, and Evangelicals, were present on the Maidan, offering refuge and aid to the revolutionaries alongside the mainstream Ukrainian Orthodox church, indirectly claiming their belonging and role in Ukrainian society. The active and visible pro-revolutionary statements of the Jewish minority proved vital to counteracting Russian propaganda of the allegedly antisemitic nature of the Maidan movement. Crimean Tatars, predominantly Muslim, also showed support for Maidan and their distrust of Russian government claims – evoking memories of Stalin's genocide against Crimean Tatars.

Feminist Message

The feminist message was less successful. On one hand, women actively participated in every aspect of the Maidan resistance: they were organizers, medics, lawyers, cooks, barricade builders, Molotov cocktail makers. As Bulatov related, "I was proud of our women: many of them were among the AutoMaidan drivers." They participated in protest rides, transported injured people, tires, firewood, risking their lives as much as their male counterparts. The creation of *Zhinocha Sotnya*, the Women's Brigade, was meant to underline women's crucial role in the revolution to counteract a sexist message.[95] Indeed, as several interviewees pointed out, the pressure to reassert gender roles was tangible on Maidan: from male activists posting signs such as "Women, do something nice: clean up," to self-defence unit members actively preventing women from accessing the battle lines with police.[96] One self-defence fighter openly described to me that while they were impressed with "athletic women with cool skate-boarding helmets, demanding to enter the battle zone," they would actively oppose them, not letting women fight alongside them.[97] In their interviews with me, some women internalized the message, defending the sexist restriction on female participation in violent action, while others challenged this approach. For example, a female revolutionary, who actively participated in the last days of the revolution, putting herself in the line of fire to treat shooting victims, shared that her experiences and discussions with others convinced her that male fighters could get distracted from their main goal if they felt they needed to also protect the women next to them.[98]

The Maidan movement exposed a tangible divide among Ukrainian feminists: responding to sexism, including violence by ultra-right groups against those promoting leftist and feminist messages, was a daunting task. On one hand, the appearance of the Women's Brigade, which claimed a place within the self-defence militia, can be seen as a degree of success: a counteraction to the strong pressure to exclude women from militia formations. On the other, a lack of condemnation by the Maidan movement of attacks by thugs on those promoting "Europe means paid maternity leave" (even when these attacks were carried out by state-paid provocateurs)[99] weakened the feminist message. Attempts to reconcile with the Maidan movement by adjusting the feminist message also contributed to a divide among the Maidan feminists.[100] This divide highlights the diversity of protest voices and at the same time the complexity of the process of negotiating the multiple ideologies of the grassroots resistance movement.

Post-Soviet countries struggled to promote a feminist message as nation-building processes often go hand in hand with discourse that suggests sustaining traditional gender roles and heterosexuality as essential for a nation's survival.[101] The pro-democratic revolutionary discourse in Ukraine relied in many ways on nation-building discourse, emphasizing the overcoming of a post-Soviet colonial past. Moreover, the eventual embrace of violent means of resistance in response to state repression meant legitimizing nationalist groups that promoted violence and traditionalism.[102] On the other hand, however, as Sarah Philips observed, while women were purposefully excluded from more violent clashes with the police, their creative responses to these exclusions have "potentially paved the way for broadening the base of Ukrainian feminism, introducing women's rights principles to segments of the population previously reluctant to embrace feminism."[103] Thus, Maidan was an important arena for intra-society dialogue about feminism: on one hand, female participants visibly contributed to all spheres of Maidan mobilization – from protesters and AutoMaidan drivers, to medics, lawyers, and logistical operatives; but, on the other hand, traditional gender roles were supported when it came to women joining fighters. As Tatiana Zhurzhenko pointed out, Ukrainian post-Soviet feminists have been navigating "between nationalist myth and anti-nationalist critique," and it is the nation-building process that engages in reinterpreting cultural heritage, where women's voices participate in rethinking tradition, searching for new ways of "inventing the nation."[104] Arguably, even Durkheim – who talked of communal solidarity as a result of revolutionary social processes[105] – had sexist notions about women's potential contribution to social evolution.[106] This study shows that feminist and pro-LGBTQ discourses were ignored (or rejected) by a majority within the movement, and, as a result, the Maidan did not produce social change in these areas. While the Maidan did not embrace a liberal feminist message, women's active participation in multiple arenas of the resistance movement and challenge of the male-focused militia formations by proclaiming the presence of the Women's Brigade triggered the resurgence of feminist debate within Ukrainian society. Therefore, Maidan, as a democratic revolution, inevitably became a process of heightened social negotiation about nation building, the pressure of violent interaction with the state shortening the timeframe of socialization processes.

LGBTQ Discourse

One example of Maidan as an arena of negotiation for a common anti-state ideology is the experience of leftist groups. In an in-depth account provided by Channell-Justice, we see that rather than abandoning Maidan after their anti-neoliberal (anti-EU) and pro-LGBTQ discourse was rejected, leftists were galvanized by state violence and repression.[107] They embraced the Maidan movement by focusing on the "common enemy" – targeting the Yanukovych administration and adjusting their language to challenge the "police state."[108] These strategies were developed over a series of meetings, where they succeeded in switching from being seen as "provocateurs" to being at the forefront of promoting the language of being "anti-police, against repression, for the freedom of peaceful gathering, for the freedom of perspectives."[109] Maidan's plurality and continuous negotiations of belonging became its strength at negotiating a pro-democratic message. While sidelining feminist and LGBTQ narratives, the Maidan movement maintained multi-ethnic and multi-religious diversity, and focused on sustaining the general language of freedom from state repression.

Failure of the Ultra-Right to Hijack the Movement

The ultra-right group, Right Sector *(Pravyy Sektor)*, attempted to hijack the Maidan movement, with the intent to gain power after the Maidan succeeded in defeating the Yanukovych administration. Russian state propaganda claimed that the revolution was carried out by ultra-right forces (often referring to the presence of Right Sector), whose ideology allegedly played a leading role in the Ukrainian Revolution. As scholars of ultra-right movements in Ukraine have shown, however, Right Sector played a negligible role in the organization and outcome of the revolution.[110] Firstly, Right Sector membership in January and February 2014, of approximately 400 people in Kyiv (with not all necessarily present at Maidan), was quite small in comparison with the number of Maidan fighters. Samooborona self-defence units alone were estimated to have around 12,000 members. Notably, a large number of fighters were not members of samooborona or political party units. Survey results among the Maidan participants showed that only a small minority of protesters were members of any political party, 7.7 per cent in January 2014.[111] Crucially, Right Sector did not have an ideological influence on the Maidan participants, and failed to garner political support after the events: Dmytro Yarosh (the Right Sector party leader) received less than 2 per cent of votes in the 2014 presidential elections, and the party failed to meet the threshold to participate in the parliament.[112] Notably, another ultra-right party, Svoboda, despite receiving 10 per cent of votes prior in the 2012 elections, also failed to meet the parliamentary threshold in 2014.[113] It's also notable that ultra-right factions gained much less support from the Ukrainian electorate after the Maidan Revolution than the ultra-right did in other European democracies.

Right Sector's ultra-right ideology was strategically concealed from Maidaners and the public in general by the group's leadership. The group, in fact, did not exist prior to the revolution, and revolutionaries recalled that they were confused when they saw the group's symbols on the square in December.[114] It was formed from several ultra-right organizations, including UNA-UNCO, Trizub, and White Hammer.[115] They gained notable support from soccer ultras, who supported the idea of violent resistance. The ideologies of these founding groups, however, were purposefully veiled: Right Sector leaders emphasized anti-corruption messages, and gained attention as they claimed that political violence was the only solution to stop Yanukovych's regime. The most informative account of the inner politics and operations of Right Sector was provided by a Ukrainian journalist who joined the group undercover to investigate. He recalled in his interview with me:

> I was surprised how much they were trying to hide it [ultra-right ideology]. For example, when speaking to the British media, Yarosh corrected a nationalistic statement by another member, suggesting it would not be understood. "We'll just say we are against oligarchs, it will be better understood, as it hits closer to home."

This anti-corruption rhetoric proved somewhat effective. In her interview, a seventy-year-old woman, whose beliefs were not consistent with ultra-right ideology, said she considered joining Right Sector during the Maidan because her son-in-law had not been promoted to become a judge due to corruption. "I was ready to give them my contacts to become a member, but I think they needed younger and stronger people."[116] The group consistently hid the anti-democratic and racist undertones of their founding parties to fit into the larger pro-democratic, multi-ethnic resistance movement. A self-reported Right Sector member I interviewed in 2014 insisted the party tolerated no racism or ethnic hatred, as he himself spoke only Russian, coming from Kharkiv.[117] Another member of Right Sector told me that he loved listening to the speeches of US Senator Ted Cruz, in response to my request to describe his ideology.[118] As the undercover journalist described, there seemed to be little ideological cohesion among the members who occupied the Right Sector main quarters in the KMDA building:

> We had lots of free time, we played chess, had discussions … There was a complete ideological mix of people. Some argued that the revolution was an anti-imperialist movement, a continuation of the national independence movement, and that Ukrainians had to lead others in the anti-imperialist movement … There were veterans from Abkhazia … Chechnya, Transnistria … People of different religions. A [soccer] ultra from Belarus – who spoke only Belorussian, refused to speak Russian, saying he would not speak in the language of occupiers; he encouraged

> us not to speak Russian … There were people promoting pan-Slavic ideology against illegal immigrants, Muslims. There were Russian nationalists. There was a Donetsk unit with miners with bald heads and swastikas with knives on their belts; there was a neo-Nazi unit … As a Jewish person, I was terrified of seeing a person with a swastika across his whole back … Only in the last days of February, a week before the tragic events, Yarosh started leading ideological discussions, meetings, with one major message: "Maidan is going to hell, Yatsenyuk and other leaders are negotiating with the state, we will take them down. We will not escalate now, because we are now with them, but remember … as nationalists we can bring order." *They made sure, though, not to let this message out.* I understood that the promised "order" was not at all what people who were fighting for the revolution had in mind.[119]

As discussed, social discourse regarding the use of political violence continued throughout the revolution. Peaceful discourse within the movement prevailed until the state began using live ammunition on protesters, whereas the ultra-right unequivocally advocated the use of violence from the beginning. As described in previous chapters, Maidan activists were able to suppress the provocations, and while violent clashes occasionally took place, general support for political violence remained low among Maidaners until the state engaged in the most severe repression in late February. As a result, most Right Sector members spent their time in their headquarters, on the fifth floor of the occupied Trade Union building throughout December and January. As the undercover journalist described:

> The Right Sector folks picked many internal fights, mainly with Svoboda [another ultra-right political party]. We'd be ordered to get dressed, get shields ready after some Svoboda and *Pravyy Sector* (Right Sector) people had a quarrel … or go storm the Kyiv City Administration building, because Svoboda people were allegedly trying to kick out UNA-UNCO [a nationalist group]. We got ready, but the commanders negotiated [a solution], so it all ended. We were on night patrol, walking on the Maidan Square, looking for suspicious or drunk people. I was lucky, my

> commander was a young guy, so we didn't have to catch anybody; when we saw drunks, we just talked to them, shamed them. Once, Pravyy Sektor caught a *titushka*, he was dragged upstairs and beaten. This was the scariest thing: people [with whom] you had ideological discussions turned into those who just wanted to beat somebody.

While they hid their intentions to promote illiberal order after the Maidan, Right Sector continued to openly agitate political violence. Ukrainian far-right parties and groups were mentioned in 20 per cent of media coverage about confrontational and violent Maidan protest events, as well as in some media coverage of assaults on state administration buildings, Lenin monuments, etc. in other parts of the country. This led Ishchenko to conclude that Right Sector played an important role in violently dismantling Yanukovych's power, particularly in western Ukraine.[120] As he recognizes, however, while the Maidan Self-Defence groups were notably more numerous, and played an active role in violent clashes with police, they were reported by the media in only 6 per cent of violent protests and in just 5 per cent of confrontations and violence together, as they were likely not recognized as an institutional entity.[121] Scholars contesting the level of Right Sector's contribution to the Maidan's victory, point out that among the hundreds of revolutionaries who died during the Maidan events, not a single one was a member of Right Sector.[122] While the level of Right Sector's contribution to the Maidan's violent clashes can be debated, their presence can't be denied. However, their role in compelling Maidaners to adopt violence is questionable. As the detailed discussion in previous chapters demonstrates, attempts to maintain peaceful resistance were a part of conscious tactics, employed by multiple Maidan activists. Their efforts decreased in response to severe state repression, which triggered a growing support for political violence among Maidaners in general as the only means to prevent the consolidation of a terror regime. In other words, I argue that the Maidan would have turned violent without the presence of Right Sector or other ultra-right groups. Moreover, without the use of political violence, the Maidan most likely would have lost, allowing Yanukovych to assert authoritarian rule, including severe repression of civil liberties.

Finally, whatever support Right Sector managed to gain from other Maidan activists, it was not only through emphasizing the use of political violence, but also through strategic veiling of their underlying ideology. Similar to leftists on the Maidan, ultra-right groups participated in the Maidan social dialogue, adjusting their message as they emphasized their desire to prevent Yanukovych from usurping power and promising to tackle corruption as part of their political agenda. Unlike the leftists, however, Right Sector had a plan to hijack the Maidan movement and institutionalize their illiberal agenda once Yanukovich was removed. As they hid their true intentions, they managed to gain some support for their promotion of political violence, which was eventually embraced by the revolutionary movement, albeit for reasons not attributable to the efforts of ultra-right groups. However, Right Sector's plan to take over power after the Maidan was not realized. As the Maidan succeeded in ousting Yanukovych, the movement's pro-democratic consensus, which focused on ending political repression and promoting civil liberties, dominated post-revolutionary democracy in Ukraine. It is within the structure of democratic institutions and fair elections that Right Sector had to compete for power, and failed.

Activism to Combat Russian Propaganda

While Ukrainian revolutionaries focused their energy on criticizing the actions of the Ukrainian government as undermining citizens' freedoms, there was an understanding that Yanukovych's step to sign the agreement with Putin's Russia was jeopardizing Ukraine's sovereignty. The latter, by default, meant a threat to Ukraine's civil rights. "Azarov's declaration that Ukraine is 'turning around,' and is entering a trade union [agreement] – made me even more cautious," shared one protester.[123] Another activist recounted his concerns about Putin's influence: "It wasn't about the quality of journalistic standards, but about the existential threat of any left-overs of freedom of the press in Ukraine. This was obvious from the steps made by Yanukovych, who was calculating Putin's actions in Moscow."[124] Another stressed Russia's threat to Ukraine's sovereignty: "While everyone else – protesters, Ukrainian politicians – were unclear about their role and strategies, Russia was a solid actor. Even at the beginning of December, we discussed that Russia's geopolitical interest lies in the destruction of Ukrainian sovereignty."[125] Another protester put it succinctly, "It's not that the EU agreement will make life easier for us, it's that it will make it harder for our politicians." In other words, a major positive outcome seen from Ukraine's closer economic co-operation with the EU were the restraints it would place on undemocratic moves by Ukraine's politicians. As shown in the first chapter, an overwhelming majority of Ukrainians supported economic ties with Russia. Aleksander Kwasniewski, who led a European Parliament monitoring mission in Ukraine, stated that the EU underestimated Putin's decisiveness, and did not offer a solid financial package to Ukraine.[126] Many Ukrainians seemed to have also underestimated the determination and nature of Russian interference. Indeed, Russia's annexation of Ukraine's territories – which was justified by the Russian government as an attempt to "save Russians from fascist Ukraine" – was difficult to fathom at the time. Many were still discovering the bold falsehoods Russian journalists were willing to construct when witnessing actual events. One activist recalled:

> An unknown journalist appeared at one of Parubiy's press conferences. She addressed me in Russian and asked, what it was about. I told her. At the time I didn't have any idea that we could have had hostile people … This woman called somebody and started saying that Parubiy and Maidan activists are getting ready to attack. I started poking her – I felt guilt since I was interpreting for her. Another journalist and I attempted to convince her: "You heard wrong, You misunderstood!" She hung up and rudely responded: "My dear, you think I don't know what I'm supposed to talk about?" …That's when we understood that there was an information war, and it was carried out in dishonest ways.[127]

While Russian government actions were seen as compromising Ukraine's sovereignty, the extent of Russia's aggressive attempts were unforeseen, and blunt falsehoods were met with shock.

The alarming discovery of continuous and purposeful deceptive propaganda carried out by Russian outlets resulted in two types of responses. Some activists gave up on their attempts to convince Russian citizens that they were being misled: "even then [in the beginning of December] it was clear: regardless of what we were going to do, Russian TV is going to falsify for itself whatever it sees as gainful." Others actively pursued ways to communicate with Russians. This led to multiple efforts, including art, posters, media, social media, and travel to convey the pro-democratic motivations of the revolutionary movement in Ukraine, and the fact that the movement had no anti-Russian or antisemitic sentiment.

The most notable communiqué during the Maidan Revolution in response to Russian propaganda was a large poster installed by activists on the Maidan New Year tree. The tree, which was at the centre of the controversy and used as justification for the initial violent dispersal was now used by protesters to post messages of resistance. In large letters, visible from across the square, it said, "We Love the Russians, We Hate Putin." The poster was not an act of spontaneity, but a thoughtfully developed action by the members of the Hromadsky Sektor – the most prominent Maidan civil initiative that organized communication for the resistance movement. As a person who participated in the project described, the poster was created on the basis of exchange with supporters of the Ukrainian revolution in Russia.[128]

Jewish Ukrainians made a number of statements in support of the revolution. An appeal to the international community regarding Russian propaganda about the social movement continued after the Maidan Revolution, in the face of the Russian annexation of Crimea. Notable Jewish public figures, scholars, artists, and businessmen published an ad in the *New York Times*, Canada's *National Post*, and Israel's daily *Haaretz*.[129] Addressed to Putin, it decried the falsehood of Russian propaganda about the treatment of minorities. Here is an excerpt from the March 2014 letter to Putin:

> The Russian-speaking citizens of Ukraine are not being humiliated or discriminated against, their civil rights have not been limited. Your certainty of the growth of anti-Semitism in Ukraine also does not correspond to actual facts. It seems you have confused Ukraine with Russia, where Jewish organizations have noticed growth in anti-Semitic tendencies last year. Yes, we are well aware that the political opposition and the forces of social protests who have secured changes for the better are made up of different groups. They include nationalistic groups, but even the most marginal do not dare show anti-Semitism or other xenophobic behavior … And we certainly know that our very few nationalists are well-controlled by civil

> society and the new Ukrainian government – which is more than can be said for the Russian neo-Nazis, who are encouraged by your security services.[130]

The tactic, utilized by the Ukrainian Jewish community, seems to have worked: Russian propaganda dropped its antisemitic claims, and focused instead on claims of supposed repression against ethnic Russians. To a large degree, the Kremlin started winning the information war, promoting falsehoods and relying on dehumanization of Ukrainians. The world knew little about the severe repression experienced in areas of eastern Ukraine, under the de facto control of Russia. Severe human rights violations, torture, and sexual violence against Ukrainians and supporters of Ukraine became the modus operandi. However, it is the accusations of alleged discrimination against Russian speakers in Ukraine that flooded the screens of Russian media (which RT widely telecasted in the Western world). The RT international television station became a crucial player in promoting the Kremlin line, infused with conspiracy theories.[131]

European countries played a very limited official role during the Maidan. Their major involvement focused on public statements condemning state violence. Thus, several EU parliamentarians were present on 1 December, addressing those on Maidan. Jacek Saryusz-Wolski of Poland said: "You are a part of Europe … so there's no exception for excessive police force [to be used against you]," adding that those guilty of violent police force should be brought to justice. The Council of Europe conducted investigations of state violence later on. The invasion of Ukraine soured Russia's relations with the West,[132] which imposed limited sanctions against Russia. Moreover, mainstream Russian media effectively engaged with far-right politicians, activists, and publicists in a number of European countries.[133] In co-operation with far-right politicians and publicists in the West, Kremlin propaganda widely promoted a justification of imperialistic Russian foreign policy.[134] Extensive trade ties remained, and the construction of Nordstream 2 was agreed upon. Western politicians maintained very civil relations with Putin. During the Minsk agreement negotiations, François Hollande justified Russian expansionism on the basis of the supposed desire of the local populations. Russian imperialism was accepted, while the Kremlin's dehumanization propaganda about Ukrainians took root in Russia, and partially succeeded in the West as well.

Conclusion

A negotiated pro-democratic consensus between the protesters facilitated volunteer and pro bono commitment and effective collaboration of the participants, overcoming a lack of financial and institutional backing. This chapter demonstrated that social resources were essential to Maidan mobilization. Most of the successful civic initiatives were formed by activists, unaffiliated with previously existing NGOs. Solidarity among participants, united to restrain the growing authoritarianism of the Ukrainian state, facilitated effective collaboration within the grassroots movement. Newly organized volunteer civic initiatives coordinated aid, provided information to protesters, organized social protest activities, mobilized the press, offered food, and secured safe transportation, housing, clothing, medical and legal aid. Maintaining the protests became an essential form of anti-state resistance. Not only did this help in overcoming the lack of financial and institutional backing, it united and focused revolutionary energy on battling the state in multiple areas of resistance.

The grassroots mode of communication also offered an arena for revolutionaries to debate the causes of mobilization and negotiate a pro-democratic consensus. As previous chapters showed, public statements and various forms of communication with the state emphasized the natural rights of citizens vis-à-vis a state that had turned to repression. Firstly, multiple volunteer groups, mobilized for the purpose of aiding protesters, including medics and lawyers, also played a fundamental role in communicating social grievances over violence and repression to the state and Ukrainian society at large. For example, medics organized press conferences, where the excessive violence and extra-legal means of state suppression were brought to light. Secondly, multiple informational, educational, and internet streaming initiatives became a forum to debate and negotiate an ideological consensus – from using the stage at night to express grievances, to initiating multiple media forums to counteract state misinformation. Thirdly, the dynamic of grassroots activists' interactions with the opposition political elite reflected negotiations over social trust of state agents, and the level of tolerance of state repression. More specifically, while opposition political elite posed themselves as social representatives, they were, in fact, distrusted by the revolutionaries, who set up grassroots social councils, parallel to those led by political forces. Contrary to Western media coverage, which portrayed the political opposition as leaders of the movement, they played little to no role in mobilizing the masses, but did occasionally contribute to protecting individual revolutionaries by leveraging parliamentarians' immunity to police/court regulations. The opposition political elite were eventually publicly rejected by the revolutionaries due to their negotiations with the Yanukovych administration after the shooting of protesters. Fourthly, the Maidan Revolution also became an arena of belonging. Jewish, Muslim, and non-Orthodox Christian communities successfully asserted their belonging by actively promoting their group identity as they publically opposed state repression and participated alongside other revolutionaries. Feminist and LGBTQ groups were less successful at incorporating their ideological cause into the Maidan movement. Finally, Maidan ideological negotiations involved leftists and ultra-right/nationalist groups, who were forced to adjust their message and instead emphasized their desire to prevent Yanukovych from usurping power. Notably, while ultra-right groups were visible during violent clashes with the police, they failed to hijack the Maidan movement and institutionalize their desired illiberal order. The pro-democratic majority consensus forced the Right Sector to consciously hide the ideological premise of their founding organizations, and subsequently obliged them to participate in the post-revolutionary democratic order (while failing to win any seats in parliament).

5

Revolutionary Socialization and Change

> January 19 – that's the day I remember the most. Nihoian dies, my wife was crying telling me this. I came to Maidan, it was snowing. I couldn't hold my tears. I saw the unity of the Ukrainian nation, regardless of religious or language differences ... There were three people next to me; they gave me a hug even though they'd never met me before. They said, "Don't cry, friend."

This personal story shared with me by an Azerbaijani immigrant to Ukraine gives insight into many aspects of the transformative power of the Ukrainian Revolution: an Azeri mourning the death of an Armenian, as they were both part of a resistance movement that superseded ethnic and other identities; a sense of community among strangers who came to Maidan. The movement forced the ousting of the Yanukovych administration, ending political repression, but the process of revolutionary socialization also affected social concepts of Ukraine, civic duty, and interpersonal trust for many of its supporters.

Political regime change is the major target of mass protests in a social revolution. The mobilization of millions of Ukrainians succeeded at preventing the consolidation of an authoritarian regime in the country and delivered a return to a democratic regime. During his presidency, Yanukovych continually expanded his powers via institutional and extra-legal means. The winter of 2013–14 witnessed a culmination of extra-legal means of suppression of dissenting opinion. Peaceful protesters were beaten and jailed without due process. Voting procedures in the parliament were severely violated to pass laws criminalizing social protest. As dissent continued, torture and live ammunition were used to suppress the opposition. When Yanukovych fled the country, extra-legal state violence against the dissent came to an end. Freedom of expression and freedom of the press were restored, allowing the elections that followed to be free and fair. A political regime is defined by the rules of the game: while many countries may showcase constitutions guaranteeing human rights, their de facto regimes are evident only through state practices. If the state systematically uses legal and/or extra-legal means to suppress political opposition, it is an authoritarian regime. The Ukrainian Maidan Revolution ended the systematic legalized suppression of the opposition and extra-legal state violence against dissent. The core features of a democratic regime – freedom of expression and of the press – were restored. Democratic elections were now possible.

On the basis of in-depth interviews with participants, this chapter examines how the experiences of Maidan shaped new attitudes for those who participated. Examination of the mechanism of these changes contributes to the perspective that the Maidan Revolution affected the growth of civil society by altering social values inherited from the totalitarian Soviet era. The revolutionary socialization process altered activists' perceptions of "civic duty" and communal trust, and, with this, the old Soviet legacy of state–society relations. Scholars have identified the following three major aspects of the Soviet legacy. First was a reliance on closely knit trust networks to obtain consumer goods and privileges during the Soviet era, which survived to cope with the harshness of oligarchic capitalism after the Soviet collapse.[1] Secondly, since the only sanctioned civic activism during the Soviet regime was state-bred, the problem in post-communist regimes lay not only in the lack of experience, but the fact that any form of civic activism was met with overwhelming social distrust.[2] The Maidan Revolution became a discussion forum for the active citizenry, where participants watched each other sacrifice time and security for a shared goal. These experiences led to a sense of community on the basis of democratic ideals, breaking the primal importance of existing trust networks. Thirdly, the experiences of Maidan participants transformed the Soviet legacy of social apathy, in which the totalitarian state was a guarantor of social goods.[3] Self-sacrifice in the face of visible risks to sustain a democratic regime transformed perceptions of "civic duty" among the revolutionaries. To put it in Durkheimian terms, the process of social integration creates a collective conscience[4] – and thus, as Goldberg observed during the Arab Spring in Egypt, the revolutionary process becomes a search to test and discover new moral communities.[5]

Political Transformation as a Result of the Revolution

The Maidan resistance movement had fundamental effects on the Ukrainian political regime. Revolution is an intensified dialogue between the state and the resisting masses, which determines the essence of resulting political and social changes. Essentially, if a mass resistance movement fails, it is categorized as a revolt, but its success makes it a revolution. Some have questioned whether the Maidan can be qualified as a revolution. Prior to the Maidan, Yanukovych came to power via free and fair elections, and a certain level of corruption existed before and after the events. This perspective, however, leaves out a crucial fact of the Maidan events: the Ukrainian government's unyielding authoritarianism leading up to the winter months of 2013–14, including dictatorial laws and severe state violence to repress its citizenry. Moreover, the scale of corruption of Yanukovych's state apparatus leading up to the repression, discussed in the introductory chapter, was substantially greater than in post-Maidan political development.

The most critical aspect of Maidan's success was the prevention of a consolidation of authoritarianism in the country. After passing the 16 January laws, which severely limited civil liberties, Yanukovych's state resorted to severe violence, torture, mockery, and shootings of protesters. As Maidaners asserted, if they had failed, Yanukovych's administration would have continued the use of violence against other forms of opposition, elections would not have been free and fair, and press freedoms would have been severely repressed. The victory of Maidan's social movement resulted in the ousting of Yanukovych and his cronies, restoration of the parliamentary-presidential constitutional regime, with free and fair elections, and widely exercised freedom of expression.

In the aftermath of the Maidan movement, electoral and civic rights have flourished in Ukraine. Voting in parliamentary and presidential elections has been consistently considered free and fair by international observers since 2014. Freedom House reported that "the collapse of the Yanukovych regime and release of Tymoshenko from jail opened the door to a flourishing of political party activity."[6] Notably, the ranking of Ukraine as "partially free" by Freedom House, and other organizations that analyze and rank state civic freedoms, was affected mainly by two factors: the rankings (1) often included the state of freedoms (or lack thereof) under "separatist-held" regions in the Donbas area, which are de-facto controlled by Russia; and (2) were affected by the Ukrainian state's choice to raid the offices of some pro-Russian newspapers and to bar Russian journalists from entering the country as a major critique of the state of press freedoms in the country. After the Russian full-scale invasion of Ukraine in 2022, and closer attention to the nature of Russian propaganda, which systematically incited mass violence against the people of Ukraine, Ukraine's minimal attempts may be seen now as justified means (even if inadequate) to counteract Russia's propaganda, rather than unfair repression of press freedoms in Ukraine.

Notably, the freedoms exercised after the Maidan Revolution in Ukraine (under government-controlled territories) radically differed from the areas under Russian occupation after 2014, as well as post-2022. Neither Crimea, which was openly controlled by the Kremlin, nor the rebel-controlled so-called "DNR" and "LNR" Donbas areas, which were de facto controlled by Russia, experienced political or civic freedoms. More specifically, in the areas of eastern Ukraine not controlled by the Ukrainian government, "there were no free and fair elections, or even meaningful laws and regulations of political institutions."[7] These regions went through an entire collapse of state institutions after coups led by Russian security services in 2014, leading to bandit-style rule and severe repression of a wide range of civil freedoms.[8] In Russian-controlled eastern Ukrainian regions since 2014, there was no due process, independent judiciary, or religious freedom; NGOs were not permitted to operate, and individuals have been systematically arrested for posting pro-Ukraine views on social media.[9] There have been numerous reports of torture and abuse in prisons, summary executions, and systematic sexual violence.[10]

Maidan was a revolution because it succeeded in radically affecting the political regime of Ukraine, preventing Yanukovych from establishing a terror regime (albeit losing some territories to Russia, where severe repression was rampant). Maidan's success was swift: it took Ukrainians only three months. The relative speed might also have contributed to the common overlooking of severe state repression occurring during the winter months, amounting to an authoritarian regime, leading to an underappreciation of Maidan's *revolutionary* success, in the full meaning of the term.

While corruption was certainly not eradicated, and many problematic aspects of local governing remained,[11] the Maidan Revolution achieved its task. Maidan also had a revolutionary effect on state–society relations via the empowerment of civil society. Unlike after the Orange Revolution, Maidan's state–society dialogue resulted in the consolidation of civil society in Ukraine. After the revolution, the state was constantly under intense scrutiny by civil society, which pushed for new regulations, anti-corruption programs, and decentralization reforms.[12] Ukraine has experienced heightened civic activism. Below is the analysis of the process of social change that took place during the Maidan Revolution.

The Process of Social Change During the Revolution

The analysis below uncovers aspects of socialization during the Maidan that affected participants' values. To maintain the protests and develop new strategies of resistance in response to growing state violence, activists continued gathering in the square, creating new initiatives to coordinate incoming masses, and watching each other sacrifice. These social interactions, intended to transform the state, created a heightened discussion forum about state–society and intra-society relations, and affected a sense of moral community. Revolutionaries created a social institution to engage with and limit the state – and with that, they developed a sense of self-power, overcoming the feeling of social weakness dominant in post-totalitarian societies. These transformations of perception included a newly gained appreciation for civic duty to their nation, now seen more as a diverse pro-democratic community. While it is challenging to disentangle the causal effects between the Maidan and the Russian invasion of 2014 on the growth of civil society in Ukraine, the discussion below uncovers the mechanism of change of perspectives among those who participated in the revolution.

Discussion Forum

The purpose of maintaining the protests was to continue pressure on the state to revert back to democratic means of governing. As discussed earlier, Maidaners debated whether the resistance should remain peaceful or become violent, and increasing state violence promoted greater creativity of resistance methods and co-operation within the movement.

The length of revolutionary engagement allowed the development of an in-depth discussion forum for participants. Since many revolutionaries sacrificed their time, money, health, and security, they were eager to discuss with each other what they were fighting for. In fact, many interviewees highlighted how much they enjoyed the conversations and exchanges constantly held among peers on the Maidan Square.

Participants were curious to learn about their fellow revolutionaries, to talk about life and politics. One activist stated: "I believe it was important to be present: it was interesting to watch people, sense Maidan's mood, understand what people think, and listen to what they are talking about."[13] A journalist I spoke with resigned from a national TV station during the Maidan, because he believed they purposefully provided inadequate coverage of the events. He noted how much he enjoyed being there as a participant, to observe "not for writing, but to understand the changes" that were taking place. Similarly, one of Ukraine's leading rock stars, Sviatoslav Vakarchuk, emphasized his own role as an ordinary participant: "I'd come as a participant, to listen to discussions."[14]

Maidan became a place to generate ideas about governing. While such social discourses always take place in societies (even authoritarian ones), they are more dispersed through time and space, inevitably distorted by the media, especially when media sources are controlled by the state. Maidan (the actual Maidan Square as well as other arenas of revolutionary resistance) was a space of social conglomeration devoted to political change – in other words, a small space for many people who are devoted to the same social purpose and struggle together. An exchange of ideas and heightened political and philosophical debates are inevitable. Many noted how inspired they were by meeting peers driven by ideas of better governing. One described the reasons she became engaged in the protests, "I am generally not for protests, tents … [but] I liked the people who were there, they had an idea, a bright thought, a wish to have a better country, better government."[15] Such interactions led to appreciation for the pro-democratic cause of the movement, prompting many to join in the fight against the state, in the name of the newly developed sense of collective. A Maidan medic who ended up risking her security on numerous occasions while providing medical aid to protesters, describes her initial inspiring encounter with the protesters, and her consequent willingness to aid them:

> At the beginning, people my age did not believe in this Maidan. I participated in the Orange Revolution, even receiving an award after, but this time … we were pessimistic: we fought for the Orange Revolution, we thought we were fighting for our choice, for our leader, but then we found out we were mistaken in the choice of that leader. There was disappointment, I was trying to leave the country, lived abroad, studied in the Sorbonne. I felt disrespected by my country as a physician. In November, I met medical school students from Lviv. They were so inspired … I was enthused by their passionate spirit (*zapal*). The next night [29 November 2013] when I watched the news, I felt these were the very students with whom I fell in love. I told my daughter I was inspired by their generation, who are driven by ideas. As I watched the news about the student beating, I felt [as though] my kids were beaten. I got ready, bought whatever was asked for – food, water, clothes, threw it all in the car, and my friend and I headed to the Mykhailivskyi monastery. That was the beginning for me.[16]

Maidan's forum debated the principles of governing and achieving a better Ukraine. In the self-organized *Rada Maidanu* (Maidan Council), representatives from Maidan civic initiatives gathered to design a plan of mass action and stay informed about others' projects. They also discussed theoretical questions, such as future constitutional changes, referenda, and possibilities for ending Yanukovych's rule via institutional means.[17] A participant in the council's discussion shared that they raised specific questions of legality and constitutionalism, addressing, for example, provisions for presidential impeachment in the Ukrainian constitution.[18] While discussions involved a wide range of social problems and solutions, a pro-democratic orientation prevailed, and solutions from these forums affected not only the movement's strategies but also the institutional consolidation of a democratic regime after the revolution. Building on these discussions, activists continued to pressure politicians during and after the revolution to limit presidential powers by returning to the 2004 constitution. As discussed earlier, the revolutionaries indeed succeeded: not only were elections free and fair after the revolution, but the parliament voted to restore the constitution, considerably limiting presidential powers.

It is estimated that four million people participated and contributed directly to the resistance movement.[19] Maidan included people with various political views. Even popular protester chants were questioned and negotiated. For instance, the chant "Ukraine above All" was questioned by some for its nationalistic undertone, while others called for its reinterpretation as prioritizing internal problems in society, or emphasizing the Kremlin's attempt to control Ukraine.[20] The most successful tactic to undermine the chant was the successful promotion of "Humans above All" and "Human Rights above All" to replace it. In other words, negotiating chants became a process of negotiating common values. While feminist, LGBTQ, and economically left messages were suppressed during the revolution, their presence contributed to the Maidan dialogue. For example, on 27 November, a "left" student group organized a silent action, holding posters such as "Organize a trade union instead of praying for Europe," and "Being scared of gender – not going to Europe." When they were surrounded and threatened by a "right" group, they chanted "To Europe without violence!" Thus, as pointed out by an activist, even in such instances, a common ideology was being negotiated.[21]

The stage on the revolutionaries' square served the purpose of making announcements and exchanging ideas between various groups and movements within Maidan. While the central stage was mostly accessible to more influential participants (initiative leaders, pro-Maidan parliamentarians, singers, religious leaders, etc.) during the day, activists had more access to the stage at night to offer other revolutionaries the opportunity to express their thoughts. The flow of people willing to discuss the movement's actions and theories on governing, or to express concerns about the movement or its challenges, continued to grow. As one stage manager described, to accommodate the growing interest in idea exchange, an open mic was set up next to the stage. Moreover, when people expressed concerns about the movement, the organizers encouraged them to provide constructive feedback and attempt to actively solve it themselves:

> When we saw we couldn't invite all to the stage, but knowing that people came to Maidan to express their ideas – we decided to have an open mic. So, next to the stage, we [set up the mic] to give people the opportunity to say whatever they wanted.

> Politicians didn't like it: people would say something contrary to their speeches, for example, people criticized politicians for their inability to respond to the needs of society. We'd try to direct people to certain initiatives – what can *you* do? [we'd ask] What is *your* idea? That was our group's initiative, some said this idea was risky: some people were swearing, or tak[ing] the mic away from each other. However, overall the atmosphere on Maidan was phenomenal, and when someone would act awkwardly, immediately a more adequate person would respond … In a way, this showed the diversity of society. Maidan became an arena [to discuss] what is going on, and how to move on.[22]

Thus, the decentralized grassroots organization of the movement promoted not only the exchange of ideas, but also constructive feedback, which was incorporated to strengthen resistance methods. In his book on the 1917 Russian Revolution, Robert Roeder emphasized that the stern hierarchical construct of the Bolshevik party contributed to the totalitarian structure of the post-revolutionary Soviet regime.[23] In sharp contrast, as Yaroslav Hrytsak points out, societies in which values of self-expression dominate are less prone to authoritarianism.[24] The decentralized nature of the Maidan movement promoted continuous discussion, making it difficult for radical groups to hijack the movement.

As described previously, the poster template created by the designers of the Strike Plakat initiative led to thousands of customized iterations by protesters, providing their personal interpretations of state–society relations. Maidan became a discussion forum: an arena where protesters who felt obliged to resist state violence and injustice debated methods of resistance, ideas of governing, constitutional rights, and belonging. They met new people and, while organizing resistance activities, constructed new social meanings of social powers and responsibilities. As Nadia Trach points out in her study of Maidan revolutionary rhetoric, the social resistance movement transformed the word Maidan itself.[25] "Maidan" now commonly referred to "people, Ukrainians, who take part in a meeting; it's a phenomenon that no longer needs to be translated to other languages … It's a concentrated disclosure of the will of the people, their colossal positive energy."[26]

Sense of Community

A majority of interviewees commented about the positive atmosphere on the Maidan Square. Mutual help, positive attitude, and friendly smiles[27] were descriptors interviewees brought up frequently when recollecting their presence on the square. Maidan became a bonding experience on the basis of a shared pursuit of democracy, contributing to a growing sentiment of unity, and providing the courage to face risks in the name of a newly discovered social community. As one founder of Strike Poster reflected: "I was particularly impressed with one of the banners: the girl wrote 'I am proud of each of you.' She used the template we created for protesters, but changed the beginning as well, saying 'I am proud of each one of you.' It was simple, and yet emotional, because when you are standing there, you feel that it wasn't about you, that you were indeed proud of all the brave people who came … Indeed, it was very dangerous at that time, you could get hit on the head, you could be followed; there were phone calls to workplaces to check who was absent."[28] Mass presence and positive exchange served not only as continuous pressure on the state, but also as reaffirmation for participants of the value of their revolutionary purpose.

In the process of expressing anti-state protest, revolutionaries exchanged ideas, discovering they had more in common with other countrymen than they previously assumed. A Jewish Ukrainian activist described, for example, that he had assumed any form of Ukrainian patriotic discourse to be antisemitic due to Russia's media coverage.[29] As he communicated with those who presented themselves as Ukrainian nationalists, he found that he "didn't feel any repulsion; they appeared completely normal and not at all aggressive." As he concluded, "Police violence … forced us to meet people whom we would have otherwise never met. Regardless of political victories, Maidan turned out to be a place to meet fantastic friends … Usually you trust only your childhood friends, maybe those you met in the army … But from the moment we met on Maidan – we became brothers. Now I perceive the concepts of friendship and like-mindedness in a very different way."[30] Vakarchuk, the singer who performed on stage during the Maidan, noted that he purposefully avoided singing certain songs, including *Ne Zdavaysia bez Boju* ("Don't Give Up without a Fight"). Rather, he saw his purpose as "playing for people from different areas of Ukraine, with different views – to show that we stand together as Ukrainians."[31] The feeling of Maidan kinship was described by one of the activists in the following way:

> Without culture and art, there would be no Maidan, as this was the spirit of Maidan. *Viche* became a meeting of friends, to see those who are alive and get strength to continue. It was like one long day which started on 29 November. As Maria Berlinska wrote, 'we don't have time for disappointment, we don't have the luxury of being pessimistic' … All people were magical, I wish I could write books about them.[32]

A number of interviewees commented on the socio-economic diversity of the participants: "During Maidan I was inspired by the fact that all social statuses, professions, very different, rich, middle class, very poor, it didn't matter … people were so different, it was obvious that people were tired of it all."[33] Several people highlighted the participation of wealthy citizens, commenting on the expensive winter coats or foreign cars the other protesters possessed, suggesting that all were united by democratic values, contrary to assumptions that revolutions are driven solely by economic deprivation.[34]

Participants emphasized the many contributions of local communities. Watching the elderly and students[35] giving away their last resources for the revolution served as reaffirmation to many of the rightness of their cause. Most interviewees commented on the positive atmosphere on the Maidan as factors that attracted them to the square. More specifically, the words "kindness" and "helping" were brought up repeatedly by interviewees, many commenting that these qualities reassured them that they were among a community devoted to a morally right cause. A participant described: "What I saw were people who were full of light, [they] were very polite. When it was raining, somebody would come and put a rain jacket on you. Even when we heard the announcement [from the government] that [they were carrying out] an 'anti-terrorist' operation,[36] and you understand they can bury you, you are standing next to people whose eyes are full of positive light."[37] Observing others making sacrifices was a powerful connector with a new community of those devoted to the revolutionary cause, while disconnecting with those who were apathetic:

Figure 5.1 Maidaners painting on a common canvas in the aftermath of the 22 January shootings of revolutionaries. Inscriptions say, "Shame to Yanyk, he is ruining our Ukraine," "Mother Ukraine, I saw your tears," "Serhii Nihoian, you are in our hearts forever."

> People brought tea, coffee; a bunch of businesses [contributed]. It was so touching to see when an elderly woman came and brought a can of peas. She brought what she could. It was also touching when a young couple brought sour cream. Everyday people would bring something … Elderly women who barely walked brought what they could … I divorced my husband – he sat at home the whole time while I was on Maidan.[38]

The new communal bond was based on mutual sacrifice for a common goal of the betterment of the community as a whole. A representative of the Mykhailivskyi monastery, which served as a refuge and then the base for a makeshift hospital, compared the developing community of mutual help on Maidan to a family: "I felt happiness to see that Kyiv residents came to bring food, took some [people] home to help … It was like a big family, all who were here." With continuing co-operation and increasing danger from the state, the sense of communal attachment to others within the ideological group grew:

> It was so hard – you go to the church in Lviv, [you see] people cry. [I remember a moment] when we were carrying [collected donations] onto the bus. I stepped on the bus to see if I know somebody… I will never forget that moment: I am coming up – huge bus, there are young men sitting there, they don't know what to expect. At that time we knew anything could happen: shootings, beatings. I was in pain … looking at them.[39]

Many participants commented on their continuing devotion to a new community despite deprivations (most described experiencing sleep deprivation, among others). The following description from a volunteer in charge of provisioning housing for revolutionaries is characteristic of many others: "I didn't want to go home: I knew there were people here who needed to sleep and eat, they might not have enough money."

Maidan socialization broke a number of socio-economic boundaries that had been dominated by ethnic, language, and religious identities. As a representative of the Ukrainian Center for the Studies of History and Culture of East European Jewry noted, "The solidarity that existed on Maidan never existed in prior life. There were no forms of xenophobia. On the contrary, there was Joseph's[40] presentation from the Maidan stage alongside leaders of the Ukrainian revolution, there was a speech by a Rabbi alongside other church representatives, there was a presentation by a Klezmer ensemble. Lots of my friends, Jewish and not Jewish, took part in the revolution." Addressing Kremlin propaganda that portrayed Maidan protesters as antisemites, the leaders of Jewish organizations shared, "we would always say the opposite: Maidan is a struggle for human dignity, fight for freedom and independence, and European choice of the Ukrainian people."[41]

As discussed in the previous chapter, the participation of ultra-right groups in the Maidan movement raised concerns of ultra-nationalism and antisemitism within the movement. Their occasional visibility, in addition to violent fights with police, included the walk of some members during Maidan in January to mark the birthday of Stepan Bandera, the leader of an anti-Soviet rebel militia, who fought alongside Nazi soldiers in the Second World War.[42] The Bandera walk was generally ignored by most Maidaners, while some raised concerns. One Maidaner described in her interview, "I went to those young people, and yelled at them, 'What do you think you are doing?' I told them. This was not acceptable."[43] As discussed previously, the negotiated pro-democratic consensus forced ultra-right groups to conceal the illiberal and nationalistic premises of their founding groups' ideology. Perhaps somewhat ironically, Kremlin propaganda to discredit the Ukrainian pro-democratic movement promoted the efforts by Maidaners – including the Jewish activists – to emphasize, and with this, promote the inclusive atmosphere on Maidan.

An occurrence discussed by Russian media as an example of xenophobia on Maidan, were occasional chants of "whoever doesn't jump is a Moscal," (*khto ne skache, toi Moscal*) the latter term being a derogatory word for Russians (most commonly, citizens of Russia). When asked about these incidents, interviewed revolutionaries asserted the chant was referring to the rivalry with Russian citizens, and frustration with those in Russia (including friends and relatives) who chose to believe the propaganda, rather than support their democratic aspirations. A member of *Rada Maidanu* described the systematic effort they invested in sending the message to Russian citizens that Maidan represented an anti-authoritarian movement, and therefore disapproval of Kremlin pressure, not Russians/Russian citizens. One of the most notable efforts was the colossal sign, "We Love Russians, but Hate Putin," visible on the Maidan New Year tree in the centre of the square. Another activist, in an interview with me, recalled discussions with their Russian friends about Maidan and supposed xenophobia that once culminated in a bet, suggesting that they each hold a flag of another country a few days after the Maidan succeeded. He recalled, "When my son stood on Maidan with the Russian flag, numerous people came to thank them for their support. After hours, he left because he got cold. However, when his friend stood on Red Square with a Ukrainian flag, it took only minutes before the OMON (Russia's law enforcement) showed up and took the flag away." Maidan participants included not only ethnic Russians and Russian speakers, but a number of Russian citizens. With the inclusivity emphasized, the rivalry between the Maidan narrative and the anti-Maidan narrative of the events was an essential part of the discourse. Anti-Russian chants (directed at Maidan haters) notwithstanding, Maidaners describe the overall inclusive atmosphere, with notable diverse groups present on the Maidan. Popular Ukrainophobia in Russia is rarely addressed, but was present and increased after the Maidan, and the Kremlin in fact institutionalized anti-Ukrainian hatred, making Ukrainian symbols illegal.

Both Ukrainian and Russian languages were used on Maidan interchangeably, reflecting the predominantly bilingual nature of Ukrainian society. One Maidan medic pointed out: "as a Russian speaker from Donetsk, I never experienced any problems. In fact, I was always very open about my origin. We'd gather around a barrel [for warmth],[44] and discuss various issues, we expressed all kinds of views, to help us understand each other; we didn't fear each other."[45] As scholars of Ukraine describe, conversations often take place using either or both languages, with people at times having no recollection of which language was used during their last interaction. Notably, while most people in Ukraine whose native language is Ukrainian are bilingual, many people whose native language is Russian speak only Russian as a result of the Soviet-era legacy, for example: (1) the use of the Ukrainian language was purposefully suppressed by Soviet policies; (2) Russian was the lingua franca of the country; and (3) due to the legacy of Soviet-era culture, Ukrainian speakers would yield to Russian-speakers' choice even if both speakers were fluent in both languages. Thus, on Maidan, there were many who could speak only Russian. Post-Soviet Ukrainian policies and associated politics battled substantially with the attempt to restore the use of the Ukrainian language, eventually making it the state language. Many interviewees noted the use of both languages on Maidan. One revolutionary highlighted that her husband, being from Odessa, spoke only Russian and never encountered any issues. A leader of a Ukrainian Jewish organization asserted that "Maidan solved the language problem," suggesting not only the use of both languages on Maidan but also the consolidation of a bilingual society in Ukraine, where language identity, and the use of the Russian language more specifically, was not associated with patriotism or hurting communal identity in Ukraine. "Civilizational identity … unites people."[46] While such Maidaners' language appears idealistic (a number of interviewees spoke of "civilizational identity"), it testifies to the discourse surrounding a search for a common moral community – building on principles of legality, rather than on an ethnic/language basis.

Socialization during Maidan turned the square into an arena for learning about other group identities. An activist, volunteering in the kitchen, described her emotional response when she heard others sing in Ukrainian when they were preparing food for the protesters:

> When they were singing, I was crying. I realized that I live in Ukraine, but speak only Russian. I don't know any Ukrainian songs. But we do the same things. Because this is all ours. This process united us. It was overwhelming to realize all this, while just a month prior [to the revolution] one could think that our nation was so weak. "What Maidan?" I said at the beginning. However, now I'd seen that this was working, and we had to follow it through to the end.[47]

Another revolutionary also described his experience as transformative, as he developed a new moral bond with other revolutionaries, who embraced rather than erased his religious identity:

> Maidan changed my attitude toward Christianity in a fundamental way. It changed my perception from viewing it as a hostile religion to seeing it as a spiritual way for people. I perceive it now as a way to see the world/God in a slightly different way from Judaism. [During the revolution] I heard everything I was used to, even the same prayers. It was a very important moment for me. Because of Maidan, I went inside a church for the first time. It was my friend's funeral. The priest saw me, as I was wearing a yarmulke, shook my hand with respect, there was no demand to take my headwear off or anything like that. He understood everything. I ask myself, is it ok to be here – under their canon? But on the other hand, my brothers died and there was nothing more important than to honour them, as it is the most sacred thing. It is important for me as an orthodox Jew to cross over some conditionality for the sake of not being disrespectful. With this, the boundaries are erased. There are people of your spirit, and then there are people of an alien spirit.[48]

Thus, the new communal identity among revolutionaries was based on shared support for a democratic Ukraine, often overcoming ethnic, language, and religious differences.

Self-Sacrifice

The new communal identity born of Maidan was reinforced by self-sacrifice. Observing other people sacrifice security and life for democratic values reinforced revolutionaries' commitment to these values, and aided their sense of belonging to the new ideational community. New states have a challenging task in creating a national identity. While it is commonly a state-led process, a society-led nation-building process is likely to gain more legitimacy among the populace. Moreover, European national identities tend to centre around ethnicity. Thus, Ukraine's diverse society, with its bilingualism, large number of ethnic minority groups, and varied imperial historical legacies, was seen as unfavourable to its nation-building process. While ethnic Ukrainians were more likely to join the movement, the Maidan Revolution united multiple ethnic and linguistic groups, solidifying a new ideational, socially driven national identity. Mutual self-sacrifice played a fundamental role in the social unification process.

Most interviewed revolutionaries retold the shock they experienced as state suppression continued to rise, and the differences between methods used by each side became starker: "So many tears, shock. People would get a stick and a wooden shield, and [they] go against a Berkut policeman, who is [highly] equipped, with ammunition. The Berkut policeman is allowed to shoot, while the Maidan guy can't. That's real heroism."[49] Similarly, interviewees recounted their impressions of the defencelessness of protesters in the face of state aggression: "It was phenomenal: people without any shields were facing bullets – I watched this myself."[50] Common sacrifice in the face of injustice and significantly more powerful state agents provided a potent unifying factor: "I was standing next to people I never met before, we knew there could be some provocations, and we could become meat: they have all the equipment, and we were bare handed. [We were there] just to protect people, to hold police [back], to take their assault on us."[51]

The revolutionary struggle was seen by many as a fight for peace. Notably, some revolutionaries compared their experiences to images from the Second World War:

> I'd become overwhelmed with a horrible feeling when these guys, covered in black, would bring a pot for the front line. [As] we put soup, kasha [in the pot], I'd visualize World War II scenes with

> dirty soldiers in a makeshift kitchen. I couldn't believe this was the twenty-first century, that they are shooting us there ... It was so scary to realize it was happening to us.[52]

The Ukrainian flag acquired a symbolic character, now associated with revolutionary struggle, bringing comfort and safety when carried by others:

> I remember walking with revolutionary pamphlets, "Don't Be Scared, Don't Be Aggressive" (*Ne Biysia, Ne Byysia*), information on how many people disappeared, who are titushky, how to conduct yourself safely, and why the 16 January laws are bad, I saw in my apartment complex entry five young men, holding something heavy ... When I saw that they had blue-yellow ribbons, I was able to breathe. They had organized [an anti-state] defence.[53]

The dangers and sacrifices were presented as a "natural" response to state aggression. Some recounted humour, addressing the faults of government officials as a unifying factor for a diverse group of protesters:

> The Trade Union building was burning ... People came to help carry out patients. We were throwing everything in the fire. Met an old friend ... a lawyer, he was digging cobblestones out. We were speaking Russian and Ukrainian to each other, he is Jewish ... He said, "We have to decide something very important: how do we express public appreciation to the former Kyiv mayor, Omelchenko, for putting cobblestones so badly that it's so easy to dig them out?" [He was saying] this when bullets were flying, and everything was burning.[54]

As state aggression increased, many referred to the necessity of self-sacrifice to help others. One activist recounted his most memorable moment: when he received a text from medics that people were now being shot, his initial shock was replaced by a determination to "just get there on time, build barricades on time, be there with everybody."[55] It was precisely the experience of seeing others sacrifice themselves that was recounted as contributing greatly to the creation of a common identity:

> The spirit of Maidan was fascinating; a unity factor appeared: common losses, we didn't expect it would be so painful … From the first shots in January, from the first Armenian shot, first Belorussian shot … All tenets of the Russian propaganda fell apart … People who didn't live through this didn't understand it fully; if they would see the Heavenly Hundred being shot … Those who saw how four hundred people stood for Maidan under fire, they think differently now.[56]

Witnessing others sacrifice for the shared idea of a more democratic country created a feeling of belonging to a newly created community, a community seen as worth sacrificing for. The following account underscores the newly acquired emotional attachment to a community that resulted from observing mutual sacrifice:

> Before, I used to think there is nobody in this country to marry. No good men. But during the revolution, there were cases when somebody would come forward and protect you from the bullets. The way people helped each other: a separate book should be written about it. I keep remembering the day, 19 February. They started killing … The Trade Union building was burnt down – that's where there was storage with medicine, food … But now people started bringing medicines, whatever money they had, they knew people on Maidan suffered … Tears … We were in line to give blood: my friend was there for eight hours: not because it was too slow, but because [there were] four floors of people [in line]. People understood that there was something more important than money. Events of the revolution showed that [people] didn't spare money or their own blood … When they brought the coffins through, people yelled, "Heroes!"[57]

As discussed in earlier chapters, state violence contributed to people's resolve to resist in order to prevent consolidation of authoritarianism. Importantly, as seen in these accounts, a newly acquired sense of anti-state community promoted further participation to protect their compatriots.

New Trust Networks

Svoi chelovek (*my person*, in Russian)[58] is a Soviet-era concept referring to a person you can trust. It was at the very core of social function: state–society relations were such that citizens expected to be penalized for things they did every day.[59] To obtain basic consumer goods, Soviet citizens had to constantly rely on their elaborate social trust networks.[60] For example, *svoi chelovek* in a grocery store could hide away a few sticks of butter for you, which meant that your closely knit network of family and friends had access to a *deficit* product. Others within this network were expected to reciprocate by obtaining access to other needs: perhaps, through their connections, they could influence a bureaucrat to assign your child to a better job. Such tactics of survival in the Soviet-style economy were widely used and yet obviously illegal, which meant that a given social network was infused with an aura of secrecy, and limited only to those who were *proverennyi* – somebody who had proven they could be trusted. Privatization policies after the Soviet collapse resulted in monopolization and oligarchization of Ukraine's economy – where a few elites profited via extra-legal means, and a shadow economy of overcoming bureaucratic hurdles and obtaining (now unaffordable) goods became status quo. The creation of new social networks, where trust is based on shared democratic values, to confront the state and promote civil liberties, seemed impossible unless GDP were to improve dramatically. The Maidan Revolution proved the contrary: while old networks were utilized during the revolution (to obtain certain information about potential state actions), new strong ones were built solely on the basis of shared ideational values.

As described previously, revolutionary activity, and association with it, presented clear dangers to the participants. "We knew we could get caught for helping those who were throwing [cobblestones]," described a hospital volunteer, "you never knew who was on whose side, you couldn't trust even the housekeeping staff."[61] However, as civic initiatives to resist the state grew, so did the ability to connect and support fellow revolutionaries. A new bond would appear on the basis of revolutionary activity that would allow you to trust a stranger with your life:

> At some point we found out that we, the Red Cross volunteers, were hunted. We had acquaintances who worked in state agencies – a friend of a friend called and warned: "be careful, walk in four- to five-person groups because a reward has been offered for you." Specifically, for medics. I saw a medic was grabbed, and then several people had to run to pull him out – they attempted to kidnap two medics. They were wearing civilian clothes. It became dangerous for me to drive, so I'd go on Facebook, post that I need a ride, and … complete strangers – would drive up to my house and drive me to Maidan. There was a closed Facebook group, a community where people were trusted.[62]

New networks involved not only those you knew personally through familial or friendship bonds, but an imagined community – tied by common ideals. Others' specificity of appearance or actions were often recognizable as connected to revolutionary activity, prompting many to help complete strangers:

> People would help each other in stores. It was obvious from seeing the collection of goods one was buying that you are going to Maidan – a large number of plastic plates, or a large quantity of any certain product. We were in line behind men who were purchasing all canned products they could find there, they just kept placing it on the conveyer belt. Then it was my turn: I picked up something for Maidan as well. In comparison to their purchase, it was so little, and when I placed my stuff on the belt, as they were paying for theirs, they saw mine and said to the sales person: "We'll pay for this as well." But I said, "Thank you. I want to do it on my own, this is my contribution."[63]

The aid to strangers who were fellow revolutionaries became characteristic of the Maidan Revolution. Most interviewees commented on mutual help in different capacities: from receiving help to carry products to Maidan, to receiving free taxi rides, to medical and legal aid. In many cases, this aid helped save lives. A revolutionary described: "When I had an injured guy on the [February] 18, we were carrying him, he had a bullet [wound] … Suddenly a little car appeared, a fragile woman came out, a medic volunteer, and offered to give us a ride, I don't know what would happen to us if not for her."[64]

A new division within society appeared on the basis of their support for Maidan: several interviewees noted the stark difference in the people of Kyiv: "In stores, you could see that people lived in a different world. I'd buy plastic plates, while somebody next to me was buying champagne in preparation for the New Year celebration. And you understand we live in different worlds ... It was surprising: there was Maidan, its territory, and then there is a night life, expensive stores. Society was divided."[65]

Those who were connected via revolutionary activity developed a new basis for overwhelming trust: "We knew we could trust each other, cover each other, say where we were."[66] One revolutionary concluded, "These Maidan communities, these events opened a crack in people's consciousness."[67]

Changing Perceptions of "Civic Duty" and State–Society Relations

Participation in the Maidan created a new socially accepted perception of the concept of "civic duty." A notable Soviet legacy was civic apathy and an expectation of the state to deliver services. Scholars identified that the Soviet regime, which deprived the masses of agency, resulted in a habitually unengaged public and distrust in civic organization years after the Soviet collapse. Post-socialist scholars argue that Soviet state-sponsored social services engineered a post-totalitarian culture of apathy, fear of retaliation for criticism of the state, and expectation of the state to deliver social goods. The growth of democratic values in Ukraine over time led to the Orange Revolution's successful assertion of freedoms of expression but did not contribute to a robust civil society. Yanukovych's anti-democratic moves led to protests in 2011 and 2012, as well as the appearance of civic groups, but not yet to a strong civil society nationally. The Maidan Revolution, however, contributed to significant growth and solidification of civil society in Ukraine. Firstly, it forced the concerned pro-democratic majority to learn how to organize resistance.

Secondly, as discussed above, mutual self-sacrifice during Maidan nurtured a new community on the basis of common pro-democratic values, breaking old Soviet-style trust networks. Finally, the severe risks of participation and co-dependency on other revolutionaries for survival promoted a sense of civic duty to persist for the sake of the common good. As an AutoMaidan leader pointed out, "It was the first time in the history of Ukraine when real civil society was born. Before, it was suppressed. Perhaps, we could see some potential in 2004, but now on a more fundamental level." Severe state violence against the youth in November of 2013 promoted the sense that undefended civilians needed protection. As one activist described: "It was obvious that the student beatings [by police] were absolutely not normal; it was abnormal treatment of Ukrainian citizens by the state. This angered me. I didn't care how many people would come, I knew I had to come: there was a strong feeling of civic duty, that you can't just watch what was happening."[68] As discussed earlier, widespread democratic values in Ukraine provided for such a condemnation of state violence, resulting in a strong emotional response. However, the experience of sharing this determination to resist the state and the success of the grassroots movement transformed people's perceptions of social responsibility and their ability to help. As a makeshift kitchen volunteer described:

> One could walk through Maidan, and there were so many emotions … I was shaking. None of us experienced anything like that: fighting for our opinion, for what we can and cannot do. Before, we didn't believe that one's small donation could save a child, for example. This experience changed people: they saw that two to three hryvnas could make a difference … So, today's socially funded *Tabletochka* collects two to three million hryvnas a month. According to the publicly available account, most donations are very small – as little as ten hryvnas. So, Maidan changed conscience for many of us.[69]

Participation on the Maidan broke the social apathy inherited from the Soviet era. A volunteer medic asserted: "People started living not for themselves only. And this continues: the number of volunteer organizations grew. Now we dress the army, and fix tanks and personnel carriers." Vakarchuk, a singer who spent months in the United States as an academic fellow, expressed this sentiment in American terms: "Revolution changed the country: it empowered lots of volunteers, NGOs, who are not asking what the country can do for them, but asking what they can do for the country."[70] Perhaps more importantly, the high price paid by fellow Maidaners brought an additional sense of responsibility:

> After I watched how people died for ideals, I can't let myself act in a wrong way. I can't participate in some sort of corrupt scheme, I can't imagine I would betray someone's ideals. Fundamental human concepts have woken up. People changed: while before one could find excuses for wrongdoings, now that internal egotism – which could always tell you that some violation is not a big deal, and that you can do the right thing later, is gone. Now lots of people lost that little inner devil. Lots of people died – and we need always to be grateful to them.[71]

After the Maidan, a number of revolutionaries commented on the feeling of obligation to do the morally right thing in a democratic society:

> I think now selling votes will be harder: people now believe that one kilogram [of buckwheat] or 100 hryvnas are not worth selling your vote for, in order to then wait for five years for that person to leave the elected post. Now we will think harder when voting. People changed. This time, unfortunately the price was too high, and people have to internalize, analyze [the events of Maidan], and realize that some paid their lives as a price.[72]

Thus, Maidaners' hard-won victory contributed to a feeling of moral responsibility to maintain democratic practices. More importantly, activists gained a sense of empowerment vis-à-vis the state. The totalitarian Soviet regime affirmed the supremacy of the state to assert political ideology, dictate social actions, and punish dissent, producing a social mentality of fear, apathy, and helplessness. Active participation in the Maidan grassroots movement, and the success of the revolution, contested these social assumptions. An immigrant from Azerbaijan who participated in battles with the police stated: "Maidan decided the destiny of the Ukrainian nation, its future. The people who paid the price with their lives, and hard work, they decided the fate of Ukraine."[73]

The multiple complex tasks successfully performed by Maidaners and the effectiveness of social organization emboldened Ukrainians. A volunteer physician who helped run medical aid after the state began using live ammunition, shared the following:

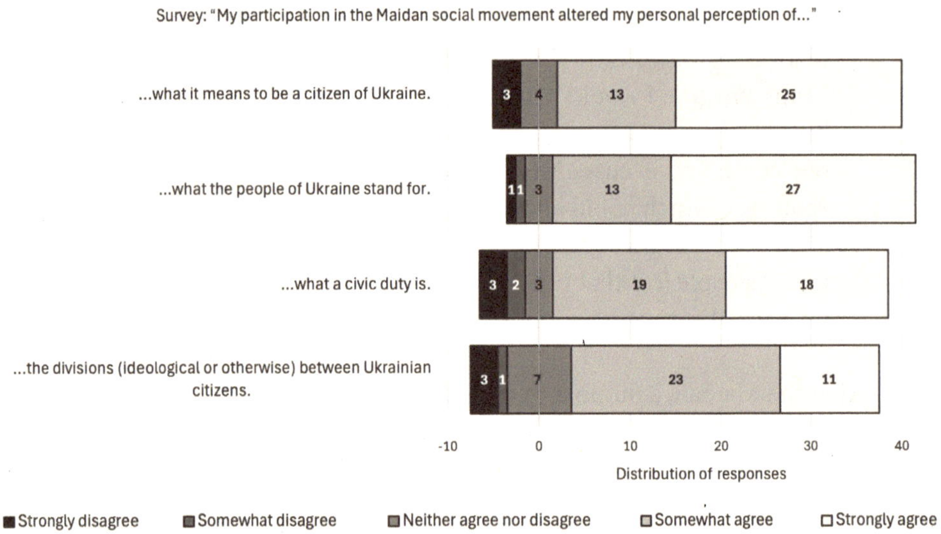

Figure 5.2 Revolutionaries' perceptions of socialization and change.
Source: Author's survey of Maidan protesters.

> Our volunteers were able to make arrangements with ministries of foreign affairs of different countries, including Israel, Poland, Italy … We could never imagine that common people were able to decide issues on an international level … Issues, such as special planes to carry injured people, ambulances on the Germany–Poland border … Young, motivated people who spoke various languages, without any previous experience, were able to carry out such operations much faster than any bureaucratic agencies.[74]

While forced to counteract the state and aid their fellow revolutionaries, Maidaners witnessed the potential and effectiveness of their own activism. A volunteer in one of the makeshift kitchens on the Maidan described her discovery of social collective capacity:

> When you were there [on the Maidan], it was an amazing and different world: everybody was smiling, everybody was helping each other, everything was so organized … We've never seen anything like that done by the state administration, such [efficient] traffic regulation or cleaning of snowy roads … While

> the rest of the city was dirty, Maidan was clean, people would just grab shovels and clean, and it would be done fast. This self-organization impressed me more than anything; that we could do this without any institution sitting above us. It was becoming clear that we can actually do anything. People of Ukraine can do more than they assume. People were used to top-down orders, we'd passively do it. Now, we are dressing the army; the function of the state is now played by the people.[75]

The Maidaners discovered that social expectations of the state to deliver public goods, which often peculiarly coexisted with public disappointment during Soviet and post-Soviet times, could be abandoned in favour of social responsibility and oversight. As a leader of a Ukrainian Jewish organization pointed out, "Maidan's most important lesson was, 'we can count only on ourselves, nobody will do it for us.'"[76] The revolutionaries emphasized that they learned to produce socially desired results through finding creative ways to counteract state repression: "Several times, the government closed the subway … so people were walking. It became dangerous to [get around] because of police and titushky, so taxi drivers would drive people for free."[77] The successful creation of grassroots social networks and initiatives, which served various functions, from food supply to housing, medical and legal aid, a number of revolutionaries said they trust socially run organizations more than state-run ones. Maidaners felt empowered with their ability to self-organize and their knowledge of political institutions. One activist who participated in the Maidan council described: "In the council, we developed a proposal for constitutional changes … We developed ideas to make experimental models, promoting development in Ukraine and other countries, advancing the birth of the network community."[78] Some went even as far as dismissing the need for a state altogether: "During the Maidan, people cooked everything, did everything … People created a structure with clear rules, people knew what to do. I started feeling, 'why do we need government?'"[79] Importantly, Maidaners' empowerment vis-à-vis political power also came from relatively small input into the success of the revolution from opposition politicians. All interviewed revolutionaries, who discussed the role of political parties in the Maidan, expressed skepticism as to their effect. One revolutionary described: "Politicians just ended up in the right place at the right time.

Imagine a good horse running by, whoever jumps on it first, gets it; that's what they did."[80] As a leader of a Ukrainian Jewish organization put it, "Maidan was self-organized, [opposition] leaders tried to catch up, enjoy the rays … but people didn't accept them. They believed they were useless, but worked with them somewhat, which was wise." The Maidan Revolution became a state–society dialogue, in which society was determined to demonstrate their ability to be in charge of political life of the country, and the civic right to make political choices:

> It was important to us, young people, to show [our capacity] to the generation of politicians who assumed that it was their business to run the country and that we were incompetent … We wanted to show that we could do our job right, we could achieve results, and we assumed responsibility for our actions. They should communicate with us on the same level. During Maidan, I got phone numbers of a number of politicians who responded to phone calls and helped out, or they called and you helped. [These events] really inspired me: people with different experiences, education, background, statuses united on Maidan for the sake of one purpose. We knew we wanted a different life, one with dignity.[81]

Maidan was a process of rewriting the nation's *social contract.* As a volunteer medic put it, "Maidan was an expression of the social desire to be taken into account. The government forgot that they were just managers hired by us – people who pay their salaries. They forgot about it, they decided they were gods. So, people decided to be heard."[82] Maidan changed state–society relations in Ukraine, putting people at the wheel of political life in the country: reasserting democracy.

Changing Perceptions of "Ukraine"

"I lived in Ukraine my whole life, but I never before witnessed a gathering of women singing Ukrainian folk songs. It was so beautiful. Ukrainian culture was kept away from us," shared a Maidan kitchen volunteer. Revolution is a process of socialization, where activists learn about members of their own community. The diversity of participants during the Ukrainian Revolution meant that people from various regions of the country, various social statuses and ideologies, learned about others' circumstances. Ukraine's revolution also offered a social dialogue to address its cultural heritage, which was actively repressed during the Soviet era. Hearing folk songs in person helped some urban dwellers experience Ukrainian culture in a new way. The revolution was a process of new discoveries and communal bonds.

As the diversity of backgrounds on the Maidan – religious, ethnic, regional – was accepted, and in fact celebrated, to emphasize support for the movement by a diverse population, this further contributed to the unification of previously compartmentalized groups within the country. A retired physician, who was a volunteer medic throughout the entire revolution, described the process: "They said pray the way you want … and this was a unification of diverse Ukraine, this was the birth of Ukraine."[83] The concept of *Ukraine* was reconsidered by activists as they revolutionized the political regime of the country.

The concept of Ukraine for the revolutionaries (and beyond) became closely intertwined with democracy and freedom of expression as a result of the Maidan. "We walked around with posters 'Ukraine above all' – we meant that we'd had enough of being silenced, we had to fight for our country, we didn't want to become like Russia; we wanted to prevent Ukraine from suspicious economic unions [with Russia], as we had a feeling we were pushed into the union with Belarus and Russia, where people don't have freedom of expression, where people don't have rights."[84] With Maidan's assertion of democracy, the revolutionaries contemplated the vitality of Ukraine's sovereignty away from Russia's influence. "People now changed their attitude toward their state," described a volunteer medic. "Independence was a gift, but in reality we didn't have it. We fought it out only now. Ukraine became truly independent only now. Maidan was also a revolution for independence."[85] An activist and immigrant from Azerbaijan described his vision of the change Ukrainian society underwent as a result of the Maidan Revolution:

> I've lived here for so many years, and yet it was like I never lived here before. This nation changed entirely … Only the Baltics became truly independent from Russia [after the Soviet collapse], [and] maybe Georgia. Ukrainians lived under de-facto Russian dictatorship all these twenty-five years. Only now has Ukraine become independent. Maidan changed my opinion about

> Ukrainians: these people can stand up for themselves. In the post-Soviet world, Ukrainians were always considered kind, the ones who would give away their last possessions. They are fighters, they can fight for themselves. I gained so much respect for them. That's why I volunteered for the Ukrainian army [in 2014]. A year I'm there. I saw there as well what great heroes they are.[86]

The Maidan movement had ambitious goals, and the process of socialization of a grassroots revolution of such scale contributed to a change of social perceptions about the country. As a Maidan activist put it, "This revolution is not only on the streets – it's in people's minds – we are changing a certain mentality … we wanted to show to the world that this is a resurrection (*vidrodzhennia*), the birth of a new Ukraine."[87] Not only did Maidan restore a democratic regime, but the concepts of Ukraine and self-sacrifice for the aim of democracy became intertwined. One volunteer physician described that watching revolutionaries sacrifice their lives for the cause in February 2014 changed his perceptions of his countrymen, and, as he asserted in 2015, transformed self-perceptions of Ukrainian citizens:

> If Russians wanted to kill us, they would by now – but they can't destroy us, because everything would be covered in blood: Ukraine's army is different, people are stronger … Self-sacrifice: this word gained a [new] meaning now, now it's people's names, doctors, economists, accountants, political scientists, construction workers, anybody, regardless of education – it's people who [showed] the value of self-sacrifice for future generations, children, neighbours. I think Europe needs to learn from us to get what we have now. Ukrainians are strong … I used to want to immigrate, I've worked in a medical centre in Austria, but I no longer want to move and become an Austrian, or a Pole, or a Canadian. They are all beautiful, but we have strong potential to build a strong state. Our spirit is higher now.[88]

Thus, state–society relations were renegotiated. From the revolutionary dialogue among social groups emerged a renewed social contract of Ukraine: where citizens dictate the terms of distribution of political powers and responsibilities.

Post-Maidan Civil Society

Studies have shown a notable change in socio-political identities after 2014.[89] While ethnic identities and language practices changed little, there has been a "significant increase in the proportion of people thinking of Ukraine as their homeland."[90] As scholars point out, the Maidan Revolution brought a "dramatic change in Ukrainian national identity," as national identity became more salient in relation to other territorial and non-territorial identities in the country.[91] Post-Maidan media discourse included frequent "assertions of individuals' increased self-identification as Ukrainian, greater pride in being a citizen of the Ukrainian state, stronger attachment to symbols of nationhood, enhanced solidarity with compatriots, increased readiness to defend Ukraine or work for Ukraine, and increased confidence in people's power to change the country for the better."[92] In 2015, volunteers spent more time volunteering in comparison with the pre-Maidan era:

> The share of those who dedicate a few hours per month to this has increased significantly (from 10 per cent in 2012 to 35 per cent in 2015) … There is also a noticeable dependence of the level of volunteer activity on the age of the respondents: young people spend more time on such activities … During 2015, 41 per cent of respondents provided material support for charitable events and support of charitable organizations. This is almost twice as much as was recorded in the 2012 survey (when 21 per cent declared such support).[93]

A comprehensive study conducted from November 2015 to December 2018, and involving 1,325 citizens aged sixteen to eighty years from different regions of Ukraine, concluded that "volunteerism has become the new watchword in Ukraine's political lexicon and the embodiment of a new form of civic activism."[94] Not only do volunteers dedicate more hours to civic activism, but "about 10 to 15 per cent of volunteers ran as candidates in 2015 municipal elections."[95] In the aftermath of the Maidan Revolution, new informal network associations and volunteer groups appeared in all regions of Ukraine,[96] including NGOs, charities, and human rights organizations.[97] Intensive civic engagement in the Ukraine refugee crisis responded to numerous new needs of Ukrainian citizens facing the Russian invasion, such as the resettlement of people escaping from occupied Crimea and the military conflict in the Donbas.[98] The growth of extended social networks enacted "civic engagement and mobilization of resources, eventually contributing to social mobility."[99] A number of newly established organizations have redirected to focus almost exclusively on providing immediate assistance to conflict-affected people. These were citizen-led initiatives that assumed an active role in the protection of activists and the support of Ukrainian servicemen in the east. Importantly, internally displaced Crimean Tatars freely organized to preserve their cultural identity in areas of displacement, and new organizations were created by internally displaced persons to work on the defence of their rights.[100]

Since Russia invaded Ukraine, two days after the Maidan Revolution, and many volunteers engaged in supporting the army and assisting those displaced from occupied territories, it is challenging to disentangle the causal variable behind the post-2014 mobilization. The discussion in this chapter detailing the transformative effects on participants' views about state–society relations suggests that these changing social views contributed to a rapidly developing civil society in Ukraine after 2014 and volunteer activism after the full-scale Russian invasion of 2022.

Over half of the revolutionaries I interviewed reported that they participate in some form of volunteer work, or volunteered for the armed forces of Ukraine. The range of their civic engagement was wide, from promoting rule of law in the country, to meeting the needs of the armed forces after Russia's invasion. Some of the lawyers who offered pro bono aid for Maidan activists chose to continue volunteer work and/or engage with the new government to work on projects addressing corruption in the legal system. Maidan medics and those engaged in logistical organization during the Maidan became organizers collecting donations for the Ukrainian army. For example, one Maidaner I interviewed was a human rights activist whose participation during Maidan initially focused on monitoring court proceedings to record due process violations. As the Maidan events unfolded, and the state began using live ammunition, he organized the retrieval and hiding of the bodies of killed revolutionaries before they could be taken to the state morgue, as it was suspected state agents stole and cremated fallen revolutionaries to hide evidence of illegal shootings. After the Maidan, he further increased his civic activism to promote human rights in Ukraine.

Most notably, Oleksandra Matviichuk and the Ukrainian Center for Civil Liberties, who were behind the Euromaidan SOS civic initiative to organize volulnteer aid for detained revolutionaries, played a key role in reporting tens of thousands of war crimes committed by the invading Russian army – receiving the Nobel Peace Prize in 2022. In her 2022 interview, she asserted that participation during the Maidan changed the movement's participants by providing a sense of empowerment. Providing examples of the impact of their volunteer engagement, she explained:

> People learned that they can make a much greater impact than they could ever imagine … We stood for something good, and that's why we were supported. Euromaidan SOS was a huge initiative, because we united thousands of people. We started legal work because hundreds of people were persecuted, beaten, tortured, accused of fabricated crimes … We were helping the relatives of those who were – unfortunately – killed … Thousands of volunteers and hundreds of volunteer lawyers joined this initiative, aiding … 16,000 [people]. My main lesson learned from the Maidan was the following. At the time we fought against the authoritarian state machine, and it was very difficult, I must admit, because the paramilitary group, titushky, co-operated with prosecutors, [and] prosecutors were in line with the court. The former president, and majority of the government, wanted the peaceful protests to be liquidated … In these circumstances, it is very easy to say, *How can we use law when the law does not work? We can do nothing in this regard, because all institutions who were meant to protect human rights now start to prosecute protesters, and kill and torture them.* But because our lawyers and our volunteers fought very honestly for each person, and for each procedural measure, it made a huge difference. And suddenly we understood that we were working not only on the legal level, but on a symbolic level. When … [on one hand] everybody on the Maidan knew that there were no guarantees: you can be beaten, arrested, tortured, even killed, but [on the other hand] there is a group of people who will never leave you alone, who will fight for you and for your release … who will take care of your family. And this understanding provided people with energy and strength to

> overcome the fear. So this was our main input into the Revolution of Dignity … You can face challenges … your own efforts can seem senseless, but you have to continue your fight honestly, and the result will unexpectedly be achieved.[101]

The decentralized nature of the Maidan movement provided continuing social discourse about natural rights and civic engagement to protect them. Experiences of mutual sacrifice and support helped solidify a new moral community, based on the principles of democratic governing and civic responsibility to defend natural rights. Maidan activists and participants remained the core contributors to continuing Ukrainian social discourse about the principles of governing, natural rights and freedoms.

Conclusion

The account in this chapter demonstrates how participation in the Maidan Revolution, and its success, transformed participants' perceptions of social capacity, transforming the Soviet legacy of social apathy. In the process of negotiating a social contract with the state by applying pressure via protesting, challenging injustice in courts, and fighting with the police, Maidaners created a forum to discuss the principles of governing among social groups who otherwise would not have engaged. Continuing co-operation under conditions of mutual sacrifice promoted the sense of a new moral community, united on the basis of the pro-democratic cause rather than ethnic/regional identities. Trusting and bonding with complete strangers for the mutual support of Maidan not only allowed more successful co-operation, but, as interviewees described, occasionally saved lives. As one Maidaner put it, these experiences of creating new "Maidan communities" caused "a rupture in people's consciousness." Witnessing the social capacity to self-organize and, with it, effectively challenge the state, transformed for many participants their view of social power: "It was becoming clear that we can do anything we put our mind to. The people of Ukraine can do much more than they assume. People were used to top-down orders, and passively following them."[102] These transformed notions of social power are in stark contrast to the social apathy observed by scholars of post-Soviet societies, and likely became a contributing factor to the notable growth of civil society in Ukraine after 2014.

The idea of value transformations within a moral community is consistent with Durkheim's argument that with certain social developments, the underlying basis of solidarity or unity within the social order also tends to evolve.[103] Ellis Goldberg explored this idea within the context of the Arab Spring protests, arguing that various forms of demonstrations "had in common claims about the nature of moral community in Egypt."[104] The Ukrainian Maidan Revolution, which challenged the state's attempt to impose new terms of legality, became the process through which new moral communities built new bases of solidarity. The accounts of Maidaners about value transformation might seem idealistic, but they point to a pattern of the effects of the revolutionary socialization process on discourses vis-à-vis a common moral community. Participation in the revolution forced Ukrainians to learn about other identities and search for commonalities on the basis of moral governing (and inclusivity).

While a majority of Ukrainians supported the Maidan as necessary to oust Yanukovych and prevent the "police state" from consolidating, post-Maidan social discourse simultaneously included a heavy dose of disappointment regarding continuing corruption in the country. While democratic revolutions may bring new institutional rules, undercutting authoritarian suppression of civil rights, they don't instantly resolve corruption in state and social institutions. This requires prolonged systematic processes of social and systemic changes. This chapter, rather, focused on the social changes that took place alongside the political regime change. Revolutionary participation became a socialization process, where boundaries were crossed between group identities as principles of governing were debated. This allowed the revolutionaries to envision a new Ukraine – one whose national narrative is intertwined with the principles of democratic governing. Historically, nation-building processes, with their promotion of national symbols and values, are assumed to be state-driven. Maidan was an event in Ukrainian history where thousands of activists were able to debate, negotiate, and contribute to the creation of a new moral community. Not only did many of the revolutionaries remain active contributors to Ukraine's growing civil society after the Maidan, the revolution is referred to as a transformative event for the social consciousness – a symbol of struggle against the police state, a struggle for people's will for freedom against repression.

6

Conclusion

Revolution as State–Society and Intra-Society Dialogue

The Maidan was a grassroots democratic revolution, a change from authoritarian to democratic regime. As a detailed analysis of the events and interview data in this book demonstrate, the Maidan Revolution was a response to state violence, which grew into a movement to restore democracy. While Yanukovych came to power through democratic means in 2009, he enacted a number of constitutional and institutional reforms, and extra-judicial mechanisms to allow further suppression of political opposition. Crucially, authoritarianism was institutionalized in the winter months of 2013–14: the government passed laws on 16 January to severely restrict freedom of expression and protest; court trials against activists involved blatant violations of due process. The government turned to extra-legal means to injure, torture, kidnap, and murder revolutionaries. The Maidan movement, which encompassed multiple forms of grassroots mobilization, pushed back against repression and new terms of legality, succeeding at forcing Yanukovych to flee the country, and reverting Ukraine back to democracy. With Yanukovych gone, violence by police and special forces against protesters ended, and democracy was restored. Thus, the movement's victory resulted in a radical change of state–society relations, altering the rules of the game from openly repressive to democratic. Vitally, if the resistance movement had failed, the authoritarian regime in Ukraine would have consolidated and worsened.

Accounts that summarize the Maidan movement as "pro-EU" protests are misleading at their core: the pro-EU protests, held 24–29 November, came to an end with only a few hundred peaceful protesters remaining on that last night. It was the openly ruthless police violence against unarmed youth and seniors – unprecedented in post-Soviet Ukraine – that brought 800,000 protesters from all over Ukraine, who now started mobilizing into a movement to fight against the injustice. Increasing state repression throughout the Yanukovych administration, which grew violent in 2013, provided motivation and determination for activists to end the repressive regime. Many among the movement supported ties with the EU – as potential additional external leverage to promote democracy in Ukraine. Putin's active support for the Ukrainian authoritarian leadership was seen as detrimental to Ukraine's democracy. Moreover, presenting Maidan as a "tug of war" between the West and Russia, as some scholars have done,[1] misleadingly oversimplifies the events and, most importantly, deprives Ukrainians of agency. A major contribution of this book is giving voice to the participants of the events, presenting a systematic study of the revolutionaries' motivations, organization, and strategies of resistance.

The book has traced how the interactions between activists and security forces gradually changed the perceptions revolutionaries held about the state's intentions, leading the resistance to eventually embrace political violence as the only viable means to stop the consolidation of an authoritarian regime. The nature of the resistance reveals the pro-democratic motives of the revolutionary movement. Protesters, minority groups, and religious organizations engaged in a dialogue on the meanings of justice, condemning state violations and asserting the need for state actions to honour inalienable human rights. Volunteer lawyers defended protesters in the courts, becoming non-violent agents, brokering dialogue between state and society, and participating in the construction of social meanings of justice. The Maidan experience underlined the ability of a unifying ideational factor to make social mobilization possible, despite resource scarcity: if a goal is perceived as essential for democracy, activists can achieve success by volunteering their time and skills rather than relying solely on monetary resources. While fighting the state, groups with varying philosophies negotiated a common pro-democratic ideology, preventing ultra-right groups from hijacking the movement, while, on the other hand, suppressing feminist and LGBT discourses.

This in-depth analysis of the Maidan reveals that a revolution is a socialization process, showing how social change takes place, and that ideational debates are at the core of such transformations. Socialization, as an essential part of the grassroots revolutionary movement, forced Maidaners to rethink social values and concepts of civic duty, which had been inherited from the Soviet era. Revolutionaries' mutual sacrifice and the ability to defeat authoritarianism by bottom-up mobilization helped them rethink the role of citizens in state–society relations. Maidan struck at the heart of Soviet-inherited social apathy, transforming its participants.

Contribution to Scholarship on Social Mobilization and Post-Communist Studies

This book about the Maidan Revolution – a detailed account of the events, social activism, and their aftermath – supplements scholarship on contentious politics by reinforcing constructivist scholarship on revolutions and social mobilization. Firstly, on the basis of my analysis of the Maidan, I propose adding complexity to the term "democratic revolution." I emphasize dialogical aspects of a democratic revolution, seeing it as a process of socialization and negotiation between the state and a social movement, and among activists themselves. Secondly, my analysis of Maidan informs literature on the paradox of repression: a puzzle addressing continued mobilization despite state suppression. This study supplements constructivist literature by showing that social mobilization in response to repression is contingent on activists' *interpretation* of state violence. In other words, social values and perceptions matter, as they inform political violence. Thirdly, I show that a lack of existing monetary and institutional resources is not a decisive factor in precluding social mobilization. I derive my argument from socio-legal scholarship that emphasizes activists' use of protest and litigation to dispute existing constraints rather than being driven by them. A common pro-democratic goal helps unite activists, who can rely on volunteer work and donations from the pro-democratic masses to overcome a lack of resources. Finally, I build on constructivist literature of post-communist societies, which addresses the post-totalitarian legacy of former communist states. I show that Maidan became a discussion forum of active citizenry, and that revolutionary experiences led to a sense of community on the basis of democratic ideals, altering the social apathy present in post-communist societies.

Adding Complexity to the Term "Pro-Democratic Revolution"

Maidan helped us understand that a revolution is a process of contentious exchange, through which participants learn about each other, and themselves undergo a substantial change. Thus, I propose to incorporate constructivist elements in definitions of pro-democratic revolution. According to the classical definition by Skocpol, a revolution is a "purposive, mass-based movement … that consciously undertakes to overthrow the existing government and perhaps the entire social order," by fighting "it out with the authorities or dominant class and, if it wins, undertakes to establish its own authority and program."[2] Goldstone sees revolution as a mass mobilization against perceived injustices, culminating in a forcible overthrow of government.[3] While scholars disagree when it comes to the motivations of revolutionaries, there is agreement about two major aspects: revolution has to include a mass-based movement, and has to result in substantial political and social change. Goldstone asserts that a modern revolution brings "a fundamental break with the past … revolutionaries can create something entirely new by force of will and frame a government using the principles of reason."[4] However, herein lies the assumption that a fundamental post-revolutionary change is dictated by the actors with a predetermined and unchangeable set of principles. The most illuminating definition of a revolution was provided by Ellis Goldberg, who in his work on the Arab Spring emphasized:

> Public gatherings literally embody the participation of society in politics and, at least for the last hundred years, have widely been understood to be protected as [forums] for the exercise of individual freedom of assembly and speech. Unlike strikes or boycotts, mass demonstrations usually raise political demands rather than express more limited economic demands … Revolutions began with an accumulation of grievances and injustices and concluded with the successful elimination of the systemic causes of those grievances.[5]

I agree that a pro-democratic revolution is first and foremost the *participation of society in politics*. Moreover, Goldberg pointed out "the nature of moral community in Egypt and its role as the basis for political action and political community."[6] As this book shows, pro-democratic revolutions can have a strong dialogical component – as negotiating new terms of legality was carried out via the exchange of demands, threats, and violence between state and society (and among social groups themselves), creating, in the process, new bases for morality and solidarity among social groups. In other words, the revolutionaries' own beliefs change during the process. On the basis of my inductive work on Maidan, I propose the following definition of a democratic revolution:

> A *democratic revolution* is a contentious, accelerated state–society dialogue, in which violent and non-violent actions are used to negotiate the terms of social contract; and a socialization process, which negotiates a post-revolutionary moral community.

Some might question the use of the word *dialogue* to describe contentious state–society interactions, as the term is often used to refer to a verbal conversation, a respectful exchange in search of a solution. Therefore, violent actions are often not seen as part of a dialogue, but rather something that brings an end to it. This study of the Maidan movement showed that contention and violence are a meaningful part of state–society dialogue. Relying on the intrinsic meaning of the term, we can see any human action toward another as an expression that sends a message, and is open to interpretation by another party. Every state action – most certainly including violent repression – is a message, as it is meant not only to suppress the individual against whom the action is directed, but rather to issue a threat to others who might challenge the state. Through an analysis of the Maidan events I traced the process of *changing* social interpretations about state intentions as a result of growing state violence – as one revolutionary explained, "I had not realized the extent to which our police are sadists"; in the words of another, "if not for Maidan, then everything would be in the hands of the state, in Yanukovych's hands … That's why even though I am not a supporter of political violence as an idea, I understood that in the existing situation it was appropriate for me to take part in … a non-peaceful Maidan." Thus, when state violence in Ukraine was used to consolidate dictatorial power, the pro-democratic resistance sent violent and non-violent messages that legitimacy lies only with a democratic state. As yet another revolutionary put it, "I was glad that people showed the state that they were the strength, because it's not people who should be afraid of the state, but the state that should be afraid of the people." This account of state–society dialogue negotiating the terms of social contract supports literature on communicative violence in mass communication, political violence, and genocide studies. Andrew Calabrese asserts that violence is used as a means of political communication by activists as well as the state, building on Hanna Arendt's argument "On Violence," where she asserts that violence "serves to dramatize grievances and bring them to public attention," undermining power,[7] as well as David Apter's argument that political violence serves as a discourse.[8] Calabrese emphasizes that is it misleading, even idealistic, to assume that violence happens only when communication breaks down, and the state (not only social movement groups) constantly relies on violence as a method of communication – including the death sentence in the US, where "the state is effectively communicating to the rest of society that crime does not pay, but that one must pay the ultimate price for the worst crimes,"[9] and when military dictatorships kidnap and torture opposition members to silence others, and when Serbian forces employed mass rape as a weapon not only toward the victims, but "against a culture, a nation."[10] The use of violence as a tool of communication is supported in Richardson's work on terrorism,[11] and in the works of Kalyvas, Straus, and Hook, addressing the logic of political violence in civil wars and other conflicts.[12]

When sending this message to society via violent suppression, the state attempts to assert new rules that shift the boundaries of power – an essential part of the state's role in negotiating a social contract. Hess and Martin showed that the state often covers up repressive actions knowing that appearing unjust may undermine the regime.[13] The state can stigmatize dissent, rely on media censorship, or reinterpret state aggression as self-defence.[14] This leads to a "legitimation battle," when state and social groups engage in an active discourse over the legitimacy of the means and ends of repression.[15] Indiscriminate state violence against peaceful protesters is likely to damage the state's legitimacy and build more support for the opposition.[16] To highlight government injustice, social movements may adopt constitutional rhetoric.[17] As I analyze the Ukrainian Revolution, I show that such *legitimation battles* are at the heart of a revolutionary process. I draw attention to statements of multiple actors, for example clergymen, who reasserted that the state's violations of citizens' constitutional norms during the revolution was a violation of moral bounds, drawing on religious dogma. Thus, the Ukrainian Revolution was democratic theory at work – a deliberation about constitutional boundaries of power and the meaning of democracy. Scholars of revolutions unfortunately overlook that battles over the concepts of justice also took place in courts.

As this book has established, the Yanukovych regime continuously exercised violence, increasing the range and level of violent actions against activists over time, in order to assert new terms of legality and therefore revise the existing social contract. In other words, not only did the state attempt to suppress the opposition, it attempted to normalize repression, creating a new order where anti-state resistance is not tolerated. Social dissent against state repression is also a message – that of social rejection of new state rules. Maidan taught us that this message can take multiple forms during a revolution. In response to state violence in Ukraine, people conducted their dialogue by carrying banners, making posters, arguing in courts, and deriding politicians. Maidaners said clearly: we will not let you normalize repressive behaviour. Simultaneously, a dialogue was happening among the protesters. People began talking to each other about democracy, belonging, and the meaning of *Ukraine*. They turned Kyiv's central Independence Square, or Maidan (Nezalezhnosti), into a revolutionary square and an arena of heightened social discourse. Of course, any non-revolutionary period also involves a dialogue between state and society about the boundaries of power. As Hanson points out, time is an essential characteristic of revolutions.[18] Revolution drastically speeds up the exchange: stakes are high, attention is focused, and people who care about social issues are right next to each other. Thus, revolutions are an accelerated dialogue between state and society.

Revolution is a *socialization process of value negotiations*. First of all, protesters learn about the ideological commitments of state agents while interacting with them. Coming to Maidan to protest Yanukovych's decision to not sign the treaty with the EU, protesters did not expect violence. However, even after the state began violently beating and detaining protesters, revolutionaries did not expect that the state would eventually start using live ammunition and torture. In multiple accounts throughout this book, Maidaners related their shock regarding the type and range of repressive state actions, which continually increased. Thus, the process of interacting with the state during the revolution affected activists' image of the state. This book's chapters on state–society dialogue have shown that as a result of the changing image of the state among activists, the commitment to maintaining peaceful resistance waned, and those who advocated a violent solution began to receive more support from the participants. Importantly, the interview data show that the vital factor behind the changing of the state's image was not only the understanding of how much power the state holds and is willing to use, but rather the personal interactions with Berkut police, which moulded the image of state agents as those who intend to abuse rather than defend the rights and lives of the citizens, and whose opinion can't therefore be changed via peaceful means. While discovering the state's intent, revolutionaries discovered each other. As this study of Maidan showed, anti-state resistance contained multiple groups, who had several disagreements on ideological grounds. Looking for common ground, these various groups negotiated a common ideology. During the Maidan, participants continually debated the provisions of the Ukrainian constitution and whether or not violence was an acceptable means of resistance. To assert the moral boundaries of state–society interaction, activists resisted attempts by state agents to reconceptualize the norms of state behaviour vis-à-vis citizens' rights. Thus, revolution promoted the active engagement of various citizens to interact and engage in state–society dialogue on the meaning of governance and state–society relations. The pro-democratic discourse of the majority dominated, forcing ultra-right groups to veil their radical agenda and preventing them from hijacking the anti-state movement. Maidan also involved intra-society negotiations of belonging. Such negotiations, for example, successfully led to further inclusion of Jewish and Muslim groups into the concept of an all-Ukrainian identity, but on the other hand, led to further exclusion of feminist and LGBTQ discourse. Thus, state–society and intra-society dialogues revolve around questions of human rights: actors negotiate boundaries of state power to assert citizens' individual rights vis-à-vis the state, and the rights of minorities against the dominance of majority values.

The final aspect of the proposed definition asserts that *revolutionary dialogue determines political and social change*. Once again, not only is the change dictated by the power dynamic between involved actors, but participation in anti-state resistance and conceptual negotiations transforms both political institutions (if the resistance succeeds), and also social values. As we saw in the case of Maidan, the emerging grassroots movement offered social experiences that forced participants to rethink their own notions of *nation* and *civic duty*, contributing to the shifting of social-wide paradigms, and eclipsing the Soviet legacy of social apathy – thus, engaging in the process of creating a new Durkheimian "moral community." The proposed emphasis on the dialogical aspect of revolutions also reflects Goldberg's discussion of pro-democratic protests as a process of creating a new moral community that reflects the social revolutionary discourse.[19]

Revolutionary Dialogue and the Paradox of Repression

Seeing a revolution as a contentious state–society dialogue enhances scholarly literature on repression-dissent. At the end of November 2013, peaceful Ukrainian protesters were surrounded and ruthlessly beaten by police. As a result, hundreds of thousands of people came from all over the country to Kyiv to protest. The state intensified its abuses: arrests, torture, brutality, live ammunition. Yet people maintained the resistance. A large body of scholarship, in fact, addresses the *paradox of repression*: continued mobilization despite state suppression.[20] Repression, thus, may become a transformative event that intensifies mobilization.[21] Sharp famously dubbed this effect *political jiu-jitsu*, referring to a form of martial arts where one's power is used against them by their opponent.[22] Backfire often occurs in the aftermath of excessive police force used against peaceful protesters,[23] or imprisonment, censorship, and arrests,[24] and other forms of political abuse and harassment.[25] Violent acts can trigger mobilization in defence of groups suppressed by structural violence: state violence becomes a "transformative event" that helps "consolidate existing activist networks ... historical memory, and interpretive frames."[26] Why do people continue to resist despite the fear of violent suppression? Considering the dialogical aspect of democratic revolutions helps us look beyond the assumptions that a threat should be considered only as a dynamic of power (and therefore, force the resistance into submission). Threat can also be interpreted as state communication: the promise to use violence indefinitely, as a tool to rewrite the social contract and normalize repression. Therefore, when we try to explain why activists embrace political violence, we must consider social interpretation of state actions as a linking, intervening variable. In other words, it is not an individual fear of repercussion, but a group fear of what future state–society relations entail. In other words, a concern for the public good, rather than a fear of individual cost, is the key for predicting social rebellion. Social interpretation of the morality of state actions, in turn, depend on majority values.

Rational-choice scholars insist that "the risk of injury during the fighting" as well as "rewards and punishments offered by the two sides" determine the possibility of resistance.[27] Thus, state repression is seen as a deterrent of political collective action due to the high costs of opposition,[28] thus having negative effects on social-movement organizations.[29] Lichbach argues that the opposition protests violently in response to state repression of non-violent protests, but abandons violent behaviour in response to state repression of violent dissent.[30] Moore supports Lichbach's model and concludes that states can shape dissident behaviour by choosing the nature of suppression.[31] Unless protection is offered by insurgent organizations against state violence, revolutionaries are expected to abandon resistance.[32] While insightful, these studies do not help understand why protest activity was maintained in Ukraine in 2013–14 despite security forces' violent crackdown that significantly increased the costs for participants. Lucan Way insists that the success of protest movements in post-Soviet authoritarian states depends on the vulnerability of the state.[33] He argues that the Ukrainian state failed to suppress the pro-democratic Orange Revolution because it lacked major "sources of authoritarian strength – a single, highly institutionalized ruling party; an extensive battle-tested, and well-funded coercive apparatus; or state discretionary control over the economy."[34] According to these parameters, the Ukrainian state gained considerable strength by the winter of 2013–14. As described in the introductory chapter, Yanukovych had a strong grip on the Party of Regions, which voted in support of authoritarian laws on 16 January with blunt procedural violations. Berkut security forces have exhibited strong skills in using unlawful methods of violence and torture and only increased their determination and brutality by the end of the revolutionary events. While independent businesses continued to function, Yanukovych's government gained strong extra-judicial control over the tax revenue apparatus, successfully using it to repress the economic section. Also, as this book indicates, the Maidan movement was enabled by continuous widespread individual donations (as well as from larger businesses). One might argue that in comparison with some other cases of state repression, Ukraine's case could be still be seen as one of "low" state repression, given that "only several hundred" revolutionaries were shot, tortured and injured, or imprisoned. And yet, the level and nature of violent repression in Ukraine in 2013–14 substantially exceeded many other cases where protest movements crumpled (for example, in Belarus in 2020 or Kazakhstan in 1986).

Rich interview data, analyzed in this book, present a conceptual counterargument to the "weak state repression" argument. More specifically, revolutionaries shared that they had high expectations of being imprisoned, injured, or killed. Thus, solely focusing on the "few hundred murders" as a sign of state "weakness" overlooks the cost to each individual activist (after all, rational-choice theory insists on individual rationality as a key element of understanding mass behaviour).[35] Thus, on an individual level, the "weak state" variable did not mean that the Ukrainian revolutionaries perceived they faced less risks of being injured. Despite the severe risks, Maidaners consciously chose to fight against a violent authoritarian state to restore democracy.

We can't understand why resistance prevails without understanding why revolutionaries risk their lives, and how they negotiated a common ideological consensus. This book shows that the discourse among Maidan revolutionaries emphasized the primacy of natural rights. This finding supplements constructivist literature on social movements. Notably, Cirtautas's extensive study of the Polish Solidarity movement showed that its success in undermining the oppressive one-party system was grounded in risky mass protests and underground activity, and would have never taken place if activists had been governed by pragmatic calculations or fear of repercussion. Cirtautas emphasizes that the Solidarity movement was centred around "the belief in the freedom and equality of individuals as an absolute value, as a *cause worth dying for*,"[36] a shared belief in the primacy of natural rights or Weberian value rationality, which is seen to trump instrumental rationality in the mass decision-making process.[37] Vitally, it was the communist regime's firm commitment to reject the concept of natural rights and the repressive martial law in Poland that "helped to sustain the revolutionary potential of natural rights ideology in Eastern Europe."[38] In other words, we cannot conceptualize repression as a cause of fear alone, but as a motivation to resist. Indeed, scholars have shown that repressive state tactics may backfire,[39] creating public "outrage to an event that is publicized and perceived to be unjust."[40] In other words, state violence becomes the state's weakness, as it motivates social forces to mobilize. Thus, many scholars have observed that state suppression may create support for those who were attacked and stimulates social protest,[41] at times radicalizing dissent.[42] Why would protesters support those who were attacked if they just witnessed that the state did not hesitate to use violence and other forms of repression? The answer is obvious: people were outraged, they viewed it as morally wrong, and they wanted state injustice and violence to stop. Elizabeth Wood showed that emotional and moral motives were essential to the emergence and consolidation of insurgent collective action in rural El Salvador.[43] Resistance appears when the state loses legitimacy.[44]

Seeing revolution as a state–society dialogue also reminds us that it is a continuing process of exchange, and depends on how each phase of the dialogue is interpreted. For example, Tilly and Tarrow, who are considered the leading scholars of contentious-politics literature, lead with an account of the Maidan in their latest book, focusing their description on Yanukovych's refusal to sign the EU deal, which brought "Western Ukrainians – including most of the residents of the country's capital," and concluding that state violence turned peaceful demonstrations into violent ones.[45] While this somewhat typical account does not provide incorrect information, it leaves out the major aspects of the revolutionary events in Ukraine, as become evident from my analysis: comprehensive changes in legal, judicial, and police behaviour to establish authoritarian rule. Moreover, in the rest of the book, Tilly and Tarrow's (and other mainstream) analyses of the Maidan leave out not only the broader grassroots mobilization, which became the necessary core to sustain protests, but also the process of how social perception about the state changed as a result of interactions between state and society. As Della Porte emphasizes, political radicalization is better understood by examining the dynamic of conflict over time, "in a trajectory of action and reaction" between state and social groups.[46] The detailed account in this book about the interactions between Maidan revolutionaries and the state showed the changing nature of perceptions that determined the social response. This study of the grassroots nature of the Ukrainian Revolution supports Gamson's approach in analyzing social discourse in order to understand how participants respond to encounters with the state.[47] As McCann put it, legal norms are an "intersubjective force that mediates meaning-making activity among and within contending groups … [they] shape and express the terms of resistance, aspiration, and tactical struggle."[48] It is, therefore, essential to see not only the way norms are imposed by the state, but the way they are understood and practised by social actors.[49] Building on Gamson's and McCann's approaches, I argue that we need to analyze social discourse with the state during a revolution more comprehensively. Thus, we need to analyze how state actions are *interpreted* by social groups, and how social interpretations, in turn, structure social response. This will help us understand what motivates the participants, and what determines the means of resistance.

State Action → Social Interpretation → Social Response

Ukrainian revolutionaries consciously maintained a peaceful means of resistance after exhaustive intra-activist deliberation. This supports literature showing that social activists attempt to maintain non-violent means of resistance in order to highlight the movement's moral superiority over state aggression.[50] However, as the state turned to torture and live ammunition, Maidaners had a tough choice: how would their pro-democratic message be affected if they were to support political violence? A significant factor is necessary to compel activists to abandon peaceful means of resistance, as the legitimacy of their action is bound to be undermined. Building on a "threat" model of social mobilization,[51] a number of scholars emphasize that radicalization follows state aggression if it is perceived as threatening.[52] An erosion of rights and state violence can trigger collective resistance[53] as masses respond to the closing down of political space.[54] As White's analysis of the micro-mobilization of the provisional Irish Army showed, a complex social reaction to repression must take place before activists choose political violence, as they must redefine their beliefs "to make them congruent with organized political violence."[55] If we study the dynamics of state–society interaction over time, we are better equipped to understand whether state action is (eventually) interpreted as a substantial threat, leading to the social justification of political violence. First, for political violence to be supported by the masses, not only must activists perceive state violence as unjust, but acts of state aggression must be interpreted as a substantial threat, and evidence of a worsening regime. Secondly, therefore, activists have to become disillusioned with state actors' ability to change. The process of interacting with the state during the conflict may affect activists' image of the state and state actors' commitment to democratic means, making activists believe violence is the only option to secure change. The flowchart below captures the theory of dynamic revolutionary dialogue: initial state repression causes a particular social interpretation, which structures social response: in the case of Ukraine, mass protests. Mass protests, in turn, may lead to increased state repression – Ukraine's police turned to torture, kidnappings, and live ammunition in January of 2014. This state repression generated a different social interpretation, namely that social failure to stop the state would lead to a terror regime. Such interpretation leads to growing support for political violence to prevent the consolidation of authoritarianism.

State Repression 1 → Social Interpretation 1 → Social Response 1 →
State Repression 2 → Social Interpretation 2 → Social Response 2

Consider the following dichotomy: in 1970 the US National Guard fired at students during a peaceful march at Kent State University against the US bombing of Cambodia, killing four and injuring nine others. The shootings led to nationwide student strikes and affected social discourse across the country. Importantly, however, this severe state violence did not trigger a revolution. In contrast, in Ukraine, excessive police violence and detentions of peaceful protesters led to a mass uprising and eventually social violence against the state, calling for an end to political repression and the resignation of the president. According to constructivist scholars, an "injustice frame" – that is, social perception of certain government action as unjust – determines social response.[56] While the state shooting at Kent State University led to social condemnation, there was no revolutionary movement because state violence was perceived as a malfunction of the current system, rather than a sign of authoritarianism. In other words, a change *within* the current regime was consequently pursued. In contrast, continuous state violence throughout the winter months in Ukraine was perceived by many as a sign of increasing authoritarian practices – a dangerous escalation of previous institutional changes undertaken by Yanukovich before the Maidan. While, initially, a commitment to non-violent methods was ardently pursued, interaction with state agents altered the social image of the existing government, pushing many to justify political violence as the only means to restore democracy. Activists perceived that if the state was not stopped, terror practices would become routine and democracy would be lost indefinitely.

Revolutionary Dialogue and "Volunteer Culture" as a Resource

While most accounts of the Maidan focus on the protest events, the detailed account in this book uncovers the complex social networks of mutual assistance that were created in order to maintain resistance. Creative grassroots mobilization became a major part of the state–society dialogue. Rather than giving in to state threats, various activists throughout the capital, the country, and the world mobilized to deliver their message in reply to the state. Support for protest efforts of the Revolution of Dignity communicated that basic civil liberties should remain in the social contract. Study of the Maidan also supports the notion that people resources[57] are a vital part of the social mobilization puzzle: perception of social injustice is vital for mobilization, while lack of resources (economic and political) can be overcome if an ideational commitment is present. In fact, during the Maidan, a lack of political opportunities became the very trigger for volunteer lawyers' mobilization – to fight against judicial abuses of power rather than being constrained by them. Finally, while debating the social contract with the state, the various Maidan groups engaged in negotiating individual rights within society. While some groups were unable to promote their group rights, the majority consensus on civil liberties within the movement suppressed ultra-right attempts to hijack the movement.

This Maidan study supplements constructivist social-mobilization literature, showing that activity-based participation compensates for a lack of financial resources.[58] Resistance against authorities depends on the level of grievances and citizens' adoption of an injustice frame.[59] Much of the Maidan movement participation was based on volunteer work, which offset a lack of financial resources, supporting Lofland

and Jamison's and Snow's[60] conclusions. Ideals led the Maidan activists to persist despite financial scarcity, supporting studies on Indigenous mobilization in Latin America.[61] Ukrainian lawyers offered pro bono aid as they empathized with clients, supporting scholarly literature on legal mobilization where lawyers are shown to mobilize motivated by empathy with those experiencing deprivation,[62] or are devoted to the cause of the resistance movement.[63] A detailed account of the Maidan challenges studies in which higher income,[64] national prosperity,[65] or groups' financial resources[66] are seen as decisive factors for participation. In short, those studies see discretionary financial resources as essential[67] – for example, higher-income families are more likely to participate in protests or social movement organizations[68] due to "more disposable income."[69] The causality between the amount of discretionary resources and activation of a social mobilization sector is based on assumptions that a social mobilization sector is a "low priority competitor of resources."[70] However, as Snow puts it, resource mobilization scholars *assume* a "constancy of mobilizing grievances" – that is, social grievances are assumed to be always present, and financial resources are necessary to translate them into social movements.[71] Detailed interviews with the Maidan activists, and the account of their activities, show that volunteer activism and individual donations – driven by pro-democratic ideology – offset a lack of financial resources. Moreover, the fundamental resource for social mobilization is an effective co-operation between activists and other social groups, rather than the professional organization per se. In other words, while some scholars argue that professional movement organizations are found to be instrumental in social mobilization,[72] and the stronger the professional organizations, the more likely activists will mobilize,[73] the Maidan experience showed that the major value of professional movements for mobilization is in providing a *network* to coordinate resistance efforts. Thus, this Maidan study supports scholarship that emphasizes that the success of social mobilization depends on the ways in which activists cultivate relationships with other movement organizations, affecting the strength of collaboration and sharing of skills, information, and knowledge.[74] Most importantly, the common pursuit of social justice promotes the building of new trust networks, which cultivate new relationships and share knowledge and skills, delivering the function otherwise delivered by professional organizations.

The analysis of the Maidan Revolution in this book also supports studies which show that interest groups turn to mobilization despite their expectations of significant political or institutional constraints.[75] Scholars have shown that rather than being restrained by these limitations, groups can reshape existing institutional restrictions through their participation.[76] For example, losing a court case may, in fact, be a litigation strategy in itself: to highlight a policy gap, gain media attention, or possibly mobilize the public.[77] Thus, activism should not be seen strictly as a strategy to alter policy, utilized only with favourable institutions and elites. Rather, restrictions can be used by activists as a powerful tool to alter existing structures, elite practices, or social discourse. The Maidan analysis in this book supplements socio-legal scholarship that emphasizes activists' use of litigation to challenge existing constraints rather than being driven by them. More specifically, the blossoming of pro bono legal mobilization during the Maidan supports McCann's analysis of cause lawyers, who deploy courtroom encounters beyond an attempt to win a case and alter a policy.[78] Even such motions as bailing protesters out of jail show support for disruptive tactics.[79] Importantly, Maidan courtroom experiences confirmed studies showing that cause lawyers often do more than mount a conventional defence to secure an acquittal: they can turn a courtroom into a political forum.[80] In the Ukrainian courts, cause lawyers and social activists challenged the state's imposition of an alternative vision of legality. These conclusions challenge literature that sees political and legal opportunity structures as decisive factors behind social mobilization. It is argued that social movements are more likely to develop under favourable political opportunity structures (POS), adapting their strategies accordingly.[81] So, if a political system is designed to offer open access to the administration in the policy area concerned, interest groups are likely to rely on lobbying; if the political system is "closed," interest groups are more likely to rely on protest.[82] Similarly, some scholars emphasize that legal opportunity structures (LOS), such as institutional access to courts and various procedural requirements, determine interest groups' choice to litigate, emphasizing that the opportunity needs to be evaluated in terms of political and judicial receptivity,[83] as "poor political and legal opportunities"[84] limit mobilization activity. These studies focus on the barriers to effective mobilization, but do not address the rise of legal mobilization in repressive environments – a notable element of the Maidan revolutionary movement. Maidan experiences support socio-legal studies showing that cause lawyers become "brokers" between state and society.[85] As Maidan demonstrated, the most fundamental brokering between state and society in a democratic revolution lies in activists' ability to uncover the state's attempts to assert illiberal legality. Maidaners didn't just look for available resources and institutional opportunities, but insisted on questioning the rules of the political game decreed by the state, dictating their terms of the social contract.

Intra-Society Revolutionary Dialogue and a New Moral Community

Studies on post-Maidan Ukraine have shown notable social changes, including the growth of civil society and changes in social attitudes. However, the authors of these studies seem to be torn when it comes to identifying the major factor behind those changes: the Maidan itself, or the Russian invasion in 2014, as a lot of volunteer work was focused on remedying the effects of the invasion, including the associated migration crisis. While both may be at play in explaining post-Maidan changes, the rich interview data presented in this book help identify the *mechanism* behind the effect of the Maidan mobilization on activists' changing values. Thus, while the Maidan was a discussion forum for negotiating the social contract with the state, it also became a bonding experience for those who risked their security in the name of democracy. This ideational identity provided the basis for a new communal identity in Ukraine, overcoming ethnic, language, and religious differences. Not only bearing risk, but witnessing others sacrificing for the idea of democracy, created feelings of belonging to a new community, forcing the participants to redefine concepts of *Ukraine* and *belonging*. Newly created grassroots networks also became tools to break dependence on existing trust networks inherited from the Soviet era, striking at the heart of the totalitarian legacy of social apathy and expectations that the state is the deliverer of goods and safety. Analysis of the Maidan experience traces the change of activists' perceptions of civic duty, as they start seeing themselves as responsible for political change. This account has additional value in understanding post-Maidan changes, as many Maidaners continued their activism after the revolution, such as organizing aid to the Ukrainian army, to internally displaced persons, and to anti-corruption campaigns, and therefore are at the heart of continuing changes in Ukrainian society.

This book revealed the underbelly of the revolutionary process, showing how the defining elements of revolutionary grassroots mobilization change the very people who organize it. To maintain the protests and develop new strategies of resistance in response to growing state violence, Maidan activists continued gathering in the square, creating new initiatives to coordinate the incoming masses, and watching each other sacrifice. These social interactions directed to transform the state created a heightened forum about state–society and intra-society relations, and generated a sense of community on the basis of a shared goal they were determined to achieve above all individual cost. Revolutionaries created a social institution to engage with and limit the state – and with that, they developed a sense of self-power, overcoming lingering post-totalitarian perceptions of social weakness vis-à-vis the state. Such transformations of social perceptions included newly gained appreciation for civic duty, and even their own nation, now seen more as a diverse pro-democratic community.

Post-Revolutionary Social Change

Post-socialist scholars point out the difficulty of transitioning to a democratic regime due to legacies of the Soviet regime. Leninist totalitarian ideology asserts the primacy of the state's decision making, which claims to guide workers through a transitional socialist stage. A number of scholars argue that decades of the Soviet regime, which deprived the masses of agency, resulted in a habitually unengaged public.[86] They point out how belief in Leninist ideology has lingered. Mistrust of the political sphere, as post-Soviet populations distrust political parties and politicians, or any civic organization, prevailed years after the collapse of the Soviet Union. Post-socialist scholars argue that severe penalties for challenging the state, state-established organizations, and state-sponsored social services (from healthcare to vacations) engineered a complacent post-totalitarian society with individuals who expect the state to deliver social goods and are inexperienced with the function of NGOs in a democratic setting. Thus, Leninist ideology is argued to have transformed state and social institutions, leading post-socialist society to freeze in "habitual socialism." Jowitt and Hanson point out that the Leninist legacy argument is based on a Weberian assumption that institutions are set by charismatic ideas.

Therefore, if new ideas and beliefs take hold, social and state institutions may change. In other words, the consolidation of democratic values has the power to overcome "post-communist democratic deficit." Moreover, looking at post-Soviet development through a post-colonial prism suggests that non-Russian former Soviet states may stress nation building with an emphasis on the national question while sacrificing individual rights.[87]

As stated in chapter 5, the Maidan Revolution was a forum for negotiating new, transformative governing principles. The idea of such a transformation within a community is consistent with Durkheim's argument that social developments may contribute to new bases of solidarity or unity, creating new moral communities.[88] These experiences led to a sense of community based on democratic ideals, breaking the primal importance of existing trust networks. Further, the Maidan transformed the Soviet legacy of state–society relations, in which perpetual social apathy had resulted from a view of the state as the guarantor of social goods.[89] Self-sacrifice in the face of visible risks to sustain a democratic regime affected perceptions of "civic duty" among the revolutionaries, challenging the Soviet legacy of social communal distrust.[90] Post-revolutionary social transformation can indeed be seen as a litmus test for true revolutionary changes.[91] Ellis Goldberg explored the vital role of a revolution in creating a new moral community, as he theorized about the Arab Spring:

> The various forms of street demonstrations – whether they voiced demands for political rights, economic grievances, or sectarian identity – had in common claims about the nature of moral community in Egypt and its role as the basis for political action and political community. The long debate about religion and secularism can be seen not so much as a quarrel about identity or law but about the nature of membership in the moral community that informs political membership … I propose that demonstrations, of many kinds, over the past several years have been an important way for Egyptians to imagine what kind of community they inhabit and to test various possibilities against not only membership in a nation but in other possible configurations of moral community.[92]

The Ukrainian Maidan Revolution, which challenged the state as it attempted to impose new terms of legality, became the process through which new moral communities were built on new bases of solidarity.

Scholars have observed that contemporary revolutions target mostly regimes, focusing on those in power,[93] which led some to conclude that these revolutions, keeping with liberal political traditions, tend to be less transformative.[94] Some even argue that such processes are less revolutionary, as resistance pressures incumbent regimes without seizing power.[95] This focus on elites in power causes us to ignore the most important aspect of revolutionary change: regime change – that is, a change in the rules of the game, which fundamentally transform the exercise of civil liberties. In other words, revolutions of earlier centuries, which were seen as "more transformative," as they led to the collapse of state institutions and seizure of power by new elites, did not, in fact, guarantee a regime where people could exercise more individual power. The Ukrainian Maidan Revolution prevented the consolidation of an authoritarian regime, restoring basic democratic freedoms: freedom of expression and the right to criticize and contest the state. Moreover, a revolutionary process of negotiation and self-sacrifice reformed Ukrainian society, crushing the prevalence of post-Soviet legacies in social attitudes.

Applying the Lessons of the Maidan

How can lessons from the Ukrainian Revolution be applied to analyze resistance in other states? The argument of this study focuses on understanding how changing social perception of the state led to the eventual embrace of violent means of resistance; and tracing how the pro-democratic consensus was negotiated among the movement – eventually leading to adoption of a new social contract, affecting broader social values. But what can the study teach us about the possibility of the success or failure of other resistance movements? Why did the 2020 protests in Belarus, challenging the legitimacy of elections, fail to oust Lukashenko? Why were they so insignificant in Russia? Can we try to apply the lessons learned to consider anti-state resistance in Iran and Hong Kong? Belarus could be seen as one of the closest cases, due to a number of shared external factors: post-Soviet totalitarian legacy,

Kremlin influence, and, at the same time, proximity to Western democracies. Some would argue that Belarus presented the case of a stronger state – with stronger repression. Notably, however, the Yanukovych administration eventually adopted severe repression tactics: torture, live ammunition, and even the use of snipers to shoot at revolutionaries, with the latter increasing the chances for anyone to be shot, even if they chose to stay back from the line of contact with police. As the detailed discussion in this book demonstrates, many Ukrainian revolutionaries expected to be jailed, tortured, or shot. A constructivist approach might be more applicable, considering that support for the pro-democratic resistance appeared to be stronger among the Ukrainian population. The discussion in this book also suggests several other factors to be considered when comparing the different outcomes in Ukraine and Belarus. The 2020 Belarus protests did not see the same level of activist mobilization and did not rely on political violence. Unlike the case of Belarus, the Ukrainian Maidan became more than just protest, expanding to include extensive grassroots mobilization, which helped sustain the revolution by organizing food, housing, and medical and legal aid. Secondly, the support for violent means of resistance as the only way to defeat the authoritarian state grew among the majority of Maidaners. In fact, it is very unlikely Maidaners would have been able to restore democracy in Ukraine without violence. The use of violent means, extensive grassroots networks, and support for Maidan among the majority of the Ukrainian population, presented a counter-power to the Yanukovych state.

The case of Hong Kong in 2019–20, then, appears closer to Ukraine: support for the pro-democratic movement was similarly very strong among the local population, and mobilization was even stronger. I would argue that if it were the people of Hong Kong vs. the state of Hong Kong, the resistance would have succeeded – similarly to Ukraine's Maidan. However, Hong Kong protesters also faced the government of China. Additionally, a critical factor to consider is that the people of China did not aid the people of Hong Kong. The discussion in this book about the process of negotiating a common resistance ideology among the revolutionaries should also be considered in future studies of the Iranian civil unrest of 2022 (and likely future resistance movements against its repressive state). The resistance in the aftermath of the murder of the Mahsa Amini by morality police embraced the slogan,

"Woman, Life, Freedom" – essentially, becoming the first truly feminist democratic resistance movement. The challenge of this premise, as this book would suggest, is that of truly majoritarian support for a feminist movement (even if centred around a discourse on human rights). Thus, in future studies of the Iranian resistance it will be vital to trace whether/how a common resistance ideology is negotiated – whether a consensus is found to mobilize and sustain an effective majoritarian pro-democratic movement.

What about Russia? Put simply, there was never enough support among the majority of the Russian population to oust Putin. While civil society organizations, anti-state protests, and pro-democratic parties existed and resisted putinist authoritarianism, the pro-democratic opposition was always in the minority. It is vital to remember that, unlike Russia, Ukraine was not burdened by a post-imperial syndrome. The collapse of the Soviet Union was empowered by Ukrainians' disillusionment with the regime, which brought them not only an underperforming/ineffective economy, but also Chernobyl, and – as unearthed archives showed – Holodomor.[96] In contrast, Russian pro-democratic attempts were subdued by a popular nostalgia for the Soviet Union's "great power" status, where the Kremlin controlled other Soviet republics and states of Eastern Europe, and played a decisive role on the global political stage.[97] Scholars refer to such popular attitudes as post-imperial syndrome, a "nationalist irredentism and an ambition to return to the status quo ante of a 'great power.'"[98] Post-imperial syndrome, in both Weimar Germany and post-Soviet Russia, is a main reason why democratization processes faced challenges, as a "culture of defeat" overshadowed the democrats' appeals for liberal reforms.[99] Democrats in Russia had to compete with Zhirinovsky's fascist party, which held a constant presence in the Russian parliament, and Alexander Dugin's fascist ideology, which was steadily gaining popularity.[100] According to Dugin's "neo-Eurasianism" theory, Russia holds a unique status,[101] in need of being saved from Western liberalism. When Ukraine became a democracy, as a result of the peaceful pro-democratic 2004 Orange Revolution, it inspired the Russian democratic political elite and civil society: anti-Putin and pro-democratic protests gained momentum. In response, Putin introduced a number of measures designed to promote an anti-Western radicalization of Russian society,[102] and encouraged anti-Ukrainian propaganda. He succeeded at suppressing the democrats and advanced illiberal policies, building on his irredentist claims, which appealed to a majority in Russia.[103]

Ukraine's Maidan democratic revolution was an accelerated state–society dialogue, in which violent and non-violent actions were used to negotiate new terms of social contract, and an intra-society dialogue which affected post-revolutionary values. As pro-democratic values dominated in Ukraine, millions headed to the Kyiv Maidan Nezalezhnosti Square in reaction to police brutality against peaceful protesters. Interactions with the state became a dialogue – where beatings, torture, sham trials, and shootings changed social actors' image of the state; many became more likely to support violence as the only path to reassert a democratic social contract. Massive grassroots mobilization enabled the resistance, and witnessed the successful negotiation of a common ideological consensus among the various groups of revolutionaries. The process of mutual self-sacrifice and active social discourse also helped consolidate post-revolutionary values. It is precisely the pro-democratic and pro-sovereignty values, born among the majority of Ukrainians during the Maidan, that contributed to successful resistance against the powerful Russian state's full-scale military invasion in 2022. With the invasion came bombings, rocket launches, and rape and torture chambers. Most observers in the West expected Ukraine's immediate demise, but social resistance, with the masses volunteering to fight, deliver food and supplies, and donate to the army, offered a strong counter to Russian military might. When Russia carried out its massive full-scale invasion of Ukraine, heavily relying on mass atrocities against the civilian population, Ukrainian civilian engagement was one of the key factors behind the successful deterrence of Russian armed forces. Ukrainians' civic activists, skilled at functioning as a decentralized resistance, greatly contributed to the success of anti-Russian resistance. The more the West would have known about the Maidan, the less surprised they would have been at Ukraine's success.

Epilogue

The Maidan and Kremlin Propaganda

> I was telling my own brother who lived in Moscow, on the phone, saying, "I'm standing right here, I'm telling you, I'm treating [injured] people who are protesting against the repressive Yanukovych government ... It's not a fascist [movement] ... Don't you think I can see things better, standing right here, on Maidan, [knowing] what we are doing?" But he'd always insist, "You just don't get it, we understand the whole picture better from here."

This story, told by a physician who volunteered during the revolution, represents a typical exchange between revolutionaries and their friends and relatives residing in Russia. Interviewees shared a common pattern: many of their Russian relatives believed the false statements aired on Russian TV about events in Ukraine, and didn't trust the testimony of their close relatives, who participated in the revolution themselves. During the Maidan Revolution, the Kremlin unleashed systematic propaganda, promoting falsehoods about the revolution, and justifying the invasion of Ukraine in 2014, and then their full-scale aggression in 2022. Legal analyses, addressing the genocidal nature of the Russian war against Ukraine, point out that understanding Russian state propaganda is essential in uncovering the intent behind the systematic war crimes committed by the Russian army in Ukraine.[1]

According to Jonathan Maynard's analysis of different ideologies that justify mass violence, there are six major similarities, in which mass violence against civilians is made to appear justified to perpetrators.[2] On the basis of examples from ideologies that were used to justify mass atrocities by Nazi Germany, Soviet Stalinism, Mao's China, the Rwanda genocide of 1994, and former Yugoslavia in the 1990s, he developed a framework of six common "justificatory mechanisms": (1) dehumanization, (2) guilt attribution, (3) threat construction to characterize the victim of atrocities, (4) de-agentification, (5) virtue talk, and (6) future bias.[3] As he explains,

> The justificatory mechanisms reveal some sort of common features of how perpetrators genuinely perceived and thought about the world – features of their "actual political thinking" … When individuals – both the policy makers who decide that atrocities should occur and the killers who actually carry out the violence – buy-in to these justificatory mechanisms, it is predictable that the commission of atrocities will come to look like a legitimate, beneficial and perhaps necessary course of action … Atrocity perpetrators can, in theory and practice, acknowledge the humanity of their victims, yet still conceive of them as guilty and threatening enemies, and still see killing them as a virtuous activity, an act they are not responsible for, and/or an act ultimately justified by some massive future benefit.[4]

The discussion that follows shows that Russian state propaganda about the Maidan Revolution (and Ukraine, Ukrainians, and Ukrainian culture more generally) follows all six characterizations. The effects intertwine and overlap, but can be divided as follows.

Dehumanization

The first characteristic mechanism is the *dehumanization* of a victim group. The effect of "moral exclusion,"[5] or an ideological construction of moral otherness, is to "push victims beyond the protection of moral (and potentially legal) norms."[6] Terms like "cancer," "microbes," "rats," "poison" are examples used by ideologues across the world to elicit fear[7] and to dehumanize by erasing a human image, and depicting the targeted group as threats to be eradicated before they can eradicate the actual perpetrator. Notably, dehumanization may lead to other justificatory ideologies, including threat construction, as the "basic fear and revulsion it can cause … [is] unsurprisingly conducive towards violence and supportive to processes of threat-construction."[8] As a result, mass killings obtain a third element of dehumanization: a euphemistic reference to aggression that supports the "psychological processes of moral evasion," often referred to as a form of "cleansing."[9] This process of dehumanization transforms victims into mere concepts, which is conveniently placed outside of the moral boundaries of the perpetrator.[10]

Russian propaganda systematically repeated the claim that the Maidan Revolution was an illegal overthrowing of a legitimate president.[11] The Russian political establishment and state media referred to post-Maidan Ukraine as a "junta" run by radicals.[12] The repeated claims of a supposed "illegitimate government" and "public disorder" were presented as a failure for Ukraine and Ukrainians, suggesting the inferior status of the entire group, who were unable to properly govern themselves. After the Maidan Revolution, Russia saw a sharp increase of fiction and non-fiction publications claiming the "collapse of the Ukraine project," the "artificial" nature of the Ukrainian language and identity, and questioning the right of Ukraine to exist.[13] For example, the book *Ukraine Is Russia* claimed the revolution was a CIA-organized "brown coup," showcased an offensive term used in Russia for Ukrainian revolutionaries (and simultaneously for people with Down syndrome – *Maidowns*), and asserted that anti-Soviet sentiment meant Russophobia.[14] Russian news media increased the use of offensive and derogative descriptions of Ukrainians, claiming that Russians have a "right" to control the Ukrainian government.[15]

The second element of dehumanization was the systematic representation of Ukrainians as "pawns of the West." The Maidan Revolution was presented as a coup, organized by "puppets of America (D.C./White House)," who illegally usurped power and forced the country into a US-dictated fascist regime.[16] The conspiracy presenting the Maidan Revolution as being US-sponsored and organized relied on Soviet propaganda tactics.[17] The West/US conspiracy became the centrepiece of the Russian narrative, and was promoted by the political elite, and media.[18] Promotion of this conspiracy became mainstream, repeated in various forms – from fake news stories, to fabricated documentaries, to books depicting the Maidan Revolution as a US-organized coup that enabled Ukrainian fascists.[19] Titles such as *Ukraine: Chaos and Revolution as Weapons of the Dollar*, a Saint-Petersburg Press book, speak for themselves. A propaganda piece, published by a Moscow press, *The Tragedy of Ukraine: A Concentration Camp Instead of a Paradise?* supposedly presented a "secular and spiritual" analysis, arguing that Maidan "bore poisonous fruit," due to "naïve" Ukrainians, who let the US and EU "rule over them."[20] Ukrainians as a group were presented as subhuman: incapable of self-governing, and in need of Russia's "strong hand."

Putin often stated that the Maidan Revolution was "organized" to threaten Russia's security.[21] It was claimed that Ukrainians, who were presumably fooled by the evil forces of the West, presented a threat to Russia's existence. The "threat" element was emphasized by depicting the pro-democratic Maidan movement in Ukraine as "extremist, fascist, Nazi." This conspiracy was at the centre of Russian propaganda, portraying the Maidan Revolution as an ultra-right extremist movement, and claiming it was similar to the Nazi overthrow of the Weimar regime.[22] The propaganda strategy utilized Stalin's tactic, which often declared opposition to his rule (including Ukrainian anti-Soviet nationalism) to be "fascist," or a "fascist collaboration." Numerous fake news stories, performances, social media posts, and books spread the "fascist/Nazi" conspiracy. For example, an image of Ukrainians singing the national anthem were claimed to represent them "swearing allegiance to Hitler," an image of a prison being constructed in Ukraine was claimed to be a concentration camp in the making.[23] Ukrainian national symbols, or images of Ukraine, were promoted as associated with fascism/Nazism. With the unfolding of the Ukrainian Revolution, the Kremlin introduced a wide range of prohibitions. Any support for the Maidan Revolution, or protests against the annexation of Crimea, were immediately suppressed. Carrying Ukrainian national symbols and flags or singing the Ukrainian anthem became illegal in Russia.

Guilt Attribution

The second characteristic mechanism to justify mass violence against civilians is a method of guilt attribution. According to Maynard, guilt attribution is the "assertion that victims have committed moral or legal crimes, and thus moved out of the universe of obligations by their own actions."[24] The guilt attribution element of Russian propaganda focused on the claim that the Maidan Revolution was a violent overthrow of a legitimate regime by "fascists," who took over power and unleashed atrocities. Russian propaganda promoted conspiratorial claims that violent acts against the protesters during the Maidan Revolution were a series of provocations, organized by the opposition to take power.[25] Discussion of the revolution contained frequent references to the Right Sector, suggesting that ultra-right ideology was behind the revolutionary movement as a whole. Any support for the pro-democratic Maidan Revolution in Ukraine was equated with public support for fascism.

As Maynard points out, guilt attribution relies on "rumors, unsubstantiated assertions by authorities, and the incessant repetition of isolated anecdotal cases ... to create a confident social perception of victim guilt."[26] Russian state-controlled propaganda and disinformation became an essential feature of Russian policy after the Maidan Revolution,[27] and opposition news sites (such as *Lenta*) had their editorial team replaced or evicted from their premises.[28] The systematic deception was strategic,[29] and followed methodical steps to suppress press freedoms and centralize control of the media by the Kremlin. During and after the Ukrainian Revolution, journalists were forced to present information about the revolution as directed by the ITAR TASS Russian news agency. A number of journalists who refused to repeat the false coverage resigned, were fired, and/or left the country.[30]

Centralized Russian government control of the news media, and a heavy investment in social media troll factories, allowed consistent distribution of rumours, falsehoods, and conspiracy theories.[31] False stories were often aired by state-run media, and then rigorously promoted through social media.[32] After the revolution, social media continued to be flooded with rumours about atrocities planned by nationalist extremists: stories about poisoned water supplies, fascist gunmen lurking in the woods, pro-Ukrainian circulars with poison absorbed by touch.[33] A telling example of such rumour-based promotion is a story, aired on Russian TV Channel One, about a three-year-old boy who was supposedly "tortured and crucified in a public square by the Ukrainian military."[34] While proven to be false by Ukrainian and Russian journalists, the story continued to be widely disseminated on social media. The distribution of purposefully false rumuor-based information was state-controlled, strategically developed, and systematically promoted via multiple Russian media sources to create an image of Ukrainians as guilty of committing or promoting crimes against Russians in Ukraine, and as supposedly likely to unleash crimes against Russians in Russia.

Critically, ideologies that justify mass violence often present a victim group guilty as a *collective*, deserving collective punishment for the specific crimes of some "members."[35] This tactic became an imperative part of the Russian state message. Labelling participants of the mass-based Maidan Revolution as Nazis, fascists, and antisemites promoted the message that Ukrainians as a group share fascist ideology,[36] and as a group are guilty of supposed atrocities. The Ukrainian post-Maidan government, supported by a majority in Ukraine, was continually dubbed a "fascist junta" that planned to confiscate the properties of Russian speakers, use violence, and prohibit Russian language.[37] Emotional TV hosts on Russian channels repeatedly argued these numerous conspiratorial claims,[38] suggesting that Ukrainians as a whole presented a threat. News coverage of the Russian occupation claimed that Ukrainian libraries were "full of books with Nazi swastikas," when images in fact show Ukraine history books (including those detailing Russian war crimes in 2014).[39]

Threat Construction

Atrocity-perpetrating regimes utilize threat construction, "saturating the discourse of reference to victims with labels that assign them threatening status," and developing a stable lexicon for defining their victims.[40] For example, the Nazis argued they fought "Judeo-Bolsheviks" or "International World Jewry"; Stalinists targeted "socially harmful elements"[41] and kulaks. As Maynard points out, the elasticity of these terms, and fuzzy boundaries of their meaning "contribute to their lethal potential," allowing them to be applied to almost any individual, and therefore convert these individuals into a legitimate target for killing.[42] As discussed earlier, the term "coup" was consistently used to undermine the democratic nature of the Maidan Revolution, often accompanied by claims that it was organized by the United States to suggest an international conspiracy. The term "junta" was used to undermine the post-Maidan political regime in Ukraine. Most importantly, the terms *fascists, Nazis*, and *Banderovites* became the core labels of Ukrainian civilians as part of the Russian propaganda strategy. These terms were consistently used to refer to Maidan revolutionaries, and after the revolution to large portions of Ukrainians. The terms were borrowed from the Stalinist era, when they were used to undermine opposition to the Soviet regime in Ukraine, and became major threat-constructing labels used by the Putin regime. The term *banderovites (banderovtsy)* relies on ambiguity of meaning; it means "Bandera-followers,"[43] and suggests that Ukrainians supposedly praise the atrocities committed by the Nazis and their collaborators. The term implicates a large portion of modern Ukrainians in the crimes of the Second World War, and labels all those who support democracy in Ukraine and opposition to Kremlin aggression as "banderovites." Propaganda also used the term *nedobitye banderovtsi*, the adjective *nedobitye* meaning "those who have not been beaten/killed."[44] This verbiage attempts to justify violence against civilians of modern Ukraine, as it suggests this to be a "continuation" of Second World War Soviet violence against Nazi Germany. According to Maynard, threat construction has a double purpose for ideologies that justify atrocities – as a characterization of the victim group, but also as a presentation of mass murder as self-defence, turning a criminal act into a heroic one.[45] Labelling Ukrainian civilians as *nedobitye banderovtsi*, Kremlin propaganda was preparing the Russian populace to embrace or be apathetic to atrocities against large groups of Ukrainian civilians.

De-agentification

Maynard defines de-agentification as an "ideological portrayal of killers as lacking meaningful agency or responsibility in causing atrocities to occur … [while presenting] the overall atrocity … as an 'inevitable' or 'necessary' result of irresistible forces or unavoidable circumstances beyond the control of human agency."[46] Russian propaganda presented the Maidan Revolution as a "Western-organized coup," arguing that this "forced" Russia to act militarily:

> The corridors of power in Washington D.C., as ever under the thumb of large transnational capital, have zeroed in on Russia as the main target of their next attack. A war with Russia, unleashed by the hands of Ukrainian Nazis, will assuredly lead to an abrupt economic downturn both in the post-Soviet space and in the EU. To this end, in February 2014, the United States, aided and abetted by EU officials, staged a coup in Ukraine, bringing neo-Nazis to power. By organizing the genocide of the Russian population in the southeast of Ukraine, they want to provoke Russia into military action, thus aiming to start another world war in Europe.[47]

The protection of Western liberalism in general was presented as a threat, for example, portraying LGBTQ rights in the West and Ukraine as "euro-Sodom," a supposed threat to Russian civilization.[48] Military aggression was presented by the Russian government as the only viable option to "save" Russia from this threat.[49]

Virtuetalk

Virtuetalk is "ideological conceptions of attractive, admirable and praiseworthy character to portray killing as a laudable act," and usually references the perpetrators as virtuous, "tough, dutiful, loyal, vigilant,"[50] and glorifies violence by connecting it to entrenched social values.[51] Kremlin propaganda depicts an image of Russian soldiers as "liberating" Ukraine from fascism.[52] The Russian state masterfully restored the Second World War cult,[53] as schoolchildren in Russian elementary schools were photographed in Second World War uniforms with automatic weapons, and "trained" to throw toy grenades at a Ukrainian flag. Numerous films and books in the fantasy genre focused on the topic of a war with Ukraine.[54] A propaganda piece in the form of "sci-fi literature," *Bloodied Ukraine: The Banderite Genocide*, published immediately after the Maidan Revolution in Ukraine, promoted an image of Ukrainians as Nazis led by "American masters," and presented the Russians as saviours from the imminent genocide. The publisher's summary reads:

> The imminent future. The Kyiv junta, on the orders of its American masters, unleashes a genocide against the Russian population in southeastern Ukraine ... [Southeastern Ukraine] is hemorrhaging but isn't giving up. Unable to defeat the rebel militia, Nazi death squads request the help of NATO troops. The United States stage a direct intervention in Ukraine. The forces are too unequal; without outside help, the Donbas is doomed to destruction. Its last hope is Russia – the only power that can stop the Banderite genocide.[55]

The Russian violence-inciting concept of *nedobitye banderovtsy* also comes through in another "sci-fi" propaganda piece by a Moscow press, *Callsign Wolfhound*, which promotes the idea that modern Ukrainian civilians are descendants of Second World War fascist collaborators, who should have been murdered. In the book, a modern anti-Ukraine fighter travels in time to 1941 with the aim to "not just to live to see the victory, but to get to the forerunners of modern Banderites and burn down their forest hideouts."[56] After the full-scale invasion of Ukraine, this premise was at the heart of public calls by Russian officials for genocide against the entire population of Ukraine: "In general, what appeared in the place of Ukraine is an existential threat to the Russian people, Russian history, Russian language and the Russian civilization. If we do not put an end to them, as, unfortunately, our grandfathers did not do away with them, we will have to die, but end up at an even greater cost to our grandchildren. So let's get this over with. Once and forever. For our grandchildren."[57]

Future Bias

Finally, future bias, according to Maynard, "defines a broad moral posture of reckless, speculative and unsubstantiated consequentialism" that presents "ends justify the means" arguments.[58] The Kremlin justified the future vision of a larger empire as a result of expansionist wars,[59] with the "necessity" to annihilate Ukrainian identity and culture after the invasion.[60] The war, with atrocities and destruction, was presented as a justifiable cost for the benefit of Russia's imperialism.

Conclusion

Kremlin propaganda presented Ukrainian Maidan revolutionaries as an intellectually inferior group who are "fascist," unable to govern themselves, and therefore, pawns of the West. The approach is consistent with the ideologies of mass violence that not only present the victim group as inferior, but also assigns the entire group a "collective responsibility," falsely depicting them as a threat to the perpetrator group's existence. For example, Nazi propaganda presented Jewish people as inferior, while also emphasizing the supposed "Judeo-Bolshevik threat." Russian propaganda after the Maidan Revolution led up to the 2022 full-scale invasion, and with the ongoing atrocities, the propaganda only intensified – calls to kill Ukrainian civilians en masse, including children and the elderly,[61] became common, as even Russian Orthodox priests called for "burning them all out."[62] The systematically false depiction of the Maidan Revolution remained, however, a cornerstone of propaganda meant to justify the Russian invasion – even during UN Security Council meetings.[63]

Prior to the full-scale invasion, Putin asserted that Ukraine was "invented by Lenin," and should be governed by Russia.[64] The underlying argument of Putin's repeated claim that "Russians and Ukrainians are the same people," was that Ukrainians are really Russians,[65] albeit an "inferior version" of them. The Kremlin denied Ukraine's sovereignty and Ukrainian identity, referring to the entire nation as a "Bolshevik invention." These dehumanizing claims became a must-read for Russian soldiers.[66] The words, "Ukraine" and "Ukrainians" appeared in quotation marks in instruction manuals for Russian soldiers. The propaganda stated that the name "Ukraine" should be erased.[67] As Russia began its full-scale invasion in 2022, Russian forces openly carried out multiple massacres, and set up torture and rape chambers. Many people have been buried alive under the rubble of targeted civilian homes, hospitals and other shelters. Tens of thousands of children were abducted by the Russian military and forcefully taken to camps across Russia, where they are forced to deny their Ukrainian identity and trained to perform military exercises to eventually fight against their own country[68] (a genocidal war crime, for which the International Criminal Court issued an arrest warrant for Putin in 2023). These actions represent a systematic, methodical targeting of Ukrainians. It reflected Russian state ideology which called for "deukrainization," declaring that "Ukrainianism is an artificial anti-Russian construct that has no civilizational substance of its own, a subordinate element of an extraneous and alien civilization."[69]

Ukrainian democracy, won by the Maidan, meant a truly sovereign Ukraine, as citizens were now much less likely to vote again for Russian-controlled politicians promoting authoritarian measures. Ukraine's democracy was therefore problematic for the Kremlin for two major reasons: (1) the Ukrainian pro-democratic movement could empower democrats in Russia, and present a threat to Putin's regime;[70] (2) a sovereign Ukraine meant it could not be controlled by the Russian government. The full-scale invasion, with its accompanying atrocities, would not have been possible to carry out in 2014 – the Russian populace was not ready to support a genocidal war against Ukraine. It took eight years of systematic propaganda, which dehumanized Ukrainians and depicted all those who supported the Maidan Revolution as a threat to Russia. While democratic Ukraine was not a threat to Russia, it did threaten Russian imperialism in Ukraine.

APPENDICES

Appendix 1

The Heavenly Hundred – Maidan Casualties*

One hundred seven Maidan participants, killed by state security officers and titushki mercenaries, received the title of the Heavenly Hundred.[1] Other deaths may have occurred, as a number of Maidan participants went missing and remain unaccounted for.[2] While a limited number of Berkut officers, police, SBU officers, and titushki were charged with killing protesters and abuse of power, most crimes committed against revolutionaries remain unpunished. Many alleged perpetrators fled to Russia, which granted citizenship to eighteen former police officers suspected of killing Ukrainian revolutionaries, in addition to other high-ranking officials suspected of organizing the killings.[3]

Following are the names of the Heavenly Hundred, by date of death.

December 2013
Pavlo Mazurenko: beaten by unknown men in state uniforms.
Taras Slobodyan: abducted, his body found near the city of Sumy with his arm severed from an explosion.

21 January 2014
Yurii Verbytskyi: abducted from hospital, interrogated and tortured, froze to death after being left in a forest.
Serhii Nihoian: shot by police with a hunting rifle.

22 January 2014 (clashes near the Dynamo Stadium)
Mykhailo Zhyznevskyi and Roman Senyk: shot using ammunition made to stop vehicles.

27–8 January 2014
Viktor Khomyak: body found with signs of torture, hanging from Christmas tree frame on Maidan Square.

Bohdan Kalyniak and Maksym Goroshishyn: died of pneumonia as a result of water cannon exposure and gas poisoning on 19 January.
Oleksandr Badera: beaten by special forces on Hrushevskoho Street on 22 January (died on 28 January).

13 February 2014
Serhiy Synenko: shot and burned in his car in Zaporizhzhya region.

18–19 February 2014
Serhii Didych, Antonina Dvorianets, Ivan Horodniuk, Volodymyr Kishchuk, Andrii Korchak, Zurab Khurtsiia, Artem Mazur, Ivan Nakonechnyi (Holodomor survivor), Anatolii Nechyporenko, Yakiv Zaiko: died of injuries received in clashes with police.
Oleksandr Klitynskyi and Volodymyr Topii: died in Trade Union building fire.
Viacheslav Veremii, journalist: beaten and shot by titushki after filming them from a car.
Dmytro Pahor, and Liudmyla Sheremet: shot during the revolutionaries' storming of the SBU office in the city of Khmelnytskyi.
Volodymyr Naumov: kidnapped from Maidan on the night of 18 February, found with signs of violent death on Trukhaniv Island, Kyiv.
Dmytro Maksymov: died of blast trauma.
Oleksandr Kapinos: died of open head injury.
Viktor Prokhorchuk: found dead with his throat cut.
Viktor Chernets: run over in Podibna, Cherkasy region, while blocking the path of a police car that was clearing the way for special forces on their way to Kyiv.
Volodymyr Boikiv, Serhii Bondarev, Valerii Brezdeniuk, Andrii Chernenko, Volodymyr Kulchytskyi, Viktor Orlenko, Yurii Paskhalin, Oleksandr Plekhanov, Vasyl Prokhorskyi, Ihor Serdiuk, Serhii Shapoval, Viktor Shvets, Yurii Sydorchuk, and Vitalii Vasiltsov: died on the Maidan from gunshots, or soon after, as a result of gunshot wounds inflicted on the Maidan.

20 February 2014 Massacre
Vasyl Aksenyn, Heorhii Arutiunian, Serhii Baidovskyi, Oleksandr Baliuk, Ivan Bliok, Serhii Bondarchuk, Oleksii Bratushka,

Volodymyr Chaplinskyi, Viktor Chmilenko, Ihor Dmytriv, Andrii Dyhdalovych, Mykola Dziavulskyi, Ustym Holodniuk, Eduard Hrynevych, Roman Huryk, Bohdan Ilkiv, Serhii Kemskyi, Oleksandr Khrapachenko, Anatolii Kornieiev, Ihor Kostenko, Yevhen Kotliar, Vitalii Kotsiuba, Volodymyr Melnychuk, Vasyl Moisei, Andrii Movchan, Valerii Opanasiuk, Mykola Pankiv, Ivan Pantelieiev, Ihor Pekhenko, Yurii Parashchuk, Leonid Polianskyi, Andrii Saienko, Oleksandr Shcherbaniuk, Yosyp Shilinh, Maksym Shymko, Vitalii Smolenskyi, Bohdan Solchanyk, Ivan Tarasiuk, Ihor Tkachuk, Roman Tochyn, Oleksandr Tsariok, Oleh Ushnevych, Roman Varenytsia, Bohdan Vaida, Nazarii Voitovych (17 years old), Anatolii Zhalovaha, Volodymyr Zherebnyi, and Vladyslav Zubenko: indiscriminately shot and killed by police/snipers on Maidan, mainly on Instytutska Street. Andriy Tsepun: beaten to death.

Maidan-Related Deaths after 20 February

Ihor Bachynskyy (died 25 February), Olha Bura (died 10 March), Petro Hadzha (died 22 March), Mykhailo Kostyshyn (died 26 February), Andriy Pozniak (found shot to death on 3 March), Vasyl Sheremet (died 5 March): died due to traumas and/or gas poisoning received during the clashes with police. Oleksandr Podryhun: beaten to death on 21 February. David Kapiani: died of heart failure immediately after his participation in 20 February events. Yuriy Diakovskyy, Yuriy Popravka, Volodymyr Rybak, Vasyl Serhiienko participated in the Maidan; they travelled to the Donetsk region in April 2014, where they were captured, tortured, and killed by the separatists; Dmytro Cherniavskyy was stoned to death by the separatists on 13 March 2014.

Appendix 2

Survey Demographics

Demographic information for survey participants. Survey data collected by the author, 2016–17 (figures 2.3, 3.6, 3.8, 3.11, 4.4, 5.2).

Gender of participants by age group

Age	*Male*	*Female*	*Total*
25–34 yrs	12	8	20
35–44 yrs	10	7	17
45–54 yrs	3	1	4
55–64 yrs	2	1	3
65–74 yrs	-	1	1
Total	27	18	45

Responses to the question, "Do you identify yourself with any of the following ethnic groups?"

	Number of respondents	*Per cent of respondents*
Ukrainian	28	62%
Russian	1	2%
Jewish	1	2%
I have multiple ethnic roots in my ancestry, and therefore do not identify myself with any of the groups in particular	11	24%
I do not believe in the concept of ethnicity	3	7%
Other	1	2%
Total	45	100%

Responses to the question, "What is your native language?"

	Number of respondents	*Per cent of respondents*
Ukrainian	16	36%
Russian	11	24%
I consider both Ukrainian and Russian as my native languages	14	31%
Other	4	9%
Total	45	100%

Appendix 3

Number of Protesters and Protester Injuries

An account of the sources of data presented in figure 2.1

Number of Protesters per Day in 2013–14

11/22 2,000 protesters reported in "EuroMaidan Rallies in Ukraine – Nov. 21–23 coverage," *Kyiv Post*, 25 November 2013. Accessed 21 March 2016. http://www.kyivpost.com/article/content/ukraine/euromaidan-rallies-in-ukraine-nov-21-23-coverage-332423.html.

11/24 50,000 protesters reported in "World Digest: Nov. 24, 2013," *Washington Post*, 24 November 2013. Accessed 21 March 2016. https://www.washingtonpost.com/world/world-digest-nov-24-2013/2013/11/24/dfeffa08-5516-11e3-8304-caf30787c0a9_story.html.

100,000 protesters reported in Leonid Ragozin, "Ukraine Turmoil Pits Russia-Friendly President Against Pro-Western Protesters," *Time*, 27 November 2013. Accessed 21 March 2016. http://world.time.com/2013/11/27/ukraine-turmoil-pits-russia-friendly-president-against-pro-western-protesters.

11/25 5,000 protesters reported in "EuroMaidan Rallies in Ukraine – Nov. 25 coverage," *Kyiv Post*, 27 November 2013. Accessed 21 March 2016. http://www.kyivpost.com/article/content/ukraine/euromaidan-rallies-in-ukraine-nov-25-coverage-332512.html.

11/26 Over a thousand protesters reported in "EuroMaidan Rallies in Ukraine – Nov. 26 coverage," *Kyiv Post*, 28 November 2013. Accessed 21 March 2016. http://www.kyivpost.com/article/content/ukraine/euromaidan-rallies-in-ukraine-nov-26-coverage-332571.html.

11/27 5,000 protesters reported in "World Digest: Nov. 27, 2013," *Washington Post*, 27 November 2013. Accessed 22 March 2016. https://www.washingtonpost.com/world/world-digest-nov-27-2013/2013/11/27/784e5d3c-577c-11e3-835d-e7173847c7cc_story.html.

11/28 15,000 protesters reported in "EuroMaidan rallies in Ukraine – Nov. 28 coverage," *Kyiv Post*, 1 December 2013. Accessed 22 March 2016. http://www.kyivpost.com/article/content/ukraine/euromaidan-rallies-in-ukraine-nov-28-coverage-332728.html.

11/29 10,000 protesters reported in "Ukraine Opposition Set to Call General Strike," *Al Jazeera and Agencies*, 30 November 2013. Accessed 22 March 2016. http://www.aljazeera.com/news/europe/2013/11/ukraine-opposition-calls-general-strike-20131130133021985378.html.

11/30 250,000 protesters reported in "Fresh Demonstrations Held in Ukraine," *Al Jazeera and Agencies*, 7 December 2013. Accessed 22 March 2016. http://www.aljazeera.com/news/europe/2013/12/fresh-demonstrations-held-ukraine-201312714758524461.html.

12/1 300,000 protesters reported in Oksana Grytsenko and Shaun Walker, "Ukrainians Call for Yanukovych to Resign in Protests Sparked by EU U-Turn: Hundreds of Thousands Take to Streets in the Largest Protests the Country Has Seen since the 2004 Orange Revolution," *The Guardian*, 1 December 2013. Accessed 24 October 2018. https://www.theguardian.com/world/2013/dec/01/ukraine-largest-street-protests-orange-revolution.

12/2 3,000 protesters reported in "Protests Continue in Ukraine," *Washington Post*, 12 December 2013. Accessed 22 March 2016. https://www.washingtonpost.com/world/protests-continue-in-ukraine/2013/12/02/b9d23462-5b5b-11e3-bf7e-f567ee61ae21_gallery.html.

12/3 Over 10,000 protesters reported in "EuroMaidan Rallies in Ukraine – Dec. 3 coverage," *Kyiv Post*, 4 December 2013. Accessed 21 March 2016. http://www.kyivpost.com/article/content/ukraine/euromaidan-rallies-and-updates-on-dec-3-332985.html.

12/4 7,000–10,000 protesters reported in "EuroMaidan Rallies in Ukraine – Dec. 4 coverage," *Kyiv Post*, 5 December 2013. Accessed 21 March 2016. http://www.kyivpost.com/article/content/ukraine/euromaidan-rallies-in-ukraine-dec-4-333067.html.

12/5 5,000 protesters reported in "EuroMaidan Rallies in Ukraine – Dec. 5 Coverage," *Kyiv Post*, 6 December 2013. Accessed 21 March 2016. http://www.kyivpost.com/article/content/ukraine/euromaidan-rallies-in-ukraine-dec-5-333124.html.

12/7 7,000 protesters reported in "EuroMaidan Rallies in Ukraine – Dec. 7 Coverage," *Kyiv Post*. 8 December 2013. Accessed 21 March 2016. http://www.kyivpost.com/article/content/ukraine/euromaidan-rallies-in-ukraine-dec-7-333236.html.

12/8 Tens of thousands of protesters reported in "Protests Continue in Ukraine," *Washington Post*, 12 December 2013. Accessed 21 March 2016. https://www.washingtonpost.com/world/protests-continue-in-ukraine/2013/12/02/b9d23462-5b5b-11e3-bf7e-f567ee61ae21_gallery.html.

12/9 5,000 protesters reported in "EuroMaidan Rallies in Ukraine – Dec. 9 coverage," *Kyiv Post*, 10 December 2013. Accessed 21 March 2016. http://www.kyivpost.com/article/content/ukraine/euromaidan-rallies-in-ukraine-live-updates-332341.html.

12/10 2,000 protesters reported in "Ukraine Protesters Defy Riot Police," *Al Jazeera and Agencies*, 10 December 2013. Accessed 21 March 2016. http://www.aljazeera.com/news/europe/2013/12/ukraine-protesters-defy-riot-police-201312108579858958.html.

12/11 25,000 protesters reported in "EuroMaidan Rallies in Ukraine – Dec. 11 coverage," *Kyiv Post*, 12 December 2013. Accessed 21 March 2016. http://www.kyivpost.com/article/content/ukraine/euromaidan-rallies-in-ukraine-dec-11-coverage-333500.html.

12/12 10,000 protesters reported in "Kiev Protesters Gather, EU and Putin Joust," *Reuters*, 12 December 2013. Accessed 23 March 2016. http://www.reuters.com/article/ukraine-idUSL6N0JR2IQ20131212.

12/15 200,000 protesters reported in Will Englund, "In Ukraine, U.S. Sens. McCain, Murphy Address Protesters," *Washington Post*, 15 December 2013. Accessed 23 March 2016. https://www.washingtonpost.com/world/in-ukraine-us-sens-mccain-murphy-address-protesters/2013/12/15/be72cffe-65b0-11e3-997b-9213b17dac97_story.html. Between 150,000 and 200,000 protesters reported in Daryna Krasnolutska, Kateryna Choursina, and Olga Tanas, "Ukraine Protests Surge before Yanukovych Meets Putin," *Bloomberg*, 15 December 2013. Accessed 23 March 2016. http://www.bloomberg.com/news/articles/2013-12-15/ukraine-protests-surge-before-yanukovych-meets-putin.

12/16 5,000 protesters reported in "EuroMaidan Rallies in Ukraine – Dec. 16 coverage," *Kyiv Post*, 17 December 2013. Accessed 23 March 2016. http://www.kyivpost.com/content/ukraine/euromaidan-rallies-in-ukraine-monday-dec16-live-updates-333739.html.

12/17 Tens of thousands protesters reported in "EuroMaidan Rallies in Ukraine – Dec. 17," *Kyiv Post*, 18 December 2013. Accessed 23 March 2016. http://www.kyivpost.com/content/ukraine/euromaidan-rallies-in-ukraine-tuesday-dec17-live-updates-333787.html.

12/18 25,000 protesters reported in "Ukraine Timeline: Developments since Political Crisis Erupted in Kiev," ABC *News*, 20 November 2014. Accessed 23 March 2016. http://www.abc.net.au/news/2014-02-19/ukraine-protest-timeline-political-crisis-kiev/5268676.

12/20 100,000 protesters reported in "Timeline: Political Crisis in Ukraine and Russia's Occupation of Crimea," *Reuters*, 8 March 2014. Accessed 23 March 2016. http://www.reuters.com/article/us-ukraine-crisis-timeline-idUSBREA270PO20140308\.

12/21 3,000–5,000 protesters reported in Olena Goncharova, "A Month Later, EuroMaidan Beat Goes On," *Kyiv Post*, 12 December 2013. Accessed 23 March 2016. http://www.kyivpost.com/article/content/ukraine-politics/a-month-later-euromaidan-beat-goes-on-334112.html.

12/22 100,000 protesters reported in Olzhas Auyezov and Jack Stubbs, "Ukraine Opposition Urges More Protests, Forms Political Bloc," *Reuters*, 22 December 2013. Accessed 23 March 2016. http://www.reuters.com/article/us-ukraine-idUSBRE9BL09220131222.
40,000–100,000 protesters reported in "EuroMaidan Rallies in Ukraine," *Kyiv Post*, 22 December 2013. Accessed 24 March 2016. http://www.kyivpost.com/content/ukraine/euromaidan-rallies-in-ukraine-live-updates-333965.html.

12/25 Thousands of protesters reported in James Marson and Katya Gorchinskaya, "Ukrainian Activist Reporter Hospitalized after Beating," *Wall Street Journal*, 25 December 2013. Accessed 21 March 2016. http://www.wsj.com/articles/SB10001424052702304753504579280802060016982.

12/29 20,000 to over 50,000 protesters reported in "Fresh Ukraine Protests Draw Thousands onto Kiev Streets," *BBC News*, 29 December 2013. Accessed 24 March 2016. http://www.bbc.com/news/world-europe-25543067.

12/31–1/1 200,000 protesters reported in "Euromaidan Draws 200,000 People for New Years Party," *Kyiv Post*, 1 January 2014. Accessed 21 March 2016. http://www.kyivpost.com/content/kyiv/euromaidan-draws-200000-people-for-newyears-party-334544.html.

1/1 15,000 protesters reported in http://www.cepolicy.org/publications/remembering-maidan-chronological-summary. Accessed 21 March 2016.

1/5 10,000 protesters reported in "Kiev Activists Target Rally Revival after First Clashes of 2014," *Bloomberg*, 5 January 2014. Accessed 21 March 2016. http://www.bloomberg.com/news/articles/2014-01-11/kiev-activists-target-rally-revival-afterfirst-clashes-of-2014.

1/12 50,000 protesters reported in G.C., "Will Maidan Live On?," *The Economist*, 14 January 2014. Accessed 21 March 2016. http://www.economist.com/blogs/easternapproaches/2014/01/ukraine-0.

1/19 100,000 protesters reported in Richard Balmforth and Natalia Zinets, "Protesters Clash with Police at Large Ukraine Rally," *Reuters*, 19 January 2014. Accessed 21 March

2016. http://www.reuters.com/article/us-ukraine-rally-idUSBREA0I09U20140120.

1/20 10,000 protesters reported in Richard Balmforh and Natalia Zinets, "EuroMaidan Rallies in Ukraine (Jan. 20 Updates)," *Kyiv Post*, 21 January 2014. Accessed 21 March 2016. http://www.kyivpost.com/article/content/ukraine-politics/euromaidan-ralles-in-ukrainejan-20-updates-335302.html.

1/22 More than 20,000 protesters reported in "Standoff Remains Today after Jan. 22 Clashes Kill Five Protesters, Injure More than 300," *Kyiv Post*, 23 January 2014. Accessed 21 March 2016. http://www.kyivpost.com/article/content/ukraine-politics/standoff-remainstoday-after-jan-22-clashes-kill-five-protesters-injure-more-than-300-335387.html.

1/23 2,000 protesters reported in "EuroMaidan Rallies in Ukraine (Jan. 23 updates)," *Kyiv Post*, 24 January 2014. Accessed on 21 March 2016. http://www.kyivpost.com/article/content/ukraine-politics/euromaidan-rallies-in-ukraine-jan-23-live-updates-335389.html.

1/24 5,000 protesters reported in Iryna Stelmakh and Claire Bigg, "Activists on Wheels: Ukraine's Embattled Automaidan Protesters," *Radio Free Europe / Radio Liberty*, 24 January 2014. Accessed 21 March 2016. http://www.rferl.org/content/ukraine-activists-automaidan/25241507.html.

1/26 10,000 protesters reported in "EuroMaidan Rallies in Ukraine (Jan. 26–27 updates)," *Kyiv Post*, 28 January 2014. Accessed 21 March 2016. http://www.kyivpost.com/article/content/ukraine/euromaidan-rallies-in-ukraine-jan-26-27-live-updates-335614.html.

2/2 50,000 protesters reported in "Ukraine Protesters Rally as Yanukovych Plans to End Sick-Leave," *Bloomberg News*, 2 February 2014. Accessed 21 March 2016. http://www.bloomberg.com/news/articles/2014-02-01/ukraine-opposition-to-rally-as-leader-warns-of-delicate-balance.

2/3 10,000 protesters reported in "EuroMaidan Rallies in Ukraine (Feb. 1–2 updates)," *Kyiv Post*, 3 February 2014. Accessed 21 March 2016. http://www.kyivpost.com/article/content/ukraine-politics/euromaidan-rallies-in-ukraine-feb-1-2-live-updates-336083.html.

2/4 More than 50,000 protesters reported in "Protests against Government Continue in Ukraine," *Washington Post*, 4 February 2014. Accessed 21 March 2016. https://www.washingtonpost.com/world/protests-against-government-continue-in-ukraine/2014/01/29/b0346cc4-88ea-11e3-a5bd-844629433ba3_gallery.html.

2/5 Tens of thousands of protesters reported in David Stern, "Ukraine's Forever Revolution: Why the Country's Political Crisis Will Persist, Even if the Protesters Win," *The Atlantic*, 5 February 2014. Accessed 21 March 2016. http://www.theatlantic.com/international/archive/2014/02/ukraines-forever-revolution/283615//.

2/9 70,000 protesters reported in "Ukraine Timeline: Developments since Political Crisis Erupted in Kiev," *ABC News*. 18 February 2014. Accessed 21 March 2016. http://www.abc.net.au/news/2014-02-19/ukraine-protest-timeline-political-crisis-kiev/5268676.

8,000–50,000 protesters reported in "Kiev Rally Draws Thousands as Opposition Warns of Default," *Bloomberg*, 10 February 2014. Accessed 21 March 2016. http://www.bloomberg.com/news/articles/2014-02-09/kiev-rally-draws-thousands-as-opposition-warns-of-default.

2/16 Tens of thousands reported in Guido Girgenti, "Ukrainians Bring Down Yanukovych Regime, 2013–2014," Global Nonviolence Database, 21 April 2014. Accessed 21 March 2016. http://nvdatabase.swarthmore.edu/content/ukrainians-bring-down-yanukovych-regime-2013–14/.

30,000 protesters reported in "EuroMaidan Rallies in Ukraine (Feb. 16 live updates)," *Kyiv Post*, 16 February 2014. Accessed 21 March 2016. http://www.kyivpost.com/article/content/ukraine/euromaidan-rallies-in-ukraine-feb-16-live-updates-336916.html.

2/18 20,000 protesters reported in "EuroMaidan Rallies in Ukraine (Feb. 18–19 night live updates)," *Kyiv Post*, 19 February 2014. Accessed 21 March 2016. http://www.kyivpost.com/article/content/ukraine-politics/police-advance-on-euromaidan-following-a-government-ultimatum-live-updates-337067.html.

2/19 Thousands of protesters reported in Marie-Louise Gumuchian, "Stop the Ultimatums, Russia Tells Ukraine Protesters," CNN, 3 February 2013. Accessed 21 March 2016. http://edition.cnn.com/2014/02/03/world/europe/ukraine-protests/index.html.
Thousands of protesters reported in Aliaksandr Kudrytski and Daryna Krasnolutska, "Ukraine Fighting Leaves at Least 18 Dead as Kiev Barricades Burn," *Bloomberg,* 18 February 2014. Accessed 21 March 2016. http://www.bloomberg.com/news/articles/2014-02-18/ukraine-fighting-leaves-at-least-18-dead-as-kiev-barricades-burn.
5,000 protesters reported in "EuroMaidan Rallies in Ukraine (Feb. 19 live updates)," *Kyiv Post,* 20 February 2014. Accessed 21 March 2016. http://www.kyivpost.com/article/content/ukraine-politics/euromaidan-rallies-in-ukraine-feb-19-live-updates-337098.html.

2/20 10,000–20,000 protesters reported in "Ukraine Death Toll Rising on Feb. 20 with at least 42 People Killed, Most by Gunshots from Police," *Kyiv Post,* 20 February 2014. Accessed 21 March 2016. http://www.kyivpost.com/article/content/ukraine-politics/ukraine-death-toll-rising-on-feb-20-with-at-least-42-people-killed-most-by-gunshots-from-police-live-updates-video-337236.html.

Number of Protester Injuries per Day in 2013–14

11/30 75/79 protesters' injuries reported in "75 Were Injured during Nov. 30 Dispersal of EuroMaidan," *Kyiv Post,* 5 December 2013. Accessed 3 April 2016. http://www.kyivpost.com/content/ukraine/75-were-injured-during-nov-30-dispersal-of-euromaidan-333103.html.

12/1 50 protesters' injuries reported in David M. Herszenhorn, "Thousands Demand Leaders' Resignation of Ukraine," *New York Times,* 2 December 2013. Accessed 3 April 2016. http://www.nytimes.com/2013/12/02/world/europe/thousands-of-protesters-in-ukraine-demand-leaders-resignation.html.

12/7 150 protesters' injuries reported in "Euromaidan Rallies in Ukraine," *Kyiv Post*, 7 December 2013. Accessed 3 April 2016. http://www.kyivpost.com/article/content/ukraine/euromaidan-rallies-in-ukraine-dec-7-333236.html.

12/10 More than 10 protesters' injuries reported in "Euromaidan Rallies in Ukraine," *Kyiv Post*, 7 December 2013. Accessed 3 April 2016. http://www.kyivpost.com/article/content/ukraine/euromaidan-rallies-in-ukraine-dec10-333425.html.

12/11 More than 100 protesters' injuries reported in Askold Krushelnycky, "The Fight for the Maidan: How Long Can Ukraine's Protesters Hold Out against Yanukovych's Thugs?" *Foreign Policy*, 13 December 2013. Accessed 3 April 2016. http://foreignpolicy.com/2013/12/13/the-fight-for-the-maidan/.

1/19 103 protesters' injuries reported in "Protesters Appear to Be Preparing for Battle," *Washington Post*, 20 January 2014. Accessed 3 April 2016. https://www.washingtonpost.com/world/in-ukraine-protesters-appear-to-be-preparing-for-battle/2014/01/20/904cdc72-81bd-11e3-9dd4-e7278db80d86_story.html.

1/20 More than 100 protesters' injuries reported in "Euromaidan Rallies in Ukraine," *Kyiv Post*, 21 January 2014. Accessed 3 April 2016. http://www.kyivpost.com/article/content/ukraine-politics/euromaidan-ralles-in-ukraine-jan-20-updates-335302.html.

1/22 300 protesters' injuries, at least 3 killed, reported in "Euromaidan Rallies in Ukraine," *Kyiv Post*, 23 January 2014. Accessed 3 April 2016. http://www.kyivpost.com/article/content/ukraine/euromaidan-rallies-in-ukraine-feb-1-2-live-updates-336083.html.

1/27 40 journalists' injuries reported in "Euromaidan Rallies in Ukraine," *Kyiv Post*, 28 January 2014. Accessed 3 April 2016. http://www.kyivpost.com/article/content/ukraine/euromaidan-rallies-in-ukraine-jan-26-27-live-updates-335614.html.

2/18 More than 1000 protesters' injuries reported in "Police Advance on Euromaidan," *Kyiv Post*, 23 January 2014. Accessed 3 April 2016. http://www.kyivpost.com/article/content/ukraine-politics/police-advance-on-euromaidan-following-a-government-ultimatum-live-updates-337067.html.

2/20 577 protesters' injuries, 77–100 dead reported in Phil Black, Nick Paton Walsh and Michael Pearson, "Ukraine Protests," CNN, 3 February 2014. Accessed 3 April 2016. http://www.cnn.com/2014/02/20/world/europe/ukraine-protests/index.html.

Notes

Chapter One

1 George Lawson, *Anatomies of the Revolution.*
2 Plokhy, *The Last Empire.*
3 Plokhy, *Chernobyl.*
4 Pipko, "The First Rally in Kyiv in 1988."
5 Wanner, *Burden of Dreams.*
6 Maidan Museum, "The Revolution on Granite"; Harvard Ukrainian Research Institute, "Revolution on Granite."
7 Onuch, "The Legacy of the Revolution on Granite."
8 Maidan Museum, "Ukraine without Kuchma."
9 Onuch, "The Maidan and Beyond."
10 Wolf, *Inside the Orange Revolution.*
11 Onuch. *Mapping Mass Mobilization,* 183–200.
12 Aslund and McFaul, *Revolution in Orange.*
13 Popova, "Authoritarian Learning and the Politicization of Justice."
14 Freedom House, "Freedom House Report," 5.
15 Freedom House, "Freedom House Report," 5.
16 Freedom House, "Freedom House Report," 11.
17 Freedom House, "Freedom House Report," 11.
18 Popova, "Authoritarian Learning and the Politicization of Justice."
19 Popova, "Authoritarian Learning and the Politicization of Justice."
20 Popova, "Ukraine's Politicized Courts."
21 Popova, "Ukraine's Politicized Courts."
22 Popova, "Authoritarian Learning and the Politicization of Justice."
23 BBC, "Mass Protests in Kiev."

24 Ukrainian Helsinki Human Rights Union, *Human Rights in Ukraine – 2007.*
25 Fedorova and Lysenko, "The Rights of Peaceful Assembly," 20.
26 Antonovych, *Ukrayinska Revoliutsiya Hidnosti*, 20.
27 Ukraine's Human Rights Helsinki Association, "Civic Organizations State."
28 Decree of the Soviet Presidium of the Supreme Soviet of the USSR, "On the Order of Organization and Carrying Out Gatherings, Meetings, Street Marches and Demonstrations in the USSR," and Decree of the Soviet Presidium of the Supreme Soviet of the USSR, "On the Responsibility for Violation the Established Order of Organization and Carrying Out Gatherings, Meetings, Street Marches and Demonstrations." In Antonovych, *Ukrayinska Revoliutsiya Hidnosti.*
29 Ukrainian Helsinki Human Rights Union, Human Rights in Ukraine, 155–6.
30 Antonovych, *Ukrayinska Revoliutsiya Hidnosti*, 26.
31 Antonovych, *Ukrayinska Revoliutsiya Hidnosti*, 24.
32 Tillmann, "Ukraine Press Freedom under Threat."
33 Freedom House, "Freedom of the Press 2012 – Ukraine."
34 Freedom House, "Freedom on the Net 2013 – Ukraine."
35 Radio Free Europe / Radio Liberty, "From Maidan to Berkut."
36 Peculiarly, Vadym Titushko himself disapproved the use of the term, claiming he supported the Maidan movement.
37 *Kyiv Post*, "Yanukovych Changes Tax Law after Protests."
38 *Kyiv Post*, "Yanukovych Changes Tax Law after Protests."
39 Lyachynka, "Battle Intensifies over Podil's Hostynny Dvir."
40 Lyachynka, "Battle Intensifies over Podil's Hostynny Dvir."
41 Lyachynka, "Battle Intensifies over Podil's Hostynny Dvir."
42 Faulconbridge, Dabrowska, and Grey, "Toppled 'Mafia' President."
43 Ukraine Crisis Media Center, "Ex President Yanukovych Suspected of Laundering."
44 Ukraine Crisis Media Center, "Ex President Yanukovych Suspected of Laundering."
45 Stecklow, Piper, and Akymenko, "Scams and Shakedowns."
46 Stecklow, Piper, and Akymenko, "Scams and Shakedowns."
47 Stecklow, Piper, and Akymenko, "Scams and Shakedowns."
48 Stecklow, Piper, and Akymenko, "Scams and Shakedowns."
49 *Radio Free Europe / Radio Liberty*, "High Profile Rape Trial."
50 *Radio Free Europe / Radio Liberty*, "High Profile Rape Trial."
51 *Radio Free Europe / Radio Liberty*, "Ukrainians March to Kyiv."
52 International Foundation for Electoral Systems, Survey Findings, 4.
53 International Foundation for Electoral Systems, Survey Findings, 14.
54 D'Anieri, *Ukraine and Russia.*
55 Hrytsak, "Ukrainians."

56 Hrytsak, "Ukrainians."
57 D'Anieri, *Ukraine and Russia*, 110–13.
58 Hrytsak, "Ukrainians."
59 Note the ominous use of the term "the Ukrainian question" in Kremlin circles, similar to the Nazi use of "the Jewish question." As addressed in this book, Russia's imperialistic denial of Ukraine's identity and sovereignty has a genocidal underpinning.
60 Hrytsak, "Ukrainians."
61 Wilson, "Elements of a Theory."
62 Warsaw Institute, "How Yanukovych Facilitated the Annexation of Crimea."
63 Warsaw Institute, "How Yanukovych Facilitated the Annexation of Crimea."
64 *Radio Free Europe / Radio Liberty*, "Yanukovych Defends Russian Naval Base Extension."
65 *Radio Free Europe / Radio Liberty*, "Yanukovych Defends Russian Naval Base Extension."
66 Polovetskyi, "Росія розв'язала торговельну війну проти України."
67 Shcherbina and Lyamets, "Rosiya pochala poglinati Ukrainu" ["Russia Has Started to Pressure Ukraine"].
68 Aslund, "Ukraine's Choice."
69 Yanukovych, "Vystuplenie Prezidenta na torzhestvenom sobranii po sluchayu Dnya Nezavisimosti" ["Speech by the President at the Festive Celebration of Independence Day"].
70 Yanukovych, "Vystuplenie Prezidenta vo vremya otkrytiya tret'ei sessii Verkhovnoi Rady sed'mogo sozyva" ["Speech by the President at the Opening of the Third Session of the Seventh Supreme Council"].
71 Panin, "Ukrainian Imports Barred."
72 Podrobnosti, "Approximately 1,000 Trucks Have Been Accumulated on the Russian-Ukrainian Border."
73 AKS-Inform, "Ukraine Might Lose More Than 30 Million USD."
74 Ukrainska Pravda, "Russia Is Preparing a Reaction."
75 Balmforth and Polityuk, "Ukraine Drops Plan."
76 Balmforth and Polityuk, "Ukraine Drops Plan"; Herszenhorn, "Ukraine Halts Plans."
77 Wilson, "The Ukrainian Revolution."
78 *Kyiv Post*, "EuroMaidan Rallies in Ukraine."
79 BBC, "Huge Ukraine Rally."
80 Channell-Justice, "Flexibility and Fragmentation," 58, 59–65.
81 Herszenhorn, "Ukraine in Turmoil."
82 Taylor, "Days of Protest in Ukraine."
83 Onuch, "The Maidan and Beyond."
84 Nikolayenko, "The Significance of Human Dignity."

85 Krasynska, Marples, and Mills, "Digital Civil Society"; Korzh, Kovalchuk, and Marshall, "Euromaidan Abroad."
86 Channell-Justice, *Without the State*; Wanner, *Everyday Religiosity*; Lokot, *Beyond the Protest Square.*
87 Wanner, *Everyday Religiosity.*
88 Lokot, *Beyond the Protest Square.*
89 Cirtautas, *The Polish Solidarity Movement*; Kenney, *A Carnival of Revolution.*
90 Shveda, "The Revolution of Dignity."
91 Walker, "Between East and West."
92 Fedunyak, "The Ukrainian Revolution."
93 Popova, "Why the Orange Revolution Was Short and Peaceful."
94 Onuch and Sasse, "The Maidan in Movement."
95 Channell-Justice, *Without the State*, 77.
96 Wanner, *Everyday Religiosity.*
97 Lokot, *Beyond the Protest Square.*
98 Hanson, *Time and Revolution.*
99 Otrishchenko, "Voices of Euromaidan"; Krapfl and Kühn von Burgsdorff, "Ukraine's Euromaidan."
100 Cirtautas, *The Polish Solidarity Movement.*
101 Krapfl, "From Leipzig to Kyiv through Brussels," 1016.
102 Brier, *Poland's Solidarity Movement*, 3.
103 Brier, *Poland's Solidarity Movement*, 17.
104 Cirtautas, *The Polish Solidarity Movement*, 166–91
105 Calabrese, "Sending a Message," 110.
106 Calabrese, "Sending a Message," 110–11.
107 Fearon and Laitin, "Ethnicity, Insurgency, and Civil War"; Stathis Kalyvas, *The Logic of Violence*; Leonard and Straus, *Africa's Stalled Development.*
108 Straus, "Destroy Them to Save Us"; Richardson, *What Terrorists Want.*
109 Onuch, "The Maidan and Beyond."
110 Channell-Justice, *Without the State.*
111 Shore, *The Ukrainian Night.*
112 Shore, *The Ukrainian Night*, xvi.
113 Arel, "How Ukraine Has Become More Ukrainian"; Kulyk, "Shedding Russianness."
114 Sereda, "I Am a Man and an Active Citizen."
115 Frye, "What Do Voters in Ukraine Want?"; Eleches and Robertson, "Identity and Political Preferences."
116 Otrishchenko, "Beyond the Square," 160.
117 Wynnyckyj, *Ukraine's Maidan, Russia's War*, 6.
118 Alexeev, "War and Sociopolitical Identities."
119 Yom, "From Methodology to Practice," 625.

120 Yom, "From Methodology to Practice," 626.
121 Yom, "From Methodology to Practice," 626.
122 Bennett and Checkel, "Process Tracing."
123 Bennett and Checkel, "Process Tracing," 9
124 Bennett and Checkel, "Process Tracing," 7.
125 Jacobs, "Process Tracing."
126 Beach and Pedersen, "Selecting Appropriate Cases."
127 Bennett and Checkel, "Process Tracing."
128 Collier, "Understanding Process Tracing," 827.
129 Keesing et al., "Anthropology as Interpretive Quest"; Leavy, Introduction to *The Oxford Handbook of Qualitative Research.*
130 Migdal, "Book Review."
131 Migdal, "Book Review," 216
132 Yom, "From Methodology to Practice."
133 Keesing et al., "Anthropology as Interpretive Quest," 161.
134 Kubik and Aronoff, *Anthropology and Political Science,* 25.
135 Kubik and Aronoff, *Anthropology and Political Science*, xxiii.
136 Research and Branding Group, "Euromaydan – 2013."
137 Beesley, "Euromaidan."
138 Beesley, "Euromaidan," 246.
139 Beesley, "Euromaidan," 247.
140 Beesley, "Euromaidan," 247.
141 Gladun, "Impact of repression on mobilization."
142 Krasynska, Marples, and Mills, "Digital Civil Society"; Korzh, Kovalchuk, and Marshall, "Euromaidan Abroad."
143 Arksey and Knight, *Interviewing for Social Scientists,* 52–7.
144 Finberg and Holovach, *Maidan. Testimonies* (2016); Finberg and Holovach, *Maidan. Testimonies* (2018).
145 Ukrainian Institute of Memory, *Maidan Vid Pershoi Osoby.*
146 The most common responses were being present as a form of protest, collecting information about the events, and communicating the goals and events to the wider public. Only 36 per cent of respondents engaged in "protection of protesters against police attacks," i.e., engaged in direct (sometimes violent) confrontation with the police. This study, therefore, allows us to test for support for the use of violent tactics by the movement among those who did and did not directly engage with the police. Moreover, the survey included a distribution of Ukrainian and Russian speakers. Thirty-six per cent of respondents identified Ukrainian as their native language, 27 per cent identified Russian as their native language, and 31 per cent stated that they perceive both Ukrainian and Russian as their native languages.
147 Migdal, "A Model of State–Society Relations," 294.

148 Migdal, "Researching the State," 162–92.
149 Tilly, *Repression, Mobilization, and Explanation.*
150 Earl, "Political Repression."
151 Davenport, "State Repression."
152 Migdal, "A Model of State–Society Relations," 293.
153 Ilko Kucheriv Democratic Initiatives Foundation and Kyiv International Institute of Sociology, "Maidan-December and Maidan-February."
154 Hibbs, *Mass Political Violence*, 7.
155 Hibbs, *Mass Political Violence*, 9.

Chapter Two

1 Kryukova and Sinitsyna, *Diary of EuroMaidan*, 19.
2 *Kyiv Post*, "Police Violently Break Up Independence Square Protests." Grytsenko, Oksana, and Daryna Shevchenko, "Victims Describe Excessive, Indiscriminate Attacks."
3 Yegiazaryan, "Prikas byl ne tolko zhestoko bit, a oskorbitelno bit," in Finberg and Holovach, *Maidan. Testimonies*, 319.
4 Ilko Kucheriv Democratic Initiatives Foundation and Kyiv International Institute of Sociology, "Maidan-December and Maidan-February."
5 Koshkina, *Maidan*, 75.
6 Koshkina, *Maidan*, 76.
7 Koshkina, *Maidan*, 77.
8 Zerkalo Nedeli, "The Head of the Kyiv City Police."
9 *Ukrainska Pravda*, "The Police Explained."
10 Zerkalo Nedeli, "Azarov Was Outraged."
11 Grytsenko, "Yanukovych Says Police Beatings Not His Fault."
12 Some interviewees in the summer of 2014 suggested that, in hindsight, state violence appeared to be a *provocation* – alluding to the possible role of the Kremlin in inciting social violence, which was later cited as a justification of their annexation of Crimea.
13 Fedir, "Reportazh Z Nochi Rozhonu," in Finberg and Holovach, *Maidan. Testimonies*, 96–9.
14 Express Online, "Euromaidan Was Brutally Dispersed."
15 Grytsenko and Shevchenko, "Victims Describe Excessive, Indiscriminate Attacks."
16 Fedir, "Reportazh Z Nochi Rozhonu," in Finberg and Holovach, *Maidan. Testimonies*, 96–9.
17 Borys, "Prikaz byl ne tolko zhestoko bit, a oskorbitelno bit," in Finberg and Holovach, *Maidan. Testimonies*, 74–7.
18 Borys, "Prikaz byl ne tolko zhestoko bit, a oskorbitelno bit," in Finberg and Holovach, *Maidan. Testimonies*, 76.

19 Grytsenko and Shevchenko, “Victims Describe Excessive, Indiscriminate Attacks.”

20 Borys, “Prikaz byl ne tolko zhestoko bit, a oskorbitelno bit,” in Finberg and Holovach, *Maidan. Testimonies.*

21 Express Online, “Euromaidan Was Brutally Dispersed.”

22 Fedir, “Reportazh Z Nochi Rozhonu.”

23 Shevchenko, “Victims Describe Excessive, Indiscriminate Attacks.”

24 Ukrainska Pravda, “Беркут Розігнав Майдан” [“Berkut Dispersed the Maidan.”], 30 November 2013. Accessed 3 August 2021. https://www.pravda.com.ua/news/2013/11/30/7003683/.

25 Shevchenko, “Victims Describe Excessive, Indiscriminate Attacks.”

26 Shevchenko, “Victims Describe Excessive, Indiscriminate Attacks.”

27 Kryukova and Sinitsyna, *Diary of EuroMaidan*, 18.

28 Grytsenko and Shevchenko, “Victims Describe Excessive, Indiscriminate Attacks”; Kryukova and Sinitsyna, *Diary of EuroMaidan*, 18.

29 Shevchenko, “Back to the Middle Ages.”

30 Mykhailivskyi monastery representative, interview with author, 12 May 2014.

31 Mykhailivskyi monastery representative, interview with author, 12 May 2014.

32 Borys, “Tsya nich bula tochkoju nepovernennya dlya vlady,” in Finberg and Holovach, *Maidan. Testimonies*, 102.

33 Borys, “Tsya nich bula tochkoju nepovernennya dlya vlady,” in Finberg and Holovach, *Maidan. Testimonies*, 102.

34 Dmytro, “Lyudy pryhodyly, bachyly, shcho treba – I robyly,” in Finberg and Holovach, *Maidan. Testimonies*, 249.

35 Kseinya, “Kazhdyi prishedshyi chelovek – eto dopolnitelnaya garantija bezopastnosti,” in Finberg and Holovach, *Maidan. Testimonies*, 93.

36 The Insider, “‘Berkut’ Dispersed Euromaidan.”

37 Kseinya, “Kazhdyi prishedshyi chelovek.” In Finberg and Holovach, 93.

38 Activist 1, interview with author, 31 July 2015.

39 Court hearing, Kyiv, May 2015.

40 Express Online, “Euromaidan Was Brutally Dispersed.”

41 Borys, “Prikas byl ne tolko zhestoko bit, a oskorbitelno bit,” in Finberg and Holovach, *Maidan. Testimonies*, 74–5.

42 Council of Europe, “Report to the Ukrainian Government.”

43 *Kyiv Post*, “75 Were Injured.”

44 Kyiv-based journalist, interview with author, 24 July 2015.

45 Dzhulai, “December 1, 2013 Maidan and Bankova.”

46 Christopher J. Miller (@ChristopherJM). “As of 4pm today 22 people sought medical attention in #Kyiv emergency rooms, says City Admin. In most cases treated for chemical burns.”

47 Rudenko, “Police Attacks Demonstrators.”

48 Rudenko, “Police Attacks Demonstrators.”

49 Onyschenko, "How 'Berkut' Beat a LIGA Business Inform Journalist."
50 Shuklynov, "Forty Journalists Were Injured in Kyiv."
51 Onyschenko, "How 'Berkut' Beat a LIGA Business Inform Journalist."
52 BBC, "Azarov Is 'Deeply Outraged' by the Dispersal of Euromaidan."
53 Ukrainska Pravda. "Yanukovich Did Not Accept Responsibility."
54 Capelouto and Butenko, "Pro-EU Protesters in Kiev."
55 Radio Free Europe / Ready Liberty, "Court Banned Going to Yanukovych's House and the Christmas Tree."
56 Ukrainska Pravda, "The District Court Blocked Mass Protests in Kyiv."
57 Ukrainska Pravda. "Kyiv City State Administration Wants to Ban Rallies." Dzerkalo Tyzhnya, "Popov Banned a Rally in the Center of Kyiv."
58 Shamota, Mariia. "EuroMaidan Rallies on Dec. 1: A Rowdy Afternoon."
59 Ukrainska Pravda. "Police Received a Report of a 'Mining.'"
60 Ukrainska Pravda. "Euro-Protesters See the Metro Closure."
61 Ukrainska Pravda. "The Barricade in the Government Quarter was Dismantled."
62 Navrotskyi, "Fair, Independent and Responsible Judiciary of Ukraine," 10–14.
63 Kyiv attorney 1, interview with author, 22 June 2016.
64 Navrotskyi, "Fair, Independent and Responsible Judiciary of Ukraine," 10–14.
65 Navrotskyi, "Fair, Independent and Responsible Judiciary of Ukraine," 15–17.
66 Kyiv attorney 4, interview with author, 19 May 2014.
67 Roman Maselko, attorney, press conference, 16 November 2015.
68 Censor.net, "The Court Prohibited the Federation of Trade Unions."
69 Verkhovna Rada of Ukraine. Zasidannya Sorokove, Сесійний зал Верховної Ради України, 20 грудня 2013 року, 10 година." [40th Meeting. Session Hall of the Verkhovna Rada of Ukraine, December 20, 2013."] https://www.rada.gov.ua/meeting/stenogr/show/5138.html.
70 BBC News Ukraine. "March of Millions in Kyiv."
71 Ukrainska Pravda, "Yanukovych: Three People Were Involved."
72 Maidan Museum, "Ukraine without Kuchma."
73 Ukrainska Pravda, "Thousands of Disgruntled Kyivans Gather at Mykhailivska Square."
74 Shevchenko, "Vox Populi."
75 Reference to the Paris 1572 massacre of the Huguenots.
76 Novyny NSPU, "NSPU Demands Punishment."
77 Federatsija Profesijnyh Spilok Ukrayiny. "Statement of the Federation of Trade Unions of Ukraine." Emphasis added.
78 Fylypovych and Horkusha, *Maidan and the Church*, 229–30.
79 Fylypovych and Horkusha, *Maidan and the Church*, 233.
80 Fylypovych and Horkusha, *Maidan and the Church*, 231.
81 Fylypovych and Horkusha, *Maidan and the Church*, 267.

82 Father Mykola, in *Maidan from the First Person*, 128–30.
83 Ukrainska Pravda, "5,000 People Chant."
84 Olga Yermak in Shevchenko, "Vox Populi."
85 Shevchenko, "Vox Populi."
86 Ukrainska Pravda, "5,000 People Chant."
87 Shevchenko, "Vox Populi."
88 Shevchenko, "Vox Populi."
89 Shevchenko, "Vox Populi."
90 Shevchenko, "Vox Populi."
91 Kyiv attorney 4, interview with author, 19 May 2014.
92 Ukrainska Pravda, "Government's Provocateurs Are at the March."
93 Kryukova and Sinitsyna, *Diary of EuroMaidan*, 22.
94 Kryukova and Sinitsyna, *Diary of EuroMaidan*, 20–5.
95 Goncharova, "EuroMaidan Rallies."
96 The word *viche* (old Slavonic) is a reference to public gatherings during Kyivan Rus, to address civilian matters.
97 Maidan Museum. "Maidan Calendar."
98 The account in the book uses New Year's tree, as that is how it is referred to in Ukrainian – due to the Soviet legacy, the term Christmas tree is rarely used.
99 Kryukova and Sinitsyna, *Diary of EuroMaidan*, 22
100 Kryukova and Sinitsyna, *Diary of EuroMaidan*, 22.
101 Kryukova and Sinitsyna, *Diary of EuroMaidan*, 19.
102 Ukrainska Pravda, "Thousands of Disgruntled Kyivans Gather at Mykhailivska Square."
103 Ukrainska Pravda, "Self-Defense Units Are Forming on Mikhailivska Square."
104 Kryukova and Sinitsyna, *Diary of EuroMaidan*, 19.
105 Rudenko, "Opposition Under Fire."
106 Rudenko, "Opposition Under Fire."
107 Daryna Shevchenko. "Vox Populi."
108 Ukrainska Pravda, March of Millions."
109 Ukrainska Pravda, "March of Millions."
110 Espresso TV. "Andrukhovych: We Must Return to the 2004 Political Reform."
111 Ukrainska Pravda, "The Lenin Monument Was Demolished."
112 Plokhii, "Goodbye Lenin."
113 Plokhii, "Goodbye Lenin."
114 Zychowicz, *Superfluous Women*, 261–5.
115 Plokhii, "Goodbye Lenin."
116 Plokhii, "Goodbye Lenin."
117 See Yurchuk, "De-Canonization of the Soviet Past" and Pavlush, "Leninopad," for further discussion on the topic.
118 Polske Radio, "Round Table – with No Result."

119 BBC News Ukraine. "A Sit-in Protest was Organized near the GPU."
120 Krushelnycky, "The Fight for the Maidan."
121 UkrLit., "Statement by the Ukrainian Writers."
122 KIIS, "Address to the President of Ukraine."
123 Zhytomyr Regional Council. "An Extraordinary Eighteenth Session."
124 Mukachevo.net, "Transcarpathian Regional Council Demands Immediate Resignation."
125 Mukachevo.net, "Transcarpathian Regional Council Demands Immediate Resignation."
126 Ternopil Regional Council. "Kyiv. Independence Square."
127 Kherson Regional Council. "On the Socio-Political Situation in the State."
128 Ukrainska Pravda, "Crimean Parliament Calls on Yanukovych."
129 Unlike many previous revolutionary movements, there were no charismatic leaders during the Ukrainian Revolution. Rather, the efforts were coordinated by multiple activists stepping at the forefront of their respective campaigns.
130 Olexandra, "I worked on coordination efforts: it was scary, but someone had to do it," in Finberg and Holovach, *Maidan. Testimonies*, 200.
131 Gorchinskaya, "Instigators of Clashes."
132 Goncharova, "EuroMaidan Rallies."
133 Oleh, "On Bankova I Was Stopped by Humanism, so Those Soldiers Would Not Lie Under the Arm of the Loader," in Finberg and Holovach, *Maidan. Testimonies*, 105.
134 Oleh, "On Bankova I Was Stopped by Humanism." Bonner, B. "EuroMaidan Rallies on Dec. 1."
135 Afineevsky, Evgeny, *Winter on Fire*; BBC News Ukraine "Опозиція: на Банковій діють провокатори." ["Opposition: Provocateurs Are Operating on Bankova Street."], 1 December 2013. https://www.bbc.com/ukrainian/news_in_brief/2013/12/131201_hk_opposition_provocation.
136 Ukrainska Pravda, "Students Marched to Protest."
137 Ukraina Criminalna, "«Титушковый» штурм Банковой." ["Titushky Storm on Bankova Street."], 1 December 2013. https://cripo.com.ua/news/?p=166693/.
138 Euroradio, "Was One of the Berkut Commanders …?"
139 Liga.net, "Побоище на Банковой: фоторепортаж" ["Beating on Bankova: photo report"], 1 December 2013. https://news.liga.net/politics/photo/poboishche_na_bankovoy_fotoreportazh#1.
140 Euroradio, "Was One of the Berkut Commanders …?"
141 Dzhulai, "December 1, 2013 Maidan and Bankova."
142 Bulatov, Dmytro, interview with author, 7 August 2015.
143 Bulatov, Dmytro, interview with author, 7 August 2015.
144 Kyiv-based physician 2, interview with author, 5 August 2015.

145 Kyiv-based attorney 3, interview with author, 28 July 2015.
146 Perry, *Civil Disobedience*, 216.
147 Kyiv-based attorney 3, interview with author, 28 July 2015.
148 Kyiv-based attorney 3, interview with author, 28 July 2015.
149 Kyiv-based attorney 2, interview with author, 19 May 2014.
150 Hajjar, "Cause Lawyering in Transnational Perspective," 495.
151 Israel, "From Cause Lawyering to Resistance French Communist Lawyers," 148.
152 Kyiv-based attorney 1, interview with author, 22 June 2016; Kyiv-based attorney 5, interview with author, May 2014.
153 Kyiv-based attorney 1, interview with author, 22 June 2016; Kyiv-based attorney 5, interview with author, 20 May 2014.
154 Kyiv-based attorney 2, interview with author, 19 May 2014; Kyiv-based attorney 5, interview with author, 20 May 2014.
155 Kyiv-based attorney 2, interview with author, 19 May 2014.
156 Kyiv-based attorney 5, interviews with author, 20 May 2014, Kyiv-based attorney 4, 20 May 2014.
157 EuroMaidan SOS activist 2, interview with author, 20 May 2014.
158 Activist 2, interview with author, 22 May 2015.
159 Kyiv-based attorney 6, interview with author, 23 May 2014.
160 Kyiv-based attorney 6, interview with author, 23 May 2014.
161 Open Statement, 12 December 2013, provided by Kyiv-based attorney 6; interview with author, 23 May 2014.
162 *The New Year's Address of the Ukrainian Nation to the President of Ukraine* provided by Artist/Kraplya v Okeani activist, interview with author, 4 August 2015.

Chapter Three

1 Andrushkiv, "I Saw Sacrifices by People, Who Wanted Changes," in Finberg and Holovach, *Maidan Testimonies*, 27.
2 Verkhovna Rada of Ukraine, "On the Judiciary and the Status of Judges."
3 Transparency International Ukraine, "Summary of Laws."
4 Verkhovna Rada of Ukraine, "On the Judiciary and the Status of Judges."
5 Transparency International Ukraine, "Summary of Laws."
6 Transparency International Ukraine, "Summary of Laws."
7 Transparency International Ukraine, "Summary of Laws."
8 Popova, "Why the Orange Revolution Was Short."
9 Popova, "Why the Orange Revolution Was Short."
10 Ukrainska Pravda, "US Secretary of State."
11 Ukrainska Pravda, "The EU Called on Yanukovych to Veto Anti-Democratic Laws."

12 TSN, "94 Days. Euromaidan," 88–93.
13 Gazeta, "Don't Follow Me, I'm the Fifth."
14 TSN, "94 days. Euromaidan," 94–103.
15 Календар Майдану. 17 січня 2014 року, https://maidanmuseum.org/en/history/2014-01-17.
16 TSN, "94 Days. Euromaidan," 104.
17 Englund, "Ukraine Protest."
18 Englund, "Ukraine Protest."
19 Englund, "Ukraine Protest."
20 Englund, "Ukraine Protest."
21 Englund, "Ukraine Protest."
22 Englund, "Ukraine Protest."
23 Popova, "Why the Orange Revolution Was Short."
24 TSN, "94 Days. Euromaidan," 104.
25 Mahaletskyi, "Here on Hrushevskoho Street, This Was the First People's Resistance," in Finberg and Holovach, *Maidan. Testimonies*, 335
26 Englund, "Ukraine Protest."
27 Panteley, "Where the People Suffer, There There's a Church," in Finberg and Holovach, *Maidan. Testimonies.*
28 *Derevyanko v. Ukraine.*
29 Council of Europe, "Report to the Ukrainian Government, 12.
30 *Shmorgunov v. Ukraine and 32 Other Applications,* 15367/14, Communicated to the Ukrainian Government in 2015, European Court of Human Rights.
31 Council of Europe, "Report to the Ukrainian Government, 17.
32 Council of Europe, "Report to the Ukrainian Government, 12.
33 Council of Europe, "Report to the Ukrainian Government, 12.
34 Dyachuk et al., *Khronika Svobody Slova* , 50–68.
35 Kyiv-based attorney 2, interview with author, 19 May 2014; Afineevsky, *Winter on Fire.*
36 Olexandra, "What was left for us to do?," in Finberg and Holovach, *Maidan. Testimonies*, 273.
37 Kateryna, "One Wanted to Be Together with Them," in Finberg and Holovach, *Maidan. Testimonies*, 222.
38 Mykhailo, "The Most Difficult in This Situation," in Finberg and Holovach, *Maidan. Testimonies*, 419–20.
39 TSN, "94 days. Euromaidan," 137.
40 Pavlo, "My fur coat saved me," in Finberg and Holovach, *Maidan. Testimonies*, 537.
41 Pavlo, "My fur coat saved me," in Finberg and Holovach, *Maidan. Testimonies*, 536.
42 Activist 2, interview with author, 22 May 2014, Kyiv.

43 Eugenia, "We Walked around Maidan and Performed First Aid," in Finberg and Holovach, *Maidan. Testimonies*, 263.
44 Eugene, "People Came to Throw Molotovs out of Despair," in Finberg and Holovach, *Maidan. Testimonies*, 319.
45 Activist 3, interview with author, 5 August 2015.
46 Olexandr, "For Me, That Was the Moment of the Beginning of the Civil War," in Finberg and Holovach, *Maidan. Testimonies*, 325.
47 Pavlo, "I Believe That Even after the First Deaths There Was Space for a Non-Violent Resistance," in Finberg and Holovach, *Maidan. Testimonies*, 397.
48 Olexandr, "For Me, That Was the Moment of the Beginning of the Civil War," in Finberg and Holovach, *Maidan. Testimonies*, 324.
49 Oleh, "Here, on Hrushevskoho Street," in Finberg and Holovach, *Maidan. Testimonies*, 336.
50 Evgeniy, "It Became Clear That There Was No Other Way It Could End," in Finberg and Holovach, *Maidan. Testimonies*, 547.
51 Evgeniy, "People Started Throwing Molotovs from Not Having a Way Out," in Finberg and Holovach, *Maidan. Testimonies*, 319.
52 TSN, "94 days. Euromaidan," 126.
53 TSN, "94 days. Euromaidan," 126.
54 TSN, "94 days. Euromaidan," 114.
55 Radio Free Europe / Radio Liberty, "Abducted Kyiv Activist."
56 Radio Free Europe / Radio Liberty, "Abducted Kyiv Activist."
57 Radio Free Europe / Radio Liberty, "Abducted Kyiv Activist."
58 Radio Free Europe / Radio Liberty, "A New Video Appeared of Torturing Naked Cossack."
59 Boris, "When Guys Died," in Finberg and Holovach, *Maidan. Testimonies*, 321–2.
60 Radio Free Europe / Radio Liberty, "Beyond Kyiv."
61 Radio Free Europe / Radio Liberty, "Beyond Kyiv."
62 Radio Free Europe / Radio Liberty, "Beyond Kyiv."
63 TSN, "94 Days. Euromaidan," 145–9.
64 Lviv police officer 2, interview with author, August 2014
65 TSN, "94 Days. Euromaidan," 150.
66 Office of the United Nations High Commissioner for Human Rights, "Accountability for Killings," 10.
67 TSN, "94 Days. Euromaidan," 150–3.
68 TSN, "94 Days. Euromaidan," 150.
69 TSN, "94 Days. Euromaidan," 153.
70 TSN, "94 Days. Euromaidan," 150.
71 TSN, "94 Days. Euromaidan," 154.
72 TSN, "94 Days. Euromaidan," 157.

73 Office of the United Nations High Commissioner for Human Rights, "Accountability for Killings," 15.
74 Office of the United Nations High Commissioner for Human Rights, "Accountability for Killings," 15
75 Grigoriy, "But When We Stood with Shields Side by Side," in Finberg and Holovach, *Maidan. Testimonies*, 540–1.
76 Oleksiy, "Those Guys, Who Were Standing in the First Row with Shields," in Finberg and Holovach, *Maidan. Testimonies*, 536.
77 Wilson, "The Ukrainian Revolution."
78 Lviv police officer 1, interview with author, 28 July 2014.
79 Activist 3, interview with author, 25 July 2014.
80 *Sotnyk*, self-defence unit leader, interview with author, 1 August 2015.
81 Wilson, 'The Ukrainian Revolution."
82 Activist 1, interview with author, 31 July 2015.
83 Kyiv-based physician 2, interview with author, 5 August 2015.
84 Activist 1, interview with author, 31 July 2015.
85 See a more detailed discussion of Pravyy Sektor in chapter 4.
86 Rostyslav, "Those Things Were Absolutely Non-Glamour," in Finberg and Holovach, *Maidan. Testimonies*, 59.
87 TSN, "94 Days. Euromaidan," 161.
88 TSN, "94 Days. Euromaidan," 162.
89 Kyiv-based attorney 1, interview with author, 22 June 2016.
90 Witness, Court hearing, Shevchenkyvskyi Court, Kyiv, 29 July 2015.
91 Migdal, "Researching the State."
92 Cirtautas, *The Polish Solidarity Movement*, 168.
93 Cirtautas, *The Polish Solidarity Movement*, 171.
94 Cirtautas, *The Polish Solidarity Movement*, 170–2.

Chapter Four

1 Center for Civic Liberties, "Center for Civic Liberties."
2 Matviichuk, Oleksandra, interview with author, 22 May 2014.
3 Matviichuk, Oleksandra, interview with author, 22 May 2014.
4 Roman, "Civil Activist," in Ukrainian Institute of National Memory, *Maidan from the First Person*, 151.
5 Kyiv-based attorney 1, interviews with author, 22–3 June 2016.
6 The Ministry of Internal Affairs of Ukraine controlled the national law enforcement agency (police force), termed *militsiya.*
7 Bulatov, Dmytro, interview with author, 7 August 2015.
8 *Rada Maidanu* activist 2, interview with author, 6 August 2015.
9 *Rada Maidanu* activist 2, interview with author, 6 August 2015.

10 Open Maidan University activist, interview with author, 7 August 2015.
11 Logistical Quarters activist, interview with author, 5 August 2015.
12 Logistical Quarters activist, interview with author, 5 August 2015.
13 The Center for Civil Liberties, headed by Oleksandra Matviichuk, received the Nobel Peace Prize in 2022.
14 Kyiv-based attorney 1, interviews with author, 22–3 June 2016.
15 *Rada Maidanu* activist 2, interview with author, 6 August 2015.
16 *Rada Maidanu* activist 2, interview with author, 6 August 2015.
17 Hospital Volunteer 1, interview with author, 7 August 2015.
18 Hospital Volunteer 1, interview with author, 7 August 2015.
19 IT activist 1, interview with author, 28 July 2015.
20 Kyiv-based physician 1, interview with author, 3 August 2015.
21 Kyiv-based attorney 1, interview with author, 20 May 2014; EuroMaidan SOS activist 2, interview with author, 20 May 2014.
22 Zakrevska in Sergatskova, 29 October 2014.
23 EuroMaidan SOS activist 2, interview with author, 20 May 2014; Kyiv-based activist 7, interview with author, 20 May 2014.
24 Kyiv-based attorney 6, interview with author, 23 May 2014; Rights activist 1, interview with author, 22 May 2014.
25 Activist 4, interview with author, 6 August 2015.
26 Makeshift kitchen activist 2, interview with author, 27 July 2015.
27 Self-defence activist 2, interview with author, 30 July 2015.
28 Makeshift kitchen activist 1, interview with author, 29 July 2015.
29 Activist 9, interview with author, 15 July 2015.
30 Makeshift kitchen activist 2, interview with author, 27 July 2015.
31 *Rada Maidanu* activist 2, interview with author, 6 August 2015.
32 Kyiv-based physician 1, interview with author, 3 August 2015.
33 Kyiv-based physician 1, interview with author, 3 August 2015.
34 Kyiv-based physician 2, interview with author, 5 August 2015.
35 Hospital Physician, interview with author, 7 August 2015.
36 Hospital activist 1, 7 August 2015.
37 Kyiv-based physician 1, interview with author, 3 August 2015.
38 Bohomolets was a notable public figure in Ukraine who participated and organized medical aid during the revolution.
39 Kyiv-based physician 1, interview with author, 3 August 2015.
40 Kyiv-based physician 1, interview with author, 3 August 2015.
41 E-Plus Safety Transport Activist, interview with author, 22 May 2014.
42 E-Plus Safety Transport Activist, interview with author, 22 May 2014.
43 Sim Dniv News, "Parubiy Spoke about the Self-Defense of the Maidan."
44 Sotnya translates as "hundred," as Zaporizhzhia units usually had 100–150 Cossacks; plural: *sotni.* Zaporizhska Sich was initially centred in the region

around today's Kakhovka Reservoir and the lower Dnieper River in Ukraine, eventually coming under control of the Polish-Lithuanian Commonwealth, the Ottoman, and the Russian empires.

45 Roman, Civil Activist in Ukrainian Institute of Memory, *Maidan Vid Pershoi Osoby*, 152.
46 Oleh, Civil Activist in Ukrainian Institute of Memory, *Maidan Vid Pershoi Osoby*, 148.
47 Roman, Civil Activist in Ukrainian Institute of Memory, *Maidan Vid Pershoi Osoby*, 151.
48 Roman, Civil Activist in Ukrainian Institute of Memory, *Maidan Vid Pershoi Osoby*, 151.
49 Roman, Civil Activist in Ukrainian Institute of Memory, *Maidan Vid Pershoi Osoby*, 151. The sotni membership lists were destroyed in the aftermath of the 16 January laws, as samooborona membership would mean a jail sentence.
50 Activist 4, interview with author, 6 August 2015.
51 Activist 10, interview with author, 15 June 2015.
52 Roman, Civil Activist in Ukrainian Institute of Memory, *Maidan Vid Pershoi Osoby*, 151.
53 Sim Dniv News, "Parubiy Spoke about the Self-Defense of the Maidan."
54 Roman, Civil Activist in Ukrainian Institute of Memory, *Maidan Vid Pershoi Osoby*, 151.
55 Roman, Civil Activist in Ukrainian Institute of Memory, *Maidan Vid Pershoi Osoby*, 152.
56 Oleh, Civil Activist in Ukrainian Institute of Memory, *Maidan Vid Pershoi Osoby*, 148.
57 *Chota* was a sotnya subgroup, also named after the Cossack sotnya formation.
58 Mykola, Military Officer in Ukrainian Institute of Memory, *Maidan Vid Pershoi Osoby*, 139.
59 Mykola, Military Officer in Ukrainian Institute of Memory, *Maidan Vid Pershoi Osoby*, 140.
60 Lviv-based artist, interview with author, 17 July 2014; Mykola, Military Officer in Ukrainian Institute of Memory, *Maidan Vid Pershoi Osoby*, 140.
61 Mykola, Military Officer in Ukrainian Institute of Memory, *Maidan Vid Pershoi Osoby*, 140.
62 Activist 4, interview with author, 6 August 2015.
63 Mykola, Military Officer in Ukrainian Institute of Memory, *Maidan Vid Pershoi Osoby*, 141.
64 Mykola, Military Officer in Ukrainian Institute of Memory, *Maidan Vid Pershoi Osoby*, 141.
65 Roman, Civil Activist in Ukrainian Institute of Memory, *Maidan Vid Pershoi Osoby*, 153.

66 Mykola, Military Officer in Ukrainian Institute of Memory, *Maidan Vid Pershoi Osoby*, 141.
67 Mykola, Military Officer in Ukrainian Institute of Memory, *Maidan Vid Pershoi Osoby*, 141.
68 *Titushky* were often described as athletically built, wearing tracksuits.
69 Self-defence activist 2, interview with author, 30 July 2015.
70 Self-defence activist 2, interview with author, 30 July 2015.
71 Bulatov, Dmytro, interview with author, 7 August 2015.
72 Bulatov, Dmytro, interview with author, 7 August 2015.
73 Zakrevska in Sergatskova, 29 October 2014.
74 Kyiv-based attorney 6, interview with author, 23 May 2014.
75 Bugai et al., "Open Appeal of Advocates, Lawyers, and Human Rights Defenders of Ukraine."
76 Bugai et al., "Open Appeal of Advocates, Lawyers, and Human Rights Defenders of Ukraine."
77 Matviichuk, Oleksandra, interview with author, 22 May 2014.
78 Open Maidan University activist, interview with author, 7 August 2015.
79 Open Maidan University activist, interview with author, 7 August 2015.
80 Open Maidan University activist, interview with author, 7 August 2015.
81 Play on words: *sit* also stands for *being in prison.*
82 Artist/Kraplya v Okeani activist, interview with author, 4 August 2015.
83 Artist/Kraplya v Okeani activist, interview with author, 4 August 2015.
84 Artist/Kraplya v Okeani activist, interview with author, 4 August 2015.
85 Artist/Kraplya v Okeani activist, interview with author, 4 August 2015.
86 Bigg, "Ukraine's 'Euromaidan' Through the Lens of Russian Television"; and Wahl, "I Was Putin's Pawn."
87 *Hromadska Rada* activist 2, interview with author, 6 August 2015.
88 Lokot, *Beyond the Protest Square.*
89 Kyiv-based journalists, interviews with author, 13 May 2014.
90 Kyiv-based journalists, interviews with author, 13 May 2014.
91 Bulatov, Dmytro, interview with author, 7 August 2015.
92 *Hromadska Rada* activist 2, interview with author, 6 August 2015.
93 EuroMaidan SOS activist 2, interview with author, 20 May 2014.
94 Zisels, "Jewish People of Ukraine Participate in the Protests."
95 Martsenyuk, "Gender Issues."
96 Kyiv-based attorney 5, interview with author, 20 May 2014, IT activist 1, interview with author, 28 July 2015.
97 Self-defence activist 3, interview with author, 6 August 2015.
98 Medical aid activist 1, interview with author, 16 May 2014.
99 Mayerchuk and Plakhotnyk,"Between Time of Nation and Feminist Time."
100 Channell-Justice, *Without the State.*

101 Wilson, "Cause Lawyering."
102 Channell-Justice, *Without the State.*
103 Phillips, "The Women's Squad."
104 Zhurzhenko, *Ukrainian feminism(s).*
105 Krapfl, "From Leipzig to Kyiv through Brussels."
106 Roth, "Durkheim and the Principles of 1789."
107 Channell-Justice, *Without the State.*
108 Channell-Justice, *Without the State*, 111–25.
109 Channell-Justice, *Without the State*, 114.
110 Likhachev, *The Far Right in the Conflict*; Shekhovtsov, *Russia and the Western Far Right*; Shekhovtsov and Umland, "The Maidan and Beyond."
111 Likhachev, *The Far Right in the Conflict*, 108, Kucheriv Democratic Initiatives Foundation & Kyiv International Institute of Sociology (KDIF & KIIS), "From Maidan-Camp to Maidan-Sich."
112 Shekhovtsov, *Russia and the Western Far Right.*
113 Shekhovtsov, *Russia and the Western Far Right.*
114 Shekhovtsov, Interview with author, 23 July 2015.
115 Shekhovtsov and Umland, "The Maidan and Beyond."
116 Activist 11, interview with author, 15 June 2014.
117 *Pravyi Sektor* member, interview with author, May 2014.
118 Activist 5, interview with author, 6 August 2015.
119 Kyiv-based journalist 5, interview with author, 5 August 2015. Emphasis added.
120 Ishchenko, "Far Right Participation in the Ukrainian Maidan." 10–12.
121 Ishchenko, "Far Right Participation in the Ukrainian Maidan." 10.
122 Snyder, *The Road to Unfreedom.*
123 Andriy, journalist, in Ukrainian Institute of Memory, *Maidan Vid Pershoi Osoby*, 22.
124 Andriy, journalist, in Ukrainian Institute of Memory, *Maidan Vid Pershoi Osoby*, 21.
125 Valeriy, businessman, civil activist in Ukrainian Institute of Memory, *Maidan Vid Pershoi Osoby*, 101–2.
126 BBC News Ukraine, "Kwasniewski: The European Union Underestimated Putin's Determination."
127 Tetiana, ecologist, journalist, in Ukrainian Institute of Memory, *Maidan Vid Pershoi Osoby*, 184.
128 *Hromadska Rada*, activist 3, interview with author, 16 June 2015.
129 *Jewish Telegraphic Agency*, "Ukrainian Jews Slam Putin."
130 *Ukrainian Jewish Encounter*, "Open Letter of Ukrainian Jews."
131 US Department of State Global Engagement Center, "Special Report Kremlin-Funded Media."
132 D'Anieri, *Ukraine and Russia.*

133 Shekhovtsov, *Russia and the Western Far Right.*
134 Shekhovtsov, *Russia and the Western Far Right.*

Chapter Five

1 Wanner, *Burden of Dreams.*
2 Howard, *The Weakness of Civil Society.*
3 Kotkin, *Steeltown,* USSR.
4 Hunt, "The Sacred and the French Revolution."
5 Goldberg, "Arab Spring. Introduction."
6 Freedom House, "Freedom in the World 2015 – Ukraine."
7 Freedom House, "Freedom in the World 2022 – Eastern Donbas."
8 As reported by the Freedom House, the following took place under the guidance of the Russian state in eastern Ukraine after 2014: "Russia has established a complex, albeit opaque, web of control over the 'People's Republics' that affects all aspects of daily life, including political affairs. Local media, schools and universities, public services, and business structures are dominated by people loyal to the separatist leadership. While many of them are locals, some key positions are held by Russian citizens. Political control is ultimately enforced by the secretive 'state security' ministries of the two entities, which are thought to be directed by Russia's Federal Security Service (FSB). The military formations known as 'people's militias,' which have tens of thousands of men under arms, are believed to be commanded by regular Russian military." Freedom House, "Freedom in the World 2022 – Eastern Donbas."
9 Freedom House, "Freedom in the World 2020 – Eastern Donbas."
10 Iarmoshchuk and Wesolowsky, "For Victims of Sexual Violence"; Freedom House, "Freedom in the World 2020 – Eastern Donbas"; Miller, "The Executioners of Slovyansk."
11 Zelinska, "How Social Movement Actors Assess Social Change."
12 Balazs and Yesmukhanova, "Ukraine's Slow Struggle for Decentralization."
13 Kyiv-based journalist 1, interview with author, 14 May 2014.
14 Sviatoslav Vakarchuk, interview with author, 18 October 2015.
15 IT Activist, Interview with author, 28 July 2015.
16 Kyiv-based physician 1, interview with author, 3 August 2015.
17 *Hromadska Rada* activist 2, interview with author, 6 August 2015.
18 *Hromadska Rada* activist 2, interview with author, 6 August 2015.
19 Oleksandra Matviichuk, "We Were Doing Our Job," in Finberg and Holovach, *Maidan. Testimonies, Aid to the Wounded,* 15–32.
20 Tkach, *Nadiya, Razom – Syla,* 38–9.
21 Tkach, *Nadiya, Razom – Syla,* 40.

22 *Kolo Narodnoi Doviry* activist, interview with author, 24 June 2016.
23 Roeder, *Red Sunset.*
24 Hrytsak, "Ukraine Will Withstand This Test As Well."
25 Tkach, *Razom – Syla*, 22.
26 Trach, *Razom – Syla*, 22.
27 Contrary to many areas in the United States, it is less common to smile to strangers in public places in Ukraine (and in Europe overall).
28 Kyiv-based artist, Kraplya v Okeani activist, interview with author, 15 July 2015.
29 Russia's coverage of any pro-Ukrainian movement is rooted in Soviet and pre-Soviet Russian policies: any movement for autonomy/independence from Russia (or a fight against Russification) was seen as a threat to the empire.
30 Self-defence activist 2, interview with author, 30 July 2015.
31 Sviatoslav Vakarchuk, interview with author, 18 October 2015.
32 Kyiv-based physician 2, interview with author, 5 August 2015.
33 AutoMaidan activist, interview with author, 7 August 2015.
34 *Hromadska Rada* activist 1, physician activist 3, interviews with author, 31 July 2015 and 14 July 2014.
35 The elderly, often referred to in Ukraine as pensioners, are in a very disadvantageous position economically; many struggle to sustain themselves. Thus, the assumption that many of them shared their "last resources" (*ostanne* in Ukrainian, *poslednee* in Russian) is likely to be substantiated.
36 This refers to the government operation on 20 February – see chapter 3 for more details.
37 IT activist, interview with author, 28 July 2015.
38 Activist 9, interview with author, 15 July 2015.
39 Lviv-based artist, interview with author, 17 July 2015.
40 Representative of Ukraine's Association of Jewish Organizations and Communities (VAAD), interview with author, 8 August 2015.
41 Representative of a Jewish organization, interview with author, 14 May 2014.
42 The figure of Bandera remains highly controversial within Ukraine. He is generally unpopular, perceived as a symbol of nationalism, and his critics point to Bandera's leadership in anti-Jewish and anti-Polish pogroms alongside Hitler's army. His supporters, on the other hand, assert that his insurgent army's purpose was an anti-Soviet struggle, based on the expectation of protectorate from Germany, similar to the terms of the First World War, and emphasize that Bandera was an inmate in a Nazi concentration camp, as he eventually turned against them.
43 Maidan's Pensioners activist, interview with author, 1 August 2015.
44 Barrels were used by the revolutionaries to burn firewood in a contained space.
45 Medical aid activist 5, interview with author, 3 August 2015.

46 Representative of Ukraine's Association of Jewish Organizations and Communities (VAAD), interview with author, 8 August 2015.
47 Makeshift kitchen activist 2, interview with author, 27 July 2015.
48 Self-defence activist 2, interview with author, 30 July 2015.
49 Activist 4, interview with author, 5 August 2015.
50 Representative of Ukraine's Association of Jewish Organizations and Communities (VAAD), interview with author, 8 August 2015.
51 Medical aid activist 5, interview with author, 3 August 2015.
52 Activist 9, interview with author, 15 July 2015.
53 *Hromadskyi Sektor* activist 1, interview with author, 31 July 2015.
54 Kyiv-based physician 2, interview with author, 5 August 2015.
55 Open Maidan University activist, interview with author, 7 August 2015.
56 Self-defence activist 2, interview with author, 30 July 2015.
57 Medical aid activist, interview with author, 16 May 2014.
58 It was particularly the Russian-language phrase (and less often the Ukrainian *svoia liudyna*) that was used even among Ukrainian speakers, referring to the common unpleasant experiences of Soviet reality, brought on by the Kremlin order.
59 Wanner, *Burden of Dreams.*
60 Wanner, *Burden of Dreams.*
61 IT activist, interview with author, 28 July 2015.
62 Medical aid activist 5, interview with author, 27 July 2015.
63 Makeshift kitchen activist 2, interview with author, 27 July 2015.
64 Self-defence activist 2, interview with author, 30 July 2015.
65 Makeshift kitchen activist 2, interview with author, 27 July 2015.
66 Kyiv-based physician 1, interview with author, 3 August 2015.
67 Medical aid activist 5, interview with author, 27 July 2015.
68 Medical aid activist 5, interview with author, 27 July 2015.
69 Makeshift kitchen activist 2, interview with author, 27 July 2015.
70 Vakarchuk, interview with author, 18 October 2015.
71 Lviv-based physician 1, interview with author, 3 August 2015.
72 Activist 15, interview with author, 3 August 2015.
73 Activist 4, interview with author, 6 August 2015.
74 Lviv-based physician 2, interview with author, 3 August 2014.
75 Makeshift kitchen activist 2, interview with author, 27 July 2015.
76 Representative of Ukraine's Association of Jewish Organizations and Communities (VAAD), interview with author, 8 August 2015.
77 Medical aid activist 5, interview with author, 27 July 2015.
78 *Hromadska Rada* activist 1, interview with author, 6 August 2015.
79 Medical aid activist 3, interview with author, 3 August 2015.
80 Activist 4, interview with author, 6 August 2015.

81 Open Maidan University activist, interview with author, 7 August 2015.
82 Medical aid activist 5, interview with author, 27 July 2015.
83 Kyiv-based physician 2, interview with author, 5 August 2015.
84 IT activist, interview with author, 28 July 2015.
85 Transcarpathia-based physician 1, interview with author, 15 August 2014.
86 Activist 4, interview with author, 6 August 2015.
87 Open Maidan University activist, interview with author, 7 August 2015.
88 Lviv-based physician 1, interview with author, 7 August 2014.
89 Alexeev, "War and Sociopolitical Identities."
90 Pop-Eleches and Robertson, "Identity and Political Preferences in Ukraine."
91 Kulyk, "National Identity in Ukraine."
92 Kulyk, "National Identity in Ukraine," 588.
93 Ilko Kucheriv, Democratic Initiatives Foundation and Razumkov Center Sociological Service, "Post-Maidan Charity and Volunteering."
94 Petrovska, "Measuring Civic Identity."
95 Petrovska, "Measuring Civic Identity."
96 Sereda, "I Am a Man …."
97 Falsini and Worschech, *The Euromaidan's Effect.*
98 Sereda, "I Am a Man …"; Mikheieva and Kuznetsova, "War-Time Volunteering."
99 Falsini and Worschech, *The Euromaidan's Effect*, 47.
100 Organization for Security and Co-operation in Europe, "Civil Society and the Crisis in Ukraine."
101 Oleksandra Matviichuk, SIUE Webinar, "A Conversation with Nobel-Prize Winner, Oleksandra Matviichuk," 4 November 2022. Emphasis added.
102 Medical aid activist 5, interview with author, 27 July 2015.
103 Durkheim, *The Division of Labor in Society.*
104 Goldberg, "Demonstrations of Democracy: Cities in Revolt," 20.

Chapter Six

1 Walker, "Between East and West."
2 Skocpol, *States and Social Revolutions*, 14.
3 Goldstone, *Revolutions.*
4 Goldstone, *Revolutions*, 62.
5 Goldberg, "Demonstrations of Democracy."
6 Goldberg, "Arab Spring. Introduction."
7 Calabrese, "Sending a Message," 109.
8 Apter, "Political Violence."
9 Calabrese, "Sending a Message," 110.

10 Calabrese, "Sending a Message," 110.
11 Richardson, *What Terrorists Want.*
12 Kalyvas, *The Logic of Violence.*
13 Hess and Martin, "Repression, Backfire, and the Theory of Transformative Events."
14 Hess and Martin, "Repression, Backfire, and the Theory of Transformative Events," 251–2.
15 Hess and Martin, "Repression, Backfire, and the Theory of Transformative Events," 252.
16 Ginkel and Smith, "A Game Theoretic Explanation of Revolution."
17 Ritter, *The Iron Cage.*
18 Hanson, *Time and Revolution.*
19 Goldberg, "Demonstrations of Democracy: Cities in Revolt."
20 Kurtz and Smithey, "Nonviolent Social Movements"; Kurtz and Smithey, *The Paradox of Repression*; Schock, *Unarmed Insurrections.*
21 Aminzade et al., *Silence and Voice.*
22 Sharp, *The Politics of Nonviolent Action*, 357.
23 Barkan, "Legal Control."
24 Jansen and Martin, "Making Censorship Backfire"; Jansen and Martin, "Exposing and Opposing Censorship."
25 Almeida, *Social Movements*, 53.
26 Marat, "Transformative Violence."
27 Tullock, "The Paradox of Revolution."
28 Feierabend, Feierabend, and Litel, "Dimensions of Political Unrest"; Olzak, Beasley, and Olivier, "The Impact of State Reforms."
29 Beckles, "Black Bookstores"; Davenport, *How Social Movements Die*; Herbert and Jone, "People and Protest"; Jeffries, "Black Radicalism"; Williams, "The Politics of Homelessness."
30 Lichbach, "Deterrence or Escalation?"
31 Moore, "Repression and Dissent."
32 Kalyvas and Kocher, "The Collective Action Problem"; Hultquist, "Collective Repression."
33 Levitsky and Way, *Revolution and Dictatorship*; Levitsky and Way, "The Durability of Revolutionary Regimes"; Way, "The Real Causes of the Color Revolutions."
34 Way, "The Real Causes of the Color Revolutions," 66.
35 Sierra, *A Unified Theory.*
36 Cirtautas, *The Polish Solidarity Movement*, 3:38. Emphasis added.
37 Hanson, "From Culture to Ideology," 364.
38 Hanson, "From Culture to Ideology," 365

39 Martin, "Political Jiu-Jitsu."

40 Hess and Martin, "Repression, Backfire, and the Theory of Transformative Events," 249.

41 Almeida, "Protest Waves"; Almeida, *Waves of Protest*; Anisin, "Violence Begets Violence"; Bramsen, "How Violence Happens"; Chenoweth and Stephan, *Why Civil Resistance Works*; Ondetti, "Repression, Opportunity, and Protest"; Schock, *Unarmed Insurrections*; Sutton, Butcher, and Svensson, "Explaining Political Jiu-Jitsu"; White, "From Peaceful Protest to Guerilla War."

42 Hirsch, "Sacrifice for the Cause"; Zwerman and Steinhoff, "State-Dissident Interactions."

43 Woods, *Insurgent Collective Action.*

44 Opp, "Repression and Revolutionary Action"; Opp and Roehl, "Repression, Micromobilization, and Political Protest"; Gamson, Fireman, and Rytina, *Encounters with Unjust Authority.*

45 Tilly and Tarrow, *Contentious Politics.*

46 Della Porta, "Radicalization," 471.

47 Gamson, Fireman, and Rytina, *Encounters with Unjust Authority.*

48 McCann, "How Does Law Matter," 81.

49 McCann, "How Does Law Matter," 81.

50 Chenoweth and Stephan, *Why Civil Resistance Works*; Nepstad, *Nonviolent Revolutions.*

51 Pinard, *Motivational Dimensions*; Bergstrand, "The Mobilizing Power of Grievances."

52 Alimi, "Introduction: Popular Contention, Regime and Transition"; Almeida, "Organizational Expansion"; Trejo, "Why and When Do Peasants Rebel?"

53 Van Dyke, "Threat."

54 Goodwin, *No Other Way Out.*

55 White, "From Peaceful Protest to Guerilla War," 1281.

56 Gamson, Fireman, and Rytina, *Encounters with Unjust Authority*; Snow, Rochford, Worden, and Benford, "Frame Alignment Processes"; Young, *Bearing Witness*; White, "From Peaceful Protest to Guerilla War."

57 Peoples, "Classical and Contemporary Conventional Theories of Social Movements," 25.

58 Rodriguez, "The Analysis of Saving Behaviour"; Holland and Cable, "Reconceptualizing Social Movement Abeyance"; Lofland and Jamison, "Social Movement Locals"; Snow, Rochford, Worden, and Benford, "Frame Alignment Processes."

59 Piven and Cloward, "Collective Protest," 12; Gamson, Fireman, and Rytina, *Encounters with Unjust Authority*; Goffman, *Frame Analysis.*

60 Lofland and Jamison, "Social Movement Locals"; Snow, Rochford, Worden, and Benford, "Frame Alignment Processes," 467.

61 Rodriguez, "The Analysis of Saving Behavior," 244; Holland and Cable, "Reconceptualizing Social Movement Abeyance," 305.
62 Menkel-Meadow, "The Causes of Cause Lawyering."
63 Elveris, "Cause Lawyering in a 'Crisis.'"
64 McCarthy and Zald, "Enduring Vitality"; Epp, *The Rights Revolution.*
65 Soule, McAdam, McCarthy, and Su, "Protest Events."
66 McCarthy and Zald, "Resource Mobilization and Social Movements," 1224.
67 McCarthy and Zald, "Resource Mobilization and Social Movements," 1224.
68 Eterovic, Smith, and Wiest, "Uneven Globalization."
69 McCarthy and Zald, "Resource Mobilization and Social Movements," 1224; McLaughlin and Marwan, "The Organizational Dynamics."
70 McCarthy and Zald, "Resource Mobilization and Social Movements," 1225.
71 Jenkins and Perrow, "Insurgency of the Powerless"; McCarthy and Zald, "Resource Mobilization and Social Movements."
72 McCarthy and Zald, "Resource Mobilization and Social Movements"; Gobe and Salaymeh, "Tunisia's 'Revolutionary' Lawyers"; Tam, "Political Transition."
73 McCarthy and Zald, "Resource Mobilization and Social Movements"; Gobe and Salaymeh, "Tunisia's 'Revolutionary' Lawyers."
74 Levitsky, "To Lead with Law," 147.
75 Vanhala, "Anti-Discrimination Policy Actor," 740.
76 Andersen, "Out of the Closets"; Cichowski and Stone Sweet, "Participation, Representative Democracy, and the Courts."
77 Vanhala, "Anti-Discrimination Policy Actor."
78 McCann, "How Does Law Matter?"
79 Hilbink, "The Profession, the Grassroots, and the Elite"; Marshall, "Social Movement Strategies."
80 Kinoy, *Rights on Trial*; McCann, "How Does Law Matter"; Sarat and Scheingold "Cause Lawyering"; Sarat and Scheingold, *Cause Lawyers*; Israël, "From Cause Lawyering to Resistance"; Marshall, "Social Movement Strategies."
81 Kitschelt, "Political Opportunity Structures"; Tarrow, *Power in Movements*; Kriesi, "The Political Opportunity Structure."
82 Koopmans, "New Social Movements."
83 Conant, *Justice Contained*; Cichowski, *The European Court*; Hilson, "New Social Movements."
84 Hilson, "New Social Movements," 250.
85 Dezalay and Garth, "Introduction: Constructing Transnational Justice," 2.
86 Jowitt, *New World Disorder*; Kotkin, *Steeltown*, USSR; Lutsevych, *How to Finish a Revolution*; Hanson, "The Leninist Legacy."
87 Brubaker, "Nationalizing States and Ethno-National Boundaries."
88 Durkheim, *The Division of Labor in Society*; Krapfl, "From Leipzig to Kyiv through Brussels."

89 Kotkin, *Steeltown,* USSR.
90 Durkheim, *The Division of Labor in Society*; Krapfl, "From Leipzig to Kyiv through Brussels."
91 Motyl, *Revolutions, Nations, Empires.*
92 Goldberg, "Demonstrations of Democracy: Cities in Revolt," 20
93 Ritter, "The Missing Unarmed Revolution."
94 Beck, "Reflections on the Revolutionary Wave."
95 Bayat, "The Arab Spring and Revolutionary Theory."
96 Wanner, *Burden of Dreams.*
97 Kailitz and Umland, "How Post-Imperial Democracies Die," 8.
98 Kailitz and Umland, "How Post-Imperial Democracies Die," 3.
99 Kailitz and Umland, "How Post-Imperial Democracies Die," 3.
100 Kailitz and Umland, "How Post-Imperial Democracies Die," 35.
101 Kailitz and Umland, "How Post-Imperial Democracies Die," 5.
102 Kailitz and Umland, "How Post-Imperial Democracies Die," 6.
103 Kailitz and Umland, "How Post-Imperial Democracies Die," 6.

Epilogue

1 Hook, "The Russian Federation."
2 Maynard, *Ideologies and Mass Violence.*
3 Maynard, *Ideologies and Mass Violence,* 119.
4 Maynard, *Ideologies and Mass Violence,* 39–42
5 As coined by Susan Opotow, "Moral Exclusion and Injustice: An Introduction."
6 Maynard, *Ideologies and Mass Violence,* 110–23.
7 Maynard, *Ideologies and Mass Violence,* 125.
8 Maynard, *Ideologies and Mass Violence,* 123.
9 Maynard, *Ideologies and Mass Violence,* 125.
10 Maynard, *Ideologies and Mass Violence,* 125.
11 Fedchenko, "Kremlin Propaganda," 160.
12 Fedchenko, "Kremlin Propaganda," 160.
13 *Chytomo,* "Fifty Anti-Ukrainian Propaganda Books."
14 *Chytomo,* "Fifty Anti-Ukrainian Propaganda Books."
15 Novyi Region, " Siberian Ukrainians Blamed Russian Journalists."
16 Fedchenko, "Kremlin Propaganda," 162.
17 Fedchenko, "Kremlin Propaganda," 161.
18 Fedchenko, "Kremlin Propaganda," 161.
19 Lelich, "Victims of Russian Propaganda."
20 *Chytomo,* "Fifty Anti-Ukrainian Propaganda Books."
21 Myhal, "Putin Accused the U.S."

22 Snyder, "Ukraine: The Haze of Propaganda."
23 Fedchenko, "Kremlin Propaganda," 163.
24 Maynard, *Ideologies and Mass Violence,* 128.
25 Dolgareva, "Maidan As It Was."
26 Maynard, *Ideologies and Mass Violence,* 128.
27 Pynnöniemi, Katri, and Rácz, "Fog of Falsehood."
28 Hutchings and Szostek, "Dominant Narratives," 184.
29 Pynnöniemi, Katri, and Rácz, "Fog of Falsehood."
30 Russian journalist, interview with author, May 2014; Human Rights Watch, "Online and On All Fronts."
31 *Analysis of Russia's Information Campaign against Ukraine.*
32 Zaliznyak, "Russia's Social Media Propaganda Warfare."
33 *Analysis of Russia's Information Campaign against Ukraine,* 24.
34 *Analysis of Russia's Information Campaign against Ukraine.*
35 Maynard, *Ideologies and Mass Violence,* 129.
36 *Analysis of Russia's Information Campaign Against Ukraine,* 19.
37 *Analysis of Russia's Information Campaign Against Ukraine,* 19.
38 *Analysis of Russia's Information Campaign Against Ukraine,* 19.
39 Goodman, Korenyuk, Swinnen, and Zakharov, "War in Ukraine."
40 Maynard, *Ideologies and Mass Violence,* 134.
41 Maynard, *Ideologies and Mass Violence,* 134.
42 Maynard, *Ideologies and Mass Violence,*135.
43 Stepan Bandera was a leader of the nationalist group OUN, which initially sought collaboration with Nazi Germany in their fight for Ukraine's independence against the Soviet regime; they were implicated in atrocities against civilians in Ukraine during the Second World War in collaboration with Nazi forces.
44 *Analysis of Russia's Information Campaign against Ukraine,* 18.
45 Maynard, *Ideologies and Mass Violence,*135.
46 Maynard, *Ideologies and Mass Violence,* 135.
47 *Chytomo,* "Fifty Anti-Ukrainian Propaganda Books."
48 Malakhova, Skovoroda and Marushchenko, "Ukrainian Dream."
49 Maynard, *Ideologies and Mass Violence,*136.
50 Maynard, *Ideologies and Mass Violence,*139–40.
51 Maynard, *Ideologies and Mass Violence,* 140.
52 Champion, "Propaganda War."
53 *Ukraine World,* "Russian Cinema."
54 *Chytomo,* "Fifty Anti-Ukrainian Propaganda Books."
55 *Chytomo,* "Fifty Anti-Ukrainian Propaganda Books."
56 *Chytomo,* "Fifty Anti-Ukrainian Propaganda Books."
57 Parabolic Arc, "Roscosmos Boss Dmitry Rogozin."

58 Maynard, *Ideologies and Mass Violence*, 145.
59 Rainsford, "Putin and Peter the Great."
60 EU vs DisInfo, "Into the Heart of Darkness."
61 Russian Media Monitor, "RT's Director of Broadcasting."
62 Russian Media Monitor, "Russian Orthodox TV Channel."
63 United Nations Press Release, "Underscoring Need for Peace."
64 Plokhy, "Contextualizing Putin's."
65 Plokhy, "Contextualizing Putin's."
66 Moscow Times, "Russian Military to Make Putin's Ukraine Opus Compulsory."
67 Chytomo, "Fifty Anti-Ukrainian Propaganda Books."
68 Yale School of Public Health, "Ukraine's Stolen Children."
69 Roth, "Fears Genocidal Language in Russian Media May Prompt More War Crimes."
70 Wilson, "The Ukrainian Crisis," 67–72.

Appendix 1

* Maidan Museum, Ukrainian Institute of National Memory, United Nations Human Rights Monitoring Mission in Ukraine, NebesnaSotnya.com.
1 Maidan Museum, "Heavenly Hundred."
2 Ukraine Crisis Media Center, "Fifty Three Persons"; "Nebesna Sotnya: Heroes Do Not Die," accessed 15 April 2025, https://nebesnasotnya.com/.
3 Office of the United Nations High Commissioner for Human Rights, "Accountability for Killings in Ukraine from January 2014 to May 2016," 2–3.

Works Cited

Afineevsky, Evgeny. *Winter on Fire*. Urkstream.tv, SPN Productions, Passion Pictures, Campbell, Grobman Films. 2015. Rock Paper Scissors Entertainment.

AKS-Inform. "Украина может потерять свыше 30 млн. долл. из-за остановки экспорта овощей и фруктов в Россию." ["Ukraine might lose more than 30 million USD due to the halting of exports of vegetables and fruits to Russia."]. 14 August 2013. https://www.fruit-inform.com/ru/news/155164#.X4CjTGhKiUl. Accessed 9 October 2020.

Alexeev, Mikhail. "War and Sociopolitical Identities." *Ponars Eurasia*. PONARS Eurasia Policy Memo No 392. October 2015.

Alimi, E. "Introduction: Popular Contention, Regime, and Transition: A Comparative Perspective." In *Popular Contention, Regime, and Transition*, edited by Eitan Y. Alimi, Avraham Sela, and Mario Sznajder. Oxford University Press, 2016.

Almeida, P.D. "Opportunity Organizations and Threat-Induced Contention: Protest Waves in Authoritarian Settings." *American Journal of Sociology* 109, no. 2 (2003): 345–400.

– "Organizational Expansion, Liberalization Reversals and Radicalized Collective Action." *Research in Political Sociology* 15 (2007): 57–99.

– *Social Movements: The Structure of Collective Mobilization*. University of California Press, 2019.

– *Waves of Protest: Popular Struggle in El Salvador, 1925–2005*. University of Minnesota Press, 2008.

Aminzade, Ronald R., Jack A. Goldstone, Doug McAdam, Elizabeth J. Perry, William H. Sewell, Sidney Tarrow, and Charles Tilley. *Silence and Voice in the Study of Contentious Politics*. Cambridge University Press, 2001.

Analysis of Russia's Information Campaign against Ukraine: Examining Non-Military Aspects of the Crisis in Ukraine from a Strategic Communications Perspective. NATO StratCom Centre for Excellence. Riga, 2015. https://stratcomcoe.org/cuploads/pfiles/russian_information_campaign_public_12012016fin.pdf.

Andersen, Ellen A. *Out of the Closets and into the Courts: Legal Opportunity Structure and Gay Rights Litigation.* University of Michigan Press, 2005.

Anisin, Alexei. "Violence Begets Violence: Why States Should Not Lethally Repress Popular Protest." *International Journal of Human Rights* 20, no. 7 (2016): 893–913.

Antonovych, M.M. *Ukrayinska Revoliutsiya Hidnosti, Russian Aggression and International Law: A Monograph.* Ukrainian Association of International Law Press, 2014.

Applebaum, Anne. *Red Famine: Stalin's War on Ukraine.* Signal, 2017.

Apter, David E. "Political Violence in Analytical Perspective." In *The Legitimization of Violence*, edited by David Apter. Palgrave Macmillan UK, 1997

Arel, Dominique. "How Ukraine Has Become More Ukrainian." *Post-Soviet Affairs* 34, no. 2–3 (2018): 186–9.

– "Interpreting 'Nationality' and 'Language' in the 2001 Ukrainian Census." *Post-Soviet Affairs* 18, no. 3 (2002): 213–49.

– "Is the Orange Revolution Fading?" *Current History* 104, no. 684 (2005): 325–30.

Arel, Dominique, and David I. Kertzer. "Censuses, Identity Formation, and the Struggle for Political Power." In *Census and Identity: The Politics of Race, Ethnicity, and Language in National Censuses*, edited by David I. Kertzer and Dominique Arel. Cambridge University Press, 2001.

Arendt, Hannah. *On Revolution.* Penguin, 2006.

Arksey, Hilary, and Peter T. Knight. *Interviewing for Social Scientists: An Introductory Resource with Examples.* Sage, 1999.

Aslund, Anders. *Russia's Crony Capitalism: The Path from Market Economy to Kleptocracy.* Yale University Press, 2019.

Aslund, Anders, and Michael McFaul. *Revolution in Orange: The Origins of Ukraine's Democratic Breakthrough.* Carnegie Endowment for International Peace, 2006.

– "Ukraine's Choice: European Association Agreement or Eurasian Union?" *Policy Brief* 13, no. 22 (2013): 1–12.

Ash, Timothy Garton. *We the People: the Revolution of '89 Witnessed in Warsaw, Budapest, Berlin & Prague.* Penguin UK, 1990.

Balazs, Jarabik, and Yulia Yesmukhanova. "Ukraine's Slow Struggle for Decentralization." Carnegie Endowment for International Peace, 8 March

2017. In Mikhail Minakov and Matthew Rojansky, "Democracy in Ukraine: Are We There Yet?" in Kennon Cable, no. 30, January 2018. https://www.wilsoncenter.org/sites/default/files/media/documents/publication/kennan_cable_30_-_rojansky_minakov.pdf.

Balmforth, Richard, and Pavel Polityuk. "Ukraine Drops Plan to Go West, Turns East." *Reuters.* 21 November 2013. https://www.reuters.com/article/us-ukraine-eu/ukraine-drops-plan-to-go-west-turns-east-idUSBRE9AK0S220131121.

Barkan, Steven E. "Legal Control of the Southern Civil Rights Movement." *American Sociological Review* 49 (1984): 552–65.

Bayat, Asef. "The Arab Spring and Revolutionary Theory: An Intervention in a Debate." *Journal of Historical Sociology* 34, no. 2 (2021): 393–400.

Bayat, Esmaeel, Mohammad Mehdi Mojahedi, Alireza Azghandi, and Aboalghasem Taheri Taheri. "Mechanisms of the Export of Revolution of Iran and Russia: Similarities and Dissimilarities." *Islamic Revolution Research* 10, no. 1 (2021): 36–69.

BBC. "Азаров 'глубоко возмущен' разгоном Евромайдана" ["Azarov Is 'Deeply Outraged' by the Dispersal of Euromaidan"]. 30 November 2013. https://www.bbc.com/ukrainian/ukraine_in_russian/2013/11/131129_ru_s_maidan_riots.

– "Huge Ukraine Rally over EU Agreement Delay." 24 November 2013. https://www.bbc.com/news/world-europe-25078952.

– "Mass Protests in Kiev, Ukraine against Tymoshenko Trial." 24 August 2011. https://www.bbc.com/news/world-europe-14651329.

BBC *News Ukraine.* Квасневський: Євросоюз недооцінив рішучість Путіна." ["Kwasniewski: The European Union Underestimated Putin's Determination."] 8 Deember 2013. https://www.bbc.com/ukrainian/news_in_brief/2013/12/131208_az_kvasnevsky_ukraine_eu.

– "Під ГПУ влаштували лежачий протест." ["A Sit-In Protest Was Organized near the GPU."] 6 December 2013. https://www.bbc.com/ukrainian/politics/2013/12/131206_gpu_protest_ek

– "Опозиція: на Банковій діють провокатори ." ["Opposition: Provocateurs Are Operating on Bankova Street."] 1 December 2013. https://www.bbc.com/ukrainian/news_in_brief/2013/12/131201_hk_opposition_provocation.

– "Марш мільйонів у Києві." "March of Millions in Kyiv." 8 December 2013. https://www.bbc.com/ukrainian/mobile/politics/2013/12/131208_march_million_kyiv_8_december_ms.

Beach, Derek, and Rasmus Brun Pedersen. "Selecting Appropriate Cases when Tracing Causal Mechanisms." *Sociological Methods & Research* 47, no. 4 (2018): 837–71.

Beck, Colin J. "Reflections on the Revolutionary Wave in 2011." *Theory and Society* 43 (2014): 197–223.

– "Revolutions against the State." *The New Handbook of Political Sociology* (2020): 564–91.

Beckles, Colin. "Black Bookstores, Black Power, and the FBI: The Case of Drum and Spear." *Western Journal of Black Studies* 20, no. 2 (1996): 63–71.

Beesley, Celeste. "Euromaidan and the Role of Protest in Democracy." *PS: Political Science & Politics* 49, no. 2 (2016): 244–9.

Bennett, Andrew, and Jeffrey T. Checkel. "Process Tracing: From Philosophical Roots to Best Practices." In *Process Tracing: From Metaphor to Analytic Tool*, edited by Andrew Bennett and Jeffrey T. Checkel. Cambridge University Press, 2015.

Bergstrand, Kelly. "The Mobilizing Power of Grievances: Applying Loss Aversion and Omission Bias to Social Movements." *Mobilization: An International Quarterly* 19, no. 2 (2014): 123–42.

Bernsand, Niklas. "Surzhyk and National Identity in Ukrainian Nationalist Language Ideology." *Berliner Osteuropa Info* 17 (2001): 38–47.

Besters-Dilger, Juliane. "The Ukrainian Language in Education and Mass Media." *Harvard Ukrainian Studies* 29, no. 1/4 (2007): 257–93.

Bigg, Claire. "Ukraine's 'Euromaidan' through the Lens of Russian Television." *Radio Free Europe / Radio Liberty*, 9 December 2013. https://www.rferl.org/a/ukraine-euromaidan-russian-media/25194912.html.

Bilaniuk, Laada. *Contested Tongues: Language Politics and Cultural Correction in Ukraine*. Cornell University Press, 2005.

Binet, Laurence. "War Crimes and Politics of Terror in Chechnya 1994–2004." *Médecins Sans Frontières*, 2016.

Bishara, Dina, "The Politics of Ignoring: Protest Dynamics in Late Mubarak Egypt." *Perspectives on Politics* 13, no. 4 (2015): 958–75.

Bonner, B. "EuroMaidan Rallies on Dec. 1. The Peaceful Morning," *Kyiv Post*, 1 December 2013. https://www.kyivpost.com/article/content/ukraine-politics/euromaidan-rallies-on-dec-1-12-am-to-2-pm-euromaidan-rallies-in-ukraine-332752.html.

Bramsen, Isabel. "How Violence Happens (or Not): Situational Conditions of Violence and Nonviolence in Bahrain, Tunisia, and Syria." *Psychology of Violence* 8 no. 3, (2018): 305–15.

Brier, Robert. *Poland's Solidarity Movement and the Global Politics of Human Rights*. Cambridge University Press, 2021

Brubaker, Rogers. "Nationalizing States and Ethno-National Boundaries: A Comparative Perspective on Soviet Successor States." In *Nationalism, Ethnicity and Boundaries*, edited by Jennifer Jackson and Lina Molokotos-Liederman. Routledge, 2014.

– "Nationalizing States Revisited: Projects and Processes of Nationalization in Post-Soviet States." *Ethnic and Racial Studies* 34, no. 11 (2011): 1785–814.

Bugai et al. "Відкрите звернення адвокатів, юристів, правозахисників України до органів суддівського самоврядування, Конституційного Суду України." ["Open Appeal of Advocates, Lawyers, and Human Rights Defenders of Ukraine to the Bodies of Judicial Self-Government, the Constitutional Court of Ukraine."], quoted in "Правозащитники, адвокаты и юристы обратились к органам судейского самоуправления и КСУ." ["Human Rights Activists, Lawyers and Attorneys Appealed to the Judicial Self-Government Bodies and the Constitutional Court."], *Sudovo-Yurydychna Gazeta*, 12 December 2013. https://sud.ua/ru/news/sud-info/58298-pravozashchitniki-advokati-i-yuristi-obratilis-k--organam-sydejskogo-samoypravleniya-i-ksy.

Calabrese, Andrew. "Sending a Message: Violence as Political Communication." *International Journal of Media & Cultural Politics* 6, no. 1 (2010): 109–14.

Capelouto, Susanna, and Victoria Butenko, "Pro-EU Protesters in Kiev Call for Government's Ouster." CNN, 2 December 2013. https://edition.cnn.com/2013/12/01/us/ukraine-eu-protest-sunday.

Carey, Sabine C. "The Dynamic Relationship between Protest and Repression." *Political Research Quarterly* 59, no.1 (2006): 1–11.

Center for Civic Liberties. "Center for Civic Liberties." Accessed 8 July 2020. https://ccl.org.ua/en/pro-nas/.

Chaisty, Paul, and Stephen Whitefield. "Putin's Nationalism Problem." *Ukraine and Russia: People, Politics, Propaganda and Perspectives*, edited by Agnieszka Pikulicka-Wilczewska and Richard Sakwa. E-International Relations, 2015.

Champion, Marc. "Propaganda War over Mariupol's Destruction Is Only Just Starting." *Bloomberg News*, 22 April 2022. https://www.bloomberg.com/news/articles/2022-04-22/propaganda-war-over-mariupol-s-destruction-is-only-just-starting.

Channell-Justice, Emily. "Flexibility and Fragmentation: Student Activism and Ukraine's (Euro) Maidan Protests." *Berkeley Journal of Sociology* 58 (2014): 59–65.

– *Without the State: Self-Organization and Political Activism in Ukraine*. University of Toronto Press, 2022.

Chenoweth, Erica, and Maria J. Stephan. *Why Civil Resistance Works: The Strategic Logic of Nonviolent Conflict*. Columbia University Press, 2011.

Chytomo. "Fifty Anti-Ukrainian Propaganda Books: How Russian Publishers Stoke Hatred against Ukrainians." 4 April 2022. https://chytomo.com/

en/fifty-propaganda-books-against-ukraine-and-incitement-to-hatred-against-ukrainians-from-russian-publishers.

Cichowski, Rachel A. *The European Court and Civil Society: Litigation, Mobilization and Governance.* Cambridge University Press, 2007.

Cichowski, Rachel A., and Alec Stone Sweet. "Participation, Representative Democracy, and the Courts." In *Democracy Transformed? Expanding Political Opportunities in Advanced Industrial Democracies*, edited by Bruce E. Cain, Russell J. Dalton, and Susan E. Scarrow. Oxford University Press, 2003.

Cirtautas, Arista M. *The Polish Solidarity Movement: Revolution, Democracy and Natural Rights.* Routledge, 2002.

Coller, David, "Understanding Process Tracing." *PS: Political Science and Politics* 44, no. 4 (2011): 823–30.

Conant, Lisa J. *Justice Contained: Law and Politics in the European Union.* Cornell University Press, 2002.

Council of Europe. "Report to the Ukrainian Government on the Visit to Ukraine Carried Out by the European Committee for the Prevention of Torture and Inhuman or Degrading Treatment or Punishment (CPT) from 18 to 24 February 2014." Strasbourg, 2015.

D'Anieri, Paul. *Ukraine and Russia.* Cambridge University Press, 2023.

Davenport, Christian. *How Social Movements Die.* Cambridge University Press, 2015.

– "State Repression and Political Order." *Annual Review of Political Science* 10 (2007): 1–23

Della Porta, Donatella. "Radicalization: A Relational Perspective." *Annual Review of Political Science* 21 (2018): 461–74

Dezalay, Yves, and Bryant Garth, "Introduction: Constructing Transnational Justice." In *Lawyers and the Construction of Transnational Justice*, edited by Yves Dezalay and Bryant Garth. Routledge, 2012.

Diachuk, Kateryna, Oksana Romaniuk, and Iryna Chulivska. *Press Freedom Chronics* (*Khronika Svobody Slova*). Kyiv: National Endowment for Democracy, 2013.

Dolgareva, Anna, "Maidan Kak Eto Bylo, Bolshaia Istorija Krovaboi Revolutsii na Ukraine." [Maidan As It Was, Big Story of the Bloody Revolution in Ukraine."] *Vashy Novosti*, 31 August 2021. https://vnnews.ru/maydan-kak-yeto-bylo-bolshaya-istoriya-kr.

Dzhulai, Dmytro. "1 грудня 2013 року Майдан та Банкова у розповідях стрімерів Радіо Свобода" ["December 1, 2013 Maidan and Bankova in the Stories of Radio Liberty Streamers."] *Radio Liberty Radio Free Europe*, 1 December 2015. https://www.radiosvoboda.org/a/27400767.html.

Dzerkalo Tyzhnya. "Попов через суд заборонив мітингувати в центрі Києва." ["Popov Banned a Rally in the Centre of Kyiv through the

Court."] 1 December 2013. https://zn.ua/ukr/POLITICS/popov-cherez-sud-zaboroniv-mitinguvati-v-centri-kiyeva-132952_.html.

Earl, Jennifer. "Political Repression: Iron Fists, Velvet Gloves, and Diffuse Control." *Annual Review of Sociology* 37 (2011): 261–84.

Elveris, Idil. "Cause Lawyering in a 'Crisis'? Volunteer Attorneys at Gezi Events in Turkey." Paper presented at the Law and Society Association meeting, Seattle, 29 May 2015.

Englund, Will. "Ukraine Protest Gives Voice to Frustration with Opposition Leaders." *Washington Post*, 19 January 2014. https://www.washingtonpost.com/world/ukraine-protest-stoked-by-harsh-new-laws-gives-voice-to-frustration-with-their-leaders/2014/01/19/e850c2b4-812a-11e3-8099-9181471f7aaf_story.html.

Epp, Charles R. *The Rights Revolution: Lawyers, Activists, and Supreme Courts in Comparative Perspective*. University of Chicago Press, 1998.

Espresso TV. "Андрухович: Ми маємо повернутися до політреформи-2004." ["Andrukhovych: We Must Return to the 2004 Political Reform."] 8 December 2013. https://espreso.tv/news/2013/12/08/andrukhovych_zachytav_vymohy_mytciv.

Eterovic, Ivana, Jackie Smith, and Dawn Wiest. "Uneven Globalization: Explaining Variable Participation in Transnational Social Movement Organizations." Paper presented at American Sociological Association annual meeting, Chicago, 16–19 August 2002.

Euroradio. "Бульдозер на прорыв оцепления вел один из командиров "Беркута"?" [Was One of the Berkut Commanders Leading the Bulldozer to Breach the Barrier?"] 1 December 2013. https://euroradio.fm/ru/buldozer-na-proryv-oczepleniya-vel-odin-iz-komandirov-berkuta-video.

EUvsDisinfo. "Into the Heart of Darkness: What Russia Wants in Ukraine." 6 April 2022. https://euvsdisinfo.eu/into-the-heart-of-darkness-what-russia-wants-in-ukraine.

Express Online. "#Євромайдан жорстоко розігнали беркутівці з трьох областей України. Хлопців і дівчат переслідували навіть у подвір'ях." [#Euromaidan Was Brutally Dispersed by Berkut Officers from Three Regions of Ukraine. Boys and Girls Were Even Harassed in Their Yards."] 30 November 2013. https://web.archive.org/web/20131203035330/http://expres.ua//news/2013/11/30/97882-yevromaydan-zhorstoko-rozignaly-berkutivci-troh-oblastey-ukrayiny-hlopciv.

Falsini, Sophie, and Susann Worschech. *The Euromaidan's Effect on Civil Society: Why and How Ukrainian Social Capital Increased after the Revolution of Dignity*. Ibidem Press, 2018.

Faulconbridge, Guy, Anna Dabrowska, and Stephen Grey, "Toppled 'Mafia' President Cost Ukraine up to $100 billion, Prosecutor Says." *Reuters*, 30 April 2014. https://www.reuters.com/article/us-ukraine-crisis-yanukovich/toppled-mafia-president-cost-ukraine-up-to-100-billion-prosecutor-says-idUSBREA3T0K820140430.

Fearon, James, and David Laitin. “Ethnicity, Insurgency, and Civil War.” *American Political Science Review* 97, no. 1 (2003): 75–90.

Fedchenko, Yevhen. “Kremlin Propaganda: Soviet Active Measures by Other Means.” *Sojateadlane Estonian Journal of Military Studies* 2 (2016): 141–70.

Federatsija Profesijnyh Spilok Ukrayiny [Federation of Trade Unions of Ukraine], “ЗАЯВА ФЕДЕРАЦІЇ ПРОФЕСІЙНИХ СПІЛОК УКРАЇНИ.” [“STATEMENT OF THE FEDERATION OF TRADE UNIONS OF UKRAINE.”] 2 December 2013. https://fpsu.org.ua/pozitsiya-profspilok/2895-zayava-federatsiji-profesijnikh-spilok-ukrajini-2.

Fedorova, Alla L., and Olena M. Lysenko. “The Rights of Peaceful Assembly and Its Suppression in Ukraine.” In *Ukrayinska Revoliutsiya Hidnosti, Russian Aggression and International Law: A Monograph*, edited by M.M. Antonovych. Ukrainian Association of International Law Press, 2014.

Fedunyak, Sergiy. “The Ukrainian Revolution in International Context.” In *Ukraine after the Euromaidan: Challenges and Hopes*, edited by Viktor Stepanenko and Yaroslav Pylynskyi. Peter Lang, 2015.

Feierabend, Ivo K., Rosalind L. Feierabend, and Norman G. Litell. “Dimensions of Political Unrest: A Factor Analysis of Cross-National Data.” *Political Research Quarterly* 19, no. 3 (1966): 17–18.

Finberg, Leonid, and Yuliana Holovach, eds. *Maidan. Testimonies: Kyiv, 2013–2014*. Kyiv: Duh I Litera, 2016.

– *Maidan. Testimonies: Kyiv, 2013–2014. Aid to the Wounded. International Solidarity*. Kyiv: Duh I Litera, 2018.

Foran, John. *Taking Power: On the Origins of Third World Revolutions*. Cambridge University Press, 2005.

Freedom House. “Freedom House Report on the State of Democracy and Human Rights in Ukraine.” April 2011. https://www.freedomhouse.org/sites/default/files/inline_images/98.pdf.

– “Freedom of the Press 2012 – Ukraine.” 6 October 2012. https://www.refworld.org/docid/50757c151a.html.

– “Freedom on the Net 2013 – Ukraine.” 3 October 2013. https://www.refworld.org/docid/52663acd12.html.

– “Freedom in the World 2015 – Ukraine.” 28 January 2015. https://www.refworld.org/docid/54d0d7ad6.html.

– “Freedom in the World 2020 – Eastern Donbas.” https://freedomhouse.org/country/eastern-donbas/freedom-world/2020.

– “Freedom in the World 2022 – Eastern Donbas.” https://freedomhouse.org/country/eastern-donbas/freedom-world/2022.

Frye, Timothy. "What Do Voters in Ukraine Want?: A Survey Experiment on Candidate Ethnicity, Language, and Policy Orientation." *Problems of Post-Communism* 62, no. 5 (2015): 247–57.

Fylypovych, Lyudmila, and Oksana Horkusha. *Майдан і церква. Хроніка подій та експертна оцінка.* [*Maidan and the Church. Chronicle of Events and Expert Assessment.*] Kyiv: Sammit Knyha, 2015.

Gamson, William A. "The Social Psychology of Collective Action." *Frontiers in Social Movement Theory* 1 (1992): 53–76.

Gamson, William A., Bruce Fireman, and Steven Rytina. *Encounters with Unjust Authority.* Dorsey Press, 1982.

Gazeta, "'Не їдь за мною, я - п'ятий.' Янукович підписав 'диктаторські закони.'" ["Don't follow me, I'm the fifth." Yanukovych signed 'dictatorial laws.'"] 17 January 2014. https://gazeta.ua/articles/life/_ne-yid-za-mnoyu-ya-pyatij-anukovich-pidpisav-diktatorski-zakoni-17-sichnya/671697.

Gilligan, Emma. *Terror in Chechnya: Russia and the Tragedy of Civilians in War.* Princeton University Press, 2009.

Ginkel, John, and Alastair Smith. "So You Say You Want a Revolution: A Game Theoretic Explanation of Revolution in Repressive Regimes." *Journal of Conflict Resolution* 43, no. 3 (1999): 291–316

Gladun, Andrii. "Impact of Repression on Mobilization: The Case of the Euromaidan Protests in Ukraine." *Social Justice* 46, no. 2–3 (2019): 29–50.

Gobe, Eric, and Lena Salaymeh. "Tunisia's 'Revolutionary' Lawyers: from Professional Autonomy to Political Mobilization." *Law & Social Inquiry* 41, no. 2 (2016): 311–45.

Goffman, Erving. *Frame Analysis: An Essay on the Organization of Experience.* Harvard University Press, 1974.

Goldberg, Ellis, "Arab Spring (Introduction)." Unpublished paper, 2014.

– "Demonstrations of Democracy: Cities in Revolt." Unpublished paper, 2014.

Goldstone, Jack A. *Revolutions: A Very Short Introduction.* Oxford University Press, 2014.

Goncharova, Olena. "EuroMaidan Rallies on Dec 1: A Rowdy Afternoon." *Kyiv Post*, 2 December 2013. https://www.kyivpost.com/article/content/ukraine-politics/euromaidan-rallies-on-dec-1-a-rowdy-afternoon-332780.html.

Goodman, Jack, Maria Korenyuk, Lucy Swinnen, and Andrey Zakharov. "War in Ukraine: The Making of a New Russian Propaganda Machine." *BBC News*, 29 May 2022. https://www.bbc.com/news/world-europe-61441192.

Goodwin, Jeff. *No Other Way Out: States and Revolutionary Movements, 1945–1991.* Cambridge University Press, 2001.

Gorchinskaya, Katya. "Police Say They Identified Instigators of Clashes." *Kyiv Post.* 1 December 2013. https://www.kyivpost.com/article/content/ukraine-politics/police-say-they-identified-instigators-of-clashes-332768.html.

Grytsenko, Oksana. "Yanukovych Says Police Beatings Not His Fault." *Kyiv Post.* 30 November 2013. http://www.kyivpost.com/article/content/euromaidan/yanukovych-outraged-by-maidans-break-up-threatens-to-punish-guilty-332718.html.

Grytsenko, Oksana, and Daryna Shevchenko. "Victims Describe Excessive, Indiscriminate Attacks (UPDATES)." *Kyiv Post.* 30 November 2013. https://web.archive.org/web/20131130115832/http://www.kyivpost.com/content/ukraine-abroad/witness-steps-on-independence-square-were-all-covered-in-blood-332681.html.

Gujarati, Damodar N. *Basic Econometrics.* McGraw-Hill Education, 2009.

Gupta, Dipak K., Harinder Singh, and Tom Sprague. "Government Coercion of Dissidents: Deterrence or Provocation?" *Journal of Conflict Resolution* 37, no. 2 (1993): 301–39.

Gurr, Tedd Robert, *Why Men Rebel.* Princeton University Press, 1970.

Hajjar, Lisa. "Cause Lawyering in Transnational Perspective: National Conflict and Human Rights in Israel/Palestine." *Law and Society Review* 31, no. 3 (1997): 473–504.

Hale, Henry E. "Democracy or Autocracy on the March? The Colored Revolutions as Normal Dynamics of Patronal Presidentialism." *Communist and Post-Communist Studies* 39, no. 3 (2006): 305–29

Hanson, Stephen E. "From Culture to Ideology in Comparative Politics." *Comparative Politics* 35, no. 3 (2003): 355–76.

– "The Leninist Legacy and Institutional Change." *Comparative Political Studies* 28, no. 2 (1995): 306–14.

– *Time and Revolution: Marxism and the Design of Soviet Institutions.* University of North Carolina Press, 1997.

Harvard Ukrainian Research Institute. "Revolution on Granite." https://gis.huri.harvard.edu/revolution-granite.

Herbert, Trevor, and Gareth Elwyn Jones. *People and Protest: Wales 1815–1880.* University of Wales Press, 1988.

Herszenhorn, David M. "Facing Russian Threat, Ukraine Halts Plans for Deals with E.U." *New York Times.* 21 November 2013. https://www.nytimes.com/2013/11/22/world/europe/ukraine-refuses-to-free-ex-leader-raising-concerns-over-eu-talks.html.

– "Ukraine in Turmoil after Leaders Reject Major E.U. Deal." *New York Times*, 26 November 2013. https://www.nytimes.com/2013/11/27/world/europe/protests-continue-as-ukraine-leader-defends-stance-on-europe.html.

Hess, David, and Brian Martin. "Repression, Backfire, and the Theory of Transformative Events." *Mobilization: An International Quarterly* 11, no. 2 (2006): 249–67.

Hibbs, Douglas A. *Mass Political Violence: A Cross-National Causal Analysis.* Wiley, 1973.

Hilbink, Thomas. "The Profession, the Grassroots, and the Elite: Cause Lawyering for Civil Rights and Freedom in the Direct Action Era." In *Cause Lawyers and Social Movements*, edited by Austin Sarat and Stuart Scheingold. Stanford University Press, 2006.

Hilson, Chris. "New Social Movements: The Role of Legal Opportunity." *Journal of European Public Policy* 9, no. 2 (2002): 238–55.

Hirsch, Eric L. "Sacrifice for the Cause: Group Processes, Recruitment, and Commitment in a Student Social Movement." *American Sociological Review* 55, no. 2 (1990): 243–54.

Holland, Laurel L., and Sherry Cable. "Reconceptualizing Social Movement Abeyance: The Role of Internal Processes and Culture in Cycles of Movement Abeyance and Resurgence." *Sociological Focus* 35, no. 3 (2002): 297–314

Hook, Kristina. "Pinpointing Patterns of Violence: A Comparative Genocide Studies Approach to Violence Escalation in the Ukrainian Holodomor." *Genocide Studies and Prevention: An International Journal* 15, no. 2 (2021): 10–36.

– "The Russian Federation's Escalating Commission of Genocide in Ukraine: A Legal Analysis." *New Lines Institute*, 26 July 2023. https://newlinesinstitute.org/rules-based-international-order/genocide/the-russian-federations-escalating-commission-of-genocide-in-ukraine-a-legal-analysis.

Howard, Marc Morjé. *The Weakness of Civil Society in Post-Communist Europe*. Cambridge University Press, 2003.

Hrushetskyi, Anton. "Attitudes of Ukrainians towards Russia and Russians." *Kyiv International Institute of Sociology*, November 2021. https://kiis.com.ua/?lang=eng&cat=reports&id=1446.

Hrycak, Alexandra. "The Dilemmas of Civic Revival: Ukrainian Women since Independence." *Journal of Ukrainian Studies* 26, no. 1–2 (2001): 135–58.

Hrytsak, Yaroslav. "Ukrainians: Who Are They, and What Do They Want?" *Krytyka* 7–8, July 2011. https://krytyka.com/en/articles/ukrainians-who-are-they-and-what-do-they-want.

– "Україна витримає і це випробування." ["Ukraine Will Withstand This Test As Well."] in *Madian: Майдан. Революція духу: мистецько-культурологічний проект. [Maidan. Revolution of the Spirit: An Artistic and Cultural Project.]*, edited by Antin Muhorskiy. Kyiv: Nash Format, 2014.

Hultquist, Philip. "Is Collective Repression an Effective Counterinsurgency Technique? Unpacking the Cyclical Relationship between Repression and Civil Conflict." *Conflict Management and Peace Science* 34, no. 5 (2017): 507–25.

Human Rights Watch. "Online and On All Fronts: Russia's Assault on Freedom of Expression." 18 July 2017. https://www.hrw.org/report/2017/07/18/online-and-all-fronts/russias-assault-freedom-expression.

Hunt, Lynn, "The Sacred and the French Revolution." In *Durkheimian Sociology: Cultural Studies*, edited by Jeffrey C. Alexander. Cambridge: Cambridge University Press, 1992.

Hutchings, Stephen, and Joanna Szostek. "Dominant Narratives in Russian Political and Media Discourse during the Ukraine Crisis." *Ukraine and Russia: People, Politics, Propaganda and Perspectives*. E-International Relations, 2015.

Iarmoshchuk, Tetiana, and Tony Wesolowsky. "For Victims of Sexual Violence in Ukraine's Donbas, Justice Seems Distant." *Radio Free Europe/Radio Liberty*. 8 December 2020. https://www.rferl.org/a/ukraine-sexual-violence-donbas-victims-justice/30990565.html.

Ilko Kucheriv Democratic Initiatives Foundation and Kyiv International Institute of Sociology. "Maidan-December and Maidan-February: What Has Changed?" 6 February 2014. https://dif.org.ua/article/maidan-december-and-maidan-february-what-has-changed.

Ilko Kucheriv Democratic Initiatives Foundation and Razumkov Center Sociological Service. "Постмайданна благодійність і волонтерство-2015: результати соцдослідження." ["Post-Maidan Charity and Volunteering-2015: Results of a Social Survey."] 9 December 2015. https://dif.org.ua/article/postmaydanna-blagodiynist-i-volonterstvo-2015-rezultati-sotsdoslidzhennya.

The Insider. "'Беркут' розігнав Євромайдан." ["'Berkut' Dispersed Euromaidan."] 30 November 2013. https://web.archive.org/web/20131202031235/http://www.theinsider.com.ua/politics/529949a99804e.

International Foundation for Electoral Systems. "Survey Findings: Public Opinion in Ukraine 2009." Accessed 11 December 2020. http://www.ifes.org/publication/69a55d8398d89d3528dc34949c099858/MediaPackChartsfromIFESUkraine2009Survey.pdf.

Ishchenko, Volodymyr. "Far Right Participation in the Ukrainian Maidan Protests: An Attempt of Systematic Estimation." *European Politics and Society* 17, no. 4 (2016): 453–72.

– "Insufficiently Diverse: The Problem of Nonviolent Leverage and Radicalization of Ukraine's Maidan Uprising, 2013–2014." *Journal of Eurasian Studies* 11, no. 2 (2020): 201–15.

Israël, Liora. "From Cause Lawyering to Resistance French Communist Lawyers." In *The Worlds Cause Lawyers Make: Structure and Agency in Legal Practice*, edited by Austin Sarat and Stuart A. Scheingold. Stanford University Press, 2005.

Jacobs, Alan M. "Process Tracing the Effects of Ideas." In *Process Tracing: From Metaphor to Analytic Tool*, edited by Andrew Bennett. Cambridge University Press, 2015.

Jansen, Sue Curry, and Brian Martin. "Exposing and Opposing Censorship: Backfire Dynamics in Freedom-of-Speech Struggles." *Pacific Journalism Review* 10, no. 1 (2004): 29–45.

– "Making Censorship Backfire." *Counterpoise* 7, no. 3 (2003): 5–15.

Jeffries, Judson L. "Black Radicalism and Political Repression in Baltimore: The Case of the Black Panther Party." *Ethnic and Racial Studies* 25, no. 1 (2002): 64–98.

Jenkins, J. Craig, and Charles Perrow. "Insurgency of the Powerless: Farm Worker Movements (1946–1972)." *American Sociological Review* 42, no. 2 (1977): 249–68.

Jewish Telegraphic Agency. "Ukrainian Jews Slam Putin in Full-Page Ad in New York Times." 27 March 2014. https://www.jta.org/2014/03/27/global/ukrainian-jews-slam-putin-in-full-page-ad-in-new-york-times.

Jowitt, Ken. *New World Disorder: The Leninist Extinction*. University of California Press, 1992.

Kailitz, Steffen, and Andreas Umland. "How Post-Imperial Democracies Die: A Comparison of Weimar Germany and Post-Soviet Russia." *Communist and Post-Communist Studies* 52, no. 2 (2019): 105–15.

Kalyvas, Stathis. *The Logic of Violence in Civil Theories of Genocide and the Logics of Political Violence and War*. Cambridge University Press, 2006.

Kalyvas, Stathis N., and Matthew Adam Kocher. "How 'Free' is Free Riding in Civil Wars? Violence, Insurgency, and the Collective Action Problem." *World Politics* 59, no. 2 (2007): 177–216.

Keesing, Roger M., Malcolm Crick, Barbara Frankel, Jonathan Friedman, Elvin Hatch, J.G. Oosten, et al. "Anthropology as Interpretive Quest [and comments and reply]." *Current Anthropology* 28, no. 2 (1987): 161–76.

Kenney, Padraic. *A Carnival of Revolution: Central Europe*. Princeton University Press, 2003.

Kherson Regional Council. "№ 927 Про суспільно-політичну ситуацію в державі." ["No. 927 on the Socio-Political Situation in the State."] 2 December 2013. https://web.archive.org/web/20140107103306/http://www.oblrada.ks.ua/index.php?id=14778.

Kinoy, Arthur. *Rights on Trial: The Odyssey of a People's Lawyer*. Harvard University Press, 1993.

Kitschelt, Herbert P. "Political Opportunity Structures and Political Protest: Antinuclear Movements in Four Democracies." *British Journal of Political Science* 16, no. 1 (1986): 57–85.

Kmenta, Jan, and Bijan Rafailzadeh. *Elements of Econometrics*. University of Michigan Press, 1997.

Koopmans, Ruud. "New Social Movements and Changes in Political Participation in Western Europe." *West European Politics* 19, no. 1 (1996): 28–50.

Korzh, Alla, Serhiy Kovalchuk, and Adj Marshall. "Euromaidan Abroad: The Social Movement Motivations of Young Ukrainian Immigrants." *Nationalities Papers* 50, no. 2 (2022): 262–74.

Koshkina, Sonya. *Maidan. Nerasskazannaia Istoriia* [Maidan. An Untold Story]. Bright Star Publishing, 2015.

Kotkin, Stephen. *Steeltown,* USSR*: Soviet Society in the Gorbachev Era.* University of California Press, 1992.

Krapfl, James. "From Leipzig to Kyiv through Brussels: How the Revolution of 1989 Defined an Era." *East European Politics and Societies* 38, no. 4 (2024): 1013–25.

Krapfl, James, and Elias Kühn von Burgsdorff. "Ukraine's Euromaidan and Revolution of Dignity, Ten Years Later." *Canadian Slavonic Papers* 65, no. 3–4 (2023): 325–34.

Krasynska, Svitlana. "Digital Civil Society: Euromaidan, the Ukrainian Diaspora, and Social Media." In *Ukraine's Euromaidan: Analysis of a Civil Revolution*, edited by David R. Marples and Frederick V. Mills. Ibidem Press, 2015.

Kriesi, Hanspeter. "The Political Opportunity Structure of New Social Movements: Its Impact on Their Mobilization." In *The Politics of Social Protest: Comparative Perspectives on States and Social Movements*, edited by J. Craig Jenkins. University of Minnesota Press, 1995.

Krushelnycky, Askold. "The Fight for the Maidan. How Long Can Ukraine's Protesters Hold Out against Yanukovych's Thugs?" *Foreign Policy*, 13 December 2013. https://foreignpolicy.com/2013/12/13/the-fight-for-the-maidan/.

Kryukova, Svetlana, and Elena Sinitsyna. *Diary of EuroMaidan: The Revolution through the Eyes of 'Reporter' Journalists, Book One*. Summit Kniga, 2014.

Kubik, Jan, and Myron J. Aronoff. *Anthropology and Political Science: A Convergent Approach*. Berghahn Books, 2013.

*Kucheriv Democratic Initiatives Foundation & Kyiv International Institute of Sociology (*KDIF & KIIS*)*. "From Maidan-Camp to Maidan-Sich: What Has Changed." January and February 2014. Accessed 5 December 2015. https://www.kiis.com.ua/?lang5eng&cat5reports&id=226.

*Kucheriv Democratic Initiatives Foundation & Kyiv International Institute of Sociology (*KDIF & KIIS*)*. "Maidan 2013." December 2013. Accessed 5 December 2015. https://dif.org.ua/en/article/maidan-2013.

Kulyk, Volodymyr. "National Identity in Ukraine: Impact of Euromaidan and the War." *Europe-Asia Studies* 68, no. 4 (2016): 588–608.

– "Shedding Russianness, Recasting Ukrainianness: The Post-Euromaidan Dynamics of Ethnonational Identifications in Ukraine." *Post-Soviet Affairs* 34, no. 2–3 (2018): 119–38.

Kurtz, Lester R., and Lee A. Smithey. "'We Have Bare Hands': Nonviolent Social Movements in the Soviet Bloc." *Nonviolent Social Movements: A Geographical Perspective* 11, no. 5, (1999): 96–124.

Kurtz, Lester R., and Lee A. Smithey, eds. *The Paradox of Repression and Nonviolent Movements*. Syracuse University Press, 2018.

Kuzio, Taras. "Ukraine's Orange Revolution: The Opposition's Road to Success." *Journal of Democracy* 16, no. 2 (2005): 117–30.

Kyiv International Institute of Sociology (KIIS). "Звернення до Президента України В. Януковича Соціологічної асоціації України." ["Address to the President of Ukraine by the Sociology Association of Ukraine."] 10 December 2013. http://kiis.com.ua/?lang=ukr&cat=news&id=215&page=1.

Kyiv Post. "75 Were Injured during Nov. 30 Dispersal of EuroMaidan." 5 December 2013. https://www.kyivpost.com/article/content/ukraine-politics/75-were-injured-during-nov-30-dispersal-of-euromaidan-333103.html.

– "EuroMaidan Rallies in Ukraine." 25 November 2013. https://www.kyivpost.com/article/content/euromaidan/euromaidan-rallies-in-ukraine-nov-21-23-coverage-332423.html.

– "Police Violently Break Up Independence Square Protests at 4 a.m. Today; Many Injuries Reported," 30 November 2013. https://web.archive.org/web/20131130115550/http://www.kyivpost.com/content/ukraine/reports-police-forcefully-break-up-protest-site-on-maidan-nezalezhnosti-this-morning-332674.html.

– "Yanukovych Changes Tax Law after Protests." 3 December 2010. https://www.kyivpost.com/article/content/ukraine-politics/yanukovych-changes-tax-law-after-protests-92010.html.

Lawson, George. *Anatomies of Revolution*. Cambridge University Press, 2019.

Leavy, Patricia. Introduction to *The Oxford Handbook of Qualitative Research*, edited by Patricia Leavy. Oxford University Press, 2020.

Lelich, Milan. "Victims of Russian Propaganda." *New Eastern Europe* 3 (12) (2014): 75–80.

Leonard, David, and Scott Straus. *Africa's Stalled Development: International Causes and Cures*. Lynne Rienner, 2003.

Levitsky, Sandra R. "To Lead with Law: Reassessing the Influence of Legal Advocacy Organizations in Social Movements." In *Cause Lawyers and Social Movements*, edited by Austin Sarat and Stuart Scheingold. Stanford University Press, 2006.

Levitsky, Steven, and Lucan Way. "The Durability of Revolutionary Regimes." *Journal of Democracy* 24 (2013): 5–17.

– *Revolution and Dictatorship: The Violent Origins of Durable Authoritarianism*. Princeton University Press, 2022.

Lichbach, Mark Irving. "Deterrence or Escalation? The Puzzle of Aggregate Studies of Repression and Dissent." *Journal of Conflict Resolution* 31, no. 2 (1987): 266–97.

Liga.net, "Побоище на Банковой: фоторепортаж." ["Beating on Bankova: photo report."] 1 December 2013. https://news.liga.net/politics/photo/poboishche_na_bankovoy_fotoreportazh#1.

Likhachev, Vi͡acheslav. *The Far Right in the Conflict between Russia and Ukraine*. No. 95. Ifri, 2016.

Lofland, John, and Michael Jamison. "Social Movement Locals: Modal Member Structures." *Sociological Analysis* 45, no. 2 (1984): 115–29.

Lokot, Tetyana. *Beyond the Protest Square: Digital Media and Augmented Dissent*. Rowman & Littlefield Publishers, 2021.

Lutsevych, Orysia. *How to Finish a Revolution: Civil Society and Democracy in Georgia, Moldova and Ukraine*. Chatham House, 2013.

Lyachynka, Oksana. "Battle Intensifies over Podil's Hostynny Dvir." *Kyiv Post*. 20 August 2012. https://www.kyivpost.com/article/content/ukraine-politics/battle-intensifies-over-podils-hostynny-dvir-311788.html.

Maidan Museum. "Heavenly Hundred." https://www.maidanmuseum.org/en/node/348.

– "Календар Майдану. 1 грудня 2013." ["Maidan Calendar. December 1, 2013."] Accessed 13 November 2024. http://maidanmuseum.org/uk/node/1280.

– "Календар Майдану. 17 грудня 2013." ["Maidan Calendar. December 17, 2013."] Accessed 13 November 2024. https://maidanmuseum.org/en/history/2014-01-17.

– "The Revolution on Granite." Accessed 13 November 2024. https://www.maidanmuseum.org/en/node/361.

– "Ukraine without Kuchma." Accessed 13 November 2024. https://www.maidanmuseum.org/en/node/362.

Malakhova, Olena, H.S. Skovoroda, and Oleg Marushchenko. "Ukrainian Dream in the Mirror of Euromaidan." In *Constructing "Europe" and Spread of European Values*, edited by Liudas Mazylis. Vytoauto Didziojo Universitetas, 2014.

Marat, Erica. "Transformative Violence and Mobilization in India and Mexico." *Mobilization: An International Quarterly* 26, no. 3 (2021): 303–22.

Marshall, Anna. "Social Movement Strategies and the Participatory Potential of Litigation." In *Cause Lawyers and Social Movements*, edited by Austin Sarat and Stuart Scheingold. Stanford University Press, 2006.

Martin, Brian. "From Political Jiu-Jitsu to the Backfire Dynamic: How Repression Can Promote Mobilization." In *Civil Resistance: Comparative Perspectives on Nonviolent Struggle*, edited by Kurt Schock. University of Minnesota Press, 2015.

Martsenyuk, Tamara. "Gender Issues in Ukraine: Were the EuroMaidan Protests Patriarchal or Egalitarian?" 2015. https://ekmair.ukma.edu.ua/server/api/core/bitstreams/f90ce41f-e57d-4aa3-bce8-a785bbcb84af/content.

Marx, Karl. *Economy, Class and Social Revolution*. 1972.

Mastnak, Tomaž. "Civil Society in Slovenia: From Opposition to Power." *Studies in Comparative Communism* 23, no. 3–4 (1990): 305–17.

Mayerchuk, Maria, and Olga Plakhotnyk. "Between Time of Nation and Feminist Time: Geneologies of Feminist Protests in Ukraine." In *Feminist Circulations between East and West / Feministische Zirkulationen zwischen Ost und West*, vol. 2, edited by Annette Bühler-Dietrich. Frank & Timme GmbH, 2020.

Maynard, Jonathan Leader. "Ideologies and Mass Violence: The Justificatory Mechanics of Deadly Atrocities." PhD diss., University of Oxford, 2014.

McCann, Michael W. "How Does Law Matter for Social Movements?" In *How Does Law Matter*, edited by Bryant Garth and Austin Sarat. Northwestern University Press, 1998.

McCarthy, John D., and Mayer N. Zald. "The Enduring Vitality of the Resource Mobilization Theory of Social Movements." In *Handbook of Sociological Theory*, edited by Jonathan H. Turner. Springer, 2001.

– "Resource Mobilization and Social Movements: A Partial Theory." *American Journal of Sociology* 82, no. 6 (1977): 1212–41.

– "The Trend of Social Movements in America: Professionalization and Resource Mobilization." CRSO Working Paper #164. General Learning Press, 1973.

McLaughlin, Paul, and Khawaja Marwan. "The Organizational Dynamics of the US Environmental Movement: Legitimation, Resource Mobilization, and Political Opportunity." *Rural Sociology* 65, no. 3 (2000): 422–39.

Menkel-Meadow, Carrie. "The Causes of Cause Lawyering: Toward an Understanding of the Motivation and Commitment of Social Justice Lawyers." In *Cause Lawyering: Political Commitments and Professional Responsibilities*, edited by Austin Sarat and Stuart Scheingold, 31–68. Oxford University Press, 1998.

Migdal, Joel S. "A Model of State–Society Relations." *Comparative Politics: Critical Concepts in Political Science* 1 (2005): 288–303.

– "Researching the State." In *Comparative Politics: Rationality, Culture, and Structure*, edited by Mark Irving Lichbach, and Alan S. Zuckerman. Cambridge University Press, 2009.

– "Revolution and Rebellion in the Early Modern Period by Jack A. Goldstone (Book Review)." *Comparative Political Studies* 25, no. 4 (1993): 608.

Mikheieva, Oksana, and Irina Kuznetsova. "War-Time Volunteering and Population Displacement: From Spontaneous Help to Organised Volunteering in Post-2014 Ukraine." *Voluntary Sector Review* 15, no. 1 (2024): 74–91. https://doi.org/10.1332/20408056Y2023D000000009.

Miller, Christopher (@ChristopherJM). "As of 4 p.m. today 22 people sought medical attention in #Kyiv emergency rooms, says City Admin. In most cases treated for chemical burns." *X, formerly known as Twitter*, 1 December 2013 11:43 a.m. https://x.com/ChristopherJM/status/407203393254326272.

– "The Executioners of Slovyansk." *Radio Free Europe / Radio Liberty*, 23 July 2020. https://www.rferl.org/a/the-executioners-of-slovyansk/30743132.html.

Moore, Barrington. *Social Origins of Dictatorship and Democracy: Lord and Peasant in the Making of the Modern World*, vol. 268. Beacon Press, 1993.

Moore, Will H. "Repression and Dissent: Substitution, Context, and Timing." *American Journal of Political Science* 42, no. 3 (1998): 851–73.

The Moscow Times. "Russian Military to Make Putin's Ukraine Opus Compulsory – RBC." 16 July 2021. https://www.themoscowtimes.com/2021/07/16/russian-military-to-make-putins-ukraine-opus-compulsory-rbc-a74538.

Motyl, Alexander J. "Deleting the Holodomor: Ukraine Unmakes Itself." *World Affairs* 173, no. 3 (2010): 25–33.

– *Revolutions, Nations, Empires: Conceptual Limits and Theoretical Possibilities.* Columbia University Press, 1999.

Mukachevo.net. "Закарпатська облрада вимагає негайної відставки уряду Азарова та міністра МВС." ["Transcarpathian Regional Council Demands Immediate Resignation of Azarov's Government and Minister of Internal Affairs."] 3 December 2013. http://www.mukachevo.net/ua/news/view/84213-Закарпатська-облрада-вимагає-негайної-відставки-уряду-Азарова-та-міністра-МВС.

Mullins, Christopher W. "War Crimes in the 2008 Georgia–Russia Conflict." *British Journal of Criminology* 51, no. 6 (2011): 918–36.

Myhal, Mariana. "Путін звинуватив США в організації Майдану." ["Putin Accused the US of Organizing the Maidan."] *Hlavkom*, 22 July 2021. https://glavcom.ua/news/putin-zvinuvativ-ssha-v-organizaciji-maydanu-764293.html.

Navrotskyi, Viacheslav. "Spravedlyva, Nezalezhna ta Vidpovidalna Sudova Vlada Ukrayiny: Analiz Praktyky Zastosuvannia Trymannia pid Vartoju pid Chas Podii 'Revolutsii Hidnosti.'" ["Fair, Independent and Responsible

Judiciary of Ukraine: Analysis of Jail Practices during the Events of the 'Revolution of Dignity'"] 2015. UsAid Project "Fair Judiciary." Contract no. AID-1420- 17 (2007).

Nepstad, Sharon Erickson. *Nonviolent Revolutions: Civil Resistance in the Late 20th Century*. Oxford University Press, 2011

Nikolayenko, Olena. "The Significance of Human Dignity for Social Movements: Mass Mobilisation in Ukraine." *East European Politics* 36, no. 3 (2020): 445–62.

– *Youth Movements and Elections in Eastern Europe*. Cambridge University Press, 2017

Novyi Region, "Сибирские украинцы обвинили российских журналистов в шовинизме и начали 'кампанию общественного порицания'" ["Siberian Ukrainians Blamed Russian Journalists in Shauvinism and Began 'Public Shame Campaign'"], 20 October 2007. https://web.archive.org/web/20071020141715/http://www.nr2.ru/center/54255.html.

Novyny NSPU, "НСПУ вимагає покарати винних у кривавій розправі над студентами." ["NSPU Demands Punishment of those behind the Bloody Violence against Students."] 10 December 2013. https://web.archive.org/web/20140107151028/http://ualit.org/?p=11349.

Oberschall, Anthony. *Social Conflict and Social Movements*. Prentice Hall, 1973.

Office of the United Nations High Commissioner for Human Rights, "Accountability for Killings in Ukraine from January 2014 to May 2016." Accessed 13 December 2024. file:///C:/Users/thewi/Desktop/MAIDAN%20BOOK%20FINAL/OHCHRThematicReportUkraineJan2014-May2016_EN.pdf.

Olzak, Susan, Maya Beasley, and Johan Olivier. "The Impact of State Reforms on Protest against Apartheid in South Africa." *Mobilization: An International Quarterly* 8, no. 1 (2003): 27–50.

Ondetti, Gabriel. "Repression, Opportunity, and Protest: Explaining the Takeoff of Brazil's Landless Movement." *Latin American Politics and Society* 48, no. 2 (2006): 61–94.

Onuch, Olga. "The Legacy of the Revolution on Granite." *New Eastern Europe* 27 no. 3/4 (2017): 133–9.

– "The Maidan and Beyond: Who Were the Protesters?" *Journal of Democracy* 25, no. 3 (2014): 44–51.

– *Mapping Mass Mobilization: Understanding Revolutionary Moments in Argentina and Ukraine*. Springer, 2014.

Onuch, Olga, and Gwendolyn Sasse. "The Maidan in Movement: Diversity and the Cycles of Protest." *Europe-Asia Studies* 68, no. 4 (2016): 556–87.

Onyschenko, Yuri. "Фотофакт: как 'Беркут' бил журналиста ЛІГАБізнеІнформ" ["Photo Fact: How 'Berkut' Beat a LIGA Business Inform Journalist."] *LIGA*, 2 December 2013. https://news.liga.net/politics/articles/perevoznik_i_berkut.

Opotow, Susan. "Moral Exclusion and Injustice: An Introduction." *Journal of Social Issues* (Spring 1990). https://doi.org/10.1111/j.1540-4560.1990.tb00268.x.

Opp, Karl-Dieter. "Repression and Revolutionary Action: East Germany in 1989." *Rationality and Society* 6 (1994): 101–38.

Opp, Karl-Dieter, and Wolfgang Roehl. "Repression, Micromobilization, and Political Protest." *Social Forces* 69, no. 2, (1990): 521–47.

Organization for Security and Co-operation in Europe, O.S.C.E. "Civil Society and the Crisis in Ukraine." 11 February 2015. https://www.osce.org/special-monitoring-mission-to-ukraine/141046.

Otrishchenko, Natalia. "Beyond the Square." In *Ukraine's Euromaidan: Analyses of a Civil Revolution*, vol. 138, edited by David R. Marples and Frederick V. Mills. Columbia University Press, 2014.

– "Voices of Euromaidan: From Collection Creation to Global Visibility." Paper presented at the Online Academic Forum, "The Revolution of Dignity: On the Road to History, Museum of the Revolution of Dignity." November 2023.

Panin, Alexander. "Ukrainian Imports Barred as Relations Hit a New Low." *Moscow Times*, 15 August 2013. https://www.themoscowtimes.com/2013/08/15/ukrainian-imports-barred-as-relations-hit-a-new-low-a26815.

Parabolic Arc. "Roscosmos Boss Dmitry Rogozin Calls for Wiping Out Ukraine." 14 June 2022. http://parabolicarc.com/2022/06/14/roscosmos-boss-dmitry-rogozin-calls-for-wiping-out-ukraine.

Pavlush, Tetyana "'Leninopad': Coming to Terms with the Past in Post-Soviet Ukraine." In *Berlin Wall Falls: History, Identity and Politics*, edited by Marion Loeffler. University of Wales Press, 2024.

Peoples, Clayton D. "Classical and Contemporary Conventional Theories of Social Movements." In *The Palgrave Handbook of Social Movements, Revolution, and Social Transformation*, edited by Berch Berberoglu. Palgrave Macmillan, 2019.

Perry, Lewis. *Civil Disobedience: An American Tradition*. New Haven, CT: Yale University Press, 2013.

Petrovska, Inha R. "Measuring Civic Identity: Difficulties and Solutions." In *Psychology and Pedagogy in XXI Century: Methodological Framework of the Activities of Psychologist and Educator*, edited by A.O. Bessarab, O.I. Ivanytsky, O.M. Kikinezhdi, et al. Liha Press, 2020. doi:10.36059/978-966-397-176-6/62-82.

Phillips, Sarah D. "The Women's Squad in Ukraine's Protests: Feminism, Nationalism, and Militarism on the Maidan." *American Ethnologist* 41, no. 3 (2014): 414–26.

Pinard, Maurice. *Motivational Dimensions in Social Movements and Contentious Collective Action*. McGill-Queen's University Press, 2011.

Piontkovsky, Andrei. *Another Look into Putin's Soul*. Hudson Institute, 2006.

Pipes, Richard. "Flight from Freedom: What Russians Think and Want." *Foreign Affairs* 83, no. 3 (2004): 9–15.

Pipko, Antonina. "The First Rally in Kyiv in 1988 as a Precursor to the Maidan Protests." Paper presented at the Online Academic Forum, "The Revolution of Dignity: On the Road to History, Museum of the Revolution of Dignity." November 2023.

Piven, Frances Fox, and Richard A. Cloward. "Collective Protest: A Critique of Resource-Mobilization Theory." In *Social Movements: Critiques, Concepts, Case-Studies*, edited by Stanford M. Lyman. Springer, 1995.

Plokhy, Serhii. *Chernobyl: The History of a Nuclear Catastrophe*. Basic Books, 2018.

– "Goodbye Lenin: A Memory Shift in Revolutionary Ukraine." MAPA, *The Digital Atlas of Ukraine, Harvard Ukrainian Research Institute*, Accessed 22 January 2025. https://www.gis.huri.harvard.edu/leninfall.

– Interview with the *Harvard Ukrainian Research Institute*. "Contextualizing Putin's "On the Historical Unity of Russians and Ukrainians." 2 August 2021. https://www.huri.harvard.edu/news/putin-historical-unity.

– *The Last Empire: The Final Days of the Soviet Union*. Hachette UK, 2015.

Podrobnosti. "На российско-украинской таможне скопилось около тысячи грузовых вагонов."" [Approximately 1,000 trucks have been accumulated on the Russian-Ukrainian border."] 15 August 2013. Accessed 9 October 2020. https://podrobnosti.ua/923859-na-rossijsko-ukrainskoj-tamozhne-skopilos-okolo-tysjachi-gruzovyh-vagonov-obnovleno.html.

Polovetskyi, Mykola. "Росія розв'язала торговельну війну проти України." *Ukrainska Pravda*, 12 August 2013. https://www.epravda.com.ua/publications/2013/08/12/389401.

Polske Radio. "Круглий стіл – без порозуміння." ["Round Table – With No Result."] 13 December 2013. http://archiwum.polradio.pl/5/38/Artykul/156015.

Pop-Eleches, Grigore, and Graeme B. Robertson. "Identity and Political Preferences in Ukraine – Before and After the Euromaidan." *Post-Soviet Affairs* 34, no. 2–3 (2018): 107–18.

Popova, Maria. "Authoritarian Learning and the Politicization of Justice: The Tymoshenko Case in Context." June 2013. SSRN *Electronic Journal*. doi:10.2139/ssrn.2274168.

– "Ukraine's Politicized Courts." In *Beyond the Euromaidan: Comparative Perspectives on Advancing Reform in Ukraine*, edited by Henry E. Hale and Robert W. Orttung. Stanford University Press, 2016.

– "Why the Orange Revolution Was Short and Peaceful and Euromaidan Long and Violent." *Problems of Post-Communism* 61, no. 6 (2014): 64–70.

Pynnöniemi, Katri Paulina, and Andras Rácz. "Fog of Falsehood: Russian Strategy of Deception and the Conflict in Ukraine." In FIIA REPORT, no. 45, *The Finnish Institute of International Affairs*, 2016. https://www.fiia.fi/wp-content/uploads/2017/01/fiiareport45_fogoffalsehood.pdf.

Radio Free Europe / Radio Liberty. "Abducted Kyiv Activist 'Crucified,' Tortured; Police Put Him on 'Wanted' List." 31 January 2014. https://www.rferl.org/a/ukraine-protests-activist-tortured-kidnapped-bulatov-avtomaidan-kyiv/25248432.html.

– "Beyond Kyiv: Ukrainian Protesters Seize Control of Regional Administrations." 25 January 2014. https://www.rferl.org/a/beyond-kyiv-regional-protesters/25242538.html.

–"Суд заборонив іти до Януковича і до ялинки." ["Court Banned Going to Yanukovych's House and the Christmas Tree."] 1 December 2013. https://www.radiosvoboda.org/a/25185747.html.

– "From Maidan to Berkut: A Ukraine Protest Glossary." 4 December 2013. https://www.rferl.org/a/ukraine-protest-glossary-euromaydan/25190085.html.

– "High Profile Rape Trial Begins in Kyiv." 26 September 2013. https://www.rferl.org/a/ukraine-vradiivka-rape-case-trial/25118352.html.

– "Ukrainians March to Kyiv to Protest Police Abuses." 18 July 2013. Video, 2 min., 5 sec. https://www.rferl.org/a/25050121.html.

– "З'явилося нове відео знущань 'Беркута' над голим козаком Гаврилюком." ["A New Video Appeared of Torturing Naked Cossack by the Berkut Forces"], 27 January 2014. https://www.radiosvoboda.org/a/25243520.html.

–"Yanukovych Defends Russian Naval Base Extension." 22 April 2010. https://www.rferl.org/a/Yanukovych_Defends_Russian_Naval_Base_Extension/2021537.html.

Rainsford, Sarah. "Putin and Peter the Great: Russian Leader Likens Himself to 18th Century Tsar." BBC *News*, 11 June 2022. https://www.bbc.com/news/world-europe-61767191.

Rapawy, Stephen. *Ethnic Re-Identification in Ukraine*. No. 90. International Programs Center, Population Division, US Bureau of the Census, 1997.

Rasler, Karen. "Concessions, Repression, and Political Protest in the Iranian Revolution." *American Sociological Review* 62, no. 1 (1996): 132–52.

Research and Branding Group. "Euromaydan – 2013." 4 and 9 December 2013. Archived 10 December 2013. https://web.archive.org/. web/20131213064315/http://rb.com.ua/eng/projects/omnibus/8840.

Richardson, Louise. *What Terrorists Want: Understanding the Enemy, Containing the Threat*. Random House, 2006.

Ritter, Daniel P. *The Iron Cage of Liberalism: International Politics and Unarmed Revolutions in the Middle East and North Africa*. Oxford University Press, 2015.

– "The Missing Unarmed Revolution: Why Civil Resistance Did Not Work in Bahrain." In *Social Movements, Nonviolent Resistance, and the State*, edited by Hank Johnston. Routledge, 2019.

Rodriguez, Meyer. "The Analysis of Saving Behavior: The Case of Rural Households in the Philippines." Working paper series 8820. Philippines Institute for Development Studies, 1988.

Roeder, Philip G. *Red Sunset: The Failure of Soviet Politics*. Princeton University Press, 1993.

Roth, Andrew. "Fears Genocidal Language in Russian Media May Prompt More War Crimes." *The Guardian*, 7 April 2022.

Roth, Guenther. "Durkheim and the Principles of 1789." In *Emile Durkheim: Critical Assessments of Leading Sociologists*, vol. 3, edited by William Stuart Frederick Pickering. Taylor & Francis. 1990.

Rudenko, Olga. "Opposition under Fire for Failure to Protect Protesters." *Kyiv Post*. 30 November 2013. https://www.kyivpost.com/article/content/euromaidan/opposition-accused-of-failure-to-lead-public-protests-332713.html.

– "Police Attacks Demonstrators Sheltered in Writers' Building." *Kyiv Post*. 1 December 2013. Video, 1 min, 1 sec. Archived 1 December 2013. https://web.archive.org/web/20131201222138/http://www.kyivpost.com/content/ukraine/writers-union-saves-people-from-police-gets-attacked-too-332777.html.

Russian Media Monitor. "RT's Director of Broadcasting Anton Krasovsky Suggests Drowning or Burning Ukrainian Children." Accessed 3 April 2024. https://www.youtube.com/watch?v=8lkshypC2Rk&list=PLLWQyEN3YR07bpdyPlWscpvx2O8qSuoT1&index=39.

– "Russian Orthodox TV Channel Advocates Genocide of Ukrainians." Accessed 3 April 2024. https://www.youtube.com/watch?v=n0WAPHQX49s&list=PLLWQyEN3YR07bpdyPlWscpvx2O8qSuo T1&index=43.

Ryabchuk, Mykola. "The Ukrainian 'Friday' and the Russian 'Robinson': The Uneasy Advent of Postcoloniality." *Canadian-American Slavic Studies* 44, no. 1–2 (2010): 7–24.

Sarat, Austin, and Stuart Scheingold. "Cause Lawyering and the Reproduction of Professional Authority." In *Cause Lawyering: Political Commitments and Professional Responsibilities*, edited by Austin Sarat and Stuart Scheingold. Oxford University Press, 1998.

– eds. *Cause Lawyers and Social Movements*. Stanford University Press, 2006.

Schock, Kurt. *Unarmed Insurrections: People Power Movements in Non-Democracies*. University of Minnesota Press, 2005.

Semukhina, Olga. "The Decriminalization of Domestic Violence in Russia." *Demokratizatsiya: The Journal of Post-Soviet Democratization* 28, no. 1 (2020): 15–45.

Sereda, Viktoriya. "I Am a Man and an Active Citizen … I Did Not Betray My State!" *Revue D'études Comparatives Est-Ouest* 2, no. 2 (2018): 93–130.

Shamota, Mariia. "EuroMaidan Rallies on Dec. 1: A Rowdy Afternoon." *Kyiv Post*, 1 December 2013, 2:22pm. https://www.kyivpost.com/post/9281.

Sharp, Gene. *The Politics of Nonviolent Action: The Dynamics of Nonviolent Action*. Extending Horizons, 1973.

– *Waging Nonviolent Struggle: 20th Century Practice and 21st Century Potential*. Extending Horizons, 2005.

Shcherbina, Serhiy, and Serhiy Lyamets, "Росія почала поглинати Україну" ["Russia Has Started to Swallow Ukraine"]. *Ekonomichna Pravda*, 20 August 2013. https://epravda.com.ua/publications/2013/08/20/390584.

Shekhovtsov, Anton. *Russia and the Western Far Right: Tango Noir*. Routledge, 2017.

Shekhovtsov, Anton, and Andreas Umland. "The Maidan and Beyond: Ukraine's Radical Right." *Journal of Democracy* 25, no. 3 (2014): 58–63.

Shevchenko, Daryna. "Back to the Middle Ages on the Way to Europe: Beaten Kyiv Protesters Take Refuge in Ancient Church Yard." *Kyiv Post*, 30 November 2013. https://www.kyivpost.com/article/content/euromaidan/back-to-the-middle-ages-on-the-way-to-europe-beaten-kyiv-protesters-take-refuge-in-ancient-church-yard-332719.html.

– "Vox Populi with Daryna Shevchenko: How Should the Nation React to Police Violence Against Protesters?" *Kyiv Post*, 30 November 2013. https://www.kyivpost.com/article/content/euromaidan/vox-populi-with-daryna-shevchenko-how-should-the-nation-react-to-the-violent-night-events-at-maidan-nezalezhnosti-332711.html.

Shore, Marci. *The Ukrainian Night: An Intimate History of Revolution*. Yale University Press, 2018.

Shuklynov, Petr. "В Киеве пострадали 40 журналистов." ["Forty Journalists Were Injured in Kyiv."] LIGA, 2 December 2013. https://news.liga.net/politics/news/v_kieve_postradali_bolshe_desyatka_zhurnalistov_spisok.

Shveda, Yuriy. "The Revolution of Dignity in the Context of Theory of Social Revolutions." *Ukraine after the Euromaidan: Challenges and Hopes*. Peter Lang, 2015.

Sierra, Luis Fernando Medina. *A Unified Theory of Collective Action and Social Change*. University of Michigan Press, 2007.

Sim Dniv News. "Parubiy Spoke about the Self-Defense of the Maidan: There Are Hutsul, Boyko, and Cossack Hundreds." 13 February 2014. https://web.archive.org/web/20140223042704/https://7days-ua.com/news/parubij-rozpoviv-pro-samooboronu-majdanu-je-hutsulska-bojkivska-kozatska-sotni.

Skocpol, Theda. *States and Social Revolutions: A Comparative Analysis of France, Russia and China*. Cambridge University Press, 1979.

Snow, David A., E. Burke Rochford, Jr, Steven K. Worden, and Robert D. Benford. "Frame Alignment Processes, Micromobilization, and Movement Participation." *American Sociological Review* 51, no. 4 (1986): 464–81.

Snyder, Timothy, *The Road to Unfreedom: Russia, Europe, America*. Crown Publishing, 2019.

– "Ukraine: The Haze of Propaganda." *New York Review*, 1 March 2014. https://www.nybooks.com/daily/2014/03/01/ukraine-haze-propaganda.

Soule, Sarah, Doug McAdam, John McCarthy, and Yang Su. "Protest Events: Cause or Consequence of State Action? The US Women's Movement and Federal Congressional Activities, 1956–1979." *Mobilization: An International Quarterly* 4, no. 2 (1999): 239–56.

Sperling, Valerie. "Making the Public Patriotic: Militarism and Anti-Militarism in Russia." *Russian Nationalism and the National Reassertion of Russia*. Routledge, 2009.

– *Sex, Politics, and Putin: Political Legitimacy in Russia*. Oxford University Press, 2014.

Stebelsky, Ihor. "Ethnic Self-Identification in Ukraine, 1989–2001: Why More Ukrainians and Fewer Russians?" *Canadian Slavonic Papers* 51, no. 1 (2009): 77–100.

Stecklow, Steve, Elizabeth Piper, and Oleksandr Akymenko. "Special Report – How Scams and Shakedowns Brought Ukraine to Its Knees." *Reuters*, 17 August 2014. https://www.reuters.com/article/uk-ukraine-tax-specialreport/special-report-how-scams-and-shakedowns-brought-ukraine-to-its-knees-idUKKBN0G71ED20140807.

Straus, Scott. "'Destroy Them to Save Us': Theories of Genocide and the Logics of Political Violence." *Terrorism and Political Violence* 24, no. 4 (2012): 544–60.

Sutton, Jonathan, Charles R. Butcher, and Isak Svensson. "Explaining Political Jiu-Jitsu Institution-Building and the Outcomes of Regime Violence against Unarmed Protests." *Journal of Peace Research* 51, no. 5 (2014): 559–73.

Tam, Waikeung. "Political Transition and the Rise of Cause Lawyering: The Case of Hong Kong." *Law and Social Inquiry* 35, no. 3 (2010): 663–87.

Tarrow, Sidney G. *Power in Movement: Social Movements and Contentious Politics*. Cambridge University Press, 2011.

Taylor, Alan. "Days of Protest in Ukraine." *The Atlantic*, 2 December 2013. https://www.theatlantic.com/photo/2013/12/days-of-protest-in-ukraine/100638.

Ternopil Regional Council. "Київ. Майдан Незалежності. Рішення 47 сесії обласної ради 2 грудня 2013 року." ["Kyiv. Independence Square. Decision of the 47th Session of the Regional Council on December 2, 2013."] 6 December 2013. https://web.archive.org/web/20140107084824/http://www.obl-rada.te.ua/diyalnist/novyny/kyyiv-maydan-nezalezhnosti-rishennya-47-sesiyi-oblasnoyi-rady-2-hrudnya-2013-roku.html.

Tillmann, Pauline. "Ukraine Press Freedom under Threat." *Fair Observer*, 17 July 2011. https://www.fairobserver.com/region/europe/ukraine-press-freedom-under-threat.

Tilly, Charles. *From Mobilization to Revolution.* Addison-Wesley, 1978

– *Repression, Mobilization, and Explanation*, vol. 218. University of Minnesota Press, 2005.

Tilly, Charles, and Sidney Tarrow. *Contentious Politics*. 2nd ed. Oxford University Press, 2015.

Tkach, Nadiya. *Razom – Syla*. Kyiv, 2014

Transparency International Ukraine. "Summary of Laws Adopted by the Ukrainian Parliament on 16 January 2014." 17 January 2014. https://web.archive.org/web/20140121054645/http://ti-ukraine.org/news/4269.html.

Trejo, Guillermo. "Why and When Do Peasants Rebel?" In *The Oxford Handbook of the Social Science of Poverty*, edited by David Brady and Linda M. Burton. Oxford: Oxford University, 2016.

Tsensor.net. "Суд запретил Федерации профсоюзов занимать здание Дома профсоюзов." ["The Court Prohibited the Federation of Trade Unions to Occupy the Trade Union Building."] 13 December, 2013. https://censor.net/ru/news/263434/sud_zapretil_federatsii_profsoyuzov_zanimat_zdanie_doma_profsoyuzov.

TSN. "94 дні. Євромайдан очима ТСН." ["94 Days Euromaidan through the Eyes of TSN."] Kyiv: Osnovy Press: 2014.

Tucker, Joshua A. "Enough! Electoral Fraud, Collective Action Problems, and Post-Communist Colored Revolutions." *Perspectives on Politics* 5, no. 3 (2007): 535–51.

Tullock, Gordon. "The Paradox of Revolution." *Public Choice* 11, no.1 (1971): 89–99.

Turner, Ralph H. "Figure and Ground in the Analysis of Social Movements." *Symbolic Interaction* 6, no. 2 (1983): 175–81.

Ukraina Criminalna. "'Титушковый' штурм Банковой." ["Titushky Storm on Bankova Street."] 1 December 2013. https://cripo.com.ua/news/?p=166693/.

Ukraine Crisis Media Center. "Fifty Three Persons Who Disappeared during Maidan Events Are Still Missing – Maidan Search Initiative." https://uacrisis.org/en/40403-poshukova-initsiativa-majdanu.

– "Ukraine's Attorney General: Ex President Yanukovych Suspected of Laundering USD 100 Billion from State Budget." 5 June 2014. https://uacrisis.org/en/24718-ukraine-s-attorney-general-ex-president-yanukovych-suspected-of-laundering-usd-100-billion-from-state-budget.

Ukraine's Human Rights Helsinki Association. "Civic Organizations State – The Freedom of Peaceful Gatherings in Ukraine Are under the Threat of Disappearing," 29 January 2013. http://Helsinki.org.ua/index.php?id=1359464718.

Ukraine World. "How Russian Cinema Dehumanized Ukrainians and Laid the Ground for Today's War Crimes." 19 May 2022. https://ukraineworld.org/articles/russian-aggression/how-russian-cinema-dehumanized-ukrainians.

Ukrainian Helsinki Human Rights Union. *Human Rights in Ukraine – 2007. Report by Human Rights Organizations*. Kharkiv: Prava Ludyny, 2008. https://khpg.org/en/1217151393.

Ukrainian Institute of National Memory. *Майдан від першої особи: 45 історій Революції Гідності. [Maidan from the First Person: 45 Stories from the Revolution of Dignity.]* Kyiv: K.I.S. Press, 2015.

Ukrainian Jewish Encounter. "Open Letter of Ukrainian Jews to Russian Federation President Vladimir Putin." 4 March 2014. https://ukrainianjewishencounter.org/media/Putin20Letter1-1.pdf.

Ukrainska Pravda. "Росія готує реакцію на «самовбивчу» асоціацію України з ЄС." [Russia is preparing a reaction to "suicidal" Ukraine-EU association."] 18 September 2013. http://pravda.com.ua/news/2013/08/18/6996231/.

– "На Михайлівській 5 тисяч скандують "Хама на Йолку»." ["5,000 People Chant 'Boor Belongs on the New Year's Tree' on Mykhailivska Street."] 30 November 2013. https://www.pravda.com.ua/news/2013/11/30/7003842/.

– "Барикаду в урядовому кварталі розібрали війська, 'Свобода' втримала пікет біля АП." ["The Barricade in the Government Quarter Was Dismantled by Troops, 'Svoboda' held a picket near the Presidential

Administration."] 9 December 2013. https://www.pravda.com.ua/news/2013/12/9/7005708/.
–"Парламент Крыма призвал Януковича вводить чрезвычайное положение." ["Crimean Parliament Calls on Yanukovych to Introduce State of Emergency."] 2 December 2013. https://www.pravda.com.ua/rus/news/2013/12/2/7004344/.
–"Окружний суд на місяць заборонив масові акції протесту в Києві." ["The District Court Blocked Mass Protests in Kyiv for a Month."] 1 December 2013. https://www.pravda.com.ua/news/2013/12/1/7003925/.
– "У ЄС закликали Януковича ветувати антидемократичні закони." ["The EU Called on Yanukovych to Veto Anti-Democratic Laws."] 17 January 2014. https://www.pravda.com.ua/news/2014/01/17/7009796.
– "Євромітингувальники вбачають у закритті метро і появі 'Тигру' підготовку до Штурму." ["Euro-Protesters See the Metro Closure and the Appearance of the 'Tiger' Special Forces as Preparation for the Storm."] 9 December 2013. https://www.pravda.com.ua/news/2013/12/9/7005567/.
– "Провокатори влади на марші." ["Government's Provocateurs Are at the March."] 1 December 2013, https://www.pravda.com.ua/articles/2013/12/1/7003664/.
–"КМДА хоче заборонити акції до 7 грудня по всьому центру Києва." ["Kyiv City State Administration Wants to Ban Rallies throughout the Centre of Kyiv until December 7."] 30 November 2013. https://www.pravda.com.ua/news/2013/11/30/7003912/.
– "ПАМ'ЯТНИК ЛЕНІНУ ЗНЕСЛИ." [The Lenin Monument Was Demolished."] 8 December 2013. https://www.pravda.com.ua/news/2013/12/8/7005453/.
–"Марш мільйонів." ["March of Millions."] 8 December 2013. https://www.pravda.com.ua/articles/2013/12/8/7005244/.
– "Міліція отримала повідомлення про "мінування" метро в центрі Києва." ["Police Received a Report of a 'Mining' of the Metro in the Centre of Kyiv."] 9 December 2013. https://www.pravda.com.ua/news/2013/12/9/7005554/.
– "В міліції розказали, за що розігнали Євромайдан." ["The Police Explained Why They Dispersed Euromaidan."] 30 November 2013. https://www.pravda.com.ua/news/2013/11/30/7003736.
– "На Михайлівській площі формують загони самооборони." [Self-Defence Units Are Forming on Mikhailivska Square."] 30 November 2013. https://www.pravda.com.ua/news/2013/11/30/7003906/.
– "Студенти йшли протестувати такою колоною, що кінця не видно." ["Students Marched to Protest in Such a Column That There Was

No End in Sight."] 28 November 2013. https://www.pravda.com.ua/news/2013/11/28/7003439/.

– "На Михайлівській площі - тисячі невдоволених киян. 10 послів ЄС також на мітингу." ["Thousands of Disgruntled Kyivans Gather at Mykhailivska Square. 10 EU Ambassadors also at the Rally."] 30 November 2013. https://www.pravda.com.ua/news/2013/11/30/7003797/.

– "Держсекретар США: Верховна Рада забирає в українців майбутнє." ["US Secretary of State: Verkhovna Rada Is Taking Away the Future of Ukrainians."] 17 January 2014. https://www.pravda.com.ua/news/2014/01/17/7009863/.

– "Янукович Зняв з Себе Відповідальність за Розгін Майдану" ["Yanukovich Did Not Accept Responsibility for the Dispersal of the Maidan"] 30 November 2013. https://www.pravda.com.ua/news/2013/11/30/7003895.

– "Янукович: до прийняття рішення про розгін причетні троє." ["Yanukovych: Three People Were Involved in the Decision to Disperse."] 13 December 2013. http://pravda.com.ua/news/2013/12/13/7006722/.

UkrLit. "Заява українських письменників, діячів культури, митців, журналістів, членів творчих спілок з приводу подій в Україні." ["Statement by the Ukrainian Writers, Cultural Actors, Artists, Journalists, Members of Artistic Unions in Regards to the Events in Ukraine."] 9 December 2013. https://web.archive.org/web/20140107150919/http://ualit.org/?p=11295#comment-4162.

United Nations. "Underscoring Need for Peace, End to Suffering, Security Council Speakers Urge Russian Federation to Immediately Withdraw Troops from Ukraine." Press Release, 9470th Meeting (PM). SC/15484. 8 November 2023. https://press.un.org/en/2023/sc15484.doc.

US Department of State Global Engagement Center. "Special Report Kremlin-Funded Media: RT and Sputnik's Role in Russia's Disinformation and Propaganda Ecosystem." January 2022. https://www.state.gov/wp-content/uploads/2022/01/Kremlin-Funded-Media_January_update-19.pdf.

Van Dyke, Nella. "Threat." In *The Wiley-Blackwell Encyclopedia of Social and Political Movements*. Blackwell, 2013.

Vanhala, Lisa. "Anti-Discrimination Policy Actors and Their Use of Litigation Strategies: The Influence of Identity Politics." *Journal of European Public Policy* 16, no. 5 (2009): 738–54.

Verkhovna Rada of Ukraine. "Zasidannya Sorokove, Сесійний зал Верховної Ради України, 20 грудня 2013 року, 10 година." ["40th Meeting. Session Hall of the Verkhovna Rada of Ukraine, December 20, 2013."] https://www.rada.gov.ua/meeting/stenogr/show/5138.html.

– "Проект Закону про внесення змін до Закону України 3879 'Про судоустрій і статус суддів' та процесуальних законів щодо додаткових заходів захисту безпеки громадян." ["Draft Law on Amendments to the Law of Ukraine 'On the Judiciary and the Status of Judges' and Procedural Laws for Additional Steps to Protect the Safety of Citizens."] 14 December 2014. http://w1.c1.rada.gov.ua/pls/zweb2/webproc4_1?pf3511=49483.

Wahl, Elizabeth. "I Was Putin's Pawn." *Politico*, 21 March 2014. https://www.politico.com/magazine/story/2014/03/liz-wahl-quit-russia-today-putins-pawn-104888.

Walker, Edward W. "Between East and West: NATO Enlargement and the Geopolitics of the Ukraine Crisis." In *Ukraine and Russia: People, Politics, Propaganda and Perspectives*, edited by Agnieszka Pikulicka-Wilczewska and Richard Sakwa. E-International Relations, 2015.

Wanner, Catherine. *Burden of Dreams: History and Identity in Post-Soviet Ukraine*. Penn State University Press, 2010.

– *Everyday Religiosity and the Politics of Belonging in Ukraine*. Cornell University Press, 2022.

Warsaw Institute. "How Yanukovych Facilitated the Annexation of Crimea." 24 April 2018. https://warsawinstitute.org/yanukovych-facilitated-annexation-crimea.

Way, Lucan. "The Real Causes of the Color Revolutions." *Journal of Democracy* 19, no. 3 (2008): 55–69.

White, Robert. "From Peaceful Protest to Guerilla War: Micromobilization of the Provisional Irish Republican Army." *American Journal of Sociology* 94 (1989): 1277–1302.

Wiggins, Bradley E. "Crimea River: Directionality in Memes from the Russia-Ukraine Conflict." *International Journal of Communication* 10 (2016): 451–85.

Williams, Jean Calterone. "The Politics of Homelessness: Shelter Now and Political Protest." *Political Research Quarterly* 58, no. 3 (2005): 497–509.

Wilson, Andrew. "Elements of a Theory of Ukrainian Ethno-National Identities." *Nations and Nationalism* 8, no. 1 (2002): 31–54.

– "The Ukraine Crisis Brings the Threat of Democracy to Russia's Doorstep." *European View* 13, no. 1 (2014): 67–72.

– *Virtual Politics: Faking Democracy in the Post-Soviet World*. Yale University Press, 2005.

Wilson, Sophia. "Cause Lawyering in Revolutionary Ukraine." *Journal of Law and Courts* 5, no. 2 (2017): 267–88.

– "The Ukrainian Revolution: Repression, Interpretation, and Dissent." Special Issue, "Four Dead in Ohio: The Global Legacy of Youth Activism and State Repression," edited by Johanna Solomon. *Research in Social Movements* 45 (2021): 157–88.

Wolf, Daniel, *Inside the Orange Revolution*. Norfolk, UK: October Fims MMV for BBC, 2019. https://www.youtube.com/watch?v=StIVTkJJMWY&t=2s.

Woods, Elizabeth J. *Insurgent Collective Action and Civil War in El Salvador*. Cambridge University Press, 2003.

Wynnyckyj, Mychailo. *Ukraine's Maidan, Russia's war*. BOD – Books on Demand, 2019.

Yale School of Public Health's Humanitarian Research Lab. "Ukraine's Stolen Children: Inside Russia's Network of Re-education and Militarization." 16 September, 2025. https://files-profile.medicine.yale.edu/documents/e6294def-3f80-4d71-9cc7-91f6af70a523.

Yanukovych, Viktor. "Vystuplenie Prezidenta na torzhestvenom sobranii po sluchayu Dnya Nezavisimosti" ["Speech by the President at the Festive Celebration of Independence Day"]. 24 August 2013.

– "Vystuplenie Prezidenta vo vremya otkrytiya tret'ei sessii Verkhovnoi Rady sed'mogo sozyva" ["Speech by the President at the Opening of the Third Session of the Seventh Supreme Council"]. 3 September 2013. www.president.gov.ua.

Yom, Sean. "From Methodology to Practice: Inductive Iteration in Comparative Research." *Comparative Political Studies* 48, no. 5 (2015): 616–44.

Young, Michael P. *Bearing Witness against Sin: The Evangelical Birth of the American Social Movement*. Chicago University Press, 2006.

Yurchuk, Yuliya. "De-Canonization of the Soviet Past: Abject, Kitsch, and Memory." In *De-Commemoration: Removing Statues and Renaming Places*, edited by Sarah Gensburger and Jenny Wüstenberg. Berghahn Books, 2023.

Zaliznyak, Yuriy B., "Russia's Social Media Propaganda Warfare." In *Handbook of Global Media Ethics*, edited by Stephen J.A. Ward. Springer, 2021. https://doi.org/10.1007/978-3-319-32103-5_65.

Zelinska, Olga. "How Social Movement Actors Assess Social Change: An Exploration of the Consequences of Ukraine's Local Maidan Protests." *International Journal of Sociology* 52, no. 4 (2021): 284–303. doi: 10.1080/00207659.2021.1910429.

Zerkalo Nedeli. "Азаров возмутился разгоном Евромайдана в Киеве: власть не заинтересована в таком сценарии." ["Azarov Was Outraged by the Dispersal of Euromaidan in Kyiv: The Government Is Not Interested in Such a Scenario."] 30 November 2013. https://zn.ua/POLITICS/azarov-vozmutilsya-razgonom-evromaydana-v-kieve-133989_.html.

– "Начальник столичной милиции взял на себя ответственность за разгон Евромайдана." ["The Head of the Kyiv City Police Took

Responsibility for the Dispersal of the Euromaidan."] 30 November 2013. https://zn.ua/POLITICS/nachalnik-stolichnoy-milicii-vzyal-na-sebya-otvetstvennost-za-razgon-evromaydana-133994_.html.

Zhitomyr Regional Council. "Відбулася позачергова вісімнадцята сесія обласної ради шостого скликання." ["An Extraordinary Eighteenth Session of the Regional Council of the Sixth Convocation Was Held."] 4 December 2013. https://web.archive.org/web/20140107083258/http://www.oblrada.zhitomir.ua/index.php/news/4995-відбулася-позачергова,-вісімнадцята,-сесія-обласної-ради-шостого-скликання.html.

Zhurzhenko, Tatiana. *Ukrainian Feminism(s): Between Nationalist Myth and Anti-Nationalist Critique*. Institut für die Wissenschaften vom Menschen, 2001.

Zisels, Joseph. "Евреи Украины принимают участие в протестных акциях." ["Jewish People of Ukraine Participate in the Protests."] Interview with A. Sharon, 6 December 2013. In Lyudmila Fylypovych and Oksana Horkusha, *Майдан і церква. Хроніка подій та експертна оцінка.* [*Maidan and the Church. Chronicle of Events and Expert Assessment.*] Kyiv: Sammit Knyha, 2015.

Zwerman, Gilda, and Patricia Steinhoff. "When Activists Ask for Trouble: State–Dissident Interactions and the New Left Cycle of Resistance in the United States and Japan." In *Repression and Mobilization*, edited by Christian Davenport. University of Minnesota Press, 2005.

Zychowicz, Jessica. *Superfluous Women: Art, Feminism, and Revolution in Twenty-First-Century Ukraine*. University of Toronto Press, 2020.

Cases Cited

Derevyanko v. Ukraine, 7684/14, Communicated to the Ukrainian Government in February 2014 2014, European Court of Human Rights. http://hudoc.echr.coe.int/eng#{%22fulltext%22:[% 22ukraine%20 2013%22],%22documentcollectionid2%22:[%22COMMUNICATEDCASES %22],%22itemid%22:[%22001-141898%22]} (accessed 12 November 2015).

Shmorgunov v. Ukraine and 32 Other Applications, 15367/14, Communicated to the Ukrainian Government in 2015, European Court of Human Rights. http://hudoc.echr.coe.int/eng#{%22fulltext %22:[%22shmorgunov%22],%22documentcollectionid2%22:[%22GRAND CHAMBER%22 ,%22CHAMBER%22,%22COMMUNICATED CASES%22],%22itemid%22:[%22001 -158474%22]} (accessed 12 November 2015).

Verentsov v. Ukraine, European Court of Human Rights, March 19, 2013.

Index

McGill-Queen's Studies in Protest, Power, and Resistance

SERIES EDITOR: SARAH MARSDEN

1 New Media and Revolution
Resistance and Dissent in Pre-uprising Syria
Billie Jeanne Brownlee

2 Games of Discontent
Protests, Boycotts, and Politics at the 1968 Mexico Olympics
Harry Blutstein

3 Organizing Equality
Dispatches from a Global Struggle
Edited by Alison Hearn, James Compton, Nick Dyer-Witheford, and Amanda F. Grzyb

4 The Failure of Remain
Anti-Brexit Activism in the United Kingdom
Adam Fagan and Stijn van Kessel

5 The Participation Paradox
Between Bottom-Up and Top-Down Development in South Africa
Luke Sinwell

6 Citizens, Civil Society, and Activism under the EPRDF Regime in Ethiopia
An Analysis from Below
Edited by Camille Pellerin and Logan Cochrane

7 Intercommunal Warfare and Ethnic Peacemaking
The Dynamics of Urban Violence in Central Asia
Joldon Kutmanaliev

8 Our Subversive Voice
The History and Politics of English Protest Songs, 1600–2020
John Street, Oskar Cox Jensen, Alan Finlayson, Angela McShane, and Matthew Worley

9 States without People
Revolt and Defeat in the Middle East
Billie Jeanne Brownlee and Maziyar Ghiabi

10 Maidan
Ukraine's Democratic Revolution
Sophia Wilson